BEYOND SUNNI AND SHIA

FREDERIC WEHREY

(*Editor*)

Beyond Sunni and Shia

*The Roots of Sectarianism
in a Changing Middle East*

OXFORD
UNIVERSITY PRESS

OXFORD
UNIVERSITY PRESS

Oxford University Press is a department of the
University of Oxford. It furthers the University's objective
of excellence in research, scholarship, and education
by publishing worldwide.

Oxford   New York

Auckland   Cape Town   Dar es Salaam   Hong Kong   Karachi
Kuala Lumpur   Madrid   Melbourne   Mexico City   Nairobi
New Delhi   Shanghai   Taipei   Toronto

With offices in

Argentina   Austria   Brazil   Chile   Czech Republic   France   Greece
Guatemala   Hungary   Italy   Japan   Poland   Portugal   Singapore
South Korea   Switzerland   Thailand   Turkey   Ukraine   Vietnam

Oxford is a registered trade mark of Oxford University Press
in the UK and certain other countries.

Published in the United States of America by
Oxford University Press
198 Madison Avenue, New York, NY 10016

Library of Congress Cataloging-in-Publication Data is available
Frederic Wehrey.
Beyond Sunni and Shia: The Roots of Sectarianism in a Changing Middle East.
ISBN: 9780190876050

Printed in the United Kingdom by Bell and Bain Ltd, Glasgow

CONTENTS

CONTENTS

ACKNOWLEDGMENTS

It is a pleasure to offer my deep appreciation to the many colleagues and friends who made this collective effort possible.

First and foremost, the research behind these chapters would not have happened without the generous financial support of the Henry Luce Foundation and especially the Foundation's Director of Initiatives, Toby Volkman. An anthropologist with deep expertise in South and Southeast Asia, Toby recognized early on the need for a broad-ranging, multi-disciplinary inquiry into the roots of Middle East sectarianism, one that challenged mainstream assumptions with academic rigor but was also accessible to broader audiences. Her sustained encouragement and critical eye were vital to the endeavor's success—and she was simply a joy to work with.

The Carnegie Endowment for International Peace provided a physical and intellectual home for the project. Founded in 1910 by Andrew Carnegie to "hasten the abolition of international war, the foulest blot upon our civilization," the Carnegie Endowment is America's oldest think tank focused on international affairs. It has expanded into a global think tank with research centers in Moscow, Beijing, Brussels, Beirut, and New Delhi. I am grateful to the past and current presidents of the Carnegie Endowment—Jessica T. Mathews and William J. Burns—for their visionary leadership of this unique organization and for their support of our research.

Within the Endowment, I want to thank my colleagues within the Middle East Program. Marwan Muasher, a vice president for studies, has led the program since 2010 with an unwavering zeal for intellectual integrity and policy relevance. In addition, his own work on pluralism and inclusive governance in the Middle East has been a constant source of inspiration. The past and current Washington-based directors of the program, Katherine Wilkens and

ACKNOWLEDGMENTS

Michele Dunne, provided critical input on successive proposals and papers. Carnegie's stellar cast of editors—Rebecca White, Ryan DeVries, Samuel Brase, and Michael Young—whipped the chapters into shape, excising stilted prose and jargon while clarifying bottom-line findings. Our talented staff in both Washington and Beirut, Tiffany Tupper, John Polcari, Tara Medeiros, Hilary McGraw, Jessica Katz, Ghenwa Bazzi, and Joumana Seikaly, piloted the project across the varied terrain of workshop logistics, financial stewardship, publicity, and web design.

Over the course of the project, the contributing authors presented their research at two workshops, in Washington DC in 2015 and in Beirut in 2016. I am grateful for the wise feedback provided by outside scholars at these gatherings, none of whom needs any introduction to Middle East watchers: Bernard Haykel, Marc Lynch, Yezid Sayigh, and Bassel Salloukh.

At Hurst & Co. Publishers, I would like to thank Jon de Peyer for his guidance and encouragement and Brenda Stones for her careful editing. At Oxford University Press, I am similarly appreciative of David McBride's support. Two anonymous peer reviewers made helpful suggestions.

Finally, on behalf of every chapter author, I would like to thank our interlocutors in the Middle East: the countless activists, scholars, religious figures, government officials, and militants who shared their insights and experiences during our field research. Many did so at great personal risk, in conditions of endemic violence, state repression, or both. For many them, sectarianism is hardly an intellectual abstraction or a policy dilemma, but a lived, everyday reality, a symptom of the momentous changes afflicting their region. It is to them that this volume is dedicated.

Frederic Wehrey   August 2017

CONTRIBUTORS

Frederic Wehrey is a senior fellow in the Middle East Program at the Carnegie Endowment for International Peace. He is the author of *Sectarian Politics in the Gulf: From the Iraq War to the Arab Uprisings* (New York: Columbia University Press, 2013).

Paul Dixon is a Professor in Politics and International Studies at Kingston University, London. He is author of *Northern Ireland: The Politics of War and Peace* (2nd edn, London: Palgrave Macmillan, 2008) and editor of *The British Approach to Counterinsurgency: From Malaya and Northern Ireland to Iraq and Afghanistan* (London: Palgrave Macmillan, 2012). He is working on a book on the Northern Ireland Peace Process.

Hassan Hassan is a senior resident fellow at the Tahrir Institute for Middle East Policy. He is co-author of *ISIS: Inside the Army of Terror*, a *New York Times* bestseller chosen as one of the '*Times* of London's Best Books of 2015'. He is a contributor to the *Guardian, The National, Foreign Policy, Foreign Affairs*, and the *New York Times*.

Heiko Wimmen oversees the International Crisis Group's Iraq/Syria/Lebanon project. Prior to joining Crisis Group, he was an associate researcher at the German Institute for International and Security Affairs in Berlin and the deputy director in the Middle East office at the Heinrich Böll Foundation in Beirut. His research focuses on political activism in divided societies.

Afshon Ostovar is an Assistant Professor of National Security Affairs at the Naval Postgraduate School. Previously, he was a fellow at the Combating Terrorism Center at West Point and has taught at Johns Hopkins University. His research focuses on conflict and security issues in the Middle East, with a specialty in Iran and the Persian Gulf. He is the author of *Vanguard of the Imam: Religion, Politics, and Iran's Revolutionary Guards* (Oxford: Oxford University Press, 2016).

Fanar Haddad is a Senior Research Fellow at the Middle East Institute, National University of Singapore. He is the author *of Sectarianism in Iraq: Antagonistic Visions of Unity* (London/New York: Hurst/Columbia University Press, 2011).

Joseph Bahout is a Visiting Scholar at Carnegie's Middle East Program, where he focuses on Syria and Lebanon, as well as on identity politics in the region. Previous to that, he was a professor of Middle East politics at Sciences-Po Paris, where he earned his PhD, and served as a consultant for the French Ministy of Foreign Affairs. He also taught and worked as a researcher in Lebanon for more than ten years.

Alexandra Siegel is a PhD candidate at New York University's Politics Department and a Graduate Research Associate at NYU's Social Media and Political Participation Lab. She is a former Junior Fellow at the Carnegie Endowment for International Peace and a former CASA Fellow at the American University in Cairo. She holds a Bachelor's degree in International Relations and Arabic from Tufts University.

Justin Gengler is the Research Program Manager at the Social and Economic Survey Research Institute (SESRI) at Qatar University. Gengler's research focuses on mass attitudes, political behavior, and group conflict in the Arab Gulf states. He publishes regularly in both scholarly and policy fora on topics related to sectarian politics, fiscal reform, public opinion, and survey methodology in the Gulf region.

Staci Strobl is an Associate Professor of Criminal Justice at the University of Wisconsin-Platteville. In 2009, she won the Radzinowicz Memorial Prize for her paper in the *British Journal of Criminology* about the criminalization of female domestic workers in Bahrain. Her main areas of specialization are policing and issues of gender, ethnicity, and religious identity in the Middle East and Eastern Europe.

Cole Bunzel is a PhD candidate in Near Eastern Studies at Princeton University, where his research focuses on the history of Wahhabism in Saudi Arabia and the Jihadi-Salafi movement in modern Islam. He is the author of *From Paper State to Caliphate: The Ideology of the Islamic State* (Washington, DC: Brookings Institution, 2015).

CONTRIBUTORS

Stéphane Lacroix is an associate professor of political science at Sciences Po and a researcher at the Centre de Recherches Internationales (CERI). He is the author of *Awakening Islam: The Politics of Religious Dissent in Contemporary Saudi Arabia* (Cambridge, MA: Harvard University Press, 2011) and (with Bernard Rougier) *Egypt's Revolutions: Politics, Religion and Social Movements* (London: Palgrave Macmillan, 2016).

Alexander D. M. Henley is a Lecturer in Islam and the Study of Religion at the University of Oxford. He previously held the American Druze Foundation Postdoctoral Fellowship at Georgetown University, as well as visiting fellowships at Harvard University's Center for Middle Eastern Studies and the Brookings Doha Center.

INTRODUCTION

Frederic Wehrey

Salah Ali, a middle-aged Saudi-trained doctor with a trim beard, took the microphone. It was November 2006. The stage-lit tent facing an audience in row upon row of folding chairs was one of countless in Bahrain's lively season of electioneering.

It was a historic time on the tiny island. Four opposition blocs had ended their boycott and decided to run for the parliament, or council of representatives. Voting turnout was expected to be high. Still, citizens exuded a mix of wary optimism and cynicism. Would the elected body have real powers over the ruling royal family? Would it heal the country's divisions, or exacerbate them?

Salah Ali was campaigning for a seat from 'Isa Town, a well-to-do suburb of the capital known for its market and the national stadium. He was the chairman of the Muslim Brotherhood's party, a Sunni and pro-regime bloc. After a speech that was both exhortative and plaintive, he took questions. From the packed floor, a diminutive old man stood up.

"Isa Town is mixed," he said, matter of factly, after some perfunctory honorifics. "So why do we have Sunni and Shia parties?"

A few in the crowd applauded. Salah Ali clutched the microphone, coiled the cord, smiled, and paced. It was a question so unsparing in its directness that it caught him off guard. He delivered his response. But he could not answer it, at least to the satisfaction of his inquisitor. And in one fashion or another, Bahrain—and the entire region—has been grappling with its far-reaching implications ever since.[1]

Today, sectarianism is all the rage. A centuries-old animus between Shias and Sunnis, we are told, is plunging the Middle East into a Dante-like inferno. The horrific war in Syria has spilled across borders into Lebanon and Iraq. Rival state claimants for Islamic leadership—Sunni Saudi Arabia and Shia Iran—are funding and arming their co-religionists. Powerful non-state actors imbued with a ferocious communalism have carved out new spaces of physical and virtual sovereignty. In many places, the space for civic, cross-sectarian, or non-sectarian actors—so-called "third forces"—seems to be shrinking by the day.

Such a reading of the Middle Eastern map is not new. Despite the innovations of technology and the seeming novelty of the Islamic State's brutality, we have seen the script before. It played out during Iraq's civil war, starting in 2006, and even earlier, after the American toppling in 2003 of the supposed Sunni bulwark of the Arab world Saddam Hussein. Many trace its origins to Iran's upheaval in 1979 and the ensuing threat from Khomeinism, ironically welcomed at first by Sunnis. Still others would date the conflagration to the post-colonial borders of the Middle East, or even farther back, to the early contest for succession to the Prophet Muhammad and leadership of Muslims.

Taken in sum, these pronouncements amount to something of a reductionist and shorthand approach to a complex and multi-dimensional region. According to this school, the collapsing of Middle Eastern regimes and entire states has "lifted the lid" off ancient passions and identities. With the region in flux, a long-standing "struggle within Islam"—always present, but sometimes in abeyance for stretches of time—is once again the engine of history.

To be sure, history and religion matter. The universe of rituals, beliefs, and collective memory that the adherents of Muslim sects inhabit has meaning and consequence. But at various points in history, sectarian differences have coexisted with, or been subsumed by other affinities: national, regional, tribal, ethnic, class, generational, urban versus rural, center versus periphery, and so on. There have also been prolonged periods of Sunni-Shia coexistence and dialogue, even in what is believed to be the formative era of conflict in the early centuries of Islam.[2]

The question, then, is why have sectarian identities surfaced, and with such force? Why do they become toxic and even violent, to the exclusion of affiliations? What has made them so political? Why, in other words, are there Sunni and Shia parties?

INTRODUCTION

Sectarian waves

Anyone grappling with these questions must first contend with the narrative of three sectarian waves that have shaken the Middle East in the last half-century. While each is something of a construct that has embedded itself in both regional and Western perceptions, they are each grounded in real and discernible trends. They are a useful starting point.

The first wave arguably followed the toppling of the Shah of Iran in 1978–9, with the emergence of a Shia regional power seeking to project its influence and upend the Sunni-dominated status quo. In self-image, at least, Khomeini's revolutionary appeal to the region sought to be ecumenical, and indeed a number of Sunnis initially welcomed it. But it was local Shia who took the most inspiration from it and who received Iranian support. This in turn provoked a counter-reaction by Saudi Arabia and the Gulf states, which featured the proliferation of anti-Shiism through sermons, audio recordings, and books to delegitimize the Khomeini regime, to paint it as an aberration from the Sunni world.[3] Here, the oil boom proved crucial. It enabled under Saudi auspices the growth and spread of Salafism, a distinctive form of Sunni Islam, which, as several of our authors argue, is at its core deeply sectarian. This wave, marked also by the bloody eight-year war between Iran and Iraq and Iranian proxy intervention in Lebanon, lasted until the end of the war and the start of a Saudi-Iranian rapprochement of the 1990s, which saw a parallel reconciliation between Gulf regimes and formerly radical Shia groups. Still, the contributing drivers of sectarianism in Arab states—uneven distribution of resources, authoritarianism, and the absence of a social contract—persisted.

The second wave coincided with the deterioration of Saudi-Iranian relations under President Ahmadinejad of Iran and Iraq's descent into sectarian civil war around 2005–6. This period also saw the rise of non-state actors as enablers of sectarianism. The murderous tenure of Abu Musab al-Zarqawi in Iraq and his targeting of Shia civilians was a key culprit behind the explosion of Sunni-Shia tensions. So, too, was the Lebanese Hezbollah, albeit indirectly. The electrifying battlefield performance of the Iranian-backed group against Israel in 2006 initially received support from both Sunnis and Shias across the Arab world. But it also provoked a strong anti-Shia reaction by staid Sunni regimes and their allied clerics, who resented the fact that a Persian rival had so effectively upstaged them on the anti-Israel, Palestinian cause—a hitherto Sunni Arab "file," and frightened them with its military prowess. What ensued was a period of proxy conflict which has been called a "New Arab Cold War," ostensibly between Sunni and Shia states; but in fact the divisions were often deeper, rooted in state-society relations, challenges to the American-led order, and the Palestine question.[4]

The third wave began in the aftermath of the 2011 Arab uprisings, which injected a new component of domestic unrest and state collapse to the ongoing geopolitical rivalries. Many of the original protests were in fact cross-sectarian, demanding changes to governance that cut across communal lines. Very quickly, though, they took on a sectarian dimension. Elites invoked sectarianism in order to bolster domestic support and divide the opposition, which in turn elicited countersectarianism from their opponents. Bahrain's crushed uprising illustrated this dynamic at work. The ruling Al Khalifa set about mobilizing Sunni supporters while trying to divide the opposition through selective arrests and by exaggerating the extent of Iranian influence.

Yet the clearest and most consequential expression of the third wave of sectarianism, of a conflict becoming "sectarianized," was in Syria. Though sectarianism was deeply embedded in Syrian institutions before the uprising, Assad's policies provoked them. Proxy interventions by regional states and narratives advanced by Syrian oppositionists sharpened them. Across the border in Iraq, corruption, nepotism, and authoritarianism in the Baghdad regime under Nuri al-Maliki reinforced sectarianism, not just among aggrieved Sunnis, but other Shia. Nowhere was this more evident than in the security sector. State weakness in Syria and Iraq hastened the spread of transnational and subnational groups, whether the Islamic State or the Afghan, Pakistani, Bahraini, Iraqi, and Lebanese Shia fighters supporting Assad, appealing to collective religious identity as a basis for mobilization and support.

In many respects, the third wave represents a confluence of trends, a perfect storm, of top-down and bottom-up sectarianism. Geopolitical rivals Saudi Arabia and Iran have exploited communal identities in their foreign policy and their dealings with non- and substate actors in fractured states.[5] These local actors are themselves deeply sectarian, more so than their patrons. As war has dragged on, their bonds with fellow co-religionists across the region—whether Sunni jihadists fighting for the Islamic State's so-called caliphate, or Shia volunteers defending the Sayida Zaynab shrine in Damascus—have strengthened. What has followed is a vicious circle, a spiral of escalating identity politics so extreme that at least one Arab scholar has declared it the end of realist politics in the region.[6]

What is unique about this wave is the primacy of social media. This has allowed state actors a powerful tool to activate and shape sectarian discourse. Yet it also has lent a real-time immediacy to regional conflicts and eroded the ability of governments to manage sectarianism. Twitter, Facebook, and YouTube have created a vast echo chamber for sectarian strife to reverberate from one corner of the region to another. Social media is a real-time, instantaneous theater where audiences do not just observe, but participate in ongoing conflicts in the region. The most extreme, strident purveyors of sectarianism are given disproportionate weight on social media.

Finally, the third wave has been magnified by the oil bust of 2014, which increased uncertainty in the region and general perceptions of instability and crisis. With dwindling resources to placate dissent, the sectarian narrative assumed even greater importance to embattled regimes, particularly in the Gulf. And the resulting tensions are not confined only to Shias and Sunnis. Intra-Sunni conflict has rocked the region, leading to escalatory behavior at home and abroad.[7] The Saudi government's 2015 intervention in Yemen against the Zaydi insurgents who follow an offshoot of Shiism was at least partly undertaken to outflank the royal family's Sunni critics at home, to include its clerical establishment—to be "more Sunni than the Sunnis."[8] Even in states with a negligible Shia population, anti-Shia witch-hunts have taken root, an expression less of sectarianism and more of regime loyalty.

Beyond Sunni and Shia: the scope and structure of this study

Attempts to explain sectarianism have varied wildly, from the superficial determinism described above to more sophisticated and theoretically rich studies. The implications of this understanding are not just academic, but will rather shape policy interventions, from within and without the region.

Much of the discourse, at both the academic and public level, has oscillated between two poles. On the one hand is what Paul Dixon, one of the authors in this volume, calls a "primordial pessimism." This is a deterministic perspective that sees religious identities deeply rooted in history and collective belief. The differences are deemed almost genetic in their immutability, depriving both elites and citizens of agency. This is the "ancient hatreds" school of thought, which reached notoriety in the debates over American intervention in the Balkans in the 1990s.[9] President Barack Obama's reading of the Middle East bears traces of it. In a 2014 interview with the *New Yorker*, he asserted that "It would be profoundly in the interest of citizens throughout the region if Sunnis and Shias weren't intent on killing each other."[10]

At the other end of the spectrum is the lens of "instrumental optimism" that assigns primacy to ruling elites and states in determining the forms and spread of sectarianism. Their sins, according to this interpretation, can be both deliberate—exploiting sectarianism in both domestic and regional politics—or inadvertent and neglectful—encouraging them through misgovernance. Obama, too, displayed this inclination, imploring Iran not to "stir up sectarian discontent in other countries."[11] Other observers adopted slightly different variations, implying that it was the absence of American power as a restraining force or a sort of referee that had enabled sectarian strife to rise to the fore.[12] The inverse of this bias is sometimes advanced by voices within the region, who see in the diffusion of sectarian identities the fingerprints of an American project of "divide and rule."

The consequences of this perspective, too, can be equally misguided—a discounting of individual preference and agency, collective memory and belief, and a naïveté about the power of outside actors, top-down reform, civil society, or even modernity itself, to mediate religious differences.

This study aims to navigate a path between these two poles. It seeks first to move beyond primordial determinism—beyond Sunni and Shia—and focus on an array of more modern and worldly drivers. These include the impact of geopolitics, namely the Saudi-Iranian rivalry—though we acknowledge that the so-called Sunni-bloc arrayed against Iran is hardly cohesive, as illustrated by the Saudi-Emirati siege of Qatar in 2017. More important though, is the domestic level, specifically the pathologies of governance in the Middle East. In authoritarian states, these deficiencies include strategies of institutionalized sectarianism through the uneven access to economic capital, political exclusion, gerrymandering, and discrimination in education, the media, and security sectors, to name a few. All of these factors, independently or together, can contribute to the politicization and radicalization of micro-level religious identities. Similarly, in weak and collapsing states, we focus on why and how sectarian affiliation emerges as a mobilizing bond among transnational and substate groups.

At the same time it acknowledges the role of religion, history, and doctrinal differences as explanatory factors. Sectarianism is not solely a means to an end or the symptom of conflict over political and materialist goals. Rather, it is a deeply-rooted and locally-held belief that partially accounts for the traction that identity peddling has received.

In striving for this balance, the volume builds on a recent body of scholarly works on sectarianism that has advanced new approaches and lenses for understanding the phenomena.[13] It also acknowledges the broader literature on identity politics in domestic and foreign policy, authoritarianism, minorities, and weak states, as well as recent work on Salafism and Shiism.[14] It aims to be rigorous, innovative, and theoretically informed, but also accessible and useful for policy-makers, the informed public, and the media.[15]

Through a generous grant from the Henry Luce Foundation, the Carnegie Endowment for International Peace commissioned a series of papers exploring different facets of contemporary sectarianism in the Middle East. The study was broad ranging, geographically and thematically. The authors hailed from a wide array of professional and disciplinary backgrounds: political scientists, scholars of Islam and comparative religion, journalists, and a criminologist. The contributors used a similarly broad range of methodologies: field interviews, surveys, social media mining, and textual analysis. Over the course of the project, the scholars gathered in two separate groups, in Washington DC and in Beirut, to present their work before fellow contributors and panels of outside experts.[16]

In Chapter 1, Paul Dixon sets a comparative and theoretical framework for the study that draws upon cases outside the Middle East. He develops the opposing schools of primordialism and instrumentalism, settling for what he terms a constructivist realist approach to understanding identity politics. He offers insights into the mobilization of sectarian identity, drawing from his own work in Northern Ireland and proposes a useful metaphor of "politics as theater" to understand how conflict actors, beholden to sect-based constituencies, can both manage and de-escalate tensions through on- and off-stage "performances."

With this foundation, Part I of the book examines what are commonly thought to be the geopolitical drivers of sectarianism in the Levant, specifically the Islamic State, the civil war in Syria, and Iranian foreign policy.

In Chapter 2, Hassan Hassan investigates origins of the Islamic State's sectarianism and its effect on the inflammation of communal identities across the region. He argues that the movement's ideology, and especially its views on the religious "other," are multifaceted and cannot be traced to one individual, movement, or period. Based on a careful reading of its texts and interviews with its supporters, he frames the Islamic State's belief system as a hybridization born of *takfiri* schools in Salafism, al-Qaeda's evolution—especially the rise of Abu Mus'ab al-Zarqawi—and the local political context in Iraq and Syria. Its extreme views on the Shia and non-Muslim minorities have proven especially powerful in outbidding al-Qaeda for recruits.

In his analysis of Syria's sectarianization in Chapter 3, Heiko Wimmen argues for a more nuanced understanding of Syria's conflict, beyond the regime's invocation and manipulation of identities. Not only is such an analysis reductive, but it also denies local actors agency and casts them as puppets who are made to believe, fear, and kill by the whims of the regime. Wimmen's examination of Syria's sectarianization reveals a very ambiguous process, manifested in a dynamic where each party to the conflict pushes a competing narrative of national unity that is positioned against the alleged sectarianism of other parties, while simultaneously engaging in discourses and practices which help to entrench sectarian categories.

In Chapter 4, Afshon Ostovar assesses the role of sectarianism in Iran's foreign policy. Essentializing Iran's foreign policy as solely sectarian, he argues, obscures more than it reveals. At its core, he explains, Iranian behavior in the region is a product of self-interest, striving to protect the regime's theocracy from external and internal threats. Since the revolution, Iran's leaders downplayed Shiism in their foreign policy, focusing instead on class-based, pan-Islamic and "resistance" themes. Still, a sectarian angle exists, rooted in Iran's cultivation of relations with non-state groups. As the Middle East has grown more sectarian since the fall of Saddam Hussein and the Arab Spring, so, too, has Iran's regional behavior. Iran's regional activities, Ostovar concludes, cannot be divorced from the explosion of Sunni sectarianism across the Middle East.

Part II shifts the focus to understanding how a range of institutions—political arrangements, economy, security sectors, and media—has contributed to the rise of sectarianism.

In Chapter 5, Fanar Haddad builds on the themes developed in Part I to explain the roots of institutionalized sectarianism in Iraq—what he calls "Shia-centric state-building"—and the resulting Sunni rejectionism. Far from being unleashed by the American invasion of 2003, this dynamic is in fact the product of a homogenizing nation-building propagated by successive Iraqi regimes and the rise of an exclusivist Shia opposition in exile. He argues that the sectarianization of Iraq was not inevitable, but hastened by the post-2003 empowerment of new and pre-existing sect-centric actors. Even in the wake of the Islamic State's demise, sect-specific grievances persist and institutions, especially the Shia militia-dominated security sector, remain highly sectarianized.

Another country dealing with deeply entrenched and institutionalized sectarianism is Lebanon. In Chapter 6, Joseph Bahout takes stock of the Taif Agreement, which ended the country's civil war and set up a system of confessional representation. He takes note of a popular sentiment in the country: that despite its imperfections, the Taif remains the least bad option, especially when compared to the country's neighbors. Its system of sectarian representation is inherently unstable, to be sure, but an ethos of "no victor, no vanquished" has allowed it to endure. Bahout finds little reason to believe that the pact might be replicated elsewhere, since it was uniquely rooted in an external regulator, Syria, and an informal, deeply entrenched sectarian system that had existed in Lebanon since at least the 1940s.

In her chapter on social media, Alex Siegel explores another highly sectarianized institution that has affected all the states in this study. Utilizing unique data-mining and coding of social media content using sectarian terms, she charts the spread of sectarian rhetoric among Twitter users across the region. Based on a five-month sampling in 2015, she finds that violent events and social network structures play key roles in its transmission. She finds that while social media have facilitated Sunni-Shia interaction online, including the coordination of joint political protest movements, counter-sectarian rhetoric is unfortunately dismissed or decried by many users as pro-Shia propaganda.

Shifting to the Gulf, Justin Gengler's chapter on sectarianism and Gulf ruling strategies offers a rich, survey-informed answer to the question posed by the audience member in 'Isa Town. Under political and fiscal pressure, Gulf rulers face incentives to cultivate non-economic sources of legitimacy in order to maintain popular support, while maximizing scarce resource revenues. He argues that the activation of sectarian and other latent social divisions offers beleaguered governments a critical pressure relief valve. By feeding intercommunal distrust, sowing fear of external threats, and emphasizing their unique ability to guarantee security, ruling elites can reinforce backing among loyalists. While this argument has been made before, Gengler's chapter is the first to test it with survey data of citizens' preferences on security from four Arab Gulf states.

Staci Strobl's chapter on Gulf security sectors picks up on themes developed by Gengler. Drawing from fieldwork and both contemporary and archival sources, she argues that sectarianism is a deeply embedded, everyday routine among actors and institutions in Bahrain's and Saudi Arabia's criminal justice agencies. She traces this not only to the ruling strategies analyzed by Gengler but to the Gulf's post-colonial legacy. Britain's export of modern administrative structures to the Persian Gulf region exacerbated "long-standing sectarian social spaces," thus institutionalizing sectarianism. Strobl concludes that over-hauling criminal justice systems in the Gulf to restore sectarian balance will be a herculean challenge, requiring an array of reforms, to include truth-and-reconciliation commissions.

Part III of the book shifts to consider the role of religion, sects, and doctrines. Here, we acknowledge the very real impact of ideas and beliefs among clerics and religious parties and the political contexts in which they exist.

In Chapter 10, Cole Bunzel returns to the Islamic State, this time assessing its conflicted relationship with Saudi Arabia. He frames the struggle between "the Kingdom and the Caliphate" as a contest over shared religious heritage and doctrines, rooted in the Wahhabi school of Islam and the first Saudi-Wahhabi state (1744–1818). Through an analysis of religious texts, sermons, and statements, Cole analyzes how the Islamic State's rise—and its targeting of the Saudi kingdom—has spurred a debate in Saudi Arabia among the clerical establishment over the very legacy and future of Wahhabism. In this sense, Cole posits a novel twist on the sectarianism of the Islamic State: its wrath is directed not only at Shiism or fellow Sunnis, but within the tradition of Wahhabism itself.

In Chapter 11, Stéphane Lacroix turns to Egypt, a country of enormous consequence in the Islamic world, even if it often escapes analysis of sectarianism. Lacroix examines what he sees as a paradox among Egyptian Salafis, and especially the al-Nour party: while doctrinally sectarian and dogmatic, they have in practice been extremely opportunist, forming coalitions with rival sects when expedient and then the Egyptian regime. Such a dynamic suggests a division between creedal steadfastness and political flexibility, leading Lacroix to make the provocative case that al-Nour should not be considered an Islamist party at all. Based on extensive fieldwork with the party's leaders and followers, Lacroix's findings have important implications for understanding how sectarianism, even among the most seemingly doctrinaire actors, is both bounded and influenced by political context.

In the concluding chapter, Alexander D.M. Henley revisits some of our basic assumptions about the nature of religious authority in the region and clerics as representatives of sects. He takes as starting point the fact that religious leaders are increasingly being seen by outsiders as interlocutors with sectarian constituencies in divided Middle Eastern societies. This is particularly true of Lebanon, where state recognition of sect leaders has led to their being granted wide powers over religious affairs, including personal-status courts, wealthy endowments, places of worship, education, and centralized employment of clerics. Still, he finds that religious leadership is inherently ambiguous, their authority is not necessarily organic, and they do not exist in isolation from politics.

1

BEYOND SECTARIANISM IN THE MIDDLE EAST?

COMPARATIVE PERSPECTIVES ON GROUP CONFLICT

Paul Dixon

Introduction

The "sectarian narrative" has become a prominent explanation for conflict in the Middle East, particularly since the invasion of Iraq 2003 and the war in Syria 2011. This narrative treats the ancient conflict over the succession to the Prophet, which dates back to the seventh century between Sunni and Shia Muslims, as responsible for the descent into civil war in post-invasion Iraq. The implication is that "artificial" states such as Iraq and Syria should be broken up. The Shias believed that authority should follow the line of descent from the Prophet Muhammad. The Sunnis preferred to follow the Prophet's most trusted companions. These sectarian or "primordial" identities are then placed at the center of accounts of the historical evolution of the Middle East, with other influences or identities downplayed or marginalized. The sectarian narrative places great explanatory weight on the intra-Muslim and religious dimension of these conflicts. It describes a new "Cold War" between, on the one hand, Shia Iran, Shia-dominated Iraq, Syria, and Hezbollah against Sunni Saudi Arabia, Qatar, Turkey, and rebel groups in Syria and Iraq. The sectarian narrative in Syria depicts a civil war between a Shia/Alawite regime and Sunni rebels that is considered to be representative of a wider conflict between Sunnis and Shias in the Middle East.

The implication of the sectarian narratives is that the collapse of authoritarian states has lifted the lid off historic divisions, and the surge of sectarianism is almost inevitably going to involve the redrawing of the "artificial" borders of the Middle East in order to reflect these sectarian realities. The best that can be hoped for is that sectarian divisions are explicitly recognized, as in Lebanon—and even reinforced—so that they can be made into the pillars of a segregationist, power-sharing accommodation between sectarian political elites. More likely is the collapse of these states and the redrawing of boundaries along sectarian lines, accompanied by "sectarian cleansing" in order to produce the "homogeneous" sectarian states of a stable region. The Middle East is compared to Eastern Europe and the ethnic cleansing that produced more homogeneous states after World War II.

A range of political interests champions this sectarian narrative. Sectarians seek to mobilize support by emphasizing the importance, persistence, and inevitability of sectarianism throughout history. Al-Qaeda may hope, for example, to provoke sectarian violence in order to generate the fear and hatred that leads to the sectarianization of conflict. Conservative Realists may use the sectarian narrative to avoid military intervention because, it is argued, this "primordialism" needs to burn itself out. Alternatively, if there is to be military intervention, the sectarian narrative justifies the employment of overwhelming force and violence in order to overcome such powerful sectarian forces. Sectarianism may also be used to pass blame for civil war from the external actors to the local population. Neoconservatives and some in the Israeli state may even see political advantage in fomenting a civil war within Islam. This sectarian narrative is very simple and easy to communicate, which makes it an attractive simplifying device for politicians, commentators, the media, and the public.

The sectarian narrative presents or frames the world in a particular way that highlights the religious aspects of conflict and downplays or ignores others. The sectarian narrative (and variations on it) is, therefore, just one of a range of possible narratives available on the Middle East. What determines the success of the sectarian narrative over these other narratives? Is this narrative an accurate analysis of conflict or a self-fulfilling prophecy that seeks to sectarianize conflict? What are the political and other interests that drive the prominence of the sectarian narrative?

This raises issues around the politics of the production of knowledge. Academic debate is often considered to produce objective knowledge from people within ivory towers who are able to be objective because they are removed from the passions of political debates. From this perspective, objective academic analysis leads to objective prescriptions. The political debate, by contrast, may be subjective or partisan, and the analysis of a conflict flows from the particular ideological commitments of the political actor. A nationalist politician may consider conflict to be the result of the failure to achieve nationhood, a neoliberal the failure of the establishment of a capitalist system, and a sectarian the failure to establish the "true religion."

The Constructivist Realist approach of this chapter considers the sectarian narrative to be one possible narrative among many competing to explain the conflict in the Middle East. These narratives or analyses have contrasting implications for policy. All narratives (including this one) are seen as subjective, but some, based on the quality of argument and evidence, are considered to be better than others. The advantage of this approach is that it draws attention to the competing political interests behind the production of knowledge and the power of particular narratives at certain moments in time. Academic knowledge is not separate from but feeds into ongoing policy debates produced, for example, in think tanks, political parties, the media, and by leading political actors. The sectarian narrative is not seen as an objective description that reflects the real world, but a narrative that constructs that world in a particular way with consequent implications for policy. These "groupist" nationalist or sectarian analyses do impact on the world, but the emphasis is on explaining their construction and the political and social forces that sustain these narratives.

This chapter uses a Constructivist Realist framework to explain contrasting comparative perspectives on group conflict. First, it is argued that grand narratives and apocalyptic visions, such as the sectarian narrative, are often alarmist and generate fear in order to shape political responses. These crude over-generalizations do not do justice to the complexity of the real world. Second, the sectarian narrative is problematic because it leads to an overly simplistic framing that implies political responses that are likely to exacerbate conflict. Third, three highly generalized, contrasting, and influential grand narratives on conflict are analyzed and their implications for conflict management explained. These are:

1. Primordialism, which provides a biological explanation, such as kinship and evolutionary psychology, for conflict.
2. Ethnonationalism, which argues that conflicts are deeply rooted in cultures. Primordialists and Ethnonationalists tend to argue that antagonistic identities are so deeply rooted that they have a tribal interpretation of conflict.
3. Instrumentalism, which argues that conflict is the result of manipulation by the political elite or an "evil dictator."

Finally, a Constructivist Realist framework for analyzing conflict is outlined, which criticizes the over-simplification of the three grand narratives and argues that only a more careful analysis of the particularities and complexities of a conflict can lead to more sensitive interventions to mitigate violence. This involves realistic assessments of the multiplicity of forces that drive violence and an approach to negotiations that accepts difficult judgments and the "messy morality" that often accompanies political accommodation.

Grand narratives and apocalyptic visions: describing or creating the world?

The rise and fall of grand narratives and apocalyptic visions over time suggests the tentative nature of our knowledge, the impact of events, and the power and interests that fuel the prominence of these competing perspectives. These grand narratives are often alarmist and generate fear in order to shape political responses.

After the collapse of the Soviet Union in 1991, Cold War narratives about the global threat from totalitarian communism were obsolete. The rapidity of the Eastern Bloc's demise cast doubt on the more hardline interpretations of the Cold War. Francis Fukuyama's *The End of History* (1989) suggested that ideological development had achieved its zenith with capitalist democracy, and this fueled expectations of globalization and an integrated world pacified by a liberal or democratic peace. During the 1990s, when the war in Yugoslavia raged, Primordialist or Ethnonational explanations for violence were prominent. These asserted that conflict was driven by deeply rooted biological or cultural factors. Robert Kaplan warned of *The Coming Anarchy* (2000) and Michael Walzer of *The New Tribalism* (1992) that was going to engulf the world, resulting in endless wars as these tribes sought to create homogeneous states.

The Instrumentalist or "evil dictator" narrative contrasts sharply with the Primordialist or Ethnonationalist analysis of conflict. This stresses the political role of evil dictators in fomenting violent conflict and genocide. Once the evil head of the snake was cut off by military intervention, then the snake would die, leading to a spontaneous outbreak of peace and democracy among the "moderate" people. President Clinton's policy on Yugoslavia shifted between a tribal narrative, justifying non-intervention, and an evil dictator narrative, which suggested that the conflict was not tribal at all and that military intervention would be effective. The evil dictator narrative also provided justification for the US-led invasion of Iraq 2003. The post-invasion violence in Iraq then led to the emergence of a primordial, sectarian, or ethnosectarian analysis, which contradicted the Instrumentalist assumptions that had led to the invasion. The evil dictator narrative has since been applied to Libya (2011) and to Syria since 2011.

Samuel Huntington's *Clash of Civilizations* (1993) argued that the future would be riven by clashes between seven or eight civilizations, for example between the West and Islam. The fault lines between civilizations were supposed to be the battle lines of the future. This narrative became particularly popular after 9/11, because it appeared to explain Muslim attacks on the West. An "axis of evil" was also identified, which identified key Muslim states (Iraq, Iran) alongside other more traditional enemies (North Korea). US Undersecretary of State John Bolton also claimed that Libya, Cuba, and Syria were candidates for this axis. New wars and new terrorism were discovered as a novel, more barbaric form of Islamic violence that demanded a more violent and repressive response. In this New Cold War, the Green Menace replaced the Red Menace as a totalitarian threat to the West, and Islam was portrayed as a threat to world peace. Superterrorism connected Weapons of Mass Destruction to terrorism, and mistakenly associated Saddam Hussein with al-Qaeda in order to justify the invasion of Iraq. In the West, Muslims and their religion became the enemy within and, along with multiculturalism, threatened to undermine Western values and weaken democracy and human rights in the battle of ideas against the totalitarian threat from "Islamofascism." The new sectarian narrative of conflict between Shia and Sunni Muslims should be seen in the context of the demonization of Islam, which draws on earlier anti-Muslim narratives. This portrays Muslims as fanatics and essentializes them as violent, irrational, savage, and fanatical.[1]

The advantage of these grand narratives and apocalyptic visions is that their simplicity provides the comforting illusion that the world is easy to understand and provides simple moral lessons. Thomas L. Friedman argues in the *New York Times* that the wars in Iraq, Libya, Afghanistan, Bosnia, and Syria "are all the same war": "They are all the story of what happens when multisectarian societies, most of them Muslim or Arab, are held together for decades by dictators ruling vertically, from the top down, with iron fists and they have their dictators toppled." Sunnis and Shiites "have been fighting since the 7th century" and Muslim "civilization has missed every big modern global trend." Since there is no sense of citizenship or pluralistic ethic, "Syria and Iraq will both likely devolve into self-governing, largely homogenous, ethnic and religious units..."[2]

The danger of these grand narratives and apocalyptic visions is that they do not accurately depict the world, but are driven by powerful political interests. Their Manichaean world-view creates the conditions for violent conflict. Enemies are demonized and so must be eliminated rather than engaged or negotiated with. The demonization of the "other" means that our own narratives and intentions—including the impact of religion on "us"—need not be questioned. Sectarian Christians may promote a sectarian narrative to stimulate support for Christianity, ignoring the historical role of Christianity in violent conflict. Western policy-makers may, consciously or unconsciously, promote Christian values as Western values.

Beyond sectarianism?

Sectarianism is a derogatory term, used to describe the "other" rather than "us." The term is used in Iraq and Syria to attack political opponents. The sectarian narrative is associated with a narrative that emphasizes the role of religion and sect, rather than say politics, in explaining current conflicts in the Middle East. The *Oxford English Dictionary* defines it as "Excessive attachment to a particular sect or party, especially in religion." As an adjective it means "Rigidly following the doctrines of a sect or other group." The *Cambridge English Dictionary* defines it as "(a person) strongly supporting a particular religious group and not willing to accept other beliefs." Sectarianism, therefore, is a concept that particularly favors a religious explanation for conflict. As applied to the Middle East, it suggests that it is the excessive, intolerant and rigid (if not fundamentalist) attachment to religious beliefs that is responsible for violent conflict. Since 9/11, religion and Islam have become a prominent explanation for political violence, with some arguing that adherence to Islam leads directly to violence, like a "conveyor belt." The sectarian narrative undermines the monolithic view of Islam by acknowledging at least conflict between two groups within it, but this narrative has also focused on "Islamic violence."

Constructivist Realist critics of the sectarian narrative do not accept the ancient and enduring nature of sectarianism. They refer to the power, processes, and interests that explain the rise and fall of sectarian narratives over time. Concepts like sectarianism are not simple reflections of the world, but are used to make that world through a process of sectarianization. The danger is that the use of the concept of sectarianism and the sectarianization of the Middle East brings into being the world that it purports to describe. This does not mean to say that groups do not exist and do not have power, but constructivists focus on how these identities are brought into being and acquire power.[3] Along with Instrumentalists, they criticize simplistic arguments around the religious motivation of violence.[4]

Grand narratives: the Primordialist and Ethnonationalist analysis

Primordialism stresses the influence of biology (genes, evolutionary psychology) and Ethnonationalism the influence of culture in producing ethnonational or ethnosectarian conflict, almost to the exclusion of other factors. They are both essentialist in that they close off the possibility of changeable human behavior. These theories are structuralist, because they emphasize the constraints that biology and culture place on the possibility for political change, and so they argue that the division of the world along ethnosectarian lines is almost inevitable. The attitudes of an individual are simply derived from a perception of their biological or cultural background, and these natural divisions predispose people to violence. This is why the ethnonational or sectarian identity of people is constantly flagged, and the group, for example Sunnis, are treated as if they are unitary collective actors. They encourage generalized statements that make little reference to cross-cultural differences or previous historical variation. They have a tendency to universalize rather than capture the complexity of individual experience. Such explanations have provided the intellectual legitimacy for murderous communal chauvinism, arguing that a state for every nation is the natural and inevitable outcome of natural, primordial attachments.[5] Critics argue that acting on the basis of these explanations risks intensifying conflict in a self-fulfilling prophecy.

Primordialism emphasizes the role of biology in creating very powerful ethnic or ethnosectarian identities. The nation or ethnic group is the "family," its members are connected biologically to one another through common descent, which is real rather than imagined. Since national and ethnic identities are natural, they are very powerful, even overwhelming influences on individual and group behavior. These group identities are deeply rooted and explain persistent conflict between ethnic groups throughout history. Since they are natural and biological, it is futile to try to remake them into less antagonistic forms. Violent conflict between such primordial groups is, therefore, inevitable where they come into contact with each other. This antagonism spreads throughout the ethnic or national group, making violent conflict with rival primordial groups widespread. Neighbor turns on neighbor as these primordial identities surpass by far any rival identity for the individual's allegiance. The role of politics in mediating conflict is therefore highly limited, because ethnic or national political leaders are driven by the same primordial passions as the people that they represent. If political leaders attempt to deviate from the achievement of the nation's destiny, they are likely to be harshly punished.

Ethnonational (or culturalist) explanations emphasize the role of culture in the formation and persistence of ethnic groups, and this explains conflict (and many different forms of social action). Nearly all nations, they argue, have a core ethnic group; the implication being that all nations *should* have a core or dominant ethnic group, which provides the values around which a nation or "ethno-nation" should cohere. Since culture can be very deeply rooted, their analysis of conflict can be indistinguishable from Primordialism. Indeed, Stephen Van Evera argues that 'Primordialism Lives!' because although identity and group identity is clearly socially constructed and not biological, we should treat identity as if it were Primordial, because it is so hard to reconstruct once it is formed.[6] The use of the terms ethnic, ethnonational or ethno-symbolism by culturalists further adds to the impression that common biological descent is part of the explanation for the strength of ethnic or national identity. Ethnic explanations can range from hardline Ethnonationalists, who appear to be indistinguishable from Primordialists, to those moderate Ethnonationalists that are more accepting of a limited degree of flexibility in cultural and ethnic identities and might even accept that a non-ethnic, civic nationalism is possible. Nonetheless, this theory is structuralist because of the weight that Ethnonationalist explanations place on the cultural context for shaping or determining the possibility of political change.

Mahmood Mamdani criticizes culturalism:

> Culture Talk assumes that every culture has a tangible essence that defines it, and it then explains politics as a consequence of that essence. Culture Talk after 9/11, for example, qualified and explained the practice of "terrorism" as "Islamic." "Islamic terrorism" is thus offered as both description and explanation of the events of 9/11.[7]

A hardline ethnonationalist explanation sees politics as highly constrained by popular Ethnonationalism, and therefore tends toward a focus on eliminationist, assimilationist, and segregationist strategies in order to create ethnically homogeneous states. Moderate Ethnonationalists will see politics as less constrained, because culture is more malleable and perhaps more able to accommodate difference than a hardline interpretation. Nonetheless, these ethnic identities are so powerful that political actors have to work around them, rather than challenge or erode them through integrationist strategies of mixing. Leaders do not invent ethnonational identity, but recognize it and appeal to it. Primordialists and Ethnonationalists argue that ethnonationalism explains social action, rather than seeing ethnonationalism as a phenomenon whose creation and complexity needs to be explained.

Primordialist and Ethnonationalist accounts of history emphasize the roles of ethnicity and nation to the exclusion of other forms of identity. Class or gender, for example, are seen as being trumped by ethnicity and nationalism. Support for internationalism and universalism is seen as a cover or camouflage to disguise 'ethnosectarian' domination. The power and appeal of ethnonationalism is strong and waiting to break through these other "artificial" identities. Primordialists and Ethnonationalists tend to date the origins of ethnic conflict back through hundreds, if not thousands, of years of history to emphasize its strength and persistence over time. This suggests that these structures will strongly shape, if not determine, the future. Historians may be "present-centered," reading current divisions back through history as if they had always existed. Fanar Haddad sees sectarianism as rooted in the premodern era and myths of Sunni-Shia hostility passed down from generation to generation waiting to be "reawakened."[8]

History is told using ethnosectarian categories to emphasize its influence and this, critics argue, reproduces the arguments of "sectarian entrepreneurs." All Sunnis in Iraq, for example, are framed as collectively responsible for the crimes perpetrated by the Baathists or Saddam Hussein. The Sunni Arab mentality is described as supremacist and contemptuous.[9] This implies that the actions of some members of a sect are representative of the whole group. This leads to the concept of representative violence, where the killings by members of a sect are seen as representative of the whole group, rather than the particular individuals or group that carried out the violence.[10] This framing of sectarian violence encourages retaliation, not so much against the perpetrators but against any members of that group. The bombing of the Shia al Askariya shrine by members of al-Qaeda in February 2006 seems to have been attributed by some to the whole Sunni community and reprisal attacks made on that basis. The failure of Shia leaders to restrain this response appeared to demonstrate the limits of their control.[11]

Ethnonationalists emphasize the fragility of multi-communal states. Peter W. Galbraith argued that Iraq was "artificial" while Germany and Japan were "real nations" since they were "ethnically and culturally homogeneous." Multiethnic and multireligious states such as Iraq were prone to disintegration, like Czechoslovakia, Yugoslavia, and the Soviet Union: "In each case, nationalism overcame loyalty to the larger entity." Galbraith favored the "end of Iraq" rather than attempting to preserve this "unnatural" entity, which would result in more violence.[12] Gareth Stansfield and Liam Anderson argued that Iraq would either chaotically break up into three or more separate independent states based on the historic Ottoman vilayets of Basra, Baghdad, or Mosul, or else institutionalize ethno-sectarian identities which were "the main organizing forces of Iraqi political life."[13]

The Primordialist and Ethnonationalist explanation of the Middle East conflict is difficult to reconcile with the religious or sectarian narrative. Islam is a global religious community including people of all racial groups with diverse national, regional, and religious practices. Political Islam transcends nation and ethnicity and aspires to unite Muslims. Primordialism emphasizes biology, and this is usually not considered to explain sectarianism and adherence to Sunni, Shia, or any other Islamic sect. Ethnonationalism is typically used to explain the emergence of nations, rather than the influence of sectarian groups whose members extend across state borders and throughout the world. In Iraq, for example, the Sunnis and Shias are sects of Islam, while Kurds are majority Sunni but also Shia and members of ancient religions, with separatist, national aspirations. Primordialism and Ethnonationalism cannot explain sectarianism or take into account the influence of multiple identities that are available in the Middle East. They use concepts like ethnosectarian or ethnoreligious to make their theories relevant in the Middle East.

The Lebanese writer Amin Maalouf applies a thought experiment to discredit primordialism. He argues that an infant removed at birth and set down in a different environment would take on his identity from that new context, "And might he not one day find himself fighting to the death against those who ought to have been his nearest and dearest?"[14] Although primordialism has been widely discredited, it survives as a simple and popular explanation for conflict, and this means it has to be taken seriously. It does not appeal and survive as an explanation for some policy-makers and may be popular among the public. Ethnonationalism has been criticized for failing to capture the malleability of culture and the invention of nations out of nothing, without ethnic cores.

Grand narratives: Primordialist and Ethnonationalist prescriptions

Primordial and Ethnonationalist explanations of violent group conflict tend to lead to authoritarian, eliminationist, assimilationist, or segregationist prescriptions for the management of conflict. Since Primordialism and hardline Ethnonationalism are essential and ineradicable, Ethnonational groups will continue to kill one another until one has been eliminated, unless they can be segregated. Plural or multicultural states are inherently unstable and prone to conflict; therefore dictatorships or authoritarian states, it is argued, keep the peace between ethnic groups. There are several prescriptions for conflict management that follow from the Primordial and Ethnonationalist analysis:

"Give war a chance": Some Conservative Realists argue that the best solution to Primordial conflicts is to "give war a chance," for one side to defeat the other and ethnically cleanse territories so that ethnically homogeneous states can be created. The examples of this could be India and Yugoslavia, but violence in Iraq and Syria has also led to reports of an increasingly segregated population. War and segregation, they argue, is the only way that long-term stable settlements can be achieved. To attempt anything less is to prolong and exacerbate the agony of a more gradual separation.

Partition: The breaking up of ethnically mixed states is the logical corollary of the Primordial and hardline Ethnonationalist perspective. This might be the result of "giving war a chance," or there might be an attempt at peaceful repartition of a state to create more homogeneous states, although the danger is that such an attempt would be accompanied by war and ethnic cleansing. This, like "giving war a chance," might also leave a legacy of hatred that would lead to future conflict.

Population transfer or exchange: This proposes that ethnic populations are physically exchanged and transferred from where they were living to live among their co-nationals, thereby creating more homogeneous states. Examples of this are the population exchanges between Greece, Turkey, and Bulgaria in the 1920s.

Authoritarianism or dictatorship: This proposes strong authoritarian structures to keep the conflicting groups under control, the fear being that the end of dictatorship "lifts the lid off the cauldron of ancient hatreds."

Assimilation: This solution proposes that minorities give up their distinctive cultures and assimilate by embracing the dominant culture. Because Primordialists emphasize genetics, they are less likely to believe that assimilation is possible, whereas moderate Ethnonationalists might see this as a possibility.

Consociationalism: This theory was built on Primordialist assumptions, but it might more logically be associated with a moderate Ethnonationalist position because it does suggest a key role for political elites in managing conflict. Consociationalism seeks to maintain the unity of a plural state by explicitly recognizing and building upon communal or sectarian difference in order to make those identities into the ethnonational pillars on which communal elites construct a power-sharing settlement. By reducing the opportunities for contact and therefore conflict, Consociationalists seek to reduce the opportunities for antagonism and conflict between the pillars. Arend Lijphart argues that "Because good social fences may make good neighbors, a kind of voluntary apartheid policy may be the most appropriate solution for a divided society."[15] Each community is encouraged to create its own political parties, newspapers, educational and social institutions in order to avoid inter-mixing. Geographical segregation logically facilitates communal autonomy and segregation. This segregation, it is argued, has the advantage of demobilizing ethnonationalism. This permits government by elite cartel or Grand Coalition, in which the sectarian leaders of each communal pillar negotiate a power-sharing accommodation over the heads of, and perhaps against the wishes of, their communal group. Consociationalism is reminiscent of the corporatist model in Western European states during the post-war period, where politicians, businesspeople, and trade unionists negotiated the government of these states in smoke-filled rooms.

There are three key criticisms of Consociationalism. First is that, as the theory has evolved, it has become so ambiguous that it can be presented as all things to all people. Although a power-sharing, Grand Coalition was supposed to be at the heart of Consociationalism, Revisionist Consociationalists claim that this is unnecessary. This permits Consociationalists to claim the Iraq constitution of 2005 as Consociationalist, even though it permitted the exclusion of the Sunnis from power-sharing.[16] Second, there is an important contradiction between Consociationalism's primordialism and the assumption that sectarian elites will have the power to manage communal divisions. Primordialism is strongly structuralist and suggests that power comes from the people and the elites are therefore highly constrained. It is illogical, therefore, for Consociationalists to direct their prescriptions at the sectarian elite, because they are so highly constrained. They also make the unrealistic assumptions that these are both benevolent and capable of imposing a power-sharing settlement. A third criticism is that while Consociationalists reinforce Primordial identities into the pillars of a stable accommodation, they show little awareness that this might escalate violence by further empowering the antagonistic elites and identities that were responsible for conflict in the first place. They have little explanation for how these sectarian pillars will wither away.

Lebanon's experience of power-sharing is considered to date back to 1861. Consociationalists have claimed the National Pact of 1943–75 and the Taif Agreement of 1989 as key examples of Consociationalism in the Middle East. The informal and unwritten National Pact led to a Christian Maronite president, a Sunni prime minister, a Shiite chairperson of the legislative, and Greek Orthodox deputy chairman and deputy prime minister.[17] The breakdown of the state and the civil war, which killed approximately 150,000, cast doubt on the effectiveness of the Consociational model. Sectarianism or Confessionalism was institutionalized, but the Taif Agreement and the constitutional settlement disguised the continuing influence of the Syrian state in Lebanon. Although sectarian power-sharing was, since the end of the Ottoman Empire, supposed to transition toward a non-sectarian democracy, "at the end of each regime the sectarianism in politics was stronger and more firmly rooted."[18] The alliances of 8 and 14 March 2005 cut across traditional religious cleavages between Christians and Muslims and Sunnis and Maronites. Simon Haddad concludes: "Consociationalism has failed in its task of providing stable and properly functioning public institutions. Instead it has led to political deadlock, inviting outside interference through nonconventional conflict resolution procedures."[19]

The Primordialist or Ethnonationalist interpretation of Iraq and its dissolution contradicts support for the invasion of Iraq. Since ethnosectarian countries like Iraq are artificial and prone to division if a dictator is removed, the chaos and sectarian conflict following the invasion of Iraq should have been expected. In the wake of the invasion of Iraq 2003, Primordialists and Ethnonationalists confidently proclaimed the inevitability of the break-up of Iraq and argued that this would be the best way of minimizing violence. Consociationalists claimed the Iraq constitution of 2005 for Consociationalism, even though it did not require all significant groups to be represented in a power-sharing Grand Coalition. The constitution allowed for the exclusion of the Sunnis, and their marginalization in the post-invasion period has contributed to further violence in Iraq and the rise of Daesh. The 2005 constitution also provided for a radical decentralization of the Iraqi state and the emergence of regions—which might evolve into separate states. Leading Ethnonationalists and Consociationalists have also acted as advisors to Iraqi Kurds, who might see Consociationalism as a step toward independence.

Primordialists and Ethnonationalists argue that Syria will have to be repartitioned to reflect the new sectarian realities created by the war. Joshua Landis has contended that there will have to be a Great Sorting Out in the Middle East similar to that in Eastern Europe after World War II. This will lead to "the rearrangement of populations in the region to better fit the nation states that were fixed after WW1. Some new borders are being drawn, such as those around the Kurdish regions of Iraq and perhaps Syria, but mostly, what we are seeing is the ethnic cleansing of much of the region to fit the borders."[20] Christopher Phillips describes how the Western media and policy-makers reinforce an exaggerated, sectarian interpretation of the Iraq and Syrian war. Groups are presented as if they represent a single ethnosectarian agenda; simplified maps are produced that do not show the extent of mixing within Sunni, Shia, and Kurdish areas, promoting the idea that Syria can be partitioned into neat, ethnic areas.[21] Consociationalism has also been recommended as a solution for Syria.[22]

The apocalyptic vision of Primordialists and Ethnonationalists leads them to claim that the future is inevitably tribal and then warn that segregation and Consociationalism are the only way to mitigate the violence. While the power of group conflict should not be underestimated, neither should it be overestimated. The widely predicted racial apocalypse in South Africa did not occur. In Northern Ireland, Primordialists and Ethnonationalists were unable to account for the success of the peace process. Negotiated and peaceful transitions to democracy have taken place in South America, Eastern Europe, and the former Soviet Union. There are thousands of groups in the world on which a state might be created, but the overwhelming tendency has been for these groups to live in peace rather than, as Primordialists and Ethnonationalists claim, to seek their own state.

Fascists, radical nationalists, and sectarians with their racial, biological, and religious visions of utopia tend to favor Primordialist and Ethnonationalist interpretations of conflict and the segregationist prescriptions that follow from them. More moderate conservative nationalists argue that a nation can only cohere and have stability if it has a common cultural core that provides common values. Pluralism and multiculturalism therefore represent a threat to the nation.

External powers will use Primordialist and Ethnonationalist explanations of conflict to avoid political or military intervention. These tribalistic analyses blame the people of the Middle East for their problems, rather than attributing any responsibility to external, imperialist powers. Alternatively, if military intervention is thought to be necessary, the Primordialist analysis of a tribal or barbaric enemy may justify the use of overwhelming force, because antagonisms are so deeply rooted that it is only by using such force that the enemy will be cowed or shocked into submission.

Grand narratives: Instrumentalism or the evil politicians/dictator explanation

The Instrumentalist (or evil politicians/dictator) explanation of group conflict emphasizes the role of political elites in creating violent group conflict. This provides a sharp contrast to and critique of Primordialism and Ethnonationalism. Instrumentalists argue that group conflict is the result of competition for power between political elites (or sectarian entrepreneurs) who exploit identities such as sectarianism and nationalism to further their own interests. These elites use the media and culture to manipulate the people in their own interests. Alternatively, sectarianism may be blamed on the manipulations of external powers, and there is denial of sectarianism within the state.[23] This analysis is agency-oriented, stressing the responsibility of elite individuals and groups for conflict and popular sectarianism. This contrasts with the structuralist explanations of Primordialists and Ethnonationalists, whose political actors are highly constrained by context and the ethnosectarianism of the people. For Instrumentalists, the groups in conflict are not necessarily ethnic or national, but may be mobilized on class, sect, gender, or other forms of identity. Identities, therefore, are highly malleable and manipulated to achieve the will of the elite. Indeed, these identities, nationalism most notably, can be created out of prior traditions or else created out of nothing. They are highly critical of Primordialists and Ethnonationalists for not simply describing sectarian conflict, but for creating and legitimizing sectarian conflict. Their rhetoric is a self-fulfilling prophecy.

Instrumentalists argue that nations and nationalism have only appeared since 1789 and are the result of modern processes like capitalism, industrialization, mass literacy and education, the bureaucratic state, the decline of religion, and the rise of secularism. These processes facilitate the spread of nationalist consciousness. States make nations, rather than nations making states. The Italian nationalist Massimo d'Azeglio famously stated in 1861 that "we have made Italy; now we must make Italians." Nations do not need ancient origins, as demonstrated by the existence of the United States, Australia, and Canada. Instrumentalists emphasize the invention of tradition, and seek to demonstrate that apparently timeless traditions are sometimes recent inventions designed to promote the power and interests of powerful elites.[24] Instrumentalists may be dismissive of the influence of ethnonationalism, believing that economic integration, modernization, globalization, and cosmopolitanism are consigning parochial nationalist, ethnic, or sectarian attachments to history.

Instrumentalist accounts challenge the myths of (ethno)nationalist history by emphasizing the rise, fall, creation, and intersection of different identities over time. In the case of Iraq, for example, they would not see history through the prism of perennial Sunni against Shia conflict, but show how a range of identities—class, race, gender, tribal, regional, local, urban-rural, national, sect, clan, city quarter, guild, intermarriage, transborder groupings—interact and intersect over time. The importance of the Sunni-Shia divide in the Middle East is seen as a recent development, sometimes dated from the Iranian revolution in 1979. Jonathan Steele, for example, argues that for most of Iraq's history the Sunni-Shia divide "was not a source of hostility or violence but simply a cultural and social fact of life, and often a mark of class."[25] They would attempt to undermine the sectarian narrative by pointing to the existence of Sunni and Shia within the same tribe and the existence of intermarriage and mixed ancestry. The divisions *within* Sunni and Shia communities would also be emphasized and the solidarity between Shia and Sunni stressed. Rather than sectarianizing Saddam's rule as an attempt to impose Sunni Arab dominance over Iraq, he is portrayed as favoring his own tribe and family, with his first victims other Sunni Arabs. Shias fought for Iraq against Iran and did not mutiny or surrender. "They formed the bulk of the conscript army and held firm against the Iranian forces. ... Sectarianism had proven to be largely irrelevant politically."[26] Sectarianisation took place after Saddam's defeat in Kuwait 1991 and this was exacerbated by the occupation after 2003, particularly with the abolition of the army and de-Baathification that was seen as de-Sunnification. There was cross-community solidarity at the time of the US attack on Fallujah.[27] Although votes were initially cast along sectarian lines in 2005, the Iraq election of 2010 was seen as a vote against sectarianism. The Anbar or Tribal Awakening in 2006 resulted in some Sunnis allying with the US forces to defeat the increasingly brutal military operations of al-Qaeda. This suggested the importance of tribal identities, intra-Sunni divisions, and the flexibility of political alliances. In Syria the geographical variation of sectarianism suggests that it might be one of a number of factors in play.[28]

Instrumentalists and Constructivists are more specific in allocating the responsibility for conflict and violence to particular individuals and organizations in order to inhibit the sectarianization and escalation of conflict. They undermine Primordialist and Ethnonationalist claims about the naturalness or inevitability of ethnosectarian conflict by demonstrating the invented or constructed nature of the world. Since the world is constructed, it may be reconstructed into a less violent and unjust form. The debate over the artificiality of Iraq is between the Primordialists and Ethnonationalists, who argue that Iraqi identity is an unnatural or artificial veneer that covers powerful ethnic and sectarian identities. Instrumentalists respond that public opinion polls and other indicators suggest that the sense of Iraqi identity, and other artificial identities in the Middle East, is as strong and natural as that of most states in the world that have been constructed by force of arms and imperial power. There is, therefore, nothing natural or inevitable about their disintegration. Instrumentalists see the sectarianization of Iraq as a dynamic, complex process. Jonathan Steele argues:

> In summary, no single group can be blamed for Iraq's devastating slide towards sectarian war. Saddam started the rot. The Americans then played a significant part by emphasizing sectarian issues in their post-war policies. Iraqi Shia politicians and the death squads that were run by their militias compounded the problem and gave it a lethal dimension.[29]

The debates between Primordialists, Ethnonationalists, and Instrumentalists over Iraq are echoed in more recent arguments over Syria. Instrumentalists are critical of the religious and sectarian description of the Syrian conflict, which almost suggests that violence is biologically or culturally determined. Instrumentalists argue that sectarianism is not about intractable religiosity but about politics. Syrians have been mobilizing against Assad for reasons that are not sectarian and because the framing of the war as sectarian is not accurate. Whether or not Syria becomes a violent sectarian conflict partly depends on whether it is framed as such.[30]

Instrumentalists challenge sectarian myths and argue that sectarianism is manipulated to achieve political goals. They point out that the majority of the Syrian state's military forces are Sunnis who are supposedly fighting their own. Sunnis play an important role in sustaining the Syrian state. Although the Syrian regime is currently allied with Hezbollah, during the Lebanese civil war President Hafez al-Assad clamped down on Hezbollah killing its fighters and almost managed to assassinate Hasan Nasrallah, the current secretary general. The Russians do not bomb Syria over religion. The alliance between President Assad of Syria and Iran is not theological but political; the Alawites were only deemed an offshoot of Shia Islam forty years ago. The Iranian state has supported both Shia Hezbollah and Sunni Hamas.

Christopher Phillips argues that Syria is a semi-sectarian conflict: "Sectarianism is a factor in the war but certainly not the only one and it varies in importance over space and time."[31] He identifies sectarianisation taking place by both the Syrian state and rebel opposition, but he argues for a more complex interpretation of the conflict. He characterizes the regime as run by "some Alawis" based on the president's clan and tribe. The state did promote national identity and even prioritized Sunni culture: "Sect was officially dismissed and an inclusive, Syrian Arab nationalism encouraged, but politicized sect identities were simultaneously reproduced, either by the regime or by its internal and external enemies."[32] Heiko Wimmen argues that sectarianism was implanted in Syrian society "long before external actors started to play a significant role in the country's current war." This sectarianisation was a result of regime and opposition actions, pointing to the diversity of experiences throughout Syria with sectarianism.[33]

Since "evil politicians/dictators" manipulate and create antagonistic identities that result in violent conflict, then they must be replaced by more authentic representatives of the people who are seen as more democratic, supportive of human rights, and moderate. This reinforces Liberal Peace Theory which suggests that democratic states will not go to war with each other. These new elites could create a strong Iraqi or Syrian state with an inclusive national identity based on equal citizenship, pluralist democracy, and protection for minority rights. The Civil Society approach takes an instrumental analysis of conflict and prescribes integration and the mobilization of Civil Society in order to put pressure on the malign elites to end communal conflict, or else to replace those political elites with the more authentic voice of the people. Integration, mixing between different groups leading to understanding, rather than segregation is seen as the means by which understanding and accommodation will be achieved at the grass-roots level, and this will then be mobilized to pressure political elites toward accommodation.[34] The economic and social basis for conflict may be addressed through egalitarian reforms. The nationalist or sectarian myths of persistent antagonism are undermined and replaced with a story that emphasizes the invention of these histories and seeks to support reconciliation and integration. Instrumentalists prescribe constitutions that encourage integration and mixing; they tend to prefer voting systems that encourage cross communal parties and moderation in voting behavior.[35]

Instrumentalist and civil society accounts of conflict serve various political interests. The Instrumentalist understanding of conflict might have popular resonance because it expresses disillusion with political elites and lends itself to a conspiratorial view of politics. This narrative denies that there is a popular sectarianism and may blame sectarian differences on external manipulation. Fanar Haddad has been critical of Instrumentalism and the failure of "traditional Iraqi discourse, whether from above or from below" to address sectarianism openly because of a "veneer of ecumenical harmony." He identifies different types of aggressive, assertive, passive, apologetic, and banal sectarianism.[36] In the West, an Instrumentalist perspective can be associated with right-wing Neoconservatives and left-wing Liberal Hawks. The argument that conflicts are caused by evil dictators leads to the conclusion that the removal of these dictators through military intervention—cutting the head off the snake—will result in the end of violence and the spontaneous demand for democracy. This was the argument for the invasion of Iraq deployed by Prime Minister Blair and President Bush. The British prime minister ignored the advice of Iraq experts who warned that the invasion would unleash violent conflict.[37]

Constructivist Realism

Constructivist Realism provides a framework that arises out of a critique of Primordialist, Ethnonationalist, and Instrumentalist theories.[38] Constructivism stresses the socially constructed nature of reality and interests; the implication is that the world can be reconstructed in order to achieve more ideal outcomes. "Thick" constructivists (like Instrumentalists) tend to be idealists because they are idea- and agency-oriented. They share the assumption that rapid, radical change is both possible and desirable. Since the world is imagined, then it can be re-imagined in radically different ways through acts of will and agency. They are reluctant to accept strictures or constraints on ideal solutions to group conflict. In doing so they risk ignoring the salience of group identity, and the challenge this poses to political actors, in their determination to challenge and overcome it. This leaves them unable to answer the moral question of what to do and unable to acknowledge the constrained choices and difficult judgments involved in real politics.[39]

Constructivism and realism tend not to be seen as compatible, because realism accepts as unchanging certain assumptions about the world, whereas constructivism is often used to challenge such assumptions. A "thin" constructivism may be compatible with a "thin" realism that recognizes the world is a social construct but also that there is an objective material reality that constrains these constructions. Constructivists may, therefore, share with realists important assumptions: the ineradicable nature of power, the inevitability of pluralism and conflict. Realists also seek to unmask power relations and expose the self-interest and (inevitable) hypocrisy of political actors: "Realism of this kind expresses skepticism about the scope of reason and the influence of morality in a world in which power, and the relentless pursuit of power, is a pervasive feature ... It faces up to the folly and perversity of political life, without illusion or false hope."[40] In contrast to Constructivist Idealists (and Instrumentalists), Constructivist Realists have a greater sense of the constraints operating on political actors and the difficult and even tragic choices that may face them. This more realistic analysis of politics, they argue, is more likely to achieve better outcomes because it is based on a more accurate understanding of the world and the inevitable compromises and messy morality of politics.[41] They accept that different stories or narratives are told about conflict to further competing political ends, yet some accounts based on better arguments and evidence are more convincing than others.

Constructivist Realism shares much of Instrumentalism's critique of essentialist Primordial and Ethnonationalist interpretations of identity. Constructivist Realists accept the influence that groups and groupist ideologies play in violent conflict. In contrast to the focus of Primordialists and Ethnonationalists on biology and culture, Constructivists agree with Instrumentalists that a range of group identities may be mobilized and that these should be conceptualized, according to Brubaker, in "relational, processual, dynamic, eventful and disaggregated terms."[42]

There are a number of points of distinction between Constructivist Realists and Instrumentalists, and especially with Primordialists and Ethnonationalists.

1. *Scepticism of grand narratives and reductionism:* A Constructivist Realist approach can provide a framework, rather than a universal theory, that allows the observer to analyze how structure and agency shape particular conflicts based on a close understanding of those conflicts. They oppose the universal and reductionist explanations of grand narratives such as Primordialism, Ethnonationalism, and Instrumentalism, which lead their

advocates to make predictions that often turn out to be mistaken, for example on the end of Iraq. These theories cannot account for the diversity of group conflict and the importance of deep knowledge of the particular context. Arguably, more violence is done to the world in the name of imposing over-generalized and universal interpretations of and prescriptions for conflict than by those who would respect the diversity and complexity of conflict. Constructivists seek a middle way between pure description, which captures complexity but explains nothing, and abstract theoretical reflection, which "inflicts violence ... on the nuance and complexity of the reality it purports to explain."[43]

2. *The complexity of identities:* Constructivist Realists argue that structures and identities may be fluid and malleable or they may be sticky and hard to change, depending on the context. This makes Constructive Realists distinct from the structuralist and essentialist arguments of Primordialists and Ethnonationalists, as well as from the agency-oriented or voluntaristic arguments of Instrumentalists and Constructivist Idealists. Constructivists argue that group identities can be deeply rooted, popularly reproduced, and therefore are not necessarily easy for elites to manipulate. Because something is socially constructed does not mean that it can be deconstructed at will. These identities may be reproduced in the banality of everyday life among popular opinion, and therefore they are not necessarily easily reinvented by political elites.[44] Identities are complex so that sectarian attitudes may not necessarily result in violent behavior.

3. *Structure/agency: politics is constrained:* Constructivist Realists argue that the political elites do not stand outside the world and are likely to be affected by the sectarian and other identities and antagonisms that may be apparent among the people. They accept that the power of group identities can be very powerful (or weak) and this constrains the power of elites. Constructivist Realists argue that politics is neither determined from below by Primordialism or Ethnonationlism, nor determined from above by the manipulations of political elites; it is not necessarily easy for elite actors to make and remake identities to pursue their interests. Constructivist Realists believe that political actors are neither simply the prisoners of the people (Primordialism) nor the shepherd who leads the sheep (Instrumentalism). The concepts of structure/agency suggest that people do make their own history, but they do so within constraints. Politics is a more complex affair that involves consideration of idealism, judgment, and often a messy morality.

4. *The people are not necessarily benign:* The people may not necessarily be pro-democratic and anti-sectarian. The public may overtly reject sectarianism but privately and through their behavior reproduce it.[45] Sectarian attitudes may be indicated in popular electoral support for radical sectarian or nationalist parties, which may contrast to less sectarian attitudes expressed in opinion polls. In Northern Ireland, for example, polls tend consistently to underestimate the electoral support for hardline political parties.[46] The people may reject democracy and dictators can, depending on the context, be popular. According to one poll, President Bashar al-Assad was supported by a 55 percent majority of Syrians.[47] Other commentators have also suggested that there is significant popular support for Assad within Syria.[48]

5. *Political elites are not necessarily malign:* Political or other elite actors act within constraints and may attempt to act in a more positive or negative way to end violent conflict. Politics is important, but it is politics within constraints; political actors are not free to lead their people wherever they will. This may be apparent when a leader attempts political accommodation and then loses popular support. The key negotiators of the Oslo Peace Process, the PLO and Israeli Labor Party, were outflanked and undermined by more radical critics, resulting in a decline in their electoral and political fortunes.

6. *Political morality is messy and involves difficult judgments:* Primordialists are structuralists who suggest that political actors need to make no moral calculation because they are driven by necessity, their own biology, and the will of the Primordial masses. Instrumentalists, by contrast, are agency-oriented and argue that political actors are unconstrained and therefore able to make clear moral and ideal choices.

Constructivist realism combines realism with an idealism that distinguishes it from conservative realism. The distinction between what is and what ought to be is artificial. Constructivist realists argue (against conservative realists) that analysts bring their values and norms to their analysis and interpretation of conflict. It is not possible to explain what is and what ought to be without using moral concepts. There is an acknowledgment that reality is constructed, and different stories can be told about politics with different implications for actions and norms. Nonetheless, some stories or arguments have more evidence to support them and are more convincing than others. For constructivists, ethical reasoning must combine both principles of action with the empirical.

Constructivist Realists argue that political actors play roles and act within constraints that may become looser or tighter. These constraints mean that political actors must use their judgment to calculate the consequences of different courses of action to achieve their goals. The assumption that political actors have choices and goals suggests that there is a moral dimension to politics but that this is morality in context. The constraints and opportunities (structure/agency) that face political actors may present them with morally difficult, even tragic choices, where the choice appears to be between two equally undesirable outcomes.

This draws attention to the importance of political judgment in determining how much ideals and morality may be compromised to achieve political accommodation. This moves the debate away from the grand narratives, where moral choices appear to be clear, to the more morally grey area of real political practice where political actors may have dirty hands and use questionable political skills to achieve their goals.[49] Constructivist Realists attempt to assess the constraints and opportunities that face various actors in the conflict without allowing moral prejudice to influence these judgments. The more morally corrupt parties may be those who, pragmatically speaking, cannot move toward accommodation; and so it may be necessary that the less morally corrupt and the more victimized make a greater compromise, or have pressure exerted on them to do so.

Constructivist Realists accept the responsibility of political actors to take difficult moral judgments. This may involve some sacrifice of justice for peace. During the war in Yugoslavia, idealists were criticized for missing opportunities for peace (it was significant that this realist argument was made anonymously): "Thousands of people are dead who should have been alive—because moralists were in quest of the perfect peace. Unfortunately, a perfect peace can rarely be attained in the aftermath of bloody conflict."[50] There are also difficult judgments to be made over how far it may be necessary to acknowledge the power of sectarian identities and how far to challenge or remake them. Power-sharing may entrench sectarian identities in the short run, in the judgment that this would end violence and lead to a situation in which those identities might be remade in the longer term. The extent of political and popular antagonism to integration might lead to a situation where partition appeared to be the most popular, feasible and least bad solution (such as the two-state solution in Israel/Palestine).

The realist practice of politicians is vulnerable to (populist) anti-politics attacks by pious idealists. These seek to win political support by condemning the dirty politics or realpolitik of peacemakers, underestimating the difficulties of a negotiated accommodation, or seeking to undermine those negotiations in favor of military victory. The talking or not talking to terrorists and peace/justice debate draws attention to the morally difficult choices and judgments that are made in trying to end violent conflict.[51] The idealist approach that insists on the requirement of legal justice for peace can guarantee perpetual war.

7. *Politics against the architectonic illusion*: A Constructivist Realist framework permits a more accurate understanding of politics because it is more complex and nuanced. It is the political process—involving power struggles and ongoing negotiations—that shapes violent struggle and the possibilities of negotiating accommodation, rather than ideal models with assumptions that abstract them from political realities. Rogers Brubaker argues that the architectonic illusion is the mistaken belief that the right institutional framework can resolve national conflicts without having to relate this to politics and power relations.[52] Security issues may be more important than constitutional architecture in managing a peace process. The management of conflict should, therefore, start from an analysis of the particular conflict and its complexities, including a realistic understanding of power and the political process, in order to understand pragmatically what the opportunities are for change that would secure a more just and peaceful society.

Policy-makers need to look beyond constitutional and institutional prescriptions and consider a more holistic and dynamic approach to conflict management that considers how numerous other factors interrelate. A political accommodation is often the result of pragmatism and compromise, rather than an attempt to impose abstract ideal types on diverse conflicts. A better and more realistic understanding of the political dynamics of a conflict is essential in order to explore what the possibilities are for conflict management. This allows political actors to make more informed interventions in what are difficult to predict and constantly changing circumstances. As a handbook on *Democracy and Deep-rooted Conflict* argues, "it would be ludicrous to prescribe one overall single design for use across a variety of situations, each in many ways unique. ... Anyone can suggest ideal solutions; but only those involved can, through negotiation, discover and create the shape of a practical solution."[53] Realists emphasize the importance of having a firm grasp of reality, however unpalatable, in order to have an understanding of how political change might be achieved.

8. *The theatrical metaphor:* A Constructivist Realist analysis might use a theatrical metaphor to look beyond the front stage performances of political and other actors in order to appreciate the constraints on those actors and the possibilities of negotiating peace. The front stage propaganda war between political actors may conceal opportunities for negotiations behind the scenes. Aggressive rhetoric may be cathartic and necessary to keep important audiences on board a peace process, and this may be accompanied by moderating performances. Understanding the constraints on other actors and helping your enemy can be an important part of the sometimes tortuous task of achieving agreement.

For example, during the Middle East peace process, secrecy and deception were used to facilitate negotiations with the PLO, and a clear gap between the Israeli government's public and private positions emerged. In Uri Savir's first-hand account, the importance of presentation and the preparation of Israeli and Palestinian public opinion was stressed. In negotiations there was a combination of conflict, through propaganda and negotiating tactics, and cooperation in order to achieve a settlement. There was talk between Palestinian and Israeli negotiators of the importance of a peace propaganda plan: Israelis and the Palestinians "had habitually portrayed the other side as savages, and their peoples adopted such language."[54]

Conclusion

Steve Smith argues: "Theories do not simply explain or predict, they tell us what possibilities exist for human actors and intervention; they define not merely our explanatory possibilities but also our ethical and practical horizons."[55] This chapter has adopted a Constructivist Realist framework in order to question the appropriateness of grand narratives or universal theories for explaining conflict and its management. The concept of sectarianism is problematic because it leads toward a simplistic analysis of conflict and fails to take into account a range of other factors, notably political power, that shape both the politics of the Middle East and the debates about it. Primordialist, Ethnonationalist, and Instrumentalist explanations and their accompanying prescriptions are rejected as far too generalized to do justice to the range and diversity of conflict situations. This is not a small point, because the overwhelming tendency has been to over-simplify conflicts and their management.

Constructivist Realism provides a framework for analysis that considers the importance of specialist knowledge and the possibility that a satisfactory explanation for one conflict might not be universalized. This framework focuses on the process by which particular identities become more and less powerful. In addition to this, an appreciation of structure/agency, the idea that actors make history but not in circumstances of their choosing, allows us to see the constraints and opportunities that face political and other actors who seek to manage these conflicts. This leads to an appreciation of the pragmatic realism and flexibility—involving political skills and messy moral choices—that may be necessary to bring various groups to peaceful accommodation.

PART I

THE GEOPOLITICS OF SECTARIANISM

2

THE SECTARIANISM OF THE ISLAMIC STATE

IDEOLOGICAL ROOTS AND POLITICAL CONTEXT

Hassan Hassan

Introduction

Since the self-proclaimed Islamic State swept through large swaths of northwestern Iraq and eastern Syria in the summer of 2014, the origins of its sectarian and ultra-extremist ideology have been debated in the region and beyond.[1] The enslavement of hundreds of Yazidi women in Sinjar, the slaughter of at least 1,500 Shia soldiers in Tikrit and hundreds of Sunni tribesmen in Syria and Iraq, and the beheading of Western hostages and Syrian and Iraqi civilians triggered a collective soul-searching that soon turned into a religious and political blame game.[2] A Saudi commentator typified the debate when he said on Twitter that the Islamic State's "actions are but an epitome of what we have studied in our school curriculum. If the curriculum is sound, then [the Islamic State] is right, and if it is wrong, then who bears responsibility?"[3]

Understanding the ideological appeal of the Islamic State is crucial to addressing the challenge of extremism even after the group is defeated. Top US military commanders have repeatedly emphasized the importance of ideology in fighting the group. As Major General Michael Nagata, a former commander of the US special operations forces in the Middle East, has noted, "We do not understand the movement, and until we do, we are not going to defeat it."[4] Field commanders battling the Islamic State in Syria have likewise reported that ideology impedes efforts to mobilize forces against the group. Muslim fighters often refuse to take up arms against the Islamic State on religious grounds, even if they would not join the group themselves. This is especially the case for efforts backed by Western powers. Ideology can therefore have practical implications in the fight against the Islamic State.

There is little consensus on the factors to blame for the Islamic State's violent and confrontational ethos. Some maintain that the Islamic State is the natural heir of a long history of such behavior.[5] Others attribute its rise and brutality to the invasion of Iraq in 2003 and to Iran's expanding role in supporting Shia militias in the region. Some commentators point broadly to political Islam as the precursor to the Islamic State's intolerance, while others reduce the Islamic State to an entity whose sectarianism is driven solely by political opportunism fueled by regional political players.[6]

In fact, the Islamic State's ideology is multifaceted and cannot be traced to one individual movement or period. And relying on the titles of books and writings used by the Islamic State can distort, not inform, the understanding of its ideology. Instead, it is important to examine closely how the group selects, understands, and teaches its ideas.

In isolation, Salafism and political Islam do not produce an Islamic State member or catalyze extremism.[7] On the contrary, both Salafism and political Islam have safeguards that may inhibit the kind of extremism adopted by the Islamic State. Similarly, political or moral outrage alone does not drive people to the Islamic State. The group has flourished in a context of political oppression, governance failures, and sectarian fissures, but this same political context can, and often does, lead individuals to insurgent groups that hold moderate views.

This chapter explores the Islamic State's ideology and sectarianism in context, drawing on primary sources and direct testimonies from Islamic State clerics and members in Syria and Iraq. It discusses broader themes relevant to the group's ideology to explain the origins of the Islamic State's violent and exclusivist vision. Until the illusion that the group's ideology is traceable straight to Salafism is dispelled, the world will not be able to understand the Islamic State's appeal, or to defeat it.

The Wahhabi root

The Islamic State presents itself as the representative of authentic Islam as practiced by the early generations of Muslims, commonly known as Salafism. Many post-colonial and modern Islamic movements describe themselves as Salafist, including the official brand of Islam adopted by Saudi Arabia known as Wahhabism, named after founder Muhammad Ibn Abd al-Wahhab, the eighteenth-century cleric who helped establish the first Saudi state with the assistance of Muhammad Ibn Saud.

Wahhabism is the intellectual legacy of the thirteenth-century Islamic scholar Taqi al-Din Ibn Taymiyyah and the Hanbali school of jurisprudence, as interpreted and enforced by Ibn Abd al-Wahhab and his successors. Marked by extreme traditionalism and literalism, Wahhabism rejects scholastic concepts like *maqasid* (the spirit of sharia law), a principle that many other Islamic schools uphold; *kalam* (Islamic philosophy); Sufism (Islamic spirituality); *ilal* (the study of religious intentions in the Quran and *hadith*, sayings attributed to the Prophet); and *al-majaz* (metaphors).[8]

Its clerics also use the concept of *bidah*—an Islamic term that forbids inventing religious practices unsanctioned by the religion—to label many practices, largely Sufi and Shia, as polytheistic. Wahhabi clerics' fixation on *bidah* creates a slippery slope that sometimes leads to the declaration of a fellow Muslim as an apostate. Adopting saints or their graves as *wasila* (means or intermediaries) to worship God, for example, is considered something that automatically leads an individual out of Islam. Circumambulating graves, slaughtering animals in the name of a saint, or believing in the divine authority of imams are also deemed polytheistic practices. While mainstream Muslims agree that innovation in religion is forbidden, Wahhabi clerics go one step further, drawing on Ibn Taymiyyah's hardline stance to label as *bidah* many practices that other Muslims consider legitimate. Wahhabi clerics reject Sufi and Shia contentions that such practices are not intended as worship.[9]

The Islamic State largely borrowed from Wahhabism the penal code that is already institutionalized in Saudi Arabia and practiced less systematically in other Muslim countries. Wahhabism's greatest contribution to the Islamic State, however, may be the concepts of *wala wal bara* (loyalty to Islam and disavowal of un-Islamic ways) and *tawhid* (the oneness of God). While these concepts exist in traditional Salafism as preached by Ibn Taymiyyah and other early scholars, they are interpreted and promoted more extremely by Wahhabi clerics.

According to the concept of *wala wal bara*, it is not enough for a Muslim to dislike un-Islamic practices and non-Muslims; instead, true Muslims must reject un-Islamic practices and non-Muslims actively and wholeheartedly.[10] Ibn Abd al-Wahhab reflected this precept when he wrote, "One's Islam cannot be sound, even if they adhered to the oneness of God and worshipped none but God, without enmity to the polytheists and showing to them hate and hostility."[11] For the Islamic State, this obligation to act in enmity applies to fellow Muslims who do not fulfill the criteria of *tawhid* by recognizing the oneness of God.

A basic tenet of Islam, as preached by Ibn Taymiyyah, is that a Muslim must abide by three criteria of *tawhid*: to worship God, to worship only God, and to have the right creed as prescribed by the Quran or by the Prophet's traditions.[12] Ibn Taymiyyah drew on the three criteria of *tawhid* to excommunicate Shia and Sufis after he established that their practices and beliefs, including the veneration of imams, compromised their worship of God alone.

In areas conquered by the Islamic State, symbols of *shirk* (polytheistic practices) are systematically demolished, notably Sufi and Shia shrines and historical sites that denote a deity. After taking over a town, Islamic State clerics typically launch a campaign against what they deem polytheistic practices, including superstitions and soothsaying. The clerics' doctrine is slowly shaping societies under their control, because many of the ideas preached by the Islamic State are based in established Islamic schools.

Because of such beliefs, study of the Islamic State's rigid, hostile, and sectarian ideology has centered on Wahhabism. Also, because the Islamic State cites or preaches the writings of Salafi and Wahhabi clerics, some scholars have concluded that the group is a manifestation of those ideas. But it is overly simplistic to blame Salafism and Wahhabism for Islamic State extremism.

A hybrid ideology

The Islamic State's extreme ideology can be viewed as the product of a slow hybridization between doctrinaire Salafism and other Islamist currents.

Many of the extremist religious concepts that undergird the Islamic State's ideology are rooted in a battle of ideas best understood in the context of Saudi Arabia's *Sahwa* (Islamic Awakening) movement in the 1970s, and a similar movement in Egypt, as well as in other countries. In those countries, the interplay of Salafi doctrinal ideas and Muslim Brotherhood–oriented political Islamic activism produced currents that still resonate today. Indeed, the commingling of Salafism and Brotherhood Islamism accelerated in the wake of the Arab uprisings of 2011, filling the void left when traditional religious establishments failed to respond adequately to the aspirations and grievances of the Arab masses. The Islamic State and other Islamist and jihadi groups seized the opportunity to enforce their vision of the role of Islam.

In Saudi Arabia and in Egypt, the marriage of traditional Salafism and political Islam produced new forms of Salafism that were influenced by, and critical of, both movements.[13] Political Islam became more conservative and Salafism became politicized.

In many instances, Salafi concepts were substantially reinterpreted, appropriated, and utilized by a new generation of religious intellectuals who started to identify with a new movement. In Saudi Arabia, the *Sahwa* generation moved away from the Najdi school, the adopted name for the Wahhabi clerical establishment.

The practice of *takfir*, or excommunication after one Muslim declares another an infidel or apostate, became increasingly prominent, first during the 1960s in Egypt and then after the first Gulf War in the 1990s when veterans of the jihad in Afghanistan began to apostatize Saudi Arabia for hosting and supporting Western troops to fight Iraq's then leader, Saddam Hussein.

Politically submissive Salafism, which had rejected political rebellion, began to give way to political *takfirism* that carries the banner of caliphate, jihad, and rebellion. At the same time, the growing influence of Salafi ideals led to the Salafization of the Muslim Brotherhood.[14]

Sayyid Qutb, an Islamist theorist and leading member of the Egyptian Muslim Brotherhood in the 1950s and 1960s, drew on Salafi ideals to create an all-embracing *takfiri* ideology.[15] Qutb argued that Muslim-majority societies are living in a state of *jahiliyya* (pre-Islamic obliviousness).[16] He believed that all ideologies—including capitalism, communism, and pan-Arabism—have failed, and that the only system that will succeed globally is Islam.[17] Qutb considered Islam the only reference for society (known as *hakimiyya*, or sovereignty of God), and he urged Muslim youth to reject their societies and lead change.

Qutbism provided a political ideology that introduced Islamic supremacism and nationalism, and that rejects many aspects of modern Muslim society and political regimes. It took conservative ideas and molded them to serve as the foundations of a political ideology that has little sympathy for views that deviate from Qutb's understanding of the Islamic way of life.[18] It is inward-looking and prioritizes internal threats over foreign threats.

Qutbist concepts such as *hakimiyya* and *jahiliyya* shape the Islamic State's dealings with the religious and ethnic communities it controls. The Islamic State believes that local populations must be converted to true Islam and that Muslims can accuse one another of apostasy without adhering to traditional clerical criteria, which stipulate a series of verification measures to ensure the apostasy of an accused person.[19] The group also believes in the Qutbist idea that Muslims have fundamentally deviated from the true message of Islam and that correcting this deviation will require a radical, coercive revolution. As one Islamic State member told the author, "If you think people will accept the Islamic project [voluntarily], you're wrong. They have to be forced at first. The other groups think that they can convince people and win them over but they're wrong. You have a ready project, you should place it on society like a tooth crown and make sure to maintain it."[20]

According to Egyptian researcher Hussam Tammam, the Muslim Brotherhood influenced Salafism through at least two channels. The first was the ideas of Qutb, represented by ideologues such as Abdullah Azzam, the Palestinian-born leader of the jihad in Afghanistan.[21] The second was Mohammed Surur, a former Muslim Brotherhood leader from Syria. Surur's influence produced a current somewhere between Saudi Salafism and Salafi jihadism. This current can be discerned in the ranks of Syrian rebel groups that until 2015 made up the Islamic Front, in the group of clerics known as the Syrian Islamic Council, and, to some extent, in the Nusra Front, the al-Qaeda-affiliated group fighting in Syria.[22]

Increasingly, Salafism has shifted from being a *dawa* (proselytism) movement to a political ideology. In an interview with the London-based newspaper *al-Quds al-Arabi*, Surur said that the current named after him had "transformed Salafism from one worldview to another" and "destroyed the myth of *wali al-amr* [religiously mandated blind obedience to Muslim rulers] and the obligation to respect them."[23]

The influence of Salafism on political Islam and vice versa led to varying outcomes—broadly referred to by its adherents as *haraki* Salafism, or activist Salafism. In Saudi Arabia and Egypt, some who adopted formulations of these ideas went on to fight jihad in Afghanistan; this included, notably, Osama bin Laden. A vast number of modern jihadists have cited the influence of Islamist ideas next to their study of Salafism, including, arguably, the true spiritual father of the Islamic State, Abu Muhammad al-Maqdisi. He is a Jordanian-Palestinian ideologue who mentored Abu Musab al-Zarqawi,[24] the group's founder in 2004 when it was known as al-Qaeda in Iraq.[25] Al-Maqdisi never met Osama bin Laden, but he taught at al-Qaeda camps.[26]

The vanguard of activist Salafism transformed Salafi concepts, it did not just borrow them. Qutb's brother, Mohammed, often known as the father of the *Sahwa*, integrated Ibn Taymiyyah's three criteria for monotheism and added a fourth which he called *tawhid al-hakimiyya*, or the unity of the sovereignty of God and his laws alone. This fourth criterion was a defining contribution to the *Sahwa* and to Salafi-jihadi thought in general.[27] Jihadi clerics took the Quranic term *taghut* (false deity) and built a full-fledged ideology on it: rulers of the Muslim world have been apostatized, and based on this, a Muslim who works for the ruler—from clerics to civil servants—can be a legitimate target. Democracy has been labeled a religion and democratic institutions as "habitats of apostasy," as a *Daily Beast* article reported.[28]

The Islamic State and al-Qaeda diverge ideologically, but the former continues to rely heavily on the jihadi literature used by al-Qaeda. The Islamic State lacks the religious resources, in terms of committed preachers, both within and outside its territories to develop its own jihadi school reflecting its intense sectarianism.

The same marriage of ideas that helped produce the al-Qaeda generation in the 1990s also produced more conservative Islamist movements that are politically active without endorsing violent jihadism, indiscriminate killing, or genocide. Religious intellectuals such as Kuwaiti Hakim al-Mutairi, for example, called for progressive Salafi ideas, including a multiparty democracy, citing Salafi references.[29] Surur's followers emphasized the Salafi doctrine of *tawhid*, while vehemently criticizing the Salafi concept of obedience to Muslim leaders, although they remained committed to traditional Sunni authorities.[30]

The schools that emerged from the mutual influence of Salafism and Islamism integrated *aqadi* (doctrinal or creed-based) and *ilmi* (scholastic) aspects of Salafism with the Muslim Brotherhood's political activism and revolutionary concepts.[31] Qutb's concept of *hakimiyya* and other Islamist ideas provided the political and activist ingredients of the new hybrid formulations, while Wahhabism and traditional Salafism provided its jurisprudential and doctrinal basis.

Although the intertwining of Salafism and political Islam has led to diverse outcomes, most reflect a key feature of Salafism: its propensity to narrowly define who is a Muslim. This makes Salafism sectarian almost by definition, unlike political Islam that tends to have no exclusionary position on a Muslim's creed. Political Islam, meanwhile, galvanizes its followers and provides them with a political ideology that advocates religious rule, the implementation of religious practices, and Islam's way of life. Stéphane Lacroix, in his book *Awakening Islam*, explained:

> On theological questions connected to creed and on the major aspects of Islamic jurisprudence, the [*Sahwa* generation] adhered to the Wahhabi tradition and considered themselves its faithful heirs. But on political and cultural questions, their view of the world tended toward that of the Muslim Brotherhood, although it was partly reformulated in terms derived from the Wahhabi tradition.[32]

The Islamic State combines ideas such as *wala wal bara* (loyalty to Islam and disavowal of un-Islamic ways) and apostasy with a religious penal code to form a political ideology and a worldview actively classifying and excommunicating fellow Muslims.[33] In this sense, revolutionary religious ideas derived from political Islam are as central to Islamic State ideology as fundamentalist ones.

Takfirism to the extreme

The Islamic State is part of a legacy of *takfiri* schools and ideas to emerge from al-Qaeda. But while the Islamic State was once affiliated with al-Qaeda, the two groups have ideologically parted ways. Comparing the Islamic State's vision with al-Qaeda's, and noting where their paths diverged, helps to shed light on the evolution of the Islamic State's sectarian ideology.

Differences between al-Qaeda and the Islamic State can be traced back to early encounters between Osama bin Laden and Abu Musab al-Zarqawi. Bin Laden and al-Zarqawi differed when they were in Afghanistan in the 1980s, as their successors do today, on the use of extreme violence and the targeting of Shia civilians.[34] According to the Islamic State, the worst enemies of Islam are the enemies within. The group argues that focusing on the far enemy (the West) and ignoring the near enemy (Muslim enemies in the region, especially Shia) is ineffective. Under the Islamic State's vision, the far enemy will be dragged into the region as Osama bin Laden planned, but by attacking the near enemy. This scenario has, in fact, played out since Islamic State fighters took over the northern Iraqi city of Mosul in June 2014, drawing more than sixty countries to the fight against the group.

The Iraq war of 2003 provided space for al-Zarqawi to spread his sectarian vision. Iraq's distinctly cross-sectarian familial bonds had previously made it largely resistant to sectarianism. Yet, al-Zarqawi's followers succeeded in kindling a civil war after bombing the Shia Askari Shrine in Samarra in 2006. Extremist ideas brought to Iraq by al-Qaeda after 2003 became entrenched as al-Zarqawi's jihadi group evolved into a local movement under the leadership of Abu Omar al-Baghdadi, who ruled the Islamic State in Iraq from 2006 to 2010, and his successor, Abu Bakr al-Baghdadi, who currently leads the group. For al-Qaeda, such a focus on Shia would distract from the fight against the West. Furthermore, mainstream Sunni clergy reject a genocidal attitude toward the Shia public. Al-Qaeda's central leadership has admonished the Islamic State (and its earlier incarnations) against attacking Shia civilians. Bin Laden reportedly favored an alliance between Shia and Sunni groups that would position them for a joint attack on the West.[35]

According to a letter published by the US State Department, al-Zarqawi urged bin Laden to focus on Shia. He wrote: "If you agree with us on [targeting Shia] ... we will be your readied soldiers.... If things appear otherwise to you, we are brothers, and the disagreement will not spoil [our] friendship."[36] The Islamic State's current leaders have criticized al-Qaeda's mellow stance, as they call it, toward Shia,[37] and in May 2014 Islamic State spokesman Abu Mohammed al-Adnani said that al-Qaeda was deliberately avoiding confrontation with Iran and Shia.

In July 2005, current al-Qaeda leader Ayman al-Zawahiri addressed al-Qaeda's position on Shia in a letter he sent to Abu Musab al-Zarqawi. He cited religious and practical reasons for al-Qaeda in Iraq to steer clear of targeting the Shia public and places of worship. Referencing Ibn Taymiyyah, he wrote that "such acts affect the protected blood of women, children, and noncombatant Shia public, who are protected because they are excused for their ignorance [of true religious doctrine, unlike Shia clerics]. This is the consensus of the Sunni toward the Shia public and ignorant followers."[38]

Al-Qaeda officially disassociated itself from the Islamic State in February 2014. Generally, outside Islamic State-held territories, the Islamic State has failed to win the support of any prominent jihadi ideologues, with the exception of a few jihadi clerics. Most jihadi ideologues have criticized the group's indiscriminate violence and sectarian bent. Al-Zarqawi's old mentor Abu Muhammad al-Maqdisi has described the group as "deviant," and has criticized its public beheadings and alienation of local Muslim communities and armed groups in Syria.[39]

The Islamic State's ideological divergence from al-Qaeda is discernible in its outlook and actions toward clerics and leaders as well. The rigidity of the Islamic State's ideology stands out even in a jihadi landscape marked by rigidity. Its refusal to bend creates a culture of *takfirism* within *takfirism*, where any leniency is forbidden.

In a video interview posted online in October 2013, Sami al-Aridi—the top cleric of the al-Qaeda-linked Nusra Front—explained some of the ideas that differentiate the Islamic State from other jihadi groups, including al-Qaeda. In contrast to the Islamic State, al-Aridi cited as legitimate scholars mainstream Wahhabi clerics, such as Saudi Arabia's Grand Mufti Abd al-Aziz Al al-Sheikh and prominent theologian Abd al-Aziz Ibn Baz.[40] He noted that al-Qaeda adheres to the four Sunni schools of jurisprudence and is more accommodating than the Islamic State of Muslim clerics, often engaging them.[41]

In contrast, the Islamic State considers clerics a key factor in the persistence of tyrannical, illegitimate governments in the Muslim world. The Islamic State believes that *tabayun* (a process of investigation) is sometimes needed to determine whether a person is a true Muslim. According to al-Aridi, the Islamic State declares a Muslim to be *kafir* (an infidel or unbeliever) based on intuitive suspicion, consequentiality, and vagueness.[42]

For the Islamic State, ordinary Muslims receive their religious education from clerics who are aligned with corrupt Muslim rulers who perpetuate Western hegemony. Accordingly, the Islamic State prioritizes the fight against clerics and rulers over the fight against the West.[43]

The Islamic State's particular sectarian outlook is also characterized by the tendency to emphasize *sunna* (the Prophet's traditions) as integral to the faith—a departure from mainstream clerics who consider them non-obligatory secondary practices that only strengthen faith. The Islamic State deems a person who adheres to these traditions to be respectful of the Prophet and those who do not adhere to the traditions to be disrespectful. Abu Mariya al-Qahtani, who served as the Nusra Front's chief cleric before he was replaced by al-Aridi, wrote in February 2014 that the Islamic State distinctly integrated these traditions into Islamic jurisprudence, changing terms from "optional" and "recommended" to "obligatory" and "duty."[44]

This view was also popular among followers of Juhayman al-Utaybi, a Saudi extremist who seized the Grand Mosque in Mecca along with his followers in November 1979 and declared himself the *Mahdi* (an expected messiah in Islam). According to Abu Muhammad al-Maqdisi, religious followers of al-Utaybi would often pray in a mosque with their shoes on, and would take them off as they leave the mosque, as the Prophet Muhammad had reportedly done on occasions.[45] Mainstream clerics often dismiss such practices as signs of the Islamic State's lack of religious qualifications, but for the group, these revivalist practices are evidence of adherence to original Sunni traditions.

The Islamic State is also extreme in its application of the Salafi concept of *nawaqid al-Islam*, or nullifiers of Islam. These are a set of conditions with which doctrinaire Salafists believe all Muslims must comply. The founder of Wahhabism narrowed nullifiers to ten acts: engaging in *shirk* (polytheistic prac-

THE SECTARIANISM OF THE ISLAMIC STATE

tices); accepting intermediaries in worship; failing to deem infidels as infidels, or doubting or justifying infidels' unbelief; mocking religious practices; believing that there is better guidance or rules than those of the Prophet; despising a practice ordained by the Prophet; exercising or accepting black magic; allying with infidels against Muslims; believing some people can do without sharia; and deliberately avoiding learning about or practicing religion.

While some clerics insist that there are degrees of faithlessness and that a sinner does not necessarily become an infidel by committing certain acts, the Islamic State generally rejects gradation and believes that all acts of unbelief are effectively equal. In the same vein, it believes that a Muslim has a religious duty to identify and label infidels or apostates, and failure to do so can lead one to become an infidel or apostate himself.

According to the Islamic State, a Muslim becomes an infidel if he fails to declare as an infidel another person worthy of being declared as such. The group declared al-Qaeda leader al-Zawahiri to be an infidel because he sympathized with ousted Egyptian president Mohamed Morsi, who endorsed democracy. The Islamic State considers members of the Nusra Front as apostates because they fight alongside foreign-backed groups.

This view and its implications are particularly pronounced among adherents of a movement in the Islamic State known as the Hazmiyya. At least some Islamic State members believe that some Hazmiyya teachings permit them to kill and rob Muslims who have committed any degree of unbelief.[46] But this could mean most of the population under their control.[47] The Hazmiyya misinterpreted a fatwa issued by Saudi cleric Omar bin Ahmed al-Hazimi, who is also identified as a member of the *Sahwa* generation that merged Islamist ideas with Salafi concepts. The fatwa, which al-Hazimi later recanted, forbade "the excuse of ignorance" in matters of faith, suggesting that a Muslim would be accountable for an act of disbelief even if that person did not intend to do so.[48] "Hazmiyya say that ignorance is not an excuse," Sheikh Hassan al-Dagheem, a prominent Syrian cleric, said in an interview.[49] In December 2014, the Islamic State produced a video showing the execution of four of its members on suspicion of extremism because they had plotted to rebel against the group for failing to implement the full scope of sharia as it preaches the doctrine.[50]

The question of not excusing ignorance in matters of excommunication was at the heart of a major controversy that swept the Islamic State throughout the first half of 2017. Clerics sympathetic to the hardline view seemed to have infiltrated the highest oversight body under al-Baghdadi, namely the Delegated Committee. In May, the committee issued a directive in which it unequivocally declared that Muslims who failed to declare certain fellow Muslims as non-believers would themselves be subject to excommunication. Muslims who qualify as apostates include ordinary Muslims who vote or run for elections. For the Delegated Committee, Muslims who run for elections are claimants of divinity.

The fatwa in May was widely circulated in outlets affiliated with the group's central media body, which indicate the influence of these ideas was common in the Islamic State's highest institutions below the so-called caliph. Binali emerged as pivotal to the crisis: shortly after the Delegated Committee's directive was made, he issued a 20-page response in which he pointed out that the fatwa deviated from the consensus of Islamic jurists, especially the point that excommunication is a foundation of Islam which the edict suggested must take precedence over learning how to pray. Binali was announced dead a month after the fatwa was released, something that added to the intensity of the internal controversy since some of the group's followers considered his last treatise as a dying will. In the following September, the Delegated Committee retracted the edit it had issued in May, and admitted it had inconsistencies and religious errors. It then issued two recordings clarifying the Islamic State's creed, insisting that it would continue to apostatize fellow Muslim who accept democratic tools, but it would refrain from calling the exercise an unquestionable fundamental part of Islam since jurists differed about it.

The Islamic State's scholars of jihad

The Islamic State relies on the jihadi literature of ideologues who support its stance to wage war against nominal Muslims. These clerics adhere to a set of ideas that significantly deviate from tradition, as some of them have explicitly stated. The Islamic State typically uses their material to justify the *takfir* of the Saudi state and Muslim rulers across the Middle Eastern region and to support the rejection of all official institutions and forces within those countries. Because of the hostility between the Islamic State and many of those clerics, observers often downplay the profound influence that such ideologues have had on the organization.

Sources include Saudi clerics Khalid al-Rashed, Nasir al-Fahd, Sulaiman bin Nasser al-Alwan, Omar bin Ahmed al-Hazimi, Ali bin Khidr al-Khudayr, and Hamud bin Uqla al-Shuaibi.[51] Others include al-Qaeda ideologues Abu Muhammad al-Maqdisi and Abdul Qadir bin Abdul Aziz.

Four of these clerics—al-Fahd, al-Alwan, al-Khudayr, and al-Shuaibi—were part of a network that heavily influenced al-Qaeda in Saudi Arabia in the early

2000s as well as the transnational jihadi movement.[52] They wrote extensively on Saudi Arabia's apostasy for helping the United States in its regional interventions, especially during the first Gulf War. For the Islamic State, these writings provide the necessary theological foundations for its campaigns against apostates. The fact that these clerics were theologically trained (a rarity for jihadi ideologues)[53] makes them even more of an asset to the Islamic State. Similarly, so does their disagreement with Saudi Arabia's clerical establishment.[54] Al-Fahd has reportedly pledged allegiance to the Islamic State,[55] and the group considers al-Shuaibi's book on the impermissibility of seeking help from infidels to be influential.

Al-Khudayr and al-Rashed are heavily referenced in the territories controlled by the Islamic State. Al-Khudayr in particular offers the Islamic State a one-stop shop in his writing on one of the most defining facets of the Islamic State's ideology: he stipulates that un-Islamic systems and followers are illegitimate and that adherence to their teachings is inexcusable. Al-Khudayr is unequivocal in his position on modern legislative systems and Muslims who become involved with them. He deems Muslims who voluntarily join a parliament to be infidels. A Muslim who swears loyalty to a constitution, even if compelled to do so, is considered an apostate, and Muslims who oppose a constitution through democratic means are deemed sinners. The idea that ordinary Muslims may not know such practices are illegitimate is no excuse for al-Khudayr.

The clerics whom the Islamic State mentions in its sermons are particularly critical of Shia, preaching that ordinary Shia cannot be excused for their faith. In a series of sermons titled "The Sharp-Edged Sword on the Evil Shiites," al-Rashed attacked Shia in graphic language. Similarly, al-Fahd has written a treatise on "the permissibility of excessiveness against the *rafidha*," replete with abusive and denigrating language directed at Shia.[56] (*Rafidha*, literally rejectionists, is a pejorative word for Shia.)

Abu Muhammad al-Maqdisi has also influenced the Islamic State, arguably more than any other religious cleric outside the organization. Because he vehemently opposed the group's expansion in Syria and has criticized its approach to other jihadists, there is a tendency to downplay his ideological influence on the group. Al-Maqdisi, who grew up in Kuwait and studied in Iraq and Saudi Arabia in the 1980s, directly influenced the Islamic State's founder, al-Zarqawi, and the two were jailed together in Jordan between 1993 and 1999. His contribution to its overall ideology is profound; he recently described his influence on the Islamic State, claiming, "I am their sheikh who taught them the concept of *tawhid*."[57]

Although the Islamic State does not publicly promote al-Maqdisi's books, his ideas are cited to repudiate the group's detractors, and his books are distributed in Islamic State-controlled areas.[58] The first issue of the Islamic State's magazine, *Dabiq*, also featured an article about al-Maqdisi's writings. Ahmed Abazaid, a Syrian expert on Islamists and jihadists in Syria, described al-Maqdisi's writings as "the basis of the *takfiri* cancer and the cause of the ease with which the blood of people and mujahideen is shed."[59]

Al-Maqdisi's book *Millat Ibrahim* is particularly instrumental for the Islamic State. The book applies the concept of *wala wal bara* (loyalty to Islam and disavowal of un-Islamic ways) to label as apostates a wide range of Muslims who practice un-Islamic ideas or habits, even if they are related to the accuser. In another book, *The Unspoken Scandals on the Apostasy of the Saudi State*, al-Maqdisi declares Saudi Arabia an infidel state. He rules that because abandoning *wala wal bara* leads to *kufr* (unbelief), many of Saudi Arabia's practices—such as interest-based banking, foreign aid to non-Muslims, membership in the United Nations, and alliance with the West—render it apostate.

Al-Maqdisi's teachings are, of course, readily applicable to all Muslim communities that adhere to practices that the Islamic State deems un-Islamic, including membership of the Baath Party or alliance with Western and regional governments. Even though he is critical of the Islamic State, for example, he condemned Syrian rebels' cooperation with the US-led air campaign against the Islamic State as apostasy.[60]

Another ideologue heavily cited by the Islamic State is Abdul Qadir bin Abdul Aziz, also known as Sayyid Imam al-Sharif, and Dr Fadl, a former Egyptian jihadist who revised his extremist views after his release from prison in the wake of the 2011 uprising. His most influential book is *The Comprehensive Guide for Seeking Noble Knowledge*. Abu Ali al-Anbari, the Islamic State's high cleric, repeatedly cited the book in his lectures, even though he claimed that the author had retracted his views. In one audio lecture, he quoted Abdul Aziz to explain that a Muslim who joins a parliament is an apostate even if he intended to use the platform for advancing a religious agenda. Abdul Aziz's explanation, as quoted by al-Anbari, is directed at former Saudi mufti Abd al-Aziz Ibn Baz, who argued that membership of a parliament depended on the intention of the member.[61]

Such ideas about modern institutions and democratic norms are applied by the Islamic State to justify war against members of the military and security forces in Muslim countries. They are also used to apostatize Islamists as well as mainstream clerics who are part of official religious establishments.

Al-Anbari, the longest-serving and highest authority in the Islamic State until his death in March 2016, produced forty lectures designed to explain his group's religious ideology. The lectures centered on the illegitimacy of institutions in Muslim countries, including mosques and courts. He saved special ire for Shia, Sufis, the Muslim Brotherhood, and mainstream Salafists (he often referred to the latter as *murjia*, a pejorative term for pacifist imams). In one of his lectures, he singled out these Salafists as the "most absurd" among the Islamic State's detractors, a reflection of the fierce ideological battle between the two since the group's recent rise in Syria and Iraq.[62]

The *Sahwa* link

Many of the clerics that the Islamic State cites to justify its anti-Shia ideology come from the *Sahwa* generation or are otherwise associated with the *Sahwa* movement. These include Ibrahim al-Fares, Muhsin al-Awaji, Mohammed al-Barrak, Hamoud al-Omari, Mohammed al-Nojaimi, Saad al-Durihim, and their contemporaries from Egypt and elsewhere, such as Omar Abdulrahman, sometimes known as "the Blind Sheikh."

These clerics tend to be particularly outspoken against Shia. Al-Fares, for example, wrote extensively about Shia as an "emblem of treason," and once quoted Ibn Taymiyyah as saying: "The origin of all sedition and calamity is Shia and their allies, and many of the swords unleashed against Islam come from them."[63] Some of these clerics, however, notably Hamoud al-Omari, emphasize that while they deem Shia as a sect to be deviant, violence against Shia civilians is unacceptable, in contrast to Islamic State doctrine.

In the Islamic State, Turki al-Binali, from Bahrain, who was confirmed dead in an American strike in eastern Syria in June 2017, was second to al-Anbari in terms of influence. According to an online biography, al-Binali is a disciple of Salman al-Awda, a prominent figure in Saudi Arabia's *Sahwa*. Al-Binali claims that the two were close before al-Awda started to "deteriorate," or become more moderate.[64] Al-Binali has been associated with Hajjaj al-Ajmi, an activist Salafi Kuwaiti cleric known for his fundraising activities for radical rebel groups in Syria. Al-Binali has also been influenced by Abdul-Aziz al-Tarifi, a well-known Saudi cleric from the *Sahwa* generation, who was arrested by Saudi authorities in April 2016 presumably for criticizing Riyadh's Western-driven religious reforms.[65] He continues to speak favorably of al-Tarifi and to recommend his writings.

Before al-Binali traveled to Syria in 2013 to join the group, he had gained credibility as a jihadi mufti through close association with fourteen known clerics in the region. In 2009, al-Maqdisi authorized him to teach and to issue fatwas, which he did in prominent jihadi forums under the nom de guerre Abu Hummam al-Athari. Islamic State members highlight al-Binali's teachings and fatwas to counter attempts to downplay his religious weight by other clerics, including al-Maqdisi.

Although al-Binali is a theological lightweight compared to some clerics, his early jihadi activities help the Islamic State stake a claim in a long line of jihadi jurisprudence. This makes him particularly useful to the Islamic State in defending itself against allegations by other jihadi factions that its ideology is not sufficiently rooted in jurisprudence. One Islamic State cleric has noted that al-Binali's accepted authority prior to his membership in the Islamic State is either a testament to the group's credibility or a testament to its al-Qaeda critics' lack of credibility because they had previously approved of his credentials.

Al-Binali has been at the forefront of building legitimacy for Abu Bakr al-Baghdadi. As a former al-Qaeda associate, al-Binali is seen as well positioned to win over al-Qaeda supporters. Al-Binali was reportedly dispatched to the Libyan city of Sirte in March 2013 and in 2014 to proselytize for the Islamic State from the Rabat Mosque.[66] And he authored a booklet about Abu Bakr al-Baghdadi and his claim to the caliphate, *Middu al-ayadi li-bayat al-Baghdadi* (Extend the hands to pledge allegiance to al-Baghdadi).

Al-Binali's sectarian views and background also make him valuable to the Islamic State. In 2007 he was expelled from Dubai, where he was studying, and was later banned from Kuwait, Egypt, Qatar, and his home country Bahrain because of his *takfiri* and sectarian ideas. He has been a prolific critic of Shia and their "warped" ideology, as he and other critics see it. In July 2015, he threatened attacks against Shia mosques in Bahrain in the wake of Islamic State suicide bombings of Shia mosques in Kuwait and Saudi Arabia.

Al-Binali tends to focus on two themes that are central to Islamic State ideology: nullifiers of Islam and *tawhid* (the oneness of God). In Libya, he lectured on nullifiers of Islam, and he wrote a textbook on *tawhid* for use in Islamic State training camps.[67][68]

While the Islamic State uses terms often associated with Salafists, or Wahhabis, it also cites sermons and writings by individuals who do not belong to the traditional religious establishment. For instance, a recommended list of 196 written, video, and audio items distributed by Islamic State supporters to new members overwhelmingly features work by the clerics mentioned above.[69] On the doctrine of *wala wal bara*, new members are advised to watch sermons by clerics associated with the *Sahwa*, who often comment on the ideas of religious scholars widely accepted by mainstream Muslims.

The influence of *Sahwa*-era scholars does not, of course, absolve Salafism, particularly the Saudi version, of its contribution to legitimizing groups such as the Islamic State. Salafi traditions provide religious fodder for the Islamic State's discourse and help it to link itself to traditional Islam. But the group has moved beyond these traditions, and the Islamic State and traditional Salafists have confronted each other on religious grounds. Many of the extremist ideas of Ibn Taymiyyah and Wahhabism were already used for political and revolutionary purposes by modern religious intellectuals who influence jihadi ideologies today. The concept of *wala wal bara*, for example, was weaponized during the *Sahwa* era to target not only heretical Muslims but also the West, a reinterpretation that heavily influenced jihadists in the 1990s.[70]

Many of the Islamic State's practices are rejected by traditional Salafists. Suicide bombing, for example, is rejected by most Salafists on the grounds that suicide is forbidden by Islam in all its forms. Islamist clerics, such as Yusuf al-Qaradawi, have sanctioned suicide bombing—although he later stated that his fatwa was specific to Israel.[71] Rebelling against rulers, declaring ordinary Shia as apostates, and bombing mosques are some of the practices rejected by traditional Salafists.

Justifying savagery

The Islamic State's favored clerics offer justifications for its savagery, especially against fellow Muslims. Some of them, however, do so by stoking totalitarian and sectarian hatred rather than directly espousing the type of violence that the Islamic State exhibits.

Al-Rashed is known for his fiery remarks, often featured in weepy sermons. In one sermon, he told of the beheading of Khalid bin Sufyan al-Hadhli in the seventh century. According to al-Rashed, Muhammad asked for a volunteer to kill al-Hadhli for orchestrating attacks against Muslims. Abdullah bin Anas volunteered, and killed and then beheaded al-Hadhli. When he returned with the severed head, according to al-Rashed, Muhammad praised and rewarded him. Although this account is disputed, it is repeatedly cited by Islamic State members.

The Islamic State cites two clerics in particular—Abu Abdullah al-Muhajir and Abu Bakr Naji—to justify its gory brutality against opponents. With their justifications for beheading and similar harsh tactics, the writings of Naji and al-Muhajir are indispensable to the Islamic State. Al-Muhajir is an Egyptian who authored *Questions About the Jurisprudence of Jihad*, a book that Islamic

State founder al-Zarqawi studied and then taught at a jihadi camp in Herat. Naji (real name Mohammad Hasan Khalil al-Hakim), a former member of the Egyptian jihadist Islamic Group, wrote *The Management of Savagery*,[72] reported by an Islamic State-affiliated cleric to be widely circulated among the group's provincial commanders and members.

The book's seminal contribution is to differentiate between jihad and other faith matters. The author said that the way in which jihad is taught "on paper" makes it hard for young people to absorb its true meaning. He stated, "Those who have practiced jihad know that it is nothing but brutality, callousness, terrorism, deterrence and infliction. I am talking about jihad and fighting, not about Islam, so do not confuse the two. Fighting cannot continue and transition from one phase to another unless the first phase includes infliction and deterrence of the enemy."[73] The impact of these two ideologues on the Islamic State is not new: they heavily influenced al-Zarqawi.[74] Al-Muhajir and Naji both justify beheading as not only religiously permissible but also recommended by God and his Prophet. They claim that the spilling of an infidel's blood is "permissible in an absolute way," and that aiding infidels against Muslims is a greater unbelief, which renders a person unequivocally an infidel.[75]

Storytelling and jihad

In terms of indoctrination, the Islamic State tends to steer clear of exposing new members to teachings that are not directly derived from sharia books. New members are almost exclusively shown religious texts, according to Islamic State-affiliated clerics. Established members or commanders, in contrast, can study manuals such as Abu Bakr Naji's book.[76] Limiting new members' readings to religious texts and historical stories conforms to the group's position that it is an extension of authentic Islam rather than an organization with its own set of teachings.

Stories from early Islamic history (often from the period known as the Apostasy Wars, which followed Muhammad's death) are also cited by the Islamic State to justify beheading, crucifixion, mass killing, and similarly brutal practices to new members. Abu Asaad al-Samaan, an Islamic State cleric, cited the story of Safiyya bint Abdulmutalib, a woman from the Prophet Muhammad's time, to justify beheading as a terror tactic. According to al-Samaan, Muslim women were separated from the men in the city of Medina during the Battle of the Ditch and put in a secured place.[77] But a man, identified in the story as Jewish, managed to climb to the secured place and approached the women. Safiyya asked an old man to kill the intruder, but the old man responded that he was incapable of fighting. Safiyya, who had fought in a previous battle, killed the approaching man, beheaded him, and threw his severed head onto enemy fighters to terrorize them. Islamic State members also reference verses from the Quran that call for the "smiting of necks" and similar tactics, although mainstream Muslim clerics maintain that these verses must be understood in the context of the battlefield.

The Islamic State relies heavily on stories and events from Islamic history because they can be more powerful than the citation of Islamic principles, especially if the stories and events support Quranic verses or *hadiths*. The group makes the most of any example it can find, and borrows from what Muslim clerics consider isolated incidents that should not be followed as rules. It uses stories not always to argue a religious idea: they may be offered to help Islamic State members who struggle with committing acts of extreme violence.

The group cites the story of Islam's commander in chief, Khaled Ibn al-Walid, who killed thousands of captives after the Battle of Ullais,[78] contrary to Islamic teachings. Ibn al-Walid had pledged to God that he would make a river of his enemies' blood if he overran them. When he could not find enough people to make that river, he killed the captives and ordered a river's dam to be opened onto their bleeding bodies. The Islamic State points out that the first caliph, Abu Bakr, praised Ibn al-Walid for his victory, and the Prophet Muhammad referred to him as the "Unleashed Sword of God." When the Islamic State kills its captives, it can simply cite this story, relying on what can be described as "kinetic sharia"—events and stories, rather than mere theology.

The Islamic State deliberately employs unusual punishments to shock observers and to highlight similar incidents in Islamic history, as followers of Saudi extremist Juhayman al-Utaybi did in the case of rituals in the 1970s. In December 2014, for example, Islamic State fighters threw a twenty-year-old man accused of homosexual acts from the highest building in Deir Ezzor "as the Muslim caliph Abu Bakr did," according to statements by the Islamic State.[79] Conversations with new Islamic State members suggest that the group's clerics often dig deep into Islamic history for obscure stories or *hadiths* to impress new members and demonstrate that true Islam has been absent from their society. Islamic State member Muthanna Abdulsattar explained, "When you listen to the clerics of the al-Dawla [State, as Islamic State members refer to their group], you are shocked that most of our Islamic societies have deviated from the true religion. They follow a religion that was invented two decades ago, or less."[80]

Mainstream clerics may struggle to deal with the stories of extreme violence upon which the Islamic State relies. They typically abstain from telling such stories in public, creating space for the Islamic State to shape these stories to fit its narrative. Furthermore, mainstream clerics often find themselves unable to engage in discussions around these stories without risking sectarian implications. For example, criticism of Ibn al-Walid, who is highly revered by Sunnis and disliked by Shia, would put a cleric in the awkward position of vindicating members of the opposing sect.

Conclusion

Regardless of how the Islamic State fares militarily in the coming months and years, its ideology remains a long-term challenge. It is a symptom of a broader issue that has been largely overlooked: an unchecked shake-up in Salafism that allows new movements to derive from both Salafism and Islamism. Until the interplay of Salafi and Islamist ideas is recognized, the Islamic State's ideology will continue to be misdiagnosed. The group's emphasis on Islamic theology in its public discourse clouds its revolutionary nature and creates the illusion that its ideology is traceable to Salafism rather than to the confluence of fundamentalist and revolutionary strands.

The central role of Islamist ideas is best captured in a saying popular among Islamic State supporters, attributed to Yemeni journalist Abdulelah Haider Shaye: "The Islamic State was drafted by Sayyid Qutb, taught by Abdullah Azzam, globalized by Osama bin Laden, transferred to reality by Abu Musab al-Zarqawi, and implemented by al-Baghdadis: Abu Omar and Abu Bakr."[81]

The Islamic State has added a focus on sectarianism to a history of radical views. In particular, it has linked itself to the Salafi-jihadi movement that evolved out of the Afghan jihad. This link has helped the group to authenticate itself, and renders it less subject to ridicule or accusations of deviance. The Islamic State's brand of sectarian jihad is flourishing in the current regional climate. Sectarian polarization; the rise of similarly sectarian militias in Iraq, Syria, and beyond; and the absence of religious and political leadership help the Islamic State to appeal, recruit, and endure. Sectarian media and political rhetoric continue to provide the group with ammunition by stoking communal hatred.

Meanwhile, the messages from mainstream clerics fail to resonate, largely because of their links to authoritarian regimes. Moderate institutions were weakened in the wake of the Arab uprisings of 2011, when religious establishments were perceived as complicit with repressive regimes and as failing to address the aspirations of revolutionary youth. The Islamic State and others quickly filled the resulting vacuum, and the group appears to be on track to turn its obscure teachings into an established school as al-Qaeda did over the years, but potentially to greater effect.

3

THE SECTARIANIZATION OF THE SYRIAN WAR

Heiko Wimmen

Initially, the Syrian protesters who rose up against the regime of Syrian President Bashar al-Assad in 2011 adopted a non-sectarian approach. However, sectarian rhetoric and perceptions came to prevail in the ensuing conflict. Within a month following the first wave of protests in mid-March 2011, sectarian identity became an important, often overriding, element in the interpretation and escalation of violence.

This does not mean that Syria is exclusively, or even mainly, experiencing a sectarian civil war, as many analysts have represented it.[1] That a significant portion of Syrian Sunnis still support the regime, or that hundreds of thousands of internally displaced people from Sunni areas have sought refuge in government-controlled areas, illustrates that this is not a struggle between distinct and cohesive groups vying for supremacy and control over territory and institutions or the exclusion or extermination of other sects.

Nor can the Syrian war be attributed solely to "conflicts dating back millennia."[2] There is compelling evidence that the *immediate* reason for the uprising against Assad rule was a mismanaged economic transformation during the preceding decade. This failure exacerbated social inequalities and plunged a significant portion of the Syrian population into grinding poverty.[3]

Hence, the lines dividing rebels from loyalists did not necessarily follow sectarian and ethnic affiliation. Divisions sprang up within sectarian groups, between localities that had been affected differently by social change, and sometimes even within families, setting the marginalized against profiteers, believers against clerical establishments, and youths against elders.

Despite the considerable efforts of early anti-regime activists, the narrative of a social and political struggle—pitting impoverished rural masses and migrants, disenfranchised urban-middle and lower-middle classes, liberal intellectuals, and youths with dim prospects against an abusive authoritarian regime and its clientele of parasitic enforcers and crony capitalists—did not prevail. The narrative was soon eclipsed by interpretations that presented the events purely, or mainly, in sectarian terms. The regime and its partisans portrayed the conflict as a defense of Syria's religious pluralism against Sunni religious extremism, which external actors sought to instigate and exploit. The opposition represented it as a struggle against a regime whose sectarian Alawite character had made it implacably hostile to mainstream Sunni Islam.

As events were narrated and interpreted through sectarian lenses, these representations quickly turned into reality on the ground, thus giving them credence. Attacks on Sunni mosques, which were the only available public sanctuaries for protesters, were perceived as expressions and proof of the regime's sectarian bias rather than as attempts to extinguish centers of dissent. On the other side, assassinations of Alawite security officers were interpreted as evidence of the sectarian hatred of the opposition, not as retaliation against the enforcers of a detested regime who had met unarmed protesters with live ammunition. These perceptions affected and shaped public attitudes and behavior on both sides and fueled self-sustaining cycles of mutual recrimination, fear, and violence.

If the conflict was not caused by age-old sectarian hatreds released by a combination of regime weakness and regional and international interference, then why did the perception of an existential sectarian conflict prevail so quickly? Why did the inclusive rhetoric of the protesters fail to convince enough Syrians—in particular non-Sunnis—that "the Syrian people are one" in their struggle against the regime? Why did so many Syrians instead fall for the fearmongering of a regime that nearly everyone (including its beneficiaries) knew and loathed for its corruption, insincerity, and opportunism?

For many supporters of the uprising, the answer to these questions is clear: it was "the regime's cynical exploitation of sectarianism" that turned the uprising away from its early inclusive and civic orientation.[4] Such a perspective appears intuitively plausible, given the advantages that the process of sectarianization offered Syria's rulers. On a domestic level, portraying the uprising as being the result of Sunni sectarianism and extremism could scare religious minorities into siding with the regime. It could also scare liberal segments of the Sunni majority, who feared a turn toward state-imposed religious rigidity and conservatism, as occurred in Saudi Arabia and the rest of the Gulf. On an international level, this concern, in particular when expressed by religious figures in Christian communities, could also influence Western societies, in which Islamophobia is rife and where most observers were unaware that many of these figures had been co-opted by the regime.

Certain decisions at the regime's highest levels may also be evidence that at least some elements in the Syrian power structure sought to steer the situation toward outright sectarian conflict. Statements that attributed the first wave of protests to a "conspiracy to sow sectarian strife" and conjured up scenarios of "internal conflict" were a sure recipe to fan fears that would hasten the outbreak of the very sectarian conflict the regime was purportedly warning against.[5] Attacking mosques using crack troops—commonly perceived as Alawite-dominated—or irregulars recruited in minority, particularly Alawite, areas,[6] and releasing militant jihadists from prison certainly enhanced the sectarian dimensions of the conflict.[7]

And yet there is no conclusive evidence of a coordinated and coherent regime strategy aimed specifically at igniting sectarian conflict. The regime's responses to protests during the first few weeks were contradictory and haphazard, and sometimes elements of the regime appeared to be working at cross-purposes.[8] While the official rhetoric concerning the sectarian dimension of the contestation certainly qualified as fearmongering, it was essentially the continuation of a long-standing and "deliberately ambiguous" strategy: branding as sectarian anyone who exposed the reality of Alawite preponderance in the composition of the Syrian regime and its security apparatus and the crony-dominated economy it fostered—all this behind a facade of secularism.[9]

On the other hand, already by mid-April 2011, instances of anti-Alawite violence and protest activities bearing an unmistakably Sunni religious imprint occurred in parallel to the non-sectarian, civic rhetoric employed by the protest movement. Long before the contestation transformed into armed conflict, local and regional cycles of sectarian violence had begun. These events fed off a long-standing legacy of violence and fueled fears of the sectarian other, thus reinforcing and escalating the cycle of violence.

Sectarianism had been implanted in Syrian society long before external actors started to play a significant role in the country's current war.[10] Its extent was also greater than those who blame the phenomenon on a regime strategy to counter the uprising are prepared to admit.[11] Its origins lay primarily in the ruling practices of the Syrian regime, which have left a legacy of violence, in particular from the conflict with the Muslim Brotherhood during the early 1980s. Rather than an existential condition suppressed by a supposedly secular regime, sectarianism was the product of the political behavior of this regime. Once the regime was seriously challenged, it served as a tool for mobilization for both sides and as a fuel for violent conflict.

This distinction is important for at least two reasons. First, it represents a response to those who argue that no matter how unsavory, authoritarian regimes are necessary to manage divided societies outside the "developed world." Such perspectives merit denunciation because they are culturally deterministic and occasionally racist, but also because they tend to obscure the developed world's propensity to deepen and intensify these conflicts in pursuit of its own strategic interests. To those who defend authoritarian regimes from a realpolitik perspective, it is worth remembering that accommodating dictators is often self-defeating in that it may only delay, and likely amplify, an inevitable revolt.

Second, taking the lingering power of sectarianization seriously and understanding its origins will be necessary once Syria's conflict is over and it comes time to reconcile the society. Blaming the violence on sinister regime manipulation may lead to the simplistic conclusion that once Assad is gone, Syrians will naturally revert to the tradition of multireligious tolerance that purportedly prevailed in the pre-war era.[12] The civic spirit of the early uprising, perhaps aided by externally led peacebuilding and reconciliation measures, would then allow for the realization of what, according to opposition representatives, is the real ambition of the Syrian people: namely fulfilment of "the right for all Syrians to live in peace and dignity; to freely practice their religious and political beliefs; to be equal citizens before the law."[13] In other words, a textbook definition of a liberal state.

It is understandable that representatives and supporters of the civic opposition would attempt to project such confidence. Yet, the botched state-building projects in Afghanistan, Bosnia, and Iraq have demonstrated how identity politics tends to resist technocratic approaches to conflict management and leaves the potential for renewed hostility in the absence of a fundamental change in social relations.

Absent of such change, and barring a decisive military victory for either side, Syria is liable to end up permanently bedeviled by deep, politicized sectarian rifts, with institutions, state power, and perhaps territory divided among competing power centers that rely on sectarian mobilization and fear to appear legitimate and maintain power. Such an outcome would represent only a moderate change from (and much continuity with) the system of dispersed domination, structured by sect, clan, region, and other substate identity formations characteristic of the Assad regimes. In other words, the post-conflict system in Syria may closely resemble the system that has been in place under the Assads since the 1970s.

Alawite predominance and the security state

Syria is often described as having a "minority regime": that is, a society where the minority Alawite community (some 10 percent of the population) rules over the Sunni Arab majority that accounts for approximately two-thirds of the Syrian population. However, it can be argued that the regime exploited tribal and kinship solidarity and networks to maintain the loyalty of the security sector and that the far-reaching clout of the latter created an image of Alawite supremacy that only partly reflected social reality.

The rise of Syria's Alawites, thanks to French colonial policies, from a marginalized rural community to one that found advancement through the armed forces, has been extensively documented and analyzed.[14] One typical interpretation of the Alawite trajectory is that "both [Assad] regimes exploited state resources in order to reinforce Alawi solidarity or *asabiyya*, ensuring that public sector employment was concentrated in the hands of the Alawi community and the regime's supporters were rewarded for their commitment to the state."[15]

At least as equally important, however, was the urge to secure the regime by stacking the security agencies and the officer corps with family relations of the ruling clan and its Alawite tribal allies. These preferences at the top level were reproduced among the rank and file. Military and security institutions represented desirable career opportunities that were especially attractive to hitherto marginalized segments of society, among all sects. However, recruitment and advancement were to a large extent dependent on connections to higher officials, ideally through blood relations. Thus, Alawites related to those sections of the community that dominated the upper ranks were at a significant advantage for upward social mobility, while those with less privileged access still had an advantage when it came to filling the lower ranks. Thus, employment in the military and intelligence services became a primary vehicle for upward social mobility and was "inextricably woven into the fabric of Alawite society."[16]

Particularly after the conflict of the 1980s against the Muslim Brotherhood, the significant sway these institutions enjoyed meant that a career in the military and security institutions came with considerable social power, further benefiting the larger Alawite community. Statistically, an Alawite was much more likely to have a relative or close friend serving as a higher-ranking officer in the armed forces or security services than members of other communities—and that relative or friend was, in turn, likely to wield more influence and patronage power than counterparts from other sects.

Interviews with Sunni officers who defected from the armed forces after the uprising in 2011 reveal a clear imbalance in enrolment at the military academy, in addition to significant power differentials between branches of the Syrian armed forces. Alawites were overwhelmingly assigned to those branches receiving the best equipment and the highest funding and social prestige. According to these accounts, many Sunni officers felt pressured to overcompensate for their sectarian identity by engaging in conspicuous displays of "secularism" (for example, by consuming alcohol) and being discrete about personal religiosity, even before the uprising.[17] One assumes such tendencies must have applied even more in the opaque world of the security services.

A strong position in the security sector helped provide access to professional and material advantages—first and foremost public employment—and to the benefits of systemic corruption in the public sector. Thus, for many Syrians, their perception of Alawites was inextricably linked to experiences of unfair privilege and quite frequently to abusive practices, such as protection rackets or the extortion of bribes for access to public services.

Systematic and conspicuous discrimination in access to labor and life opportunities effectively leads to a deeper identification with the sect or other particular category on which this discrimination is based.[18] The effect was pronounced in Syria, where the state wielded strong control over much of the economy and the labor market and where formal procedures and institutional rationality were largely supplanted by extensive networks of patronage.

Revealingly, during the first phase of the protests in 2011, protesters in mixed Sunni-Alawite cities, such as Baniyas, Latakia, and Tartus, demanded the rectification of alleged pro-Alawite sectarian biases in employment in state industries and public administrations.[19] In these cities, perceived communal competition over limited state resources and benefits was also tied closely to rural migration. Migration increased the percentage of Alawites in Latakia from the single digits on the eve of independence in 1945 to around 50 percent in the first decade of this century; in Homs from near zero to about 25 percent; in Tartus from about 30 percent to 80 percent; and in Baniyas from less than 10 percent to around 60 percent during the same period.[20] Such significant demographic shifts caused tensions between the traditional urban population, comprising mostly Sunnis and Christians, and the new arrivals.

However, these local fractures were compounded in that they appeared to indicate a dramatic reversal of communal fortunes on a national scale, whereby formerly dominant groups—urban Sunnis and Christians—were supplanted to the benefit of one-time rural outcasts. Widespread rejection of intermarriage and incompatible behavioral norms (relating to alcohol consumption, the mingling of genders, and female dress code) further contributed to community divisions. For instance, in Baniyas, the seaside area of Corniche was informally divided between Sunni and Alawite residents even before 2011.[21] Thus, in mixed cities where sectarian violence first erupted in 2011, relations between Sunnis and Alawites had already been clouded by long-standing social grievances.

The post-2000 period of limited economic liberalization, which initiated more competition over dwindling public resources and increased social inequality, only exacerbated these tensions. As in other cases of economic transformation—for instance, in Eastern Europe after the Cold War—the precariousness and exploitative character of the emerging private sector actually made the public sector more attractive. Despite declining benefits and pay, public sector jobs also remained preferable to unemployment, a fate that affected a rising number of those Alawites without access to patronage.

By the middle of the first decade of the twenty-first century, shrinking opportunities for ordinary citizens of all communities contrasted with increasingly ostentatious displays of wealth by a small stratum of extremely wealthy businessmen and their entourage.[22] Connections to those at the center of power, like the protection of high-ranking individuals in the security establishment, were essential to flourish in this environment. The prevalence of kinship ties meant that, among the beneficiaries, Alawites were still prominently represented in the top tier.[23]

However, there was an increasing tendency of this "counter-society standing between the authorities and real society" to seal itself off from the populace.[24] As liberalization proceeded apace, horizontal, crosscutting class interests among the elite—visible through the incorporation of non-Alawite cronies (for example, the Sunni in-laws of Maher al-Assad from the Hamsho family; the Tlass, Shihabi, and, until 2005, Khaddam clans; or the Shia entrepreneur Saeb Nahhas)—increasingly displaced communal solidarity. As a result, a growing number of Alawites were left outside the circle of communal privilege which they purportedly enjoyed. Yet, the influence of larger-than-life Alawite business moguls, such as Bashar al-Assad's cousin Rami Makhlouf, ensured that public perceptions did not adjust to these changing socio-communal realities.

Liberalization also contributed to the exacerbation of sectarianism by diminishing the role of the Baath Party and its affiliated mass organizations. The party's entrenchment in the public sector and its resilient commitment to egalitarian values—however compromised through practices of patronage— were increasingly perceived as a nuisance by the elite. While in the past the party had offered a degree of inclusion and an avenue of influence that potentially transcended the sectarian divide, its decline served to expose the Alawites' domination of the security apparatus even more.[25] Likewise, as faith-based charities and non-governmental organizations operating under the umbrella of First Lady Asma al-Assad increasingly took charge of social services, the number of people dependent on religious groups or powerful individuals only increased.[26]

Economic restructuring, the state's withdrawal as a provider, and the continued parasitic nature of the security sector served to accentuate existing communal grievances. Yet the effects of securitization on communal relations were not restricted to material issues. The regime's response to the 1980s conflict had turned Syria into a society characterized by ubiquitous surveillance, leading to a common, probably greatly exaggerated, assumption that one in four individuals was an informer.[27] And because of the known recruitment patterns of the security agencies, Alawites were generally suspected of being informers until proven otherwise.[28] The opaque character of these agencies, their propensity for violence, and the absence of any accountability[29] further contributed to an aura of existential suspicion of Alawites, which contributed to popular views of them as a tightly knit, closed-off community with carefully guarded, secret beliefs—or, more unsettling, no beliefs at all.

Above all else, this Alawite aura inspired pervasive fear. For instance, in the early 1990s, rumor had it that on the beaches around Latakia, young women were at risk of being kidnapped by thugs suddenly appearing in speedboats.[30] The implication was that the kidnappers were part of semi-criminal smuggling networks related in one way or another to the Assad clan. While such stories may have been partly invented or exaggerated,[31] the rumor was persistently retold and believed, which inarguably deterred numerous Damascenes from vacationing on the coast—and thus expressed, as well as reproduced, the fear that was lurking under the surface of ostensibly harmonious communal relations.

One result of this generalized association of Alawites with power was that individuals with high-ranking positions in the security sector were sometimes widely assumed to be Alawites, such as, for instance, the supposed founder of the all-powerful Air Force Intelligence Directorate and current director of the National Security Bureau, Ali Mamlouk, who is a Sunni.[32]

Even in social milieux where disavowing sectarianism and exposing the insincerity of the regime's professed secularism was common, sectarian affiliation was never entirely forgotten. For example, in 2004, the sculptor Mustafa Ali was able to purchase a 500-year-old home in an area of Damascus coveted by developers of high-end restaurants and boutique hotels and established an art gallery in what became an outlet for non-conformists. His ability to do so was generally attributed to the fact that he was an Alawite and therefore well-connected by default.[33] Thus, throughout the decades preceding the uprising, sect had become a common frame of interpretation for social relations, with one particular sect—Alawites—credited with unpredictable, near magical powers.

A dispersed power structure

On the surface, the omnipresence and brutality of the security state, the absurd personality cult around the Assads, and the state's ideological posturing and militarism made the Baath Party appear similar to totalitarian parties in North Korea and earlier in former communist Romania.[34] However, as will be discussed in this section, Syrian Baathism in fact relied on a dispersed, localized power structure that allowed the regime to integrate, promote, or marginalize groups belonging to different sects according to their loyalty and their usefulness for the purpose of power maintenance.[35]

This power structure was based on the management of informal networks of power and patronage structured by subnational identities and categories: sect, region, ethnicity, and tribe. At the grass-roots level, a combination of official regime representatives, intelligence officers, and prominent members of local society would cooperate in running a specific locality as a fief, sometimes with considerable autonomy. These officials would provide their loyalty and material proceeds to the leadership in return for franchises of authoritarian power. Thus, the main currency in this system of dispersed rule, and the key to accessing privilege and resources, was not so much sectarian affiliation but rather loyalty to the regime and usefulness for its maintenance of power.

In his extensive study of the political economy of the Assad state up to the 1990s, German scholar Volker Perthes described its power structure as a system of "authoritarian corporatist group representation," similar to models found in Latin America during the 1970s and 1980s.[36] According to this view, the holders of political power manage society as an assembly of groups with discrete demands and entitlements, which the leadership, selectively and partially, serves in return for loyalty and also attempts to balance. Power—in the sense of sometimes quasi-autonomous rule and command over resources, security, and more—is distributed from the highest levels of the state and society (provinces, sectarian communities) to the lowest (neighborhoods, extended families). Those same vertical networks and intermediaries or power brokers, in turn, also serve as conduits for bottom-up interest representation, albeit in a highly selective fashion and within constantly renegotiated limits. Framed as processes of consultation or even participation, demands, grievances, and other concerns are communicated to the leadership level, which responds at its own discretion and according to its own calculations of political and material benefit and cost. In other words, legitimacy and consent are obtained through hierarchical inclusion of the ruled by the rulers rather than through popular suffrage and legal accountability. Just how much power, resources, and influence flow up and down in specific relationships within these networks mostly depends on how reliable and valuable the support is of a particular representative group—in other words, to what extent it contributes to regime maintenance in terms of political resources and support on the popular and elite levels.

Within such a framework, everyday authoritarian rule can be exercised with a comparatively low level of actual coercion, while the permanent presence of the intelligence apparatus serves as a reminder that the potential for coercion still exists. Demands, grievances, and tensions can be communicated and potentially defused at an early stage and in a framework of unequal exchange.[37] Such forms of inclusion serve to confirm and reproduce existing power relations, thus avoiding a build-up of resentment and social tension that may be generated by the absence of meaningful participation and the pronounced inequality that systems of patronage inevitably generate. They also allow for the selective integration of indispensable social and economic actors and specialists, without compromising the monopoly on leadership decisions. And while *bargaining* for resources and influence is conducted vertically and hierarchically (between representatives of regional or sectoral interests and networks on the one hand and the state and party bureaucracy on the other), *competition* will occur horizontally—that is, among networks, regions, and sectors vying for the favor of the leadership or a greater share of resources. Authoritarian domination can thus be framed as the management of and mediation between groups pursuing competing particularistic agendas rather than different visions of the common good. Broad social alliances are difficult to build under such conditions and can be easily disrupted by policies of divide and rule.

These divisive practices in the maintenance of power stand in perennial tension with the ideological foundation of corporatism and its emphasis on harmony, which imagines social groups as the composite members of an organic national body and the regime as its brain. In this regard, it is interesting how, three months into the uprising, Assad chose to portray his opponents as "germs" or hostile organisms that a healthy body—that is, a harmonious society rallying around *his* vision and leadership—would naturally repel.[38]

As for the relationship between corporatism and sectarianization, the crucial question is which types of groups would the regime acknowledge as members of the national body and attempt to integrate and accommodate? In its classical form, corporatism proposes a differentiation of society according to functions and roles (peasants, blue- and white-collar workers, industrialists, intellectuals, clerics), which justifies, indeed renders natural, differences in treatment, resource allocation, and access to participation. The Baath Party originally incorporated groups along such functional lines by setting up mass organizations and designating quotas for them in its rubber-stamped bodies, some of which survive even as the party's standing has diminished.[39] The party also successfully co-opted existing institutions of collective interest representation, such as the chambers of commerce.

As for the religious sects, their supposedly harmonious integration into the state through the co-optation of their clerical leadership served two major purposes. It testified to the regime's professed secularism by placing the sects under state authority and constituted a positive contrast to sectarian mayhem in neighboring Lebanon and later Iraq. It also recruited religious leaders for purposes of mediation, and even more so for the disciplining and surveillance of their flocks.[40] And these tended to increase in importance as the intermediary role of the Baath Party's structures receded.[41]

For instance, Sunni clerics such as Grand Mufti Ahmad Badreddin Hassoun or the renowned scholar Muhammad Said Ramadan al-Buti were employed to rally the loyalty of Syrian Sunnis. In return, they sometimes received significant concessions when the support was especially valuable. Thus, on 5 April 2011, a presidential decree revoked the license for the only casino in Syria and overturned an earlier decision that had banned from public schools hundreds of female teachers wearing the full body veil (*niqab*). Both issues had been sharply criticized by al-Buti in late 2010, though he stood by the regime after the uprising began.[42] Ironically, when protesters demanded the teachers' reinstatement during the early phase of the uprising, regime mouthpieces used their demand as evidence of the protesters' alleged Sunni extremism.[43] Even real Sunni extremists were at times tolerated or exploited for political ends, for example, when jihadi networks infiltrated by the Syrian intelligence services facilitated the transit of jihadists to Iraq to fight against the American occupation forces after 2003.[44]

Furthermore, a hidden quota system provided for sectarian balance within the leadership and throughout the Syrian administration.[45] For instance, although the de facto establishment of dynastic rule implied that the president would always be an Alawite, since the conflict in the 1980s, the posts of first vice president and foreign minister have been occupied by Sunnis. In other words, the two executive positions at the head of the state that were beyond criticism, the presidency and vice presidency, and the one minister whose portfolio was so closely tied to the president as to be beyond reproach as well, were reserved for the two sects most crucial for the regime's survival: the Alawites and Sunnis. Abdul Halim Khaddam, who took over from Hafez al-Assad's brother Rifaat after the latter's failed bid for power, held the post for twenty-one years (1984–2005). After his removal, former foreign minister Farouk al-Sharaa took over the position of vice president, with Walid Al-Muallim, also a Sunni, named as foreign minister. Sharaa remains in office despite rumors of differences with President Assad.[46]

At lower levels of the state, where the leadership would occasionally admit to evident failures and punish scapegoats, there was a rotation of the different communities in posts. Sometimes this mechanism allowed for accommodation or validation of specific sects according to current expediency. For example, the appointment of the Christian Dawoud Rajiha to the position of defense minister on 8 August 2011 was commonly understood as a move to curry the loyalty of the Christian communities.[47] It was perhaps also not a coincidence that in the two cases when Sunni prime ministers turned into public villains (Mahmoud al-Zoubi, who was scapegoated in 1999 during the anti-corruption drive that prepared the ground for the presidential succession and ostensibly committed suicide; and Riad Hijab, who defected to the opposition in 2013), their successors would also be Sunni (Muhammad Miro and Wael al-Halqi), as if to dispel the notion that the disgrace of one official could indicate a rift between the regime and community.

Despite these practices of sectarian balancing, focusing on religious sect alone would have been too blunt an instrument for managing a demographically and socially complex society such as Syria's—let alone responding to the dynamic changes after the onset of economic liberalization in the second half of the 1990s. From the perspective of maintaining power, working with and through broad categories based on *passively* acquired group membership (that is, being born into a certain sect) would have made little sense for the purpose of generating and rewarding the *active* loyalty of individuals and groups.

In particular, it would have been entirely counterproductive to marginalize collectively the majority of Syrians who are Sunnis and thus generate a shared sense of injustice, which opponents could have readily exploited for the purpose of mobilization. The regime, instead, went to great lengths to placate the Sunni clergy. It also worked consciously to downplay and obscure outward signs of Alawite religiosity and encouraged assimilation into the Sunni mainstream. During fifty years of so-called Alawite rule, the Alawite clergy never obtained any form of official recognition or institutionalization that even remotely resembled the status of the Sunnis and the other minorities.[48] Instead, Syria's Alawite presidents performed public prayers in Sunni mosques, flanked by the mufti of the republic. Alawite children, like those of other Muslim minorities, received a Sunni religious education.[49] And Sunni mosques were built across Alawite-majority areas, even though they remained empty, emulating practices applied by the Ottoman Empire a century ago.

The formation of a coherent Sunni collective opposed to the regime, with a sense of shared purpose under a unified leadership, was made all the more difficult because of other factors. The social and behavioral differences and historical animosities between Sunni agriculturalists in the south, Bedouin tribes in the north and east, bourgeois urban dwellers in Damascus and Aleppo, and the inhabitants of the small and medium towns of the central plain and the coast, ruled out such a development. Throughout their almost five decades of rule, the two Assad regimes instead accommodated and marginalized each of these groups—at different times and on different terms—in response to changing domestic and regional dynamics.

In contrast, during the early 1980s, the radical wing of the Muslim Brotherhood attempted to generate Sunni solidarity that would cut across Syria's social and regional divides. The Brotherhood sought to mobilize violent confrontation against the "heretical" Alawite regime, but only found a response among the Sunni middle classes of the northern cities of Hama and Aleppo, whose interests had been negatively affected by the Baath Party's economic policies. The Sunni populations of the countryside and the smaller cities, as well as the Bedouin, rewarded the regime's pro-rural development agenda with their loyalty, alongside the Sunni urban elite of Damascus, which the regime had made significant efforts to co-opt.[50]

This geographically differentiated treatment and incorporation of groups pointed to a key element of the Baathist corporatist arrangement, namely the dispersal of power to the local level. This only increased as the grass-roots structures of the party wilted away—and with them any effective institutional mechanism to keep local power holders in check. Managed as a "system of regions,"[51] Syria developed "not [as] a nation-state or even a territorial state, but as a state of territories ... in which the regime [was] in constant negotiation with local societies."[52]

Regions and localities, in turn, served as proxies for communal affiliation according to sect, clan, ethnicity, and region of origin. In the popular perception, most rural areas, villages, and sub-regions in Syria tended to be identified with one particular sect and, where this mattered, specific clans and tribes or other defined sub-groups. The same held true for most urban areas, where typically only the central commercial and administrative districts were considered neutral spaces. Most residential quarters, in turn, as a result of historical patterns of settlement and migration, were identified with a specific sect, with further differentiations according to region of origin, social status, and other factors.

This structure of dispersed power showed itself to be an efficient insurance policy once the regime was seriously challenged in 2011. It allowed Assad to draw on local allies who would come forward in defense of the status quo and limit the reach of the insurgency. Syria's north-east, with a mixed Christian, Kurdish, and tribal Arab population, provided an instructive example of this. Having ruled the area by working through intermediaries and treating the groups the intermediaries represented differently,[53] the regime responded to pro-democracy demonstrations in 2011 with the same violent repression as elsewhere in Syria. In contrast, parallel protests demanding Kurdish national and cultural rights were treated leniently.[54] Evidently, Kurdish self-assertion, which had been repressed violently as late as 2004, appeared to be far less of a threat than demands for democratic change. In the summer of 2012, the regime stood by when the Democratic Union Party (PYD) affiliated with the Kurdistan Workers Party (PKK) took over most areas with a sizable Kurdish population. This territory became a buffer zone between regime-controlled areas and Turkey, the PKK's mortal enemy, which by that time had emerged as a main sponsor of the Syrian opposition.

The surge of the PYD also served to split the local Arab communities and motivated many to side with the government and even provide manpower for pro-Assad militias. This is because many Arabs were settled on land originally expropriated by the Baath Party from Kurdish owners as part of the regime's "arabization" policies and feared for their property in the event that Kurds took control of their areas. At the same time, the sizable local Christian community established militias that were either co-opted into the PYD structures or allied themselves with the regime.[55] Thus, while large parts of northern and north-eastern Syria were removed from the immediate control of the Assad regime, they remained hostile to its opponents and could still be easily incorporated back into the regime's system of indirect rule.[56]

As in the north-east, the regime has been able to exploit local conditions elsewhere and mobilize clients to generate support, or at least ensure neutrality, among many Sunni communities—in addition to the middle and upper classes of large cities. Prior to the revolution, these urban classes had often complained about the excessive greed and privileges of Alawite regime cronies.[57] However, that did not mean that they were ready to risk their privileges by openly joining the rebellion.[58]

Just as the regime's strategies of rule benefited *some* Sunnis and (belatedly) Kurdish areas and communities, the impact on Alawites was likewise highly differentiated. Pronounced geographical differences existed between the degree to which certain Alawite-populated areas were incorporated into the power structure and benefited from it. In particular, a significant hierarchy exists between Alawites originating from the coast and the coastal mountains and those from the central plain.[59] These regional distinctions partly overlapped with and blurred into tribal origins, with access to power also being a function of family and tribal proximity to the ruling Assad-Makhlouf clans. The extensive field knowledge and long memory of the security services further allowed for precise differentiation between loyal supporters, fence-sitters, and likely opponents, as well as by tribal allegiance and sub-group.

Therefore, in the period preceding the 2011 uprising, social divisions in the much smaller Alawite community were as pronounced as within the Sunni community. Unlike the Sunnis, however, the Alawites lacked a developed clerical hierarchy, institutional structures, or an ideological narrative with unifying potential. This made it doubtful whether, before 2011, it would have made sense to speak of an Alawite community at all. The uprising, however, changed all that by providing a powerful impetus that would galvanize the vast majority of Alawites across Syria—and, to some extent, other minorities—into supporting the regime: fear of potential genocide.

The legacy and anticipation of violence

The transition from peaceful protest to escalating violence between Sunni and Alawite communities was accelerated significantly by a legacy of mutual fear generated by earlier violent conflict, in particular during the uprising of the Muslim Brotherhood against the Assad regime during the late 1970s and early 1980s.

On 16 June 1979, a radical faction of the Muslim Brotherhood attacked the Aleppo Artillery School, killing between thirty-two and eighty-three cadets. According to some accounts, the attackers were selective, executing Alawites and sparing Sunnis.[60] The attack was a landmark in transforming opposition to the regime of Hafez al-Assad, which escalated in the second half of the 1970s into a conflict dominated by sectarian violence.[61] More precisely, it became a confrontation between the regime and parts of the Muslim Brotherhood that had chosen armed struggle over reformism. Driven by a mix of ideology and opportunism, they chose to attack the regime over its sectarian composition rather than its foreign policy, failing economic performance, and authoritarian practices.

The response to Islamist violence was excessive, and mostly extra-legal, state violence, culminating in the Hama massacre of February 1982.[62] The regime's retaliatory actions were focused on, but hardly limited to, the Muslim Brotherhood—mere membership became a capital crime.[63] Being identified as an Alawite, in turn, implied being a potential target of lethal violence, regardless of an individual's political preferences and views of the regime. In fact, the conflict of the early 1980s illustrated that politicized identity was not only a *source* of collective violence but could also be *generated*, activated, or hardened by violence.[64] For Syrians who felt they were recognizable as Alawites—whether by name, place of birth, residence, or accent—the possibility of violence being directed against them, as well as the knowledge (typically inflated by rumor and propaganda) of attacks that appeared to be motivated by sectarian antagonism, drove home that their future in Syria was tied to that of the sectarian community to which they belonged, regardless of their own orientations.

Since the Muslim Brotherhood's rhetoric during the 1970s and 1980s explicitly emphasized the heretical character of the regime, the inevitable conclusion was that in a Syria ruled by the Brotherhood, or similar strands of politicized Islam, there would be no place for Alawites. The extreme violence of the conflict (some accounts put the number of victims of the Hama massacre alone at 40,000) instilled in Alawites a pervasive fear that one day equally violent retribution would be exacted against them.[65]

In response, some Alawites sought to hide their identity or that of their loved ones. In one case, the father of an Alawite woman, out of concern over future sectarian violence, used his influence as an intelligence officer to have her place of birth registered as Midan, a predominantly Sunni neighborhood of Damascus, rather than the family's original home in Tartus, commonly regarded as a mainly Alawite city.[66] Fear was kept alive through the taboo surrounding any mention of the conflict against the Muslim Brotherhood during the early 1980s, as well as by occasional, perhaps calculated, exceptions to this taboo.

However, alarm over possible reprisals was by no means restricted to the Alawite community. In the early 1990s, many Syrian Christians expressed their fear that if a day of reckoning were to come, the massacre of Alawites (which was taken for granted) would quickly spill over to engulf all non-Sunni communities and areas.[67]

Thus, the experience of violence not only remained present in individual and collective memories, but impressed itself on how many Syrians imagined their future in the country and their relations to others. Such unaddressed potential for violence lingered under the surface of supposedly harmonious intercommunal relations. That is why in early 2011, though only few instances of apparent intercommunal violence took place—amid considerable violence by regime forces—they were enough to trigger again the drive toward the "dead certainty" of identity politics.[68]

The storming of the Omari Mosque in Daraa on 23 March 2011, where protesters had established a field hospital and a headquarters of sorts, added a sectarian tinge to a contestation that, until that moment, had been exclusively fixated on social issues and the misconduct of the local governor. For many, the assault underlined the regime's disregard for religious sanctuaries, which was widely perceived as disregard for Sunni Islam.[69]

As a consequence, on 25 March, demonstrations in solidarity with Daraa found a strong response in many Sunni-populated localities. These included neighborhoods in the mixed Sunni-Alawite city of Latakia. Alongside confrontations between protesters and the security forces, with live fire leaving twelve people dead, sectarian altercations occurred at the edges of Sunni- and Alawite-dominated areas and on the campus of Tishreen University. For a day, the city was abuzz with rumors of an impending, full-fledged sectarian confrontation. Yet when a motorcade originating in the Alawite heartland above Latakia reached the outskirts of the city with the objective of "saving" the Alawite population, they were stopped by army and police units and eventually turned back.[70] Faced with the prospect of open sectarian warfare, municipal authorities and local community leaders cooperated and eventually succeeded in containing the situation.[71] In the following weeks, a strong security presence confined the protests to the Sunni neighborhoods and finally to the southern periphery of the city, where they were eventually crushed.

Sectarian tensions escalated further two weeks later in Baniyas. On 9 April, a cycle of violence between protesters and the security forces— allegedly also involving violent regime supporters—led to several casualties. At nightfall, a bus carrying a group of Alawite soldiers and servicemen was ambushed near the city, killing nine. At the same time, videos of atrocities with an apparent sectarian dimension started to circulate. In one, what appears to be a mixed group of security forces and armed irregulars, identifiable as Alawites by their accent and first names, is shown violently abusing the civilian population of what was supposed to be the Sunni village of Al-Bayda, about 6 miles south of Baniyas.[72] A second video from Baniyas showed the gruesome killing of an Alawite vegetable trader who was allegedly acting as a recruiter for pro-regime militias, or Shabbiha, by what was supposedly a Sunni mob.[73] Negotiations ensued between the notables of Baniyas and Assad himself, helping again to calm the threat of a larger sectarian confrontation. However, the city was stormed by the military on 7 May, putting an end to protests for months to come.

In Homs, about 200 protesters had first assembled on 18 March at the Khaled Ibn al-Walid Mosque to denounce not the regime but the local governor. He had acquired a track record for arbitrary land expropriations and shady real estate deals and was attempting to push through a futuristic urban renewal project named "The Dream of Homs" (*Hilm Homs*).[74] Resistance to the project, led by local businesses fearing for their interests, focused on its alleged hidden purpose of changing the demographic make-up in the Sunni-majority city.[75] A week later, on 25 March, police cordoned off the mosque, but protests broke out at several other Sunni mosques around town before converging on the downtown New Clock Tower Square, where portraits of the president were defaced. A loyalist counter-demonstration, allegedly fomented by the security forces and the Shabbiha,[76] set out from the Alawite quarters of Akrama, Nuzha, and Zahra. These led to clashes that were followed by a large number of arrests and allegations of torture.[77] Over the following three weeks, with New Clock Tower Square barricaded, reciprocal altercations occurred between so-called popular committees organized in Alawite quarters to protect against alleged incursions by Sunni gunmen and protesters congregating in various Sunni mosques, where a rising number of casualties were recorded. In return, Alawite members of the security forces were targeted for assassination, which was extensively covered by official media.[78] Funerals became rallying points for both sides.

Events took a new turn when demonstrations against Assad's address to the new Syrian government on 16 April were answered with gunfire. The ensuing cycle of funerals turning into protests and protests leading to new funerals generated massive rallies on 18 April, which overwhelmed the security forces and allowed protesters to reclaim New Clock Tower Square, which they renamed Freedom Square. Once there, they established a leadership committee comprising clerics, local notables, and other prominent personalities. According to participants, a major motivation for the move was the need to keep under control a sizable faction seeking to overrun Alawite quarters and exact retribution against the popular committees.[79] Furthermore, some activists set up tents and a platform specifically dedicated to national unity to underline their inclusive approach to communal relations. According to accounts by activists, a delegation claiming to represent the Christian quarters of Homs reached where the protesters were gathered and expressed its support, while activists identifying themselves as Alawites took to the podium to underline the all-encompassing nature of the protests and alleviate sectarian tensions generated by the earlier violence.[80]

The protesters thus attempted to adopt techniques similar to those applied during the protests at the Pearl Roundabout camp in Bahrain. There, as in Syria, claims by regime-dominated media and partisans that the movement was motivated by sectarianism (in the Bahraini case, Shia sectarianism) were countered by showcasing prominent opposition supporters from the sect supposedly under attack (in the Bahraini case, the Sunni minority, to which the ruling family belongs). This demonstration was accompanied by solemn expressions of cross-sectarian solidarity and unity in the struggle against oppression.[81]

Given the weeks of slowly mounting sectarian altercations that preceded the 18 April protests in Homs, it remains doubtful whether these attempts at conciliation could have succeeded had the gathering of protesters been allowed to last and develop into a protest camp along the lines of what had happened in Baghdad, Cairo, or Manama. Either way, it was violently dismantled in the early hours of 19 April, with a large number of casualties.[82] As in Latakia previously, the protest movement was thus pushed back from a central urban location that could potentially have served as a neutral meeting ground required for bolstering the narrative of "national unity in resistance" that the protesters were trying to propagate. Instead, they were forced into neighborhoods identified as Sunni, despite all attempts to sound the national unity theme there as well (including building a wooden effigy of the New Clock Tower). Quite literally, the space for cross-communal solidarity in rebellion against oppression was thus erased. Furthermore, the encouragement of violent counter-demonstrations that blurred into the recruitment of pro-government militiamen was a crucial step that turned the dynamics from a contestation between the protest movement and the regime into a conflict between social groups largely defined by sect. Over the summer, Homs, dubbed the "Heart of the Revolution," became engulfed in a furious cycle of sectarian violence, killings, and kidnappings that gradually descended into urban civil warfare.[83]

How would those who place all or most of the blame for the sectarian turn of the Syrian uprising on regime manipulation explain the different trajectories in Latakia and Baniyas, where sectarian conflict was quickly contained, and in Homs, where it was allowed to fester and turn into urban warfare? On the one hand, the differences could be attributed to the regime's use of dissimilar strategies and objectives in different regions and at different times. On the other hand, they could also be attributed to specific local conditions and different institutional and regime actors working at cross-purposes. Among such differences, one may mention the precarious demographic and economic situation of the local Alawite population, which made it a prime recruiting ground for pro-government militias, and the overwhelming Sunni majority in the city and its hinterland—a situation that is reversed on the coast. Bishara also mentions the Bedouin background of a proportion of the protesters and the geographic location, which facilitated access to smuggling networks and the procurement of light weapons.[84]

Either way, events in all three mixed cities and a number of other similar localities underlined that the regime's ruling practices over previous decades had turned social relations into a sectarian time bomb that any serious challenge to the political status quo would set off. With this kind of preparation, there was no need for the Assad regime actively to instigate sectarian conflict. Rather, mediation including community leaders and regime representatives was necessary, and possible, to *prevent* such a development. But the regime's price was submitting to its authority.

While perhaps not expecting that the turn to intercommunal violence would occur so rapidly, many intellectuals who became part of the opposition were clearly aware of the dangers stemming from the existing legacy of violence and fear.[85] Yet despite all explicit disavowals of sectarianism and solemn declarations of national unity on social media outlets and in public demonstrations, the opposition's approach remained ambiguous and contradictory. Over the summer of 2011, young Sunni activists with mostly secular outlooks would often express a wide range of inconsistent positions, swinging between patronizing expressions of tolerance for minorities in general, blanket vilification of Alawites, and proud references to prominent individual Alawites (for example, the writer Samar Yazbek or the actress Fadwa Suleiman) and representatives of other minorities (for example, the Druze or Christians) who openly sided with the uprising.[86] Those advocating inclusiveness were powerless to prevent a turn toward protest practices that adopted Sunni-inflected religious language and symbolism. The fact that mosques provided the only available meeting places for the opposition, and that the rising number of casualties turned religious rituals of burial and mourning into the centerpiece of the protest repertoire, inevitably colored the public face of the movement.

Another problem was the high visibility of religiously colored forms of expression in public protests. Salafi networks that had been growing over the past decade, in particular in marginalized areas where there had been significant migration to the Gulf, most likely represented only a small proportion of demonstrators. However, calls for martyrdom and the wearing of burial shrouds to express the bearer's readiness to die, which were observed in Baniyas and Jableh in early April, rapidly spread over social media.[87] The resort to nightly renditions of the *takbir*, where entire urban neighborhoods shouted "God is Great" (*Allahu Akbar*) from rooftops—a method borrowed from the 2009 Green Movement in Iran[88]—certainly created a sense of empowerment among Sunni protesters. However, it was hardly suitable to convince members of other communities that the protests were inherently inclusive.

Kheder Khaddour reports the feelings of a young Alawite man after participating in a large and violently repressed protest in Homs in April 2011: "Soon
afterwards, he remembers hearing loud appeals to Jihad coming from the
minarets of mosques—which to Alawites meant a holy war against them. He
says, 'Suddenly I became scared and I changed my mind, as I realized that
what was happening was no longer a revolution.'"[89] The increasingly inflammatory rhetoric of Salafi television preachers operating out of the Gulf further
fueled such fears. These became more extreme and influential as casualties
rose, while those who could have provided a civic-minded, moderate leadership were increasingly neutralized by regime violence.

Whether these mostly young people could have infused the narrative of
"national unity in the struggle against repression" with additional credibility
and vigor, or whether the protest camp in Homs could have become the
nucleus of cross-sectarian solidarity had it been allowed to last, remains
unknown. On the other hand, already in June 2011, the Syrian publicist
Yassin al-Haj Saleh, one of the intellectual leaders of the uprising, had highlighted the difficult relationship between the "civic" element in the protest
movement—made up of young, educated, mostly liberal-minded activists—
and the more "traditionalist-communalist" element.[90]

Along similar lines, the Syrian sociologist Mohammed Jamal Barout attributed the vulnerability of disenfranchised youth with regard to "populist
Salafism" to the absence or lack of efficiency of any organized Islamist political
force (such as the Muslim Brotherhood).[91] In Egypt, Tunisia, and Yemen, the
downside of the decentralized, leaderless character of the uprisings that
received so much praise from foreign observers only became manifest during
the post-uprising transitions, while in Syria, the lack of leadership may have
been a fatal liability from the beginning.[92]

Conclusion: plus ça change

As invariably happens to internal conflicts with strong identity components,
the Syrian civil war has led to speculation about resettling communities within
political or administrative borders that allow for greater homogeneity.
Comparisons with Europe's Thirty Years' War and dramatic projections of a
"great sorting out" tend to portray Syria, like Iraq, as a centerpiece of an existential struggle that can only be resolved through a break-up of the countries
into sectarian entities.[93] Long-term stability, it is assumed, is conditioned on
boundaries that create mostly homogeneous communities. Forced population
transfers and mass ethnic cleansing are an inevitable part of such a scenario.

Fortunately, the odds that this scenario will come to pass are extremely low. There are few if any local takers for such plans. None of the Syrian parties are pursuing a political project that aims for control over anything less than all of Syria. Territorial division, even federalization, is anathema for most parties except the Kurds, whose declared ambitions are, however, restricted to cultural autonomy within a unified Syrian state. Local proponents of Alawite, Druze, or Sunni statelets could perhaps be found, or built up, if the external actors involved in Syria agreed that this was a viable solution to the conflict. Yet at the present time, no one appears prepared to venture into such unpredictable territory, which risks completely unraveling the regional state order.

Attempts to end the conflict while maintaining Syria's territorial integrity may instead move in the direction of non-territorial power-sharing schemes that would integrate some elements of the opposition and enhance the representation of the Sunni community.[94] However, tinkering with representation in Syria's political institutions will be meaningless unless the regime agrees to dismantle its sprawling security apparatus, where real power is located. Given the nature of the Syrian power structure, any attempt at gradual or partial reform will be pointless—a basic fact that has remained unchanged since the abortive Damascus Spring in the early 2000s. No opposition representatives with influence and credibility will participate on such terms and put themselves at the mercy of the Assad regime's shadow army.

In all likelihood, then, the current state of fragmentation will endure for the foreseeable future, creating a situation of de facto separation into a number of fiefdoms, as was the case in neighboring Lebanon during its civil war.[95] Five or more areas ruled by authoritarian leaderships of different ideological hues may accommodate each other in an uneasy relationship characterized by a stabilized military balance, while the magnitude of the fighting declines. Over time, this may give way to the only form of power-sharing that could feasibly succeed in formally reintegrating the Syrian state: a confederation of several dictatorships, each claiming a certain sectarian, regional, or ethnic share and preserving its own military and security forces within the formal framework of the Syrian state.

In theory, the operational cooperation between the United States and Russia that was proposed by the agreement between US Secretary of State John Kerry and Russian Foreign Minister Sergei Lavrov in early September 2016 could have initiated such a process of reintegration. An established consensus about which groups should be considered terrorist, and hence be excluded from any ceasefire, and others who may not be attacked by anyone, would have helped the latter to consolidate their military position. In addition, it would have implicitly vetted them as legitimate participants in any further political process. However, the practical difficulties of establishing such a consensus appear nearly insurmountable amid mutual distrust, frequent re-alignments on the ground, and the blurring and renegotiation of borders among existing and emerging organizations. It also is difficult to see how such a scheme could be implemented as long as there is no external enforcer with troops on the ground to ensure that those excluded from the ceasefire do not spoil the process. Thus, gradual convergence appears more plausible and will likely include actors that are today considered beyond the pale, such as parts of the former Nusra Front (now rebranded as Jabhat Fateh al-Sham).

Genuine reform would thus be replaced by the incorporation of a limited number of new actors into the system of dispersed authoritarian rule characteristic of Syrian Baathism, while sectarian representation would substitute for democracy. Thus, for the civic movement that emerged during the first half of 2011 in Syria, and was pushed aside or abroad by the violent turn of the uprising, the real struggle is yet to come, once the guns fall silent.

Given these possible dynamics, Syrian actors and the international community should focus on initiatives that successfully navigate six key conditions. First, the rebuilding of community relations, and any serious political change, will depend on comprehensive security sector reform—in other words, the dissolution of the existing security institutions and their replacement by fully accountable ones. For as long as this condition is not fulfilled, even after a stable ceasefire has been put in place, cooperation with state institutions in areas under the control of the regime (with or without Assad) will only help to consolidate authoritarianism and sectarianism.

Second, in areas not under regime control, structures of civic self-government may help to attenuate sectarian tensions and should be protected and nurtured as much as possible. Any return of the regime's unreformed security agencies to these areas, in any guise and under any pretext whatsoever (such as fighting terrorism), must be prevented. At the same time, external actors who support and supply armed groups in these areas must weigh in with their clients to preserve local self-governance.

Third, sectarian power-sharing is liable to replace the dictatorship of one person with that of several. Such leaders will convert the military status they gained during the conflict into control over institutions and resources in their region, claiming to represent one community or the other. External actors should not fall for the illusion that pacification of the conflict through such means can buy long-term stability. Nor can it amount to a democratic order, even if elections take place that appear genuinely competitive, in the sense that they regulate the power balance among local leaders.

Fourth, despite these dim prospects, the post-conflict political order may still allow for margins of dissent that differ from one area to another. External actors should work with Syrian exile communities to build up political parties and movements in preparation for a post-conflict order and, as much as possible, with activists in areas outside regime control. Apart from establishing formations that cut across sectarian lines, Syria urgently needs parties with the capacity to represent the multiple forms of politicized Sunni Islam that currently exist among the population.

Fifth, in assisting Syria's post-conflict recovery, external actors should not make sectarian inclusiveness the sole criterion for choosing in-country partners. For genuine pluralism to take hold, the potential for parties, activist groups, and non-governmental organizations to challenge entrenched hierarchies is more important than ensuring that their membership accurately reflects Syria's ethnosectarian mix.

And finally, for future crises, the central lesson from Syria should be that banking on authoritarian regimes to maintain stability in societies threatened by internal ethnic, religious, and sectarian tensions and conflict is fatally misguided. Ultimately, when they are seriously challenged, authoritarian rulers will resort to exploiting, mobilizing, and militarizing these cleavages. In divided societies, today's authoritarian stability begets tomorrow's civil war, or worse, genocide.

4

SECTARIANISM AND IRANIAN FOREIGN POLICY

Afshon Ostovar

Introduction

War in the Middle East has brought more attention to Iran's regional role. The Islamic Republic's support to allies in the region's main conflicts—Iraq, Syria, and Yemen—has put it on the opposite side of most of its neighbors. That divide is more than political or strategic: it is sectarian. Iran and its main allies are all Shia or are considered as such. Together they have fought against Sunni forces backed by Sunni-led states. This dynamic has deepened the region's descent into sectarianism and has exacerbated political disputes between Iran and many of its Sunni neighbors.

Iran's critics, especially Saudi Arabia, view its foreign policies as sectarian and expansionist. They argue that Iran has been exploiting political unrest across the region to champion its militant Shia clients and undermine the Sunni-dominated status quo. They see Iran's endgame as an expansive, transnational, pro-Iranian Shia polity stretching from Iran to Lebanon and encompassing Iraq and Syria—something akin to a resurrected Persian empire, but with the Shia faith and allegiance to Iran's supreme leader as the unifying characteristics. Such a scenario is worrisome to Iran's neighbors and something that Saudi Arabia and others appear committed to preventing.[1]

The Islamic Republic's foreign policies are aimed at advancing its strategic interests. Sectarianism plays a role in those policies, but not in the single-minded, all-encompassing way that Iran's critics suggest. Indeed, for most of its history, the Islamic Republic has followed a largely non-sectarian path. Iran's leaders have long emphasized pan-Islamic ideals and courted Sunni allies. The majority of scholars who have studied Iranian foreign policy since 1979 do not describe that record of behavior as sectarian, meaning primarily aimed at advancing a pro-Shia agenda. Rather, they see Iran's decision-making as closer to realpolitik.[2]

However, the sectarian element in Iranian foreign policy has increased over the last decade. The primary catalysts for the country's shift toward a more clear-cut favoring of Shia clients and allies in the Middle East were the toppling of former Iraqi leader Saddam Hussein in 2003 and the Arab Spring beginning in late 2010. Those events and the conflicts they ignited—particularly in Iraq, Syria, and Yemen—have sharply divided the interests of Iran and its neighbors. Fearful of each other's intentions, the behavior of Iran and its Arab rivals has moved increasingly in a sectarian direction. Such sectarianism runs counter to Tehran's official positions, but close relationships with Shia allies have become the basis of Iranian influence in the region. With its allies threatened in Iraq, Syria, and Yemen, Iran has doubled down on its pro-Shia strategy as a way of protecting its regional interests and investments. This has been exemplified in the behavior and rhetoric of the Islamic Revolutionary Guards Corps (IRGC)—Iran's pre-eminent military organization and the leading agency in its strategic activities in the Middle East. In addition to being heavily involved in the region's conflicts, the IRGC has begun to portray its allies and clients as a unified Shia front with regional ambitions.

Iran's reputation and competing visions of sectarianism

In 2016, as part of their bitter feud, Iran and Saudi Arabia exchanged public accusations of sectarianism that reached as far as mainstream media outlets in the United States. In September, the *New York Times* published an op-ed by Iran's foreign minister, Mohammad Javad Zarif, entitled "Let Us Rid the World of Wahhabism."[3] Zarif contends that Wahhabist Islam has become a plague, unleashing terrorism and murderous tumult across the Middle East and throughout the world. He calls Wahhabism a "theological perversion" that has "wrought havoc" and had a "devastating" impact in Islamic communities. The violence committed by jihadist groups such as al-Qaeda is a direct result of "Riyadh's persistent sponsorship of extremism," he argues, and this violence is at the root of the current conflicts in the Middle East. He accuses Saudi Arabia of "playing the 'Iran card'" to induce its allies to take part in the Syrian and Yemeni wars, and he concludes that "concrete action against extremism is needed." Even though Riyadh caused the mess, Zarif "invite[s]" Saudi Arabia to be part of the solution. That gesture rings hollow, given the accusatory tone of the piece. It is clearly a polemic against Iran's neighbor and arch-rival, another salvo in their ongoing cold war.

However, Zarif also speaks to Iran's view of sectarianism and sectarian conflict in the Middle East. They are not organic, but rather the by-products of a misguided effort by Saudi Arabia and its Western allies to isolate Iran and curb its influence.

The September 2016 op-ed followed another that the Iranian foreign minister wrote months earlier in January. In that piece, entitled "Saudi Arabia's Reckless Extremism," the veteran diplomat argues that while Iran's president, Hassan Rouhani, has made "friendship with our neighbors, peace and stability in the region and global cooperation" priorities for Iran, as evinced by the July 2015 nuclear deal, "some countries," particularly Saudi Arabia, have stood in the way of Iran's efforts at "constructive engagement."[4]

Zarif lists several reasons why Saudi Arabia is harming regional security. Riyadh is not only obstructing Iran's efforts at compromise and friendship, but also is involved in the "active sponsorship of violent extremism." Zarif links Saudi Arabia to terrorist attacks in the West, al-Qaeda affiliates in the Middle East, and extremism around the globe. Zarif frames the Saudi war in Yemen, Saudi support for Syria's Islamist rebels, and other acts as ways to bait Iran and "derail the nuclear agreement" by exacerbating tensions in the region.[5]

The January op-ed appeared at a flashpoint in Iranian-Saudi relations. Eight days earlier, the Saudi government had executed Sheikh Nimr al-Nimr, a senior Saudi Shia cleric and political activist, along with forty-six other prisoners (mostly Sunni radicals). The incident caused ire in Iran and elsewhere, with Supreme Leader Ali Khamenei warning that the Saudi monarchy would suffer "divine revenge."[6] Iraqi Shia militias allied with Iran also promised vengeance.[7] Fury over the execution of al-Nimr culminated in a large protest outside the Saudi embassy in Tehran. During the demonstration, a group of hardliners stormed the embassy and set it on fire.

The fall-out for Iran was quick. Saudi Arabia and all of its Gulf Cooperation Council (GCC) allies (except Oman), plus Jordan, Morocco, and Sudan severed or downgraded diplomatic ties with Iran. The incident appeared to be an embarrassment for Iran. The government scrambled to stem the blowback by claiming that the attack had been the action of rogue elements and arresting some of the individuals involved. Zarif's open letter fell into that context, but instead of an apology, it was an attempt to defend Iran by casting Saudi Arabia as the real culprit of regional unrest.

Later that month, Saudi Foreign Minister Adel al-Jubeir, Zarif's counterpart, responded in kind through a *New York Times* op-ed of his own, wherein he reminds Zarif of Iran's reputation:

> We [Saudi Arabia] are not the country designated a state sponsor of terrorism; Iran is. We are not the nation under international sanctions for supporting terrorism; Iran is. We are not the nation whose officials are on terrorism [watch] lists; Iran is.[8]

Al-Jubeir further charges that, in condemning Saudi Arabia, Iran "opts to obscure its dangerous sectarian and expansionist policies," rather than making the necessary effort to transform into a "respectable member of the international community." For the Saudi foreign minister, Iran's sectarian behavior has been "consistent since the 1979 revolution." He points to Iran's stated "objective of exporting the revolution" as the basis of its foreign policy ills, and he lists Iran's support for Shia groups, "Hezbollah in Lebanon, the Houthis in Yemen and sectarian militias in Iraq" as proof of Iran's continued sectarian agenda. This behavior runs counter to Iran's stated desire for cooperation, al-Jubeir argues:

> While Iran claims its top foreign policy priority is friendship, its behavior shows the opposite is true. Iran is the single-most-belligerent-actor in the region, and its actions display both a commitment to regional hegemony and a deeply held view that conciliatory gestures signal weakness either on Iran's part or on the part of its adversaries.[9]

Those comments should not be seen simply through the lens of Saudi-Iranian tensions. Rather, Middle Eastern officials share this perspective of Iran as a sectarian and expansionist actor in the region. In March 2015, Turkey's President Recep Tayyip Erdoğan accused Iran of "trying to dominate the region" through supporting Shia groups in Iraq, Syria, and Yemen.[10] In Iraq, he highlighted the involvement of the Quds Force, a division of Iran's IRGC, as especially sectarian. Commenting on the Quds commander, Major General Qassem Suleimani, who oversees Iranian military operations abroad, Erdoğan claimed: "This is someone I know very well.... So, what is [Iran's] objective? To increase the power of Shiite[s] in Iraq. That's what they want." A number of Arab states have made similar indictments regarding Iran's activities outside its borders. Nearly the entire Arab League, which represents twenty-two states, formally condemned Iran's foreign "meddling" at its annual 2016 meeting.[11] Lebanon was the only league member not to sign the declaration.

The regional concern at Iran's perceived sectarian aspirations is mostly rooted in the rhetoric and behavior that Tehran's leaders adopted after the 1979 revolution: the ethno-nationalism of Mohammad Reza Shah Pahlavi and Iran's history as a Shia state since the early modern Safavid dynasty are deeper sources of tension, but they are not the focus here. The revolution introduced a radical form of Shia Islamism and anti-monarchical views to Iranian politics. That ideological turn worried the Persian Gulf's Arab monarchies and neighboring Iraq.[12] With political activism rising in Iraq's politically disenfranchised Shia-majority community, Saddam Hussein felt that his country was especially vulnerable to Iran's revolution. He claimed that Iraq's invasion of Iran in 1980, which set off the nearly eight-year Iran-Iraq war, was necessary to shield Iraq and the Sunni Arab world from the spread of the radical Shiism of Ayatollah Ruhollah Khomeini—the father of the revolution and Iran's first supreme leader.[13] The GCC, which was formed by the Arab sheikhdoms of the Persian Gulf to create a unified front against Iran, backed Saddam Hussein in the war. Saudi Arabia and Kuwait in particular bankrolled much of his war effort.[14]

As problematic as he was, the Iraqi leader was considered by some to be a vital bulwark against Iran's ambitions in the Middle East. He governed the most populous Shia country in the Arab world, which houses the most important Shia centers of learning and pilgrimage. Through arrests, torture, and murder, Saddam Hussein ensured that Iran's Shia revolutionary fervor would not take root in his country, or be embraced by Iraq's prominent ayatollahs and potentially spread to Arab Shia communities elsewhere in the Persian Gulf. So when he was toppled in 2003, and Shia parties began to gain political power in Iraq, fears of expanding Iranian sectarian influence and regional ambitions increased in neighboring Gulf states.[15]

Sensing Iran's growing influence in the newly established Iraqi democracy, Jordan's King Abdullah II warned in 2004 that by building a support base in Iraq, Iran was actually seeking to establish a massive Shia "crescent" that would spread from Iran through Iraq, Syria, and Lebanon.[16] This geographic bloc of like-minded polities would challenge the status quo of pro-Western Sunni dominance in the Middle East. Abdullah's caution was that if Iraq were to become dominated by pro-Iranian Shia parties, this could have a cascading effect in the region. Shia-Sunni tensions could re-emerge, which could destabilize Persian Gulf states that have sizable Shia minority populations, such as Saudi Arabia. This would "propel the possibility of a Shiite-Sunni conflict even more" outside Iraq, Abdullah argued.

From the perspectives of many Arab states and Turkey, if not that of the general observer, recent history has borne out the sectarian conflict that Abdullah warned would occur. They see Shia-dominated, post-Baathist Iraq as the genesis of what has become a series of sectarian-driven conflicts in Iraq, Syria, and Yemen, as well as in the Arab Spring protests in Bahrain and the Eastern Province of Saudi Arabia. Arab states largely do not publicly reflect on their own potentially negative contribution to these crises. Rather, Iran is blamed for all of the turmoil. To its critics, these crises are a direct product of Iran's unchecked ambitions to control the region through the sowing of sectarian discord and the establishment of powerful Shia armed groups across the region.[17]

Is Iran a sectarian actor?

Iran's activities in the Middle East are well-documented and can appear sectarian in nature. There is no question that Iran has been heavily involved in the Syrian civil war and in the war against the self-proclaimed Islamic State in Iraq. The scope of Iranian activity in Yemen is murkier and more disputed,[18] but Iran has done little to hide its support of the Zaidi Shia Houthis and their Ansar Allah movement.[19] The fact that Iran's allies in these conflicts are non-Sunnis who either share the same brand of Twelver Shiism as Iran's leaders (Lebanese Hezbollah and Iraqi militias) or identify with other forms of Shia Islam (Alawism in Syria and Zaidism in Yemen) is also not in question. Such connections have given Iran's foreign policy a clear sectarian angle. But is Iran's foreign policy driven by sectarian interests, or is it more complicated than that?

When one analyzes Iran's strategic behavior and decision-making, it is important to note that the country has two main levels of foreign policy, both of which are overseen by the supreme leader and subject to his authority, but which differ in content and form. The first level is state-to-state policy, which in most cases is managed by the elected government in Tehran. The second level is Iran's relations with non-state clients, which are overseen by the IRGC and mostly managed outside the elected government's purview.

Iran's foreign policy can seem contradictory. As the country touts the supremacy of its Islamic system of government, and remains a vocal proponent of anti-Americanism and anti-Zionism, its relationships show a more diverse picture. Although Iran's closest allies are non-state actors, mostly Shia Islamist groups, Tehran maintains productive state-to-state ties with a host of countries that espouse a number of non-Islamic systems. Iran is famously closer to India than its Muslim neighbor Pakistan, and Tehran has long favored largely Christian Armenia in its ongoing disputes with largely Shia Azerbaijan.[20] Iran's most ideologically committed civilian and military leaders have also had no difficulty developing important links with atheistic regimes, including those of China, North Korea, and Venezuela. The regime also had a complicated relationship with al-Qaeda after 9/11, which seems to have included allowing some members to operate from Iranian soil, while imprisoning dozens of others.[21]

Why does the Islamic Republic pursue relationships that are hard to square with its religious beliefs? Generally, it is because they correspond with the regime's politics and antagonism toward the United States, or because they serve some other economic or strategic purpose. Most of Iran's relationships are not driven by ideological or religious considerations. Rather, Iranian foreign policy, like that of most states, is based on a number of factors. When religion does come into play, it usually intersects with more paramount national security and strategic interests. In many ways, the Islamic Republic's foreign policy has been fueled by its own realpolitik inclinations—inclinations that have enabled it to engage in arms deals with the United States and Israel during the Iran-Iraq war, maintain a limited relationship with al-Qaeda, and strike a strategic partnership with Russia.[22]

The problem with exporting the revolution

To understand the rationale behind Iran's foreign policy, one should note that the 1979 revolution was above all a rejection of foreign dominion over Iran, especially the influence of the United States. Anti-Americanism and anti-imperialism were themes that unified Iran's diverse revolutionary movement. Revolutionaries used a popular slogan—"neither East nor West"—to assert their desire for Iran to strike a politically and ideologically independent path. The revolution included strands of Iranian nationalism and Islamism, which, echoing philosopher Frantz Fanon, framed Shia Islam as Iran's true native political system. Khomeinists also had a strong pan-Islamic agenda.

After the revolution, Khomeinists emerged as the dominant faction. Their commitment to anti-Americanism was as firm as their desire to establish an

Islamic form of government following Khomeini's thesis of clerical rule (*velayat-e faqih*). This system of theocratic government, which was adopted in the Islamic Republic's 1979 constitution, placed near-total control in the hands of a single senior Shia cleric, the supreme leader (*rahbar*), who would oversee all branches of the state and have veto power over decision-making. Iran's two supreme leaders to date—Khomeini, who held the post from 1979 until his death in 1989, and Ali Khamenei, who succeeded Khomeini that year and has been in power ever since—have seemingly acted more as stewards of the decision-making process than as micro-managers. Under Khamenei, the supreme leader's office has become more involved in the policy process than it had been under his predecessor, but even so, as long as official bodies remain within the parameters that the supreme leader sets, it appears that they are generally afforded space to pursue their agendas.

Aside from the supreme leader, other governmental institutions were created after the revolution to take on the everyday tasks of building and enforcing policy. The democratically elected executive branch is formally responsible for Iran's foreign policy, while the appointed Guardian Council—a board of Shia clerical and civilian jurists—vets candidates for office and ensures government policies comport with Shia law. Today, the Supreme National Security Council (SNSC) is Iran's most important body for strategic decision-making and is composed of top government officials, military chiefs, and representatives of the supreme leader. The SNSC is said to sign off officially on major foreign policy and strategic decisions—whether they are initially generated by the government or the IRGC—before they are put into action.

What animated Iran's decision-making calculus after the revolution was an all-encompassing trepidation that the United States or its allies would attempt to overthrow the fledgling revolutionary regime. Iraq's invasion of Iran in September 1980, and the war that followed, was a manifestation of that fear. The support that Western states and Iran's Arab neighbors provided to Saddam Hussein during the war was proof to Iran that Washington and its allies would go to great lengths to defeat the revolution.[23] Iran was surrounded by hostile states and alienated from much of the international community. Iran's only friend in the region was Syria under Hafez al-Assad, who shared a mutual antagonism for Saddam Hussein's Iraq.

Tehran's leadership did not see their alienation as an outcome of their own hostile behavior and rhetoric; rather, it was part of an imperialistic conspiracy aimed at rooting out the nascent Islamic Republic and destroying its theocratic system. As Khomeini asserted in 1984, the war was not against Iran, but against the Islam that Iran promoted:

The superpowers are intent on opposing Islam at present. The other puppet regimes would do likewise... Is it Iran that threatens them or is it Islam? If they call on the Arabs to unite, it is a call to unity against Islam. They consider Islam to be against their interests. You ... should note that all the powers have risen against Islam and not against Iran... If they find the opportunity and if you do not pay attention Islam will be uprooted.[24]

The war confirmed for Iran's leaders that in order to safeguard their revolution effectively, its ideology and politics must be spread outside Iran's borders. The best defense, in their estimation, was a good offense. Iran's leaders embraced a radical form of internationalism, which rejected the norms of liberal internationalism.[25] Their approach included a policy of exporting the revolution; an idea that meant taking the revolution's politics and ideological values to other oppressed polities—especially in the developing world—and helping like-minded liberation and Islamic movements achieve self-determination.[26]

The IRGC was the prime mechanism for this policy. As the organization stated in 1980:

> We have no recourse but to mobilize all of the faithful forces of the Islamic Revolution, and with the mobilization of forces in every region, we must strike fear into the hearts of our enemies so that the idea of invasion and the destruction of our Islamic Revolution will exit from their minds. If our revolution does not have an internationalistic and aggressive worldview the enemies of Islam will once again enslave us culturally and politically.[27]

It was under the rubric of exporting the revolution that Iran pursued partnerships with a range of non-state actors. Through the IRGC, Tehran funneled support to the mostly Sunni Palestinian movement; it also backed Christian Palestinian militants, such as George Habash and his secular Popular Front for the Liberation of Palestine. A similar effort led to the organization of non-Iranian Shia groups, which, unlike the Palestinians, not only accepted Iranian support but also adopted Khomeinist ideology as their own. Hezbollah in Lebanon is the foremost example of the IRGC's success in cultivating a closely knit allegiance with a foreign entity along shared political and religious lines. The other lasting successes are the Supreme Council for the Islamic Revolution in Iraq (SCIRI) and its Badr military wing, which were established by Iraqi Shia expatriates in Iran, and in Badr's case, trained by the IRGC during the Iran-Iraq war.[28]

The assertive behavior of supporting non-state groups in the Middle East thus became a foundational element of Iran's post-1979 foreign policy. Iran's leaders considered this approach to be essential to the long-term success and security of the Islamic revolution. Although the scope of Iran's foreign activities waned throughout the 1980s and into the 1990s as the country focused on healing its war-torn economy, it continued to support allied groups outside its borders and looked for opportunities to expand its client base, as it did in Bosnia during the Balkan war of the 1990s.[29]

Over time, these relationships became important strategic investments for Iran. With them, Iran was able to develop an outsized role for itself and its clients in the Middle East's most important conflicts and political issues, including the Israeli occupation of Lebanon, the broader Israeli-Palestinian conflict, the US occupation of Iraq, and the ongoing war in Syria. Alienated by its neighbors, Iran found value in making friends with non-state groups.

The limits of Pan-Islamism and emergence of non-state clients

Although the Islamic Republic is a distinctly Shia enterprise, Khomeini discouraged overt Shia sectarianism. Instead, he emphasized pan-Islamism and regularly made appeals to Sunnis on the basis of Islamic unity. Khomeini would charge that the enemies of Iran's revolution—the United States, Israel, and imperialism—were the enemies of Islam writ large, and that they sought to weaken the global Muslim community by exacerbating interconfessional disputes. In a 1980 declaration, Khomeini asserted:

> More saddening and dangerous than nationalism is the creation of dissension between Sunnis and Shiis and diffusion of mischievous propaganda among brother Muslims.... I extend the hand of brotherhood to all committed Muslims in the world and ask them to regard Shiis as cherished brothers and thereby frustrate the sinister plans of foreigners.[30]

Beyond such calls for unity, Khomeini also wanted Iran's version of Islamic government, which thrust clergy into positions of political authority and policy-making, to inspire other Islamic societies to adopt similar theocratic systems. He adopted pan-Islamic causes, and made the Palestinian issue paramount, to show that his movement and the interests of the Islamic Republic had common cause with the wider Muslim world. Khomeini and many of the most ardent proponents of exporting the revolution—such as Ayatollah Hossein-Ali Montazeri (the once-assumed successor to Khomeini), his son Mohammad Montazeri, and Ali Akbar Mohtashami—considered support to the Palestinian movement to be Iran's foremost foreign policy concern.[31] Ayatollah Montazeri even charged the IRGC with leading support to the Palestinians, stating:

Liberation of beloved Jerusalem is an important issue to us. Consequently, in order to realise the slogan "Today Iran; tomorrow Palestine" and to strengthen the profound bond between the Islamic revolution of Iran and the Palestine revolution, it would be appropriate for the [IRGC] to implement certain programmes both inside and outside the country in order to strengthen ideological foundations as well as to promote and expand their religious knowledge of Palestinian Muslims.[32]

Support to the Palestinians trumped any latent pro-Shia, sectarian inclinations. A prime example early after the revolution was Iran's staunch backing of former Palestinian leader Yasser Arafat's Fatah organization in its conflict with the Shia Amal Movement in southern Lebanon—an organization established by the Iranian cleric Musa al-Sadr and his lieutenant, Mustafa Chamran, himself a prominent personality in Iran's revolution.[33] The Amal Movement was a communalist enterprise focused on the social and political uplifting of Lebanon's long-marginalized Shia community. However, Amal quickly fell out of Khomeini's favor because it was seen as asserting the interests of the southern Lebanese Shia over those of exiled Palestinian militants in Lebanon—the latter had established bases in Shia areas through confiscation and coercion, thus provoking tension and conflict with Amal.[34] Iran eventually broke ties with Arafat after the Palestinian leader supported Saddam Hussein in the Iran-Iraq war, but support for the broader Palestinian movement and for Palestinian militant groups remained a priority for Tehran.

Ardent support for the Palestinians, however, did not translate into much support from Sunnis for Khomeini or his cause. Rather, the particular Shia flavor of Iran's Islamic revolution and theocratic system, which was firmly rooted in the Shia clerical tradition, mitigated the attraction of the Khomeinist model for Sunni Islamist constituencies.[35] Iran's activists tried to make inroads with Sunni Muslim movements from Eritrea to the Philippines, but the Khomeinist message remained a tough sell.[36]

Sunnis were not alone in their lack of receptivity. Senior Shia clergy outside Iran widely criticized the cornerstone of Khomeini's ideology—Islamic government ruled by the clergy—for being an errant departure from the traditional apolitical role of clergy in Shia societies.[37] Khomeini's ideas did not gain much purchase in clerical circles and were largely unattractive to lay Shia communities in South Asia and the Arab world.[38]

However, Khomeini's message did somewhat resonate with already-politicized Shia activists in Iraq and Lebanon. Iranian revolutionaries (including both clerical leaders and early members of the IRGC) had established informal networks in Lebanon and among the Iraqi Shia before the revolution. They were able to utilize their pre-existing connections with Arab Shia activists and, with state backing, transform those relationships into the formation of pro-Iranian client organizations.[39]

These efforts benefited from the social and political dislocation caused by regional conflicts. In the case of Hezbollah, the 1982 Israeli invasion of Lebanon provided a turning point for Shia domestic politics. Israel's occupation of southern Lebanon accelerated a split within Amal, the more militant activists of which moved firmly into the pro-Palestinian camp and became more receptive to the ideology and politics of Khomeini.[40] In Iraq, Saddam Hussein's suppression of Shia political groups, which escalated violently after the Iranian revolution, further radicalized Iraqi Shia activists and led to a surge of Iraqi Shia exiles settling in Iran. Iran's support to these constituencies produced Hezbollah in Lebanon and the Iraqi expatriate organizations of the SCIRI and Badr in Iran. All of these groups embraced the broad framework of Khomeinist ideology.

Iran had less success elsewhere. In the 1980s, Iran tried to develop like-minded clients among Afghanistan's Shia and Sunni Tajik Islamists. The Soviet war in Afghanistan provided an opening for Iran's support, and though that support helped develop some nominally pro-Tehran clients within the country, those groups never coalesced into a sustainable movement.[41] Iran retained contacts with Hazara and Tajik militias and continued to provide them with support during the 1990s and early 2000s, but that support did not translate into special affinity for Khomeinism or Iran's political objectives more broadly.[42] Similarly, the IRGC's intervention in the Balkan conflict of the early 1990s, where it funneled arms and support to Bosnian Muslim militias, was relatively short-lived and unsuccessful at establishing a lasting pro-Iranian movement.[43]

Ties to Hezbollah and Palestinian groups became a strategic asset for Iran after the war with Iraq. Throughout the 1990s and into the early 2000s, these relationships seemingly afforded Iran a credible deterrent against outward Israeli and US aggression. By being able to threaten escalation by proxy, Iran could leverage its clients as tools in dealing with its two primary enemies. It is likely that this dynamic crystallized for Iran the value of developing and maintaining such client networks in strategically important locations.[44]

More broadly, the fall of Saddam Hussein in 2003 was a turning point in the Middle East. It provided an opportunity for Iraq's long-oppressed Shia to return to politics, and it opened the doors to Iranian influence. Iran's allies in SCIRI, and the organization's IRGC-trained and IRGC-aligned Badr military wing, soon returned home from exile and became part of Iraq's new political reality. Internal Iraqi politics proved a complicating factor for Iran's relationships. Seeking to distance itself from the perception of being an Iranian proxy, SCIRI changed its name to the Supreme Islamic Council of Iraq (SICI), and its clerical leaders downplayed their previous commitment to Khomeinism.[45] This encouraged a split with Badr, which, under the leadership of Hadi al-Amiri, formed a new political entity dubbed the Badr Organization, which remained close to the IRGC and Tehran.[46]

The US occupation of Iraq coincided with the administration of then US president George W. Bush and its escalating rhetoric toward Iran. After being dubbed part of an "axis of evil" in Bush's 2002 State of the Union address, Iran's leaders began to worry about a growing military threat from the United States.[47] Iran's secret nuclear program, revealed to the public in the fall of 2002, gave the Bush administration a *casus belli* for ratcheting up the pressure. The presence of hundreds of thousands of US troops right across the border in Iraq, not to mention also in nearby Afghanistan, was threatening to Iran. In response, the IRGC began a covert effort to organize and train small Iraqi Shia militias and use them to target US forces.[48] Through its Shia clients, Iran possessed the ability to harass and target US forces by proxy, and it could threaten to escalate that violence should the United States ever strike Iran. Unlike Iran's more aboveboard allies in Iraq, the militias were more extreme in their politics, more in line with Iranian ideology, and directly involved in sectarian violence, particularly during the 2006–7 civil war.[49] Iran pursued a similar strategy in Afghanistan, where it provided weapons to segments of the anti-US insurgency. However, those links have not led to the creation of a client base as strong and committed to Iran's agenda as that found in Iraq.[50]

As the Iraqi militias grew in size and influence, they became a way for Iran to influence Iraqi politics from below. Combined with Iran's long-lasting contacts with Badr and the SICI, as well as with more recently groomed ties to other prominent Shia politicians, Iranian influence was able to permeate Iraqi political dynamics. Beyond giving Iran tremendous influence there, those relationships, particularly the IRGC's close proximity to extremist Shia militias, also presented Iran as a decidedly sectarian actor in Iraq.

Sectarianism and the Arab Spring

Like his predecessor, Ali Khamenei has been an advocate of Muslim unity. To Khamenei, divisions in the Muslim world are not natural, but rather the product of US propaganda and the policies of US allies. He even disputes the Shia character of the Islamic Republic, asserting, for example:

Ever since the victory of the Islamic Revolution in Iran, the arrogant powers have been trying to portray our revolution as a Shi'i revolution ... [but] if our revolution had been a Shi'i revolution, we would have become separated from the Islamic world and had nothing to do with it. They would have had nothing to do with us either. They would have expressed no hostility to our revolution. But they have noticed that our revolution is an Islamic revolution.[51]

Such claims speak to the reputation that Khamenei would like Iran to have. But these claims are undermined by Iran's actual behavior in the Middle East, especially since the Arab Spring.

Iran initially hailed the popular protests that spread across the Arab world in late 2010 and early 2011. That enthusiasm was ironic, given how Iran had suffered through its own explosion of mass unrest following the contested 2009 reelection of then president Mahmoud Ahmadinejad. Despite condemnation from the West, Iranian security forces viciously put down those demonstrations, ignoring the legitimate grievances of ordinary Iranians and dismissing the episode as a foreign plot to overthrow the regime. But when protests erupted across Bahrain and Egypt, Iran's leaders cheered the outpouring of discontent as righteous and legitimate. Iranian officials were particularly vocal regarding Bahrain, where they called on the ruling Sunni al-Khalifa family to respect popular democracy and the will of the country's people. As the Iranian supreme leader's top foreign policy advisor, Ali Akbar Velayati, saw it, the problem was simple:

The people of Bahrain have said that they are not at war with anyone. They call for [negotiations] between themselves and the regime. They are calling for a one-man-one-vote system ... It should not be that the Shi'i would be regarded as a second-class citizen in Bahrain. Between 60 to 70 percent of the people there are Shi'i. They, proportionate to that 60 to 70 percent, have to have the vote.[52]

For Velayati, the issue in Bahrain was not one of religious identity but one of fairness. Shia or not, the people of Bahrain deserved to have their voices heard. And just because Iran also happened to be majority Shia did not mean that its support for co-religionists in Bahrain was driven by sectarian interests. Rather, Velayati cited his country's broad support for all Muslims to rebuff accusations of bias:

Have we not, us the Islamic Republic, supported Hamas and Islamic Jihad who are both Sunnis? Have we not supported Bosnians who are Sunni brothers? ... These kinds of conspiracies, where they would say that as the Bahrainis are Shi'i they are acting under the influence of Iranians against a Sunni government; this has lost its meaning these days.[53]

The notion that Iran cannot be sectarian because it has Sunni friends is one of the more common arguments that Iranian authorities such as Velayati make when disputing perceived sectarian inclinations. This has not been effective at allaying the concerns of Iran's neighbors.

As Middle East experts Toby Mathiessen and Frederic Wehrey have shown, the February 2011 protests in Bahrain were not spurred by sectarianism and certainly were not engineered by Iran. It was a populist, grass-roots movement by a marginalized, yet demographic-majority community, seeking greater inclusion and political reform.[54] A Shia uprising, however, regardless of the reason, triggered the deeply ingrained fears of Gulf Arab leaders, who have long worried that Iran could use Shia populations to destabilize their monarchies. They saw Iran's hand in the unrest and moved collectively to crush it.

Iran did Bahrain's protest movement no favors by standing out as its main champion, particularly after the movement was violently put down by a Saudi-led GCC military operation. Bahraini authorities already had linked some local Shia activists to the IRGC, which made the latter an easy scapegoat used to undermine the legitimacy of the protests. When IRGC-affiliated commentators began threatening reprisals in response to the intervention, they helped make the tenuous links between Iran and the protest movement appear more substantial. An editorial in the IRGC-linked *Javan* newspaper wrote:

> Saudi and UAE troops should know that with the first bloodshed or massacre of the people of Bahrain, they will expect a harsh response that will not only render the Bahraini king and the ceremonial Saudi and UAE troops insecure, but also the US military base of 5,000 people will not remain safe and will bear a heavy blow with mutual responsibility. Eye for an eye and tooth for a tooth is the Koranic logic that is awaiting them. These countries must also accept the spread of the revolutionary movements in their own countries.[55]

The author further concluded that while Washington and its allies were losing out in the Arab Spring, Iran was making "progress with regard to its objectives."[56] He confidently asserted: "The changes in the Middle East region are in line with Iran's objectives." Such statements made it evident that, from the IRGC's perspective, the Shia uprising in Bahrain served Iran's agenda.

Iran's eager endorsement of the Arab Spring stumbled when it hit Syria. As Iran hailed the will of the people in Bahrain, it condemned the foreign plot that was causing disorder in Syria. Unlike the demonstrations in Egypt and Bahrain, which threatened unfriendly governments, the protests in Syria put Iran's foremost ally at risk. Syria under Bashar al-Assad has been Iran's only state ally in the region and, more crucially, a central node in its strategy against

Israel and the United States. Assad has been the linchpin of Iran's support to Hezbollah and a core member of Iran's axis of resistance. When the protests spread beyond the Syrian government's control, the IRGC stepped in to help Assad crush the mounting rebellion. IRGC Quds Force chief, Qassem Suleimani, explained Iran's motivation: "[America's] main goal is to break the resistance front." He added, "We will support Syria till the end."[57]

Iran's enemies and rivals have backed Syria's largely Sunni rebels. This has raised the stakes for Tehran. Iran has concluded that if Assad were to be defeated, his replacement would be the client of the United States or Gulf Arab rivals, and therefore inimical to Iranian interests. For Iran, backing Assad has not been simply a means of preserving strategic interests. It has been a necessity to prevent a virulently anti-Shia movement, patronized by Iran's enemies, from taking root in the region. As one editorial in the conservative *Siyasat-e Ruz* newspaper later put it:

> It is one of the unattainable dreams of the USA and its ally Al Sa'ud that Iran would become like Syria. They were dreaming that after the [Bashar al-Assad] regime collapses, it would be Iran's turn to be raided by takfiri, Salafi, and Al-Qa'idah groups just as they are doing in Syria. In fact, Al Sa'ud has begun a war with Iran, whose soldiers are not the army of Saudi Arabia, but rather the radical Wahhabi and takfiri terrorists who are at enmity with and hostile towards Shia Islam. The news and reports of the anti-Iranian and anti-Shi'i stances by some clerics in this group against Iran is spread to intensify the anti-Iranian atmosphere.[58]

To defend its role in the Syrian war, Iran has regularly claimed to be fighting a foreign conspiracy aimed at toppling the legitimate government in Damascus. But the sectarian dimensions of the conflict have been impossible to conceal. Iran's allies in Syria are the loyalists of Bashar al-Assad. Although these loyalists include Sunnis and Christians, Alawites—the same Shia minority community from which the Assad clan hails—have held most positions of power in the regime. As the war has progressed, Iran has facilitated the entry of Lebanese Hezbollah, Iraqi Shia militias, and eventually Shia Afghan and Pakistani mercenaries to help the loyalist effort. This has made Iran's side of the conflict distinctly Shia and sectarian, much as the Sunni rebellion has also become.

Iranian and IRGC officials have done their best to deflect the issue by rejecting any sectarian agenda out of hand, and by emphasizing that their war is not with Sunnis, but rather with terrorists and *takfiris*—a term widely used to describe the ideology of jihadist groups, such as the Nusra Front and the self-proclaimed Islamic State, which view fellow Muslims who do not share their literalist beliefs to be apostates and therefore not protected under Islamic law. However, for Iranian officials, the *takfirism* of the Islamic State is synonymous with the Wahhabi strain of Sunnism that Saudi Arabia promotes. For example, Ali Akbar Velayati has referred to Saudi Arabia as the "origin" of *takfirism*, adding: "Wahhabism is an extremist and incorrect interpretation of Islam and its exports are Daesh, al-Nusra, and al-Qaeda.... Therefore the presence of Saudis in [Syria] is closely related to Takfiri terrorist groups."[59]

Similarly, commenting on the Islamic State and other jihadists in Syria and Iraq, the Iranian speaker of parliament, Ali Larijani, has claimed that such groups have "no relationship" with Islam and that Sunnism "rejects and denies the principles and thinking" of the Islamic State and its ilk. Rather, he continued, "it is only the Wahhabis" who ascribe to such beliefs.[60] Ayatollah Sadegh Larijani, the brother of the parliamentary speaker and himself the head of Iran's judiciary, has proclaimed that "takfiri and Salafi currents are not related to Islam" or Sunnism, but are ideological sects created by the West "to weaken Islamic societies" from within.[61]

Iran's antipathy to Wahhabi and Salafi jihadism is unsurprising. Both teach that Shiism is a dangerous and deviant sect, the believers of which are outside the fold of Islam.[62] As Saudi Arabia's top cleric, Grand Mufti Abd al-Aziz Al al-Sheikh, told a Saudi journalist in September 2016: "You must understand, they [the Iranian regime] are not Muslims. They are sons of the Majous [that is, Zoroastrians]. Their hostility to Muslims is ancient, specifically with Sunnis."[63] The rhetoric of Iranian officials is rooted in that shared antipathy.

However, by equating *takfirism* and Wahhabism, Iran further muddies the water of identity politics. It is a way of confusing the sectarian dynamic in Iraq and Syria, by asserting that the other side is not actually Sunni, but rather an extreme ideological movement (*takfirism*) that is beyond the pale of Islam and, therefore, not even Islamic. Like the case of the Saudi grand mufti, such rhetoric allows Iranian officials to indulge in their own game of *takfir*—articulating who is and who is not a Muslim and justifying actions accordingly. To neutral observers of Wahhabism, such accusations might touch on truth, but as a foreign policy tool, they only beget further acrimony from Iran's Sunni neighbors.

Toward a transnational Shia movement

Through its nearly four-decade history, the Islamic Republic has acted in chiefly non-sectarian ways when it comes to its broader foreign and regional policies. There are examples in which shared sectarian backgrounds have facilitated Iran's relationships with non-state clients, primarily with Hezbollah and

Iraqi groups, but when viewed against the totality of its foreign policy actions, those relationships are not enough to suggest that Iranian foreign policy has been primarily driven by a pro-Shia impulse.

However, since the Arab Spring, Iran's regional behavior has shifted toward a more outward sectarianism. Sectarianism has become a way for Iran and its Sunni rivals to defend their interests and equities in the region's conflicts. Like its enemies, the IRGC seems to have embraced that logic, and now sees its side, and the regional political battlefield as a whole, through a sectarian lens. The statements of IRGC officials, combined with the organization's behavior, attest to that shift and suggest that its agenda in the Middle East has become dominated by confessional concerns.

IRGC Major General Qassem Suleimani has asserted that Iran's place in the Muslim world is second to none, saying: "Although a number of Islamic countries claim to lead the Islamic world today ... none are able to fulfill this perilous responsibility other than Iran."[64] What has enabled Iran to rise to such heights, when so many other Muslim countries have failed to do so? Its dedication to foreign involvement, Suleimani argues. As he puts it, "Supporting Islamic and revolutionary warriors and defending Muslims and Islam from [enemy] assaults" have allowed Iran to "take leadership of the Islamic world."[65]

Suleimani sees Iran's power as emanating from two fundamental sources: "The greatness of the Islamic revolution" and the revolution's impact on the "cherished Shiite faith." He points to Iraq as an example where "Shiites now have seized the right to govern" to illustrate the impact of Iran's influence. At no other point in history have the "struggles of the Shia or that of the Shia clergy" produced the same "global effects" as the Islamic revolution, according to Suleimani.[66]

These statements encapsulate the themes of Iranian exceptionalism that most irk Iran's neighbors. Suleimani is simultaneously claiming that Iran has leadership of the Muslim world while also linking Iranian influence to its foreign activities and Shiism. As much as Iranian officials often downplay the confessional angle of Iran's extraterritorial activism, Suleimani celebrates it, offering the achievements of the Shia in Iraq as a prime example of the revolution's political impact.

While Suleimani holds up Iran as the leader of the entire Muslim world, his meaning is much narrower. For Suleimani and Iranian authorities in general, the Muslim world is divided between those who support Islam and those who support Islam's enemies. Iran's clients and allies are part of the former, the so-called axis of resistance, and most of Iran's Western-friendly Sunni neigh-

SECTARIANISM AND IRANIAN FOREIGN POLICY

bors are part of the latter. Conflicts in the Middle East are divided along these lines and driven by Islam's enemies and their surrogates. The Islamic State and other jihadist groups are seen in that context as tools that the West has created to destroy Islam from within. As IRGC Brigadier General Iraj Masjedi explains, the "Saudis, Americans, and Zionists" are using the Islamic State to "destroy the real Islam—the front led by the Shia."[67] In describing Iran's role in Syria, another IRGC commander, Ismail Heydari, has claimed that the war is not a civil conflict, but rather a battle of "Islam against the infidels. A war of good versus evil." On the side of good are Iran, Hezbollah, and Iraqi and Afghan mujahideen—all Shia actors. On the side of evil are Israel, Saudi Arabia, Turkey, Qatar, UAE, America, France, and "other Europeans."[68]

Similarly, when discussing the plight of the Palestinians, the secretary of Iran's SNSC, Ali Shamkhani, has stated that while "Sunni states are staying silent regarding the inhumane crimes of the Zionist entity, the greatest amount of support to the oppressed Palestinian people has come from Shia Iran."[69] Shamkhani's point is that while some states only condemn Israeli policy vis-à-vis the Palestinians with words, Iran does so with actions. It talks the talk and walks the walk. But what is more interesting is Shamkhani's sectarian framing. The fact that Shia Iran is helping Sunni Palestinians is seemingly meant to shame Sunni states. This also reaffirms Iran's Shia identity.

Instead of subverting sectarian associations, Iranian officials, through such statements, feed into sectarian narratives with their own rhetoric. These statements also speak to a certain intellectual honesty, in that even Iran's officials know that their political movement—however they describe it—is largely Shia and runs counter to the interests or policies of most Sunni states. The sectarian dimensions of the Iraqi and Syrian conflicts are evident. Iran's closest allies in these contexts are Shia or perceived as such. Although Iran's leadership tries to obscure that inconvenient truth through various rhetorical lines, the religious symbols and language used to describe the involvement of Iran and its allies betray any nuance.

For example, IRGC leaders routinely assert that the war in Syria is nonsectarian, but rather a war between a legitimate government and foreign-backed terrorists. Mazaher Majdi, the deputy commander of the IRGC's Ansar al-Husayn Brigade, once even described the loyalist forces in Syria as "130,000 Sunnis defending their country [who] need our help."[70] But like the IRGC itself, its entire project in Syria is steeped in Shia confessional language and symbolism. Take the name of Majdi's own command, the Ansar al-Husayn Brigade, which translates to "Helpers of Husayn" and is a reference to Imam

105

Husayn—the third Shia imam and its most revered martyr and hero. Such names are how the IRGC marks its religious identity.[71]

Those same outward signs of confessional identity permeate Iran's network in Syria and give it an unequivocal sectarian guise. To help overstretched forces in Syria, the IRGC developed a unit known as the Fatimaiyun Brigade composed of between 3,000 and 13,000 (estimates vary) Afghan immigrants from Iran—primarily Shia Hazaras with some Sunni Tajiks.[72] Afghan immigrants are something of an underclass in Iran; they are often poor, with limited educational and employment opportunities. Most have impermanent status, and legal residency is difficult to attain. The methods used to recruit Afghans for war play to those motivations, as recruits are offered monthly stipends, work permits, or residency papers.[73] Some seem to have been recruited from jails and given pardons in exchange for military service.[74] Smaller numbers come from outside Iran, including from Afghan communities in Syria and from Afghanistan proper.[75] A similar unit, known as the Zaynabiyun Brigade, is composed of several hundred to a few thousand (again, estimates vary) Shia of Pakistani origin. Most come from the Pakistani Shia expatriate community in Iran, particularly those associated with al-Mustafa International University in the city of Qom.[76]

Neither the Afghan nor the Pakistani units are billed as mercenary forces, or even as a foreign legion. Rather, they are defined in religious terms. Retired IRGC Brigadier General Mohammad Ali Falaki, who served in Syria, has emphasized that point: "They fight in Syria due to their commitment to Islam, not because of ethnicity ... but [out] of their commitment to Shiism."[77] This idea is conveyed by the two groups' names, which both honor revered members of the Prophet Muhammad's family. Fatimaiyun (which could be rendered as Devotees of Fatima or Partisans of Fatima) is a homage to Fatima, the Prophet's daughter and the wife of the first Shia imam, Ali. It is through Ali and Fatima that the remaining eleven Shia imams are descended, making her the matriarch of Shiism. She is revered for her saintly qualities, and she holds an unparalleled station within the pantheon of Shiism similar to that of Mary in Catholicism. The name Zaynabiyun (or Devotees of Zaynab) similarly honors the daughter of Fatima, who accompanied her brother, Imam Husayn, during his last stand and martyrdom at Karbala in 680 CE. Her heroic actions in that founding episode of the Shia religion earned her a revered place in its spiritual tradition. She died as a prisoner in Damascus, where a famous mosque dedicated to her memory became a Shia pilgrimage site and the center of a largely Shia neighborhood.

Some might view such religiosity as superficial. Even if that were the case, the chosen symbolism would still be important. It is not only intentionally and self-consciously employed by the groups' overseers in the IRGC, but is also an unsubtle display of sectarianism not lost on Sunnis.[78] Both of these brigades are meant to represent Shia armies composed of pious Shia warriors. Commenting on the devoutness of his troops, the Fatimaiyun commander, known by the *nom de guerre* Karbala, has said: "The takfiris have no faith and so many fear death. But we do not fear martyrdom."[79] The commander's *nom de guerre* is significant, too. By adopting the name Karbala, the commander evokes the martyrdom of Imam Husayn and draws a linkage between his fighters and their spiritual ancestors.[80] Any hint of secularism is missing. If the goals of these groups were non-sectarian, they are concealed by the religious cloaking of their organizations.

The religious manner in which the IRGC refers to the participants in its Syrian operations and their mission is revealing. Perhaps the best glimpse the public has had into Iran's ground operations in Syria comes through film footage taken from the camera of an IRGC film-maker who was killed in an ambush by a Syrian rebel group in late August 2013. That rebel group released the footage to provide evidence of Iran's role in the conflict, and the BBC later transformed the footage into a short documentary.[81]

The video centers on an IRGC unit that oversees a contingent of Syrian militia called the Sayyida Ruqayya Brigade near the city of Aleppo. Sayyida Ruqayya is the title Shia use for the daughter of Imam Husayn. She died in prison as a child a few years after her father's martyrdom. She was buried in Damascus, where a mosque was later built in her honor. Like that of her aunt Zaynab, her name is used as a marker of both Syrian and Shia identity. It evokes the injustice of her father's martyrdom, the cruel imprisonment of his family, and the historical oppression that the Shia endured under Sunni dominion after the Karbala massacre. By adopting her name as their own, the IRGC and its Syrian allies in the film footage represent the protectors of Sayyida Ruqqaya, both literally and figuratively. They are defending the territory that holds her tomb and are fighting to preserve the legacy of the Prophet's family in Syria.

The way in which Iran describes its war in Syria, particularly in memorializing its soldiers killed there, draws on analogous religious connotations. Soldiers killed in Syria are hailed as martyrs, and they are buried with both the honors of patriotic soldiers and with the reverence of fallen religious heroes.[82] Iranian officials describe them as having died "defending the shrine of Sayyida

Zaynab"—an honorific used for the sister of Imam Husayn. The Sayyida Zaynab Mosque in Damascus, which according to Shia belief houses her tomb, became the central metaphor for Iranian involvement and sacrifice in Syria. The image of the mosque's golden dome adorns Iran's memorials of the hundreds of its Iranian, Afghan, and Pakistani soldiers killed in action.[83]

Iran describes its role in the war against the Islamic State in Iraq in similar terms. Iraq is home to the most sacred Shia shrines, including that of Imam Husayn in Karbala and that of Imam Ali in the city of Najaf. The historical legacy of Shiism in Iraq has made it sanctified ground for the Shia. When Iranian soldiers began getting killed in Iraq shortly after Iran's intervention to back up the government of then prime minister Nouri al-Maliki in June 2014, they were described as having died "in defense of the holy shrines."[84] Again, this statement had literal and figurative connotations. While Iran has defended the government in Baghdad, it has also seen itself as defending the sacred ground of the imams from the anti-Shia scourge of Islamic State. This view has been shared across Iran's leadership, with even the generally more circumspect President Hassan Rouhani vowing that Iran would not "spare any effort" to protect sacred Shia sites in Iraq.[85] As with Iran's Syrian martyrs, the placards and memorials of soldiers killed in Iraq often bore the imagery of that country's Shia shrines.[86]

In Iraq, in Syria, and in Yemen, Iran's closest allies are Shia. Lebanese Hezbollah, various Iraqi Shia militias, Afghan and Pakistani foreign legions, the largely Alawite Popular Mobilization Forces in Syria, and the Zaidi Shia Ansar Allah organization in Yemen comprise a vast network of Iranian clients that all share a broad confessional identity. That these partnerships are based in part on shared sectarian affiliations is difficult to dispute, even for Iranian authorities, who generally emphasize the non-sectarian nature of these relationships. What is more is that these partnerships appear, especially to Iran's enemies and Sunni rivals, to be transforming into a transnational movement of Shia militancy under the command of Iran.[87] This is not a misperception, but rather something the IRGC, too, feels it has achieved. As retired IRGC Brigadier General Falaki explains:

> A Shia Liberation Army has been formed. It is now under the command of Hajj Qassem Suleimani and obedient to the authority of the leader of the revolution [that is, Iran's supreme leader]. This army comprises a single front in Syria, a single front in Iraq, and a single front in Yemen. The manpower for this army cannot come [solely] from Iran's military forces. In whatever region it is deemed that this army is needed, the people of that region should be organized and provided the necessary support.[88]

Falaki describes the Shia Liberation Army as being in lockstep with Iran's leadership. Its members collectively operate "under the command of their Revolutionary Guard brothers" and share Iran's goals. Together, "with one uniform, under one flag, as one organization, and as one front they fight jihad."[89] Even though the vast collective is said to include Sunnis, Shiism is the animating force of its identity.

Falaki's comments caused a minor stir in the Arab and Western press. The explicit sectarianism of the Shia Liberation Army did not escape notice. Perhaps in an effort at damage control, the original Iranian website that published the interview, Mashregh, removed the word Shia from Falaki's quotations. Even as outward signs of sectarianism have increased, this deletion reaffirms that the sensitivity toward appearing sectarian has not declined in Iranian officialdom.

The IRGC's effort at establishing a transnational Shia movement composed of militant groups and activists from across the greater Middle East and South Asia has benefited from the hardening of confessional identities since the Arab Spring. Violent suppression of Shia protests in Bahrain and Saudi Arabia, combined with the wars in Syria, the rise of the Islamic State in Iraq, and the Saudi-led intervention against the Houthis in Yemen, have all contributed to a collective sharpening of identity among the region's Shia. Toby Matthiesen has recognized this phenomenon unfolding in what he calls "the Shia public sphere," where the symbols used to sacralize the conflicts in Iraq and Syria have widely "spread through social media and Shia satellite channels ... strengthening transnational sectarian identities."[90]

The wars in Iraq, Syria, and Yemen are not simply strategic for the indigenous Shia (or Alawis and Zaidis). They are fights for survival. Defeat in these conflicts does not mean losing leverage against enemies, as is the case for Iran: instead, it means potentially losing villages, cities, or entire confessional communities to the bloodlust of implacable foes, or at least succumbing to their brutal dominion. It is unsurprising that the region's Shia would therefore sympathize with Iran and its allies, if not support them. Iran and the IRGC have been able to harness that support because the Shia have no other power willing to side with them. Time will tell what becomes of the IRGC's network, but the signs of a burgeoning transnational movement are there. The Shia militant groups loyal to Iran already see themselves as a global association under the spiritual and political authority of Iran's supreme leader.[91] That vision has been forged by a shared unity of purpose in the region's conflicts. The longer these conflicts endure, and the more severe identity politics become, the stronger the bonds between Iran and its clients will grow.

Conclusion

As central as Shiism has been to Iranian domestic policies, how it has impacted on foreign policies has been less clear-cut. Religious identity and beliefs certainly influence Iran's approach to foreign affairs, but they do not dictate them. Religion is one of many factors that fuel Iran's behavior, and often is not the primary or even secondary consideration. The Shia character of the Islamic Republic might make Iran's leaders more predisposed to supporting Shia outside Iran than not. Yet, those inclinations are generally curbed by the regime's self-interest. It would therefore be inaccurate to label Iran's approach to foreign policy as sectarian (meaning primarily driven by Shia-centric beliefs and goals). Sectarianism is a latent and inescapable facet of Iranian foreign policy, but confessional aspirations are not what drive the bulk of Iran's decisions.

Iran might not see itself as a sectarian actor. But circumstances and an aggressive regional policy have progressively moved it in that direction. The revolution and the war with Iraq made Iran deeply unpopular with its neighbors. Alienated, and unwilling to temper its politics, Iran became increasingly dependent on its non-state clients to gain influence in the Middle East and leverage over its rivals. Despite the country's links to some Sunni groups, Iran's most important relationships have been forged with fellow Shia. These relationships have given Iranian foreign policy a sectarian guise. They have also provoked the indignation of Iran's neighbors and stiffened their own sectarian inclinations.

Since the Arab Spring, as conflict and political unrest have exacerbated communal divisions across the Middle East, Iran's policies, and the actions of the IRGC in particular, have fed the flames of difference more often than not. Iran is not alone in this regard. Saudi Arabia's decades-long sponsorship of its intolerant brand of Sunnism, both in the Middle East and globally, is an undeniable factor. The support that Arab states give to Sunni Islamist organizations across the region—not to mention these countries' sectarian policies toward their own Shia populations and more broadly—has also worsened confessional divisions. The rise of Islamist and jihadist organizations—including Ahrar al-Sham, al-Qaeda, and the Islamic State—has shaped the current conflicts in Iraq, Syria, and Yemen as much as Iran's clients have.

Who is to blame for the Middle East's current sectarian woes? Arguments can be made for various culprits. Arab states blame Iran. Iran blames the United States, Israel, and Arab neighbors, above all Saudi Arabia. Everyone blames America. But such narratives are simplistic, lack self-criticism, and selectively ignore the exogenous and the endogenous sources of identity politics. It has been a collective effort, and Iran has played its part. While Iran's foreign policy writ large exists mostly beyond the confines of confessionalism, this much is clear: as Iran's neighborhood has become more sectarian, so has its behavior.

PART II

INSTITUTIONAL SOURCES
OF SECTARIANISM

5

SHIA-CENTRIC STATE-BUILDING
AND SUNNI REJECTION IN POST-2003 IRAQ

Fanar Haddad

Introduction

The clash of visions over the Iraqi state's identity, ownership, and legitimacy, long pre-dating the US-led invasion of the country in 2003, has been the root cause of political violence in post-war Iraq. In many ways, the carnage of the past fifteen years can be viewed as part of a longer political conflict, one between two sets of ways of imagining Iraq: the more homogenizing and centralizing versions propagated by the former Baathist regime and those permitted within its redlines on the one hand; and on the other, the sect-centric and ethnocentric conceptions of Iraq advocated by the former regime's Shia-centric and Kurdish opponents. The overthrow of Saddam Hussein upset the balance of power between these camps and created the space in which attempts to redefine Iraqi state and society could be made. It also created conditions that incentivized the entrenchment of identity politics and heralded the start of an intensely violent contest over the definition of Iraq and Iraqi nationalism.

Political violence between 2003 and 2014 and the ongoing instability in Arab Iraq have been chiefly driven by the dynamic between Shia-centric state-building and Sunni rejection of this state-building project. These forces were evident soon after the fall of the former regime, quickly developing mutually reinforcing qualities, feeding off each other, polarizing society, and drawing in external actors in the process. Both are rooted in pre- and post-2003 Iraqi and regional dynamics.

As with many of the problems that have bedeviled Iraq in recent years, sectarian polarization and the dynamic between Shia-centric state-building and Sunni rejection are cumulative issues with roots that have grown and evolved over the course of the twentieth century and into the twenty-first.[1] They are chiefly the product of a history of authoritarianism, failed nation-building, and the mismanagement of communal plurality—a pattern that persists into the present. As such, although pre-2003 sectarian relations were vastly more benign than they have been over the past fifteen years, they nevertheless contained the seeds of what was to follow after regime change. This was most evident in the emergence, growth, and ultimately the centrality of sect-centric actors in the pre-2003 Iraqi opposition. By making a link with pre-2003 history, the intention here is not to assign an eternal character or any kind of inevitability to sectarian animosities in Iraq or elsewhere. What has occurred over the past fifteen years was neither mandated by preceding events, nor completely divorced from them. As such, any attempt to understand a subject as complex and as multi-layered as sectarian relations in post-2003 Iraq will yield only partial results as long as the broader sweep of modern Iraqi history is ignored.

The dynamic between Shia-centric state-building and Sunni rejection[2]

Many terms have been used to describe the toxic salience of sectarian identities in Iraq and elsewhere in the region since 2003. Mention is often made of "sectarianization" or a "sectarian landscape" or that the region has become "sectarian." As with much of the vocabulary associated with "sectarianism," the meaning of these terms is open to vastly differing interpretations in that they could refer to anything from sect-centricity to sectarian violence and anything in between.[3] Perhaps the simplest way to understand a sectarian environment such as post-2003 Iraq is to view it as one that encourages sect-coding. In such an environment, sectarian identity attains an outsized ability to influence people's social and political perceptions. As a result, significant actors and events rarely escape sectarian labeling: a political dispute becomes a sectarian dispute, a policy becomes a sectarian policy, a demonstration is invariably labeled a Sunni or Shia one, and so forth.[4] This is very much the case in Iraq and several other conflict zones in the Middle East today.

While the various causes of the conflicts in Iraq and elsewhere are debatable, what is crucial is that since 2003 there has been a tendency to perceive them as being driven by sectarian identity. This has had a considerable impact on how conflict is perceived by both policy-makers and public opinion in the post-2003 Arab world as witnessed by the outsized role of sectarian sentiment in regional mobilization, recruitment, and messaging in Syria, Iraq, and Yemen, and in understandings of regional geopolitical rivalries.[5] As such, it makes little difference where one draws the line between power politics and sectarian identity in, say, Saudi Arabian–Iranian rivalry, so long as their interplay is viewed and portrayed in such intensely sectarian terms by significant bodies of public opinion and by influential figures. Once such a pattern is in place, it develops a momentum of its own, with both elites and masses driving the sect-codification of ever-increasing facets of social and political life. Rather than sectarian entrepreneurs acting as puppeteers above masses devoid of agency, elites and masses mutually reflect and shape each other in a circular way: cynical politicians use sectarian identity to their political advantage, but only succeed to the extent that such a strategy resonates with enough people for it to be effective. A Shia Iraqi politician scaremongering the public in, for example, the elections of 2014 would be better placed trying to raise fears of a Baathist coup (code for a Sunni overthrow of the post-2003 order) rather than a Communist one: the former appeals to existing fears, existing sectarian entrenchment, and an existing conflict, whereas the latter—given the demise of Communism as a significant political force in the post–Cold War era—would simply be bizarre.

There is no single factor—least of all the mere fact of sectarian plurality—that could account for the sectarianization of post-2003 Iraq. A cumulative web of perceptual and tangible drivers, spanning the better part of a century, gave birth to and still influences the defining feature of post-2003 Arab Iraq, namely the tension between Shia-centric state-building and Sunni rejection. Firstly, it is important to understand what these terms mean. Rather than fixed, uniformly defined positions, Shia-centric state-building and Sunni rejection are two broad spectra. Sunni rejection refers to the widespread resentment toward the post-2003 order, beginning with the US-led invasion and continuing in various forms into the present.[6] The spectrum runs from ambivalence, or even begrudging acceptance, all the way to anti-state violence.

Underlying this spectrum of Sunni rejection is a latent resentment toward the post-2003 order, that in turn is founded on a deep sense of Sunni alienation, a sense of loss, and a sense of victimhood beginning with regime change in 2003.[7] This sense of resentment does not predetermine attitudes and positions; rather, and as with similar societal cleavages characterized by asymmetric power relations elsewhere in the world, people's attitudes and positions are constantly shifting. Most people are not ideological hardliners: they react to socioeconomic and political conditions and make their choices accordingly. This can be seen in changing Sunni political behavior and participation in the political process over the years: from the boycott in 2005, to violence to participation in 2009 and 2010, to protest in 2013, back to violence in 2014–15 and growing participation since then.[8] These shifts have reflected how Sunnis have perceived the permanence or transience of the post-2003 order and the prospects for political progress.

Shia-centric state-building is likewise a spectrum. At its most basic, it involves ensuring that the central levers of the state are in Shia hands (and more specifically in Shia-centric hands) and that Shia identities are represented and empowered. This could range from allowing, or even encouraging, Shia symbolism in public spaces, to incorporating the Shia calendar into the national calendar for events and holidays, all the way to attempting to endow the state with a Shia identity.[9] Whatever position a person adopts along this spectrum, the essence of it is that the Iraqi Shia are the Iraqi *staatsvolk*—Iraq's constitutive people.

As such, one way to understand Shia-centric state-building is to view it as an effort to ensure that Shias are the big brother or the senior partner in Iraq's multi-communal framework. This mindset is perfectly encapsulated in one of former Iraqi politician Ali Allawi's recollections in *The Occupation of Iraq*. In 2005, an internal document was circulated in the United Iraqi Alliance (UIA)—the grand Shia political alliance of the time, of which Allawi was a representative—that outlined a proposed vision for Iraq's future. The document's significance lies in the unabashed framing of Iraqi Shias as the new governing class, asserting that "Iraq is the Shi'a.... And the Shi'a are Iraq." Describing the document, Allawi writes: "It also marked the abandonment of the western ideal of citizenship, in favour of a constellation of lesser sects and ethnicities revolving around a Shi'a sun."[10] This, rather than classical understandings of state-building, is the essence of what is being referred to here as

Shia-centric state-building: instead of building institutions or constructing the mechanisms of a functioning administrative order, Shia-centric state-building has been far more concerned with seizing the remnants of the pre-2003 state and altering its identity so as to reify the concept of the Shias as the Iraqi *staatsvolk*.

Both spectra are fluid and inherently inconsistent in that, beyond their extreme ends, the positions and attitudes they embody are implicit rather than explicit. These spectra have to accommodate and at times compete with older frames of reference and older social and political values that Arab Iraqis—both Sunni and Shia—have been thoroughly socialized into accepting, including an inclusive Iraqi citizenship, a rejection of "sectarianism," a commitment to Iraqi unity, and other similar ideals. While these continue to resonate with many ordinary people, and while politicians are, at the very least, still obliged to pay lip service to them, the attachment to these ideals has been coming under increasing strain over the past fifteen years. It is doubtful that a critical mass of Iraqis have stopped believing in these principles—as has been consistently demonstrated in opinion polls;[11] however, despite their continued resonance, these ideals have not been mirrored in Iraqi political and social reality. Consequently, at certain junctures, the perceived interests of the moment render them irrelevant in the face of sect-centric existential fears. Indeed, it is precisely at these junctures—the battles of Fallujah, the spiraling violence of 2006–7, the Sunni protest movement of 2012–13, and the fall of Mosul in 2014, to name a few—that, out of conviction or perceived necessity, the mindsets of Shia-centric state-building and Sunni rejection gain broader support at the expense of other conceptions of Iraq.

The dynamic between Shia-centric state-building and Sunni rejection was evident almost immediately after regime change. Both spectra emerged very quickly precisely because they fed on pre-existing narratives and pre-existing elements of Iraqi society. However, the spectra being referred to here have not resulted in the coalescence of two monolithic, sect-specific camps; rather, what has emerged is a division between two largely sect-specific constellations of actors each internally competing for a sect-specific audience. This is perhaps most clearly visible in political messaging and electoral politics. By 2010, and more so by the time of the 2013 provincial elections and the 2014 parliamentary elections, an intensely segmented electoral scene had emerged, bearing no resemblance to the grand coalitions of 2005.[12] Nevertheless, a Sunni-Shia duality was clearly visible despite the intensity of intra-Sunni and intra-Shia competition: to a considerable extent, the 2010 and 2013–14 elections primarily involved two sets of political actors competing for two separate, multi-layered constituencies. While issues of class, region, political habit, ideology, and patronage animated intrasectarian competition, the division between the two sets of political actors and constituencies considerably mirrored the sectarian divide, with few exceptions.[13]

The dynamic between Shia-centric state-building and Sunni rejection has been sustained by several factors. There are far too many actors in Iraq and beyond that are thoroughly invested in this dynamic, thereby ensuring its perpetuation. Furthermore, it is difficult to break the cyclical relationship between the two spectra: as long as the mindset of Shia-centric state-building is in place and is politically empowered, Sunni resentment and rejection will persist; and as long as there is a sense that Sunnis reject the post-2003 order, the mindset of Shia-centric state-building will deepen and gain broader popular acceptance. In both cases, feelings of mistrust, fear, encirclement, and insecurity drive further sectarian entrenchment and stand in the way of compromise and reform.

The pre-2003 roots of post-2003 sectarianization

Many observers argue that 2003 marks the dividing line separating a sectarian Iraq from a non-sectarian Iraq. According to this view, the sectarian entrenchment of the past fifteen years is solely a product of the invasion and subsequent events.[14] An opposing, though no less common and no less narrow, view regards ethnosectarian entrenchment as the default setting of Iraqis: the union of Shias, Sunnis, and Kurds was never voluntary and always required the coercive force of a strong centralized state. Once this was removed, it was only natural—so the argument goes—for Iraqis to succumb to their centrifugal tendencies and innately held animosities.[15]

The most obvious tension between the two camps is in their opposing views about the viability of the Iraqi nation-state and the validity, or even existence, of Iraqi nationalism: the former cling to the idea of a transcendent Iraqi nationalism whose otherwise perpetually enduring qualities were only interrupted by the invasion of 2003, while the latter dismiss the Iraqi nation-state in favor of perennially divided Sunnis and Shias (and Kurds). Underscoring the two positions are divergent views as to whether or not Arab Iraq has always been "sectarian" and whether or not "sectarianism" was a feature of pre-2003 Iraq. From the outset, this debate is doomed to incoherence because of the incoherence of the terminology. If the understanding of "sectarianism" is restricted solely to violent sectarian conflict, widespread sectarian hate, and the empowerment of sect-centric political actors, then yes, 2003 undoubtedly becomes the moment separating a sectarian Iraq from a non-sectarian Iraq. However, such a restrictive approach obscures a far broader spectrum of sectarian competition: if "sectarianism" is taken to include not just the headline-grabbing extremes witnessed over the past fifteen years but sect-centric bias, prejudice, stereotypes, or institutional discrimination as well, then "sectarianism" in Iraq and the Arab world dates to far earlier than 2003. That year marked the empowerment of sect-centric political actors and the political institutionalization of Iraq's sectarian and other communal divides; in Arab Iraq, it marked the beginning of the contest between Shia-centric state-building and Sunni rejection. Yet, it is worth asking why sect-centric actors existed in the first place, why they were so well-placed to reap the benefits of regime change, and why Arab Iraq was so susceptible in 2003 to identity politics and to the cycle of Shia-centric state-building and Sunni rejection.

Throughout its existence, the modern Iraqi nation-state has struggled to manage communal pluralism adequately. The country's ethnic, religious, and sectarian diversity was framed in a paradoxical way: state discourse often celebrated it as a defining fact of Iraq, while at the same time regarding it with a degree of suspicion as a potential threat to national unity. This applied not only to Iraq's sectarian divide, but also to the state's relations with other religious and ethnic groups that were suspected of obstructing its conception of Iraq and Iraqi identity, as illustrated by the examples of the Kurds, the Assyrians, and the Jews. This relationship is the product of a history of exclusionary nation-building that was based on problematic conceptions of unity and pluralism.[16] Rather than fostering unity or respecting and nurturing pluralism (politically or communally), these concepts were repeatedly used to exclude dissenters whose nonconformity was deemed a threat to the body politic. Be it the Iraqi Nationality Law of 1924, Arabization policies, or the way that *tabaiyya* (dependency) and other concepts were used, time and again citizens were marginalized or excluded on the basis of their identities or their political dissent, all in the name of a very coercive understanding of unity.[17] These tools of exclusion, particularly given that they often relied on the manipulation of communal identities, considerably aided the process of turning social multiplicity into social division among some Iraqis.

Popular conceptions of unity in the twentieth century often translated into something more akin to a desire for uniformity or conformity. In this framework, unity did not equally embrace difference under an all-encompassing national meta-identity. Rather, the more commonly seen pattern was the censorship or suppression of difference; the validation of a dominant group's sense of entitlement to assert its identity, frames of reference, and owner-ship—culturally and politically—of a country; and a firm expectation that out-groups should accept the status quo and their secondary role in it as an integral part of the natural order of things.

These conditions formed the backdrop to sectarian relations prior to 2003 in Iraq. With that in mind, sectarian dynamics between the state's establish-ment in 1921 and regime change in 2003 had three key characteristics. First, Iraq had a sectarian issue that was chiefly concerned with state-Shia relations rather than Sunni-Shia relations. Indeed, it can be argued that prior to 2003 Sunnis did not have an active sectarian identity, nor did they regard them-selves in sectarian terms.[18] In that sense Iraq's sectarian issue was a Shia issue, the relevance of which varied considerably from time to time and never bore any resemblance to post-2003 sectarian relations, but it nevertheless existed. Second, sectarian dynamics never overtly challenged the nation-state; sectar-ian competition took place in the name of and within Iraq, and at no point did any significant sect-centric actor seek to alter borders or contemplate secessionist ideas. Third, while sectarian plurality was accepted (celebrated, even), sectarian identity and its expression were viewed negatively, to the point of criminalization, because the dominant discourse framed them as being detrimental to national unity.[19]

In theory, a secular state may vilify all sectarian identities, thereby acting as an equal opportunity enemy of all active sectarian identities. However, because Sunnis tended not to view themselves in sectarian terms, the issue of "sectarianism" in Iraq was one disproportionately associated with Shias, many of whom felt that state policy pressured them to dilute their sectarian identity. As such, in pre-2003 Iraq, to stigmatize sectarian identity was not to stigma-tize Sunnis and Shias equally. As a result, the pre-2003 state's stance toward "sectarianism" and toward sectarian identities proved to be one of the key drivers behind the growth of a sect-centric Shia political culture, one that was to expand throughout the twentieth century, eventually eclipsing other forms of political activism and ultimately flourishing after 2003. By the same token, the pre-2003 state's policies toward sectarian relations not only led to the growth of Shia-centric political actors, but also laid the foundations of post-2003 Sunni rejection through vilification and national excommunication of the state's sect-centric opponents.

While it is true that a certain generation of a certain socioeconomic bracket really were oblivious to their own and others' sectarian identities, what proponents of a purportedly non-sectarian pre-2003 Iraq overlook is that this was unfortunately not the general condition of Arab Iraqi Muslims. The much-lauded secularism of twentieth-century Iraq was, for the most part, an urban phenomenon that was heavily influenced by class. While the facts of coexistence and the absence of overt sectarian conflict—particularly on a societal level—remained undeniable features of twentieth-century Iraq, there was nevertheless from the earliest days of the Iraqi nation-state a Shia issue, the contours of which were essentially related to political representation, the institutional extent of organized Shiism, and the limits of Shia identity in the public space. This was not a case of Shia agitation against a Sunni state; rather, since state establishment in 1921, and unlike their Sunni compatriots, significant sections of Shia society had a politically salient and culturally autonomous structures. Nevertheless, the point is that since state establishment in 1921, and unlike their Sunni compatriots, significant sections of Shia society had a politically salient and culturally autonomous sectarian identity that demanded recognition and grated against the modern state's homogenizing impulses.

It is not that the Iraqi state wanted Shias to abandon Shiism, nor was the state anti-Shia per se; rather, it would be far more accurate to argue that the pre-2003 state was suspicious of those whose lives and identities were embedded in Shia social and religious structures (some of which are transnational) that provided parallel truths regarding Iraqi history, the Iraqi self, and the Iraqi nation, and that flew in the face of the state's narrative of Iraq. As such, social and political mobility were more readily available to Shias who were unencumbered by these parallel truths and whose Shia sectarian identity was as invisible as Sunni sectarian identity.[20] Successive governments were unwilling or unable to accommodate a salient or active Shia identity, often regarding it—and the semi-autonomous structures underpinning it—with suspicion. This was to become especially pronounced under the Baath who, due to rising internal and external challenges (both real and perceived), persecuted Shia religious figures, banned major Shia rituals, and suppressed Shia activism and the expression of Shia identity. In many ways, the Shia issue was a contestation over the relationship between Shia-Iraqi identity and an unhyphenated, state-approved Iraqi identity, and consequently the place and role of Iraqi Shias in state and society.

From the earliest days of the modern Iraqi nation-state, there were instances of certain Shia politicians, leaders, and organizations advocating specifically Shia issues—with little in terms of a Sunni counterpart, thereby further entrenching the association of "sectarianism" with Shias. For example, as early as 1922, Mahdi al-Khalisi—a militant, though far from marginal, Shia cleric known for his opposition to the government—made a series of political demands that, alongside demands for complete Iraqi independence from the United Kingdom, included calls for half the cabinet to be composed of Shias and half of all government officials to be Shias.[21] Similarly, in the 1920s, the short-lived and avowedly Shia-centric al-Nahdha Party emerged, championing the causes of Shia rights and Shia representation.[22] Another example can be found in the People's Pact (Mithaq al-shaab) of 1935. Addressed to King Ghazi, Iraq's second monarch, this document was signed by tribal and religious leaders from the mid-Euphrates region and by Shia lawyers in the capital, demanding, among other issues unrelated to sectarian identities, that Shias be better represented in government and that Shia jurisprudence be represented in the judiciary.[23]

These examples do not preclude other strands of Shia opinion and political activism (pro-state, oppositional, mainstream or clandestine), and they should not be taken as proof of hostility or interminable division. Rather, such examples reflect many Shias' latent resentment against the pre-2003 state. Regardless of whether this was a product of reality or perception, the inescapable fact is that, throughout pre-2003 Iraq's existence, some sections of Shia society firmly believed that they were treated as second-class citizens on account of their sectarian identity; as evidenced, they would argue, by their political under-representation compared to their demographic weight and the suppression of their sectarian identity. Indeed, this resentment was commented upon by Iraq's first monarch, Faisal I, who, writing in 1932, argued that the causes of Shia disadvantage were due to structural and historical reasons (such as their distance from the centers of government or their lack of state education and hence their lack of qualification for government office) rather than sectarian discrimination, but that this had nevertheless "led this majority [Shias] ... to claim that they continue to be oppressed simply by being Shi'a."[24]

It is this belief that led to the emergence of sect-centric Shia political movements. Until at least the 1960s, these were rather marginal and were overshadowed by more popular movements, such as the Iraqi Communist Party, that fought for broader conceptions of social justice beyond the prism of religious or sectarian identity. Over the decades, however, several factors conspired to reverse that. The state's ever-increasing authoritarianism was accompanied by an intensification of Shia activism, both qualitatively and quantitatively.[25] This resulted in the sharpening of the state's suspicions of political Shiism and of

SHIA-CENTRIC STATE-BUILDING IN IRAQ

the mobilization of Shia identity, which in turn served to deepen Shia resentment and broaden support for Shia-centric movements.

By the 1970s, Shia political activism was becoming more outspoken and more brazen, resulting in increasingly violent confrontations with the state. Several disturbances were witnessed in the 1970s, most notably the violent clampdown of Shia processions in 1977 and the disturbances of 1979.[26] This escalation was partly shaped by the regional environment and deteriorating relations with Iran—naturally this downward spiral only accelerated after the Iranian revolution of 1979. The demise of Arab nationalism and communism as popular mobilizers and the emergence of the Islamic Republic of Iran (and regional Islamist movements in general) further explain the growing relevance of Shia-centric movements to the opposition of the regime in Iraq and beyond. The climax was the uprisings of 1991 and their brutal suppression. In many ways this signaled an irreparable break between the regime and significant sections of Shia Iraq.[27] Beginning in the 1980s, but particularly in the 1990s, the opposition in exile was undeniably dominated by Kurdish ethno-centric and Shia sect-centric movements, both of which were viewed with intense suspicion by Iraqis subscribing in one way or another to the state's centralizing and homogenizing visions of Iraqi nationalism.[28]

The 1990s: the opposition in exile and the sectarianization of Iraq

While one can—and indeed should—highlight the role that US policy played in institutionalizing and perpetuating division and conflict in Iraq, one should not deny Iraqis agency in, and responsibility for, their political development. Various developments in the decades preceding regime change, and particularly the era of sanctions that began in 1990, created sociopolitical realities that proved conducive to the advent of identity politics, Shia-centric state-building, and Sunni rejection after 2003. Nowhere was this more evident than in the exiled opposition to Saddam Hussein and the Baath regime that came to play a key role in post-war Iraq.

Sect-centric political causes were championed by sect-centric political actors from as early as the 1920s in Iraq; but by the 1980s, and more so by the 1990s, this once-marginal sect-centricity had matured and deepened to the extent that it dominated the non-Kurdish opposition to Saddam Hussein's regime. This sect-centric political culture that had steadily grown among Shias had been built on a conviction that they were uniquely victimized by the regime, coupled with an equally strong sense of entitlement based on their demographic weight. In time, this belief in themselves as the long-oppressed majority came to alter the political identity of a significant body of Shia Iraqis and elevated the relevance of Shia-centric politics among the organized (and exiled) opposition to Saddam Hussein and the Baath regime. These developments were accelerated by a number of factors: the suppression and demise of other forms of political mobilization, such as Arab nationalism and communism; the empowerment of political Shiism in post-1979 Iran; the Gulf War and particularly the uprisings that followed it in 1991; the social costs of the sanctions era and the resultant mass migration witnessed throughout the 1990s; and the increased interest and support that opposition movements were able to garner from foreign patrons. These and other factors helped to reshape the Iraqi diaspora and diaspora politics.

The most significant effect of this was the shift away from an apologetic Shia identity that downplayed, or even diluted, Shia specificity in the hopes of placating detractors who argued that the Shia challenged the homogenizing nation-building efforts of the modern Iraqi state. Instead, in the 1990s, and particularly in diaspora circles, it became increasingly acceptable to speak in sect-specific terms, and a clearly and unambiguously differentiated Shia political identity was articulated. For example, in 1992, the London-based Al-Khoei Benevolent Foundation hosted a seminar on "The Shia of Iraq at the Crossroads." The title alone, with its specific focus on the Shia as opposed to Iraq, would have been unthinkable in earlier decades, but what was even more unprecedented was the seminar's proposal of federalism as a solution to the Shias' disempowerment.[29] This was an early example of a process that was initially triggered by the uprisings of 1991 and their costly suppression, but that unfolded throughout the sanctions era: namely, the withering away of a hitherto deeply held aversion to discussions of sects and sectarian relations and the mainstreaming of more assertive forms of Shia identity.[30]

Importantly, these developments were taking place at a time when the exiled opposition to the regime was turning into something of an industry—one largely subsidized by foreign powers, including the United States.[31] With regard to US Iraq policy, there was a positive feedback loop between the sect-centricity (and ethnocentricity) of the Iraqi opposition and US preconceptions of, and interests in, Iraq. The simplistic reduction of Iraq into oppressive Sunnis and victimized Shias and Kurds was one largely subscribed to—out of conviction or calculation—both by US policy-makers and by many of their Iraqi interlocutors in the opposition. Many if not most of these were not simply Iraqis who happened to be Shias or Kurds; rather, they were products of ethnocentric and sect-centric movements: Shia politicians, whose politics were deeply embedded in Shia identity and in the concepts of Shia victimhood and Shia entitlement, alongside Kurdish nationalists. While it is perfectly legitimate and sometimes necessary to highlight the plight of a particular community by engaging in sectional advocacy, this form of sectional politics was to dominate the Iraqi opposition, in turn shaping or at least reinforcing US views on Iraq.

Come 2003, the politics of sectional advocacy were superimposed onto national politics, turning them into the defining political principle of the new Iraq. Few examples illustrate this better than the much-maligned ethnosectarian apportionment of post-war Iraqi politics. Far from being solely a product of the past fifteen years, the major players in the Iraqi opposition had adopted the principle of ethnosectarian quotas as the arbiter of political representation and entitlement from as early as 1992.[32] There have been criticisms singling out the United States as the mastermind behind the divisive policy and behind the political elevation of ethnosectarian identities more generally, but while the obsession with ethnosectarian identities may have been a feature of US policy toward Iraq, it was also a characteristic feature of significant parts of the Iraqi opposition.[33]

The shift in Shia political consciousness was not restricted to those in exile; similar developments were under way in Iraq. The 1990s saw the rise of religious and, by extension, sectarian identities' relevance in Iraq. Equally important, Shia resentment of the state deepened and broadened during the sanctions era, as did Shia sectarian entrenchment. This did not necessarily entail any anti-Sunni social antagonisms, nor did it presage the sectarian violence that was to follow 2003. However, it did mean the further development of a Shia vision of Iraq, one largely unknown to Sunnis prior to 2003, which revolved around the triumvirate of victimhood, demographics, and entitlement. The point to be made here is that while the exiled opposition lacked a social base and often even lacked name recognition in Iraq, by 2003 its identity politics and the mindset of Shia-centric state-building resonated with a significant body of Shia opinion. As such, the most immediately noticeable manifestations of popular sentiment after the fall of the regime were to be found in the assertions of Shia identity through public displays of religiosity. As analyst Nicolas Pelham puts it, "[For Iraqi Shias] freedom was not the saccharine of Hollywood movies or American pop, both of which could already be found in [pre-2003] Baghdad. It was mass Shi'a pilgrimage and the public display of the revered trinity of Imam Ali ... and his two sons."[34]

Both in social and political terms, the power vacuum left by the fallen regime was quickly filled by varying shades of Islamist forces whose power and popularity surprised outsiders—as exemplified by the Sadrists (supporters of Shia cleric Muqtada al-Sadr).[35] The only notable reception that greeted any of the returning political exiles was the one that met Shia cleric Mohammad Baqir al-Hakim—head of the Supreme Council for Islamic Revolution in Iraq as it was then known—when he returned from his long exile in Iran.[36] Politically, the fact that identity politics and Shia-centric state-building resonated with a significant body of Shia opinion was reflected in the electoral process. For a certain constituency, regime change provided a unique opportunity through which to guarantee the empowerment of Shia political actors, thereby validating their sense of entitlement, their sense of victimhood, and their demographic weight. This partly explains the sweeping success of the UIA—the grand Shia electoral coalition—in the December 2005 election. As reported at the time by the International Crisis Group, "Even secular Shiites appear to have voted for the UIA rather than for the available alternatives... In the words of a Western diplomat, they may well have voted 'against the hijacking of a historical opportunity for the Shiites.'"[37]

Nevertheless, one should be wary of tautologies that predetermine the institutionalization of identity politics in post-2003 Iraq. Sect-centric politicians and their constituencies were just one group of voices among many in 2003. Neither they nor the positions they espoused, namely identity politics and Shia-centric state-building, were alien to Iraq, but nor were they the only voices therein. Sect-centric politicians and their parties may have formed the broadest and most organized position along Iraq's political spectrum, but that position was empowered and privileged in the new Iraq as a result of US policy, the regional environment, and the evolution of diaspora politics.

In summary, the course taken after 2003 was not inevitable but was always likely. The drivers of Shia-centric state-building came from both above and below: Shia-centric state-building was championed by Shia elites and by US policy, but it also fed off pre-existing social divisions, fears, and aspirations. The idea that Shias were the long-oppressed majority that should rule Iraq was not invented by US policy-makers, nor was it the preserve of Shia-centric politicians in exile; rather, for many Shias it was a long-held article of faith dating back to the foundations of the modern Iraqi state. Unsurprisingly, it proved problematic in post-2003 Iraq, in that its main practical implication was Shia ascendancy (through demographic weight) rather than sectarian equality. As such it was incompatible with and resistant to a non-sectarian or sect-blind approach to Iraq; for those who implicitly or explicitly advocate forms of Shia-centric state-building, a sect-blind approach would be rejected for fear that it would squander the Shias' demographic advantage and would stifle the expression of Shia identities.

As with Shia-centric state-building, Sunni rejection was rooted not only in post-war changes but also in pre-2003 prejudices, convictions, fears, and ways of imagining Iraq, which, among other things, vilified active sectarian identities. At heart, Sunni rejection was not just a reaction to occupation, regime change, and the empowerment of sect-centric and ethnocentric politicians; it is a rejection of the system of ethnosectarian power-sharing and of the elevation of subnational identities to politically relevant categories. In many cases, this has led Sunnis to deny the notion that they are a demographic minority.[38]

The ambivalence with which many Sunnis have viewed subnational identities goes back to the paradoxical way in which the subject was approached by successive regimes before 2003: communal plurality was at once celebrated as a defining feature of Iraq and vilified or feared as a potential threat to national unity. As such, the post-2003 system of ethnosectarian power-sharing not only disadvantaged Sunnis as a demographic minority devoid of sect-centric organizations, structures, and leaders, but also struck them as unfamiliar if not downright sinister. In the words of Allawi: "There was a general sense [among Sunnis] that an unnatural, alien, force had overthrown an entire system of power and authority. It had no connection to Iraq's history or experience and could not therefore be considered a legitimate arbiter of the country's destiny."[39] Political scientist Harith al-Qarawee further underlines the reasons for Sunni alarm at regime change by arguing that in pre-2003 Iraq, Sunnis had been told, and had believed, that they faced three major threats: foreign occupation, Kurdish separatism, and Shia Islamism: "In 2003, Sunni Arabs woke up and saw these three enemies (the occupiers, the Kurdish nationalists, and the Shia Islamists) sitting together and setting the rules for the new Iraq."[40]

What became clear only after 2003 and complicated Sunnis' acceptance of the new order was the extent of their obliviousness to the facts of Shia sect-centricity. Prior to 2003, many Sunnis had never encountered or even known of the existence of an alternate Shia-centric narrative of Iraqi nationalism. Because for many if not most Sunnis, a differentiated and explicitly Shia political consciousness was an alien and irredeemably negative notion that had only been visible when it was highlighted by the former regime as evidence of pro-Iranian treason, this predisposed them toward rejection of the post-2003 order. The outpouring of Shia symbolism immediately after the fall of the former regime and the empowerment of Shia-centric—even Iran-aligned—political actors validated Sunni fears that Iraq had succumbed to a Shia takeover. Even the Shias' demographic weight came as a rude awakening, with many Sunnis never having conceived of Baghdad as anything even approaching a Shia-majority city.[41]

For many Sunnis, and indeed for some anti-Islamist Shias as well, rejection was prompted not just by the mere fact of Shia empowerment; it was also a reaction to the empowerment of a particular brand of Shia: not politicians who just happen to be Shia, but Shia-centric politicians whose politics were inseparable from their Shia identity. More to the point, they were exactly the forces that had long been demonized by state propaganda as the treacherous arm of Iranian machinations in Iraq. This Sunni predisposition toward rejection of the post-2003 order was hardly ameliorated by the actions of the newly empowered Shia political elites, the regional environment, or the abject failure of the new political classes to construct a functioning state that could deliver basic services and offer hope for a brighter future.

There was also a basic obstacle facing Sunni acceptance of the new order in that it carried an overt sense of Shia ownership. Even if this contained no anti-Sunni sentiment, it would have still been difficult for Sunnis—unaccustomed as they were to thinking of themselves as a sectarian group, much less as a minority one—to subscribe to a new national mythology based on the symbols and narratives of what would formerly have been considered an outgroup. The Shias' profound sense of victimhood under Saddam Hussein meant that, generally speaking, they celebrated the downfall of the Baath Party as their salvation as much as it was Iraq's. Even if Sunnis were glad to see Saddam Hussein's downfall, it was hardly likely for them to subscribe to a celebration so heavily tinged with someone else's mythology of victimhood and entitlement, particularly given that this mythology can all too easily be construed as implicitly vilifying Sunni Arabs by associating them with the former regime. These conditions shaped the manner in which a previously non-existent Sunni identity emerged after regime change.

Ironically, despite Sunnis' long-held aversion to the assertion of subnational identities, Sunni opponents of the post-2003 order had to become as sect-centric as the system they derided for its sect-centricity.[42] Prior to 2003, Sunnis had seldom if ever had any real cause to conceive of, mobilize, or organize themselves as Sunnis. After regime change, Sunnis had to imagine themselves as a sectarian group, both as a response to Shia-centric state-building and in order to be relevant in a system fundamentally based on identity politics.

The Sunni identity that emerged was one founded on opposition to the post-2003 state. As such, Sunni rejection, be it in the form of begrudging acceptance, anti-state violence, or anything in between, is an integral part of post-2003 mainstream Iraqi Sunni identity. This has proven problematic in that Sunni leaders have often found themselves seeking greater representation in a system that many of their constituents deem illegitimate. This paradox and the consequently ambivalent relationship toward anti-state violence has led some Sunni politicians to collude with anti-state insurgents.[43] Further-more, there is also the danger that, if left unaddressed, Sunni rejection of the post-2003 order may ultimately translate into alienation from the Iraqi nation-state—something that has already been seen on the most extreme end of the spectrum in the form of the self-proclaimed Islamic State. Likewise, and particularly at times of heightened tension, the line separating Sunni rejection of a Shia political project from outright anti-Shiism can easily be blurred.[44]

Where to for Arab Iraq?

The year 2003 marked the simultaneous emergence of Shia-centric state-building and Sunni rejection. The dynamic between the two, particularly once they were politically empowered, quickly developed mutually reinforc-ing and self-perpetuating characteristics that were accelerated by the divi-siveness of the occupation; the role of external actors; Iraqi electoral politics; and the spiral of violence, fear, mistrust, and uncertainty that con-tinues to mark post-2003 Iraq.

However, Iraq did not travel a clear downward path following regime change. There were moments when Shia-centric state-building and Sunni rejection seemed to be in retreat, and hopes were raised that the cycle could be broken. The most promising period was 2008–10: violence was declining, sectarian politics were in clear retreat,[45] militia and insurgent networks had been crippled, and many were optimistic that post-2003 Iraqi politics had come of age.[46] But whatever glimmer of hope existed began to fade during the controversial parliamentary election of 2010, in which Nouri al-Maliki lost the ballot but retained power. His disastrous second term as prime minister, 2010–14, saw the retrenchment of identity politics, the deepening of Sunni alienation from the state, the reinvigoration of militant networks—partly aided by the spiraling and heavily sect-coded conflict in neighboring Syria—and ultimately the return of civil war.[47]

The summer of 2014 saw the dynamic between Shia-centric state-building and Sunni rejection reach its most extreme expression to date in the form of the Islamic State and the Hashd al-Shaabi (the Hashd hereafter).[48] The Islamic State obviously represents not just a rejection of Shia-centric state-building in Iraq, but also a rejection of the Iraqi nation-state and a genocidal rejection of Shias and others. The rise of the Islamic State and its conquest of Mosul and most Sunni-majority areas of Iraq in the summer of 2014 has seen mainstream Sunni political actors and non-Islamic State Sunni insurgent groups reduced to irrelevance, thereby accentuating the post-2003 state's Shia-centricity and limiting the presence and effectiveness of less extreme, non-Islamic State manifestations of Sunni rejection.

The Hashd is the term given to the mass mobilization of volunteers and militias to repel the Islamic State. Its origins date to the final months of Maliki's second term and prior to the fall of Mosul to the Islamic State in June 2014. However, it only gathered momentum after Grand Ayatollah Ali al-Sistani's call on Iraqis to volunteer for the security services to defend Iraq against the Islamic State. This resulted in a massive Shia mobilization that included the reinvigoration of older Shia militias and the formation of newer ones. Although officially an institution of the state, the more powerful formations in the Hashd, particularly Badr and Asaib Ahl al-Haq, are widely viewed as a parallel force competing with the Iraqi security forces. In several regards, this mirrors a broader intra-Shia struggle between Prime Minister Haider al-Abadi and his rivals on the Shia right.

The Hashd is the most popular and mainstream manifestation of Shia-centric state-building yet. It is also significant in that it is a rare example of Shia-centric state-building in an institutional sense. The gravity of the events of the summer of 2014, following on from the calamities of the preceding eleven years, resulted in a significant shift in Shia political identity further toward sect-centricity. The Hashd, and its political patrons on the Shia right, is the most visible embodiment of this shift. The Hashd's organic popularity, not to mention its military muscle and political relevance, seems destined to alter Iraqi politics in a way that may further cement the post-2003 Iraqi state's Shia identity.[49]

The issues of Shia-centric state-building, Sunni rejection, and, more broadly, Iraq's Sunni-Shia issue are at heart inseparable from questions of state legitimacy. This is best illustrated in the parallels between the reactions to impending state collapse in 2003 and 2014. In 2003, Shias were, broadly speaking, more receptive to the idea of regime change than their Sunni compatriots. The reason was not that Sunnis were pro-Saddam Hussein; rather, it was that some Sunnis accorded the state structure some measure of legitimacy regardless of their views on Saddam. Conversely, many Shias accorded the state no legitimacy whatsoever, viewing it as an oppressive apparatus that targeted them as a sectarian group. As such, Shias were more likely to view state collapse in 2003 as Iraq's, and particularly Shia Iraqis', chance to be liberated from tyranny, while Sunnis were more likely to view state collapse as an existential crisis.

In 2014, the same dynamic was evident but in reverse: as Islamic State militants surged toward Baghdad, and as the post-2003 order seemed to be on the verge of collapse, Shias rallied to the defense of the state despite the deep resentment they harbored against the government. Conversely, there was a body of Sunni opinion that would have welcomed the collapse of the entire post-2003 order if it were at the hands of practically any group other than the Islamic State—hence Sunni public discourse in the summer of 2014 downplayed the group's role while making repeated references to "tribal revolutionaries" instead.[50]

The reactions to the Islamic State threat highlighted a fundamental divergence in perceptions: while Grand Ayatollah Ali al-Sistani's calls for mass mobilization were enthusiastically answered by Iraqi Shias, they incensed several Sunni public figures who believed—or at least propagated the belief—that the mobilization was an anti-Sunni mobilization in defense of Maliki rather than the state.[51] More to the point, the fact that the events of the summer of 2014 constituted a national emergency in need of mass mobilization was self-evident to many Shias, but not, generally speaking, to Sunnis. A rhetorical question that was often heard being asked by Sunnis at the time was: Where were Sistani's powers of mobilization in 2003 when Iraq was invaded? Herein lies the crux of the matter: broadly speaking, neither Shias in 2003 nor Sunnis in 2014 wanted the state to survive, because neither considered the state legitimate; in both cases, Sunnis and Shias were divided on whether it was justifiable to defend the state. That these divergent positions were nevertheless couched in nationalistic terms is testament to the depth of division regarding the contours of what Iraq and Iraqi nationalism constitute.

The question is whether there is a breaking point. Changing the mindsets that sustain the dynamic between Shia-centric state-building and Sunni rejection will take a new generation of political and religious leaders. As evidenced by Prime Minister Abadi's faltering reform agenda and the political reactions to it, the current crop of leaders is too invested in the status quo to enact meaningful change. Likewise, battle fatigue paving the way to compromise remains a distant possibility given the zero-sum nature of the conflict—particularly where the Islamic State is concerned—and given the seemingly inexhaustible external support that various Iraqi actors continue to receive from regional and international powers.

The reality in Arab Iraq is that Shia political ascendancy—more specifically the ascendancy of Shia-centric political actors—will remain irreversible well into the foreseeable future. For Sunnis and everyone else, the distasteful implication of this is that they must either withdraw from the state by boycotting it or taking up arms, or, alternatively, they must accept a junior role in Iraqi politics. Dreams of a sect-blind Iraqi state based on citizenship will likely remain dreams for the time being. There are signs that this is increasingly happening: although it is too soon to say, the sheer enormity of the calamities visited upon Sunni-majority areas of Iraq since 2014 may have altered political calculations amongst many local-level leaders. Since 2014, many such figures have shown a willingness to seek the patronage of Shia political forces in order to secure their interests.[52] If such patterns persist and widen, we may look back on 2014 as the beginning of Shia-centric state-building's culmination—though any such proclamation would be premature at the present time of writing.

However it is achieved, the priority has to be finding an end to the war and to mass mobilization. As long as violence rages, the mistrust characterizing politics and sectarian relations will persist to the benefit of hardline actors on all sides. With Iraq in a state of undeclared but seemingly endless civil war, it will remain difficult to shift the focus meaningfully away from questions of state legitimacy toward those of state efficiency, corruption, and service delivery. Putting these universally relevant material issues on the political center stage may be the surest way toward long-term solutions and a reduction in the salience of communal identities—after all, even a somewhat discriminatory state is more likely to be tolerated if it is efficient and offers people a decent standard of living and the prospects of a brighter future. However, this is unlikely to happen before violence is dramatically reduced.

Iraq's future is being shaped today by far more than its blundering political elites and the weight of history. Violence in Iraq is inextricably linked with the Syrian civil war, which itself is perpetuated by and hostage to the conflicting policies and interests of regional and international powers. In Iraq, the rise of the Shia right after the fall of Mosul and the deepening penetration of their Iranian patrons has significantly constrained the political space for would-be reformers. Added to that is a less than benevolent economic situation prompted by plummeting oil prices and the mounting costs of war, all of which equates to a gloomy forecast for Iraq's future and for the prospects of positive change at precisely the time when a departure from current trajectories is most critically needed.

6

THE UNRAVELING OF TAIF

THE LIMITS OF SECT-BASED POWER-SHARING IN LEBANON

Joseph Bahout

Introduction

The upheavals in the Arab world that began in December 2010 and continue to this day in a number of countries shook the most solid pillars of what had been considered a stable, even immutable, Arab order. Several countries long considered solidly under the control of authoritarian regimes have fragmented, bringing to the fore realities that had largely been beneath the surface. One of these realities was the heterogeneous nature of the social fabric in a number of Arab states, and therefore the fragile relationship between this social reality and the states themselves, which were openly challenged in the revolutionary process.

All across the Middle East today, the political systems of a number of countries are eroding and states themselves are unraveling, while their societies are fragmenting, perhaps irremediably. This is particularly true in the Levant, where identity politics have come to predominate, and where, until recently, disparate sectarian, ethnic, and tribal groups coexisted in mosaic-like social environments, for the most part in heavily centralized, strongly nationalistic state systems.

Because of this unraveling, the decade-long process of nation-building in a number of mixed states proved to be elusive, despite the strong, even brutal, dynamics that were brought to bear. Instead, substate and subnational identities now increasingly appear to prevail. Their consolidation is, in part at least, a defense mechanism, the answer to perceptions of threat, which are frequently defined and described in sectarian terms. In the past, substate and subnational identities were kept in abeyance in the presence of state apparatuses much more focused on defending a privileged minority clan than on enhancing the public interest.

Today, the broader Sunni-Shia rift, which has had dramatic repercussions in the Levant in particular, is the most visible and explosive of these identity-shaped responses. However, beyond the purely sectarian question (one that takes religion as a determining factor in behavior), the question of minorities—or groups that define and perceive themselves as being marginalized by a dominant community or suppressed by an aggressive minority—is also at play in the Middle East. Identity reformation expresses itself in sectarian terms, as well as in ethnic or even tribal terms, depending on which Arab country is affected. Identity reformation tends to express itself in terms of sect in Bahrain, Iraq, Kuwait, Lebanon, Saudi Arabia, Syria, or elsewhere in the Levant and in the Gulf—where Sunnis, Shia, Christians, and other minorities often coexist. It tends to do so more in ethnic terms elsewhere—Kurds or Turkmen in northern Syria and Iraq, and Berbers in the Maghreb.

In all these cases, the dynamics of disintegration that have been unleashed will be difficult to reverse without new and inventive means of political reintegration. On the social level, and in cases of civil conflicts or wars, this will entail processes of reconciliation, justice, and the redistribution of resources. On the political level, countries will have to go through structural political change, even political re-engineering, to devise new power-sharing formulas that can take the new realities into account and come to grips with them. The challenge ahead, if the Arab world is to emerge from the long night in which it seems to have entered, will be to try to find the proper balance between a more unified national identity and sociological and political pluralism, as a prelude to democracy. Such a balance will be very difficult to attain.

Over the course of the past century, since the development of the modern Arab state system, pan-Arab nationalism has developed amid nationalistic political cultures that only partially approximated the ideal of Arab nationalism as well as substate loyalties and allegiances. These loyalties and allegiances were suppressed by authoritarian regimes through mechanisms of state centralization, which aimed to overwhelm and marginalize primordial ties in the state. The process came at the expense of individual rights and freedoms.

Of all the Arab states, only Lebanon pretended to offer a different answer. It crafted an unusual power-sharing and governing system, based on a different definition of identity than in other Arab countries. Lebanon gradually adopted a political system built on sectarian representation, itself influenced by developments during the Ottoman period. This was done as soon as the state of Greater Lebanon was formally established under French authority on 1 September 1920.

Political sectarianism in Lebanon was refined and embraced by the independence movement in November 1943 through what became known as the National Pact, an unwritten agreement that laid the foundations of a sectarian system in the post-independence republic. Surprisingly, the pact survived the civil war of 1975–90. The conflict began, in part, because of calls to abolish political sectarianism. Yet political sectarianism was reaffirmed and even consolidated in the Taif Agreement of 1989, also known as the Document of National Accord. In that regard, Lebanon has the illustrious privilege of having been a pioneer in the creation of a system based on sectarianism and also a laboratory highlighting its dysfunctions and limitations.

Political sectarianism has had its successes as well as its sad and bloody moments of failure and shame. It is worth investigating both extremes and re-examining the origins and history of Lebanese sectarianism, its translation into a political structure, and the dynamics of its unraveling in the period leading up to 1975. The conditions under which the system was resurrected and reshaped after the war and how, nowadays, it is showing its limitations also merit attention. The question of how, or whether, the confessional system can still deal with and adapt to the many structural challenges that it faces again in 2016 can be addressed by focusing on Lebanon. And, given the strong and profound relationship between Syria and Lebanon since the two countries' inception, the dynamics of the ongoing conflict in Syria, and that country's disintegration, are weighing most heavily on the future prospects of the Lebanese system.

In light of this, the many flaws in the Lebanese system have become increasingly evident. What is striking in the current regional political context, however, is that because all the experiments elsewhere in creating strong centralized states have failed, some analysts and policy-makers are willing to look at the Lebanese system, or experience, in a new way. Their interest lies in determining what can be taken from, or influenced by, Lebanon and applied to mixed Arab countries in deep crisis, and what is to be avoided at all costs. For example, analysts as well as policy-makers observing post-2003 Iraq have often referred to an "Iraqi Taif" to govern communal relations in the future—in reference to the Lebanese post-war reconciliation and power distribution agreement. More recently, some attempts to address the mayhem in Syria have led to discussions of adopting some features of Lebanon's system to bring about an eventual "Syrian Taif."

Similar calls may involve other countries in the region as the quest for new and more flexible paths to accommodate different identities, integrate societies, and allow for political power-sharing become unavoidable. This is why an assessment of Lebanese sectarianism conjures up some lessons that could have relevance for the region. The Lebanese experience may form the basis for a reflection on what may be applied elsewhere, and what, on the contrary, would best be abandoned.

A Muslim-Christian national pact

Lebanon's system of political confessionalism (*al-taifiyya al-siyasiyya*), or political sectarianism, was originally an answer to a sociological and ideological challenge. A sectarian distribution of power had already been adopted under the Ottoman Empire, since the inception of the administrative region of Mount Lebanon during the nineteenth century as the nucleus of modern Lebanon. The governing system that was introduced after the civil war in Mount Lebanon in 1860, the *mutasarrifiyya*, like the arrangement adopted earlier to end the conflict of 1840, accepted the various religious sects as political actors. In the post-1860 period, and under the authority of a non-Arab Christian Ottoman governor known as the *mutasarrif*, an administrative council was created in which seats were reserved for the six main religious sects in Mount Lebanon, proportional to their overall numbers.[1]

What is notable here is that this post-1860 power-sharing and local governance formula followed a conflict that had pitted the Druze against the Maronites, the two main communities of the semi-autonomous Mount Lebanon region. Further tensions later on, not to mention the civil war of 1975, were similarly ended through power-sharing and political rebalancing arrangements, though the pursuit of non-sectarian systems of political accommodation was never attempted.

From a multicommunal society, Lebanon was thus transformed into a multi-communal state system. The sociological reality, a relatively neutral one at the beginning, was used by the founders of the Lebanese polity to become the prime consideration of their political order. To paraphrase the Marxist formula regarding social classes and their formation, the adoption of political sectarianism in Lebanon could be considered similar to the passing from a group (or a community) in itself to a group (or a community) for itself. After that, the culture of political sectarianism became gradually entrenched in the collective consciousness and political practice of Lebanon's political and social elites.

On the ideological level, political sectarianism indirectly answered a challenge that emerged from the conditions in which the Lebanese entity was born. The formation of Greater Lebanon after 1920 could not be considered—whether by its detractors or partisans—anything more than a French colonial construct undertaken with the active complicity of Maronite elites and on their own behalf. For both the Maronites and the French, while motivated by different reasons, the aim was to provide Christians with a quasi-national homeland in a Muslim-majority Middle East. Maronite elites saw this venture as the crowning moment of a long-maturing project of a Lebanese nation.[2] In this, the ambiguous relationship between Lebanonism and political Maronitism was never resolved.[3] For France, in the midst of its growing rivalry with Great Britain, the motive was to satisfy its geopolitical interests. It sought a vanguard in the Levant that would allow France to project its ideology in the region, alongside a policy of minority protection: that of the Christians at the forefront.

Thus, from the outset, Maronite elites had to invent a founding narrative that would supersede and transcend their new state's very crude *raison d'être*. Given Lebanon's new demographic and sociological make-up, created by the enlargement of the country around a core of Mount Lebanon, a more inclusive discourse was needed to help accommodate the Muslim sects that had been integrated into the new state and that demographically were almost as numerous as the Maronites. In other words, hegemony needed to be transformed into a more commonly accepted national story in order to supersede and absorb the cleavages between the main communities.

Additionally, the plethora of competing narratives and legends surrounding the Lebanese entity and its legitimacy—from the myth of Phoenician ancestry, to the Maronite presence described by France's King Louis IX as a "rose between two thorns," to the country as an outpost of the Arab conquest of the Levant—had to be balanced.[4] The emirate (until 1841), the nucleus of Greater

Lebanon that reflected Maronite-Druze joint sovereignty, had already been grounded in the idea of a land of refuge for persecuted communities. This narrative delved into the early history of religious schisms and conflicts in the region, from the original fragmentation of primitive Christian churches to the Arab and Muslim conquest and its repercussions on the Middle East. This was thus seen as a convenient framework to encompass other religious groups, provided its scope was widened and it was granted a universal dimension. Lebanon was therefore to be considered a land of communal coexistence, mainly between Islam and Christianity, and a bridge between the East and the West, between Arab lands and Europe.

Such ideas were precisely what Bechara el-Khoury, Lebanon's president at the time, and Riad al-Solh, the prime minister, integrated into the National Pact of 1943.[5] According to Solh's formulation, the National Pact's primary aim was to "Lebanonize Lebanese Muslims and to Arabize Lebanon's Christians."[6] In the pact Christians were supposed to renounce alignment with the West (mainly France), while Muslims were to forgo any notion of integrating Lebanon into a larger Arab nation.

With respect to the details of governance and the structure of the independent state, the National Pact put in place what both Khoury and Solh considered a fair distribution of power between the two religious communities, but one that would grant a large margin of superiority to the Christians. Parliamentary representation, based on ratios reflecting communal demographics, was six to five in favor of Christians over Muslims. The same ratio was adopted in the cabinet and in the civil service.

The most fascinating aspect of the National Pact, however, is one that is frequently overlooked, and yet is the most important: the allocation of the three top positions in the state to specific communities. The pact implied that the president of the republic would be a Maronite, the prime minister a Sunni, and the speaker of parliament a Shia. This was never formally stated or spelled out, but it has been left untouched ever since, indicating the strength of the pact and its superiority over rigorously written constitutional texts. Another consequence of this implicit power-sharing pledge was the decision to reserve highly important government positions for particular communities. Maronites were to get the lion's share, especially in vital sectors of the state. The commander of the army, the heads of military intelligence and the state security services, as well as the governor of the central bank, to name a few, were all Maronites.[7]

Political sectarianism had two sides. On the one hand it allowed disparate groups to come together by providing the Lebanese people with the framework to devise a social contract. On the other hand, power-sharing almost necessarily introduced a corrosive machinery for the distribution of spoils. This allowed corruption to become an accepted form of political behavior relatively quickly; over time, it translated into state inefficiency and the paralysis of decision-making. More important, and this is the main flaw of the sectarian model, is that reinforcing sectarian identities and providing them with full-fledged political and legal status came at the expense of convergence toward a common identity.

Consociational democracy and its unraveling

By opting for a system based on political sectarianism, the founders of the Lebanese Republic effectively joined the club of so-called consociational democracies, a political model that flourished after World War II. By seeking to establish states on the basis of permanent compromise and consensus, consociationalism was an inventive way of reconciling social heterogeneity with parliamentary democracy.[8] The political unit was not only the individual but also the group. In Lebanon, religious sects were both political and legal entities, in which the rights of individuals were balanced by the guarantees given to the sects. If the notion of guarantees was mainly dear to the Christians, relating to the fears and threats they perceived in a Muslim-majority Middle East, it gradually expanded over time to encompass almost all other religious groups. Guarantees thus became another word for minority rights, a kind of material and symbolic security mechanism in which a community was assured a place in the sun whatever the changing conditions.

However, consociational democracies must meet certain conditions to function in a lasting way. These include a stable and peaceful regional environment, as well as economic growth with efficient redistributive mechanisms ensuring a socioeconomic balance between the various segments of the polity.[9]

Both conditions, in addition to many others, were cruelly lacking in Lebanon's case before 1975. Muslim political forces began demanding a greater share in a system they were more or less forced to join. Although aspirations for a unified Arab state prevailed in the Middle East, the idea that individual states were now permanent gained traction over time. If Muslims still doubted the idea of a Lebanese nation, they nevertheless began to accept the state, at least as a livable framework. Hence it became necessary for them to ameliorate substantially the conditions of their participation in this state— displaying precisely the reflexes of citizenship that their Christian partners had long demanded.

Consequently, participation (*musharaka*) became a rallying cry for Muslim politicians. This was especially true after changes in the system opened up new avenues for fundamental political change in the country.[10] The quest for greater participation emanated from highly conflictual regional dynamics, such as the escalating Arab-Israeli conflict, the rise of Palestinian militancy, inter-Arab rivalries, and the Cold War and its projections on the Middle Eastern stage. The convergence of these factors was largely the origin of Lebanon's war in 1975.

Taif's rebalancing act and the Sunni-Shia question

The Lebanese conflict was not all about political sectarianism, nor was it only about the redistribution of sectarian shares in the political system. Indeed, such issues were largely tackled, and more or less agreed upon, during the early stages of the war, well before the Taif Agreement.[11] However, the domestic dimension of the war was very much about sectarianism. When Muslim political forces began contesting the system during the 1960s, it was with the aim of rebalancing powers and prerogatives between Muslims and Christians. By the 1970s this had evolved. On the eve of the war, Muslims were demanding fundamental change and the introduction of a one-person, one-vote democratic system.[12]

Yet by 1989, after multiple rounds of fighting, more than 100,000 deaths, and immeasurable destruction, all that the Taif Agreement did about sectarianism was readjust the old system. With the exception of ties with Syria and Lebanon's relations with its regional environment, Taif was much more about reorganization than transformation.

The agreement was organized around three guiding principles: the establishment of a new balance between the unity of Lebanon and its political system and the diversity of the country's political and social structure; the transfer of executive power from the presidency of the republic to the Council of Ministers as a collective body; and the principle of parity between Muslims and Christians in the parliament, the cabinet, and the higher echelons of the civil service, regardless of future demographic developments.[13] The agreement also called for the establishment of a sectarian-based senate, which guaranteed the say of religious groups by granting them oversight on vital national affairs and matters that referred to the pact, after the deconfessionalization of parliament; introduced administrative decentralization; mentioned revising the civil status law system; and called for the creation of a national committee to discuss the abolition of political sectarianism, though probably with little expectation that it would be implemented. Furthermore, Taif laid the groundwork for privileged relations between Lebanon and Syria, with implications for the two countries' political environment. Of the three principles, the first two are the most relevant to this discussion of Lebanese sectarianism. However, the third would, arguably, turn out to be the most important.

Behind the benign facade of a transfer of executive prerogatives from a once-omnipotent presidency to the Council of Ministers, Taif reorganized constitutional powers and apparatuses. It also put in place an entirely new paradigm for a sectarian balance of power by ending the political and symbolic hegemony exercised by the Maronite establishment. However, the destination of the transferred presidential powers remained unclear. By vesting such powers in the cabinet, where religious parity was a formal guarantee of equality among communities, Taif also disseminated and diffused power, making it difficult to locate and exercise. Nor was it clear who was to be held accountable for decisions. This situation was exacerbated by several provisions of the agreement that were, probably intentionally, left vague and subject to interpretation.

At first sight, the Sunni prime minister appeared to be the main beneficiary of this transfer of power. Nevertheless, other measures were adopted to avoid such an outcome. As the master of cabinet agendas, the prime minister had to draft them with the speaker of parliament. Taif stipulated that the executive and legislative branches were separate but that they "should work in synergy and coordination" to optimize political action. To that was added the fact that the prime minister was to be nominated after obligatory consultations between the president and speaker and the president's consultations with parliamentary blocs in the presence of the speaker. In the Council of Ministers all important decisions required a two-thirds majority, giving implicit veto power to one of the three larger anticipated blocs of ministers: those of the president, the speaker of parliament, and the prime minister. This was repeatedly true of the Shia ministers, more homogeneously organized and disciplined than the others, held together by the tight alliance between the Amal Movement (a Shia political party created in the 1970s) and Hezbollah, backed by Syria.

So if the Sunni prime minister appeared to some as the new king, the ultimate kingmaker was nevertheless the Shia speaker—at least that is what the experience of Taif's implementation has shown until now. The speaker has been granted enhanced powers, and the speaker's term has been extended to correspond with that of parliament, normally four years. The speaker has also been granted extensive control over legislative activity and potentially has major influence over the votes of Shia ministers and parliamentarians.

At best, behind the formal facade of parity between Muslims and Christians, what has really animated political life and reality since the Taif Agreement is the three-tiered interaction among Christians (with the Maronite component gradually melding into the broader Christian community), Sunnis, and Shia. Maronite pre-eminence was indeed ended by Taif, but it was in turn replaced by the rising and competing pre-eminence of the two principal Muslim sects, and this happened well before Sunni-Shia polarization came to characterize the Middle East.

Syria as Taif's first and ultimate regulator

Beyond the text, Taif was largely shaped by the way it was implemented after 1990 and how Lebanon was governed, both by its new leaders and Syria, which exercised control—or tutelage—over the country. From the outset, many observers and critics of Taif determined that the shortcomings in the means of governance outlined by the agreement were intentional, for reasons pertaining to Syrian power. The international guarantors of Taif had unanimously accepted that Syria be allowed to impose a de facto protectorate over Lebanon and its political life. Taking full advantage of the leeway it was granted, Syria played a permanent and subtle balancing act between Christians and Muslims in general, between Maronites, Sunnis, and Shia more particularly, and between Sunnis and Shia specifically, initiating many of the tensions that are present today.

More important, Syria's management of Lebanon was defined exclusively by its own priorities. These were of two sorts: the first was regional, pertaining to Syria's position on the Middle Eastern chessboard, and its relations with the Arab world and with the West, the United States in particular; the second related to maintaining delicate balances inside Syria, expertly manipulated by then president Hafez al-Assad and increasingly affected by the imperative of ensuring his own succession.

Syria's tutelage over Lebanon was accepted by the international community in exchange for Damascus's constructive participation in the peace process with Israel, an outgrowth of the Madrid Conference of 1991. From Syria's perspective, in line with its first priority, this role allowed it to gain leverage in the negotiations by manipulating the still-open front in Israeli-occupied southern

Lebanon, in which Hezbollah played an important role. At the same time Syria was the overseer and de facto protector of the lucrative reconstruction process in Lebanon, guided by Rafik Hariri, the indispensable prime minister as of 1992. This allocation of roles allowed Syria to award Hariri's political patron, Saudi Arabia, as well as other Gulf and Sunni-majority Arab states, a stake in stabilizing the country, while at the same time extracting enormous financial profits for its own elite through this protection mechanism.[14]

Assad's highly accurate reading of power relations in Lebanon and the region permitted him to play effectively on both levels. At moments of stalemate or crisis in the negotiations between Syria and Israel, Hezbollah operations in southern Lebanon would all of a sudden escalate, sometimes culminating in mini-wars, leading to rapid intervention by international actors. When, on the contrary, the process was smoother, or when Assad's relations with France, the United States, or Saudi Arabia were good, the obstacles faced by Hariri's governments were eased, projects were passed on to parliament and swiftly approved, with notable acceptance by all Shia and pro-Syrian ministers in the cabinet. Resistance and reconstruction became the dual Syrian options in Lebanon, while also reflecting the polarization existing in the region. Metaphors aimed at illustrating this balancing act flourished. Some were even devised by the actors themselves, such as the Druze leader Walid Jumblatt, who characterized Lebanon as both "Hanoi and Hong Kong"—a reference to the country's simultaneous embrace of militancy and its pursuit of profit mainly through the Hariri-led reconstruction effort.[15]

Translated internally in Lebanon, however, resistance and reconstruction divided the major political forces in the country: the Shia community, through Hezbollah, which increasingly manifested the communal ethos and aspirations and embodied the project of resistance to Israel; and the Sunni community, represented by Hariri and his allies, who were the caretakers of economic and financial reconstruction. Assad, between his aim of simply ameliorating Syria's position at the negotiating table or waging open warfare against Israel, something more in line with Iranian aims, left the endgame ambiguous. For Syria, both options coexisted and competed with each other, an attitude that soon permeated Lebanese political culture.

These contending approaches gradually became opposing projects for Lebanese society. Their imposed coexistence created cracks in the political system thanks to their mutual exclusiveness. The Hariri project was economically and politically liberal, insofar as it was linked to globalization and ties to the West that Hariri willingly cultivated through his relations in France and elsewhere. In contrast, the Hezbollah project was increasingly perceived as one of a country and society endlessly at war, mobilized against Israel and the West. This was implicitly confirmed in the party's inclination toward the idea of an economy focused on war. To Hezbollah, such an economy was opposed to one whose orientation would be geared toward regional interdependency and integration, always suspected as being one facet of an eventual Arab-Israeli peace process. That is not to mention Hezbollah's palpable support for a parallel society in the areas under its control.

The second part of Syria's balancing act related to the ways in which Hafez al-Assad had stabilized his rule within Syria since 1970, when he seized power and began forming a tightly knit apparatus of control. His method of rule blended ruthlessness with the subtle maintenance of sectarian, regional, and sectoral balance inside Syrian society and among its elites. With his grip firmly on the process of Lebanon's political rehabilitation, Assad put in place a system that incorporated the Lebanese and Syrian political spheres in a complementary way. Marginal adjustments in the Syrian system were made through the influence exercised by Syrian actors in Lebanon—a way for Assad to expand the pie, thereby distributing more wealth and power and allowing him to reinforce his supremacy.

Toward the end of the 1990s, the succession question in Syria became a growing worry for the aging and increasingly ill president. The balance between the different wings constituting the inner core of his regime had to be sustained to facilitate the smooth handover of power to his son Bashar. Reconstruction and resistance became Syrian agendas as well, each one embraced by a segment of the regime's men, so that even in Syria cracks appeared in the edifice of Assad rule.

Things became clearer in 1998, when the Syrian president effectively handed the Lebanese file to Bashar. The two-decade-old game of balancing power began to falter, caused by a number of factors. Foremost among these was the fact that the dynamics of succession in Syria needed to rest more firmly on a foundation of external resistance and steadfastness. One reason for this was Bashar's defiance toward the Sunni old guard that had loyally accompanied his father to power, and which he perceived was resisting his own rise. This paralleled his developing antipathy toward Hariri, his ways, and what he represented. For Bashar and his entourage, Hariri became increasingly dispensable, even as the Syrian heir apparent was more comfortable with individuals such as Hezbollah's secretary general, Hassan Nasrallah. To this was added his strong suspicion that Hariri had deeply penetrated his father's system and even bought off senior Syrian officials, the implicit assumption being that this was done with a specific anti-Alawite intent on his part.[16]

On the Lebanese scene, the clear-cut signal of an underlying shift in Syria came with the election as president of the army commander, Emile Lahoud, in 1998 and the rapid removal of Hariri as prime minister. Few analysts doubted that these two crucial decisions had been taken by the younger Assad, with the backing of an entourage that had started to paint Hariri and Harirism as the potential spearhead of a Wahhabi plot to weaken or dismantle the regime in Damascus.[17]

The end of ambiguity: Lebanon regionalized

The early stages of Sunni-Shia tension in Lebanon lie in the country's post-war order as well as the dynamics in Syria. Not always hidden, such tensions were nevertheless contained by the presence in Lebanon of the Syrians and the reflexes of a consociational culture that discouraged overt sectarian behavior. The tension was to become uncontrollable, however, and to transform itself into outright conflict when the many changes affecting Lebanon's political environment began to accumulate. It was because of regional dynamics that the sectarian balance, with its many ambiguities since the time of the Taif Agreement, was undermined.

In short, the international consensus around Syria's effective protectorate of Lebanon started to erode after 2001, and then became more openly questioned. The post-11 September paradigm shift in Washington and the invasion of Iraq in 2003 were crucial turning points. Regionally, Israel's unilateral withdrawal from Lebanon in May 2000, followed by the death of Hafez al-Assad in June, brought about a new Lebanese landscape in which the idea of resistance became a source of discord. Meanwhile, Syria was growing wary of developments in the region, fearing that after the fall of Saddam Hussein's regime in 2003, Bashar al-Assad's was next. Assad's belief that his regime was encircled and besieged was confirmed in his mind with the passage in September 2004 of the French- and US-backed United Nations Security Council Resolution 1559 that called for Syria's withdrawal from Lebanon, the restoration of normal political life in the country, and the disarmament of Hezbollah.[18]

Only time will tell if, as Syria and its Lebanese allies asserted, Rafik Hariri was responsible for, or at least an active partner in, the passage of the resolution, his aims being to force a Syrian pull-out from Lebanon and even induce regime change in Damascus. The anti-Hariri feeling, already prevalent in Bashar al-Assad's circles, with all its sectarian underpinnings, reached a climax. Not only had Hariri reneged on the original contract with Syria's leadership when he came to power, namely to be the caretaker of Syrian interests in Lebanon and an obedient instrument on behalf of the Sunni community; he was now perceived as a vital threat to the Assad regime itself, on behalf of his Saudi patrons and probably, in Assad's mind, of France and the United States.

This was the political climate that surrounded Hariri's assassination in February 2005.[19] His death was without doubt a quasi-fatal blow to the balance put in place in Lebanon after 1990. It was the first and strongest earthquake in the Sunni-Shia balancing act that until then Syria had successfully managed. It also ended Syrian oversight of Lebanon's governance structure that had prevailed until that time. In this regard, Hariri's assassination brought on the clinical death of Taif.

This upheaval almost completely transformed the mechanisms of sectarian competition in Lebanon by eliminating one of its main local pillars, Hariri, and by undermining Syria's role as the main regional arbiter in the country. The latent tension between the two main sectarian contenders for power, the Sunnis and Shia, suddenly came out into the open. The gloves were off, and violence emerged as an ever-present possibility.

When, in the weeks after Hariri was killed, large numbers of Lebanese descended on Martyrs' Square in central Beirut to protest the Syrian presence in their country and demand that those behind political assassinations in Lebanon face justice, it was evident that one main component of the country, the Shia community with its political representatives, was absent. This absence was an indication of the sharp divide in Lebanon at the time, which has only widened since then. For Lebanon's Sunnis, Hariri's assassination represented an unbearable offense, one whose sectarian impact would increase amid suspicions that Hezbollah was involved. The indifference of the Shia was perceived as a breach of the tenets of peaceful sectarian coexistence that had prevailed until then.

The years that followed, between Hariri's assassination in 2005 and the beginning of the uprising in Syria in 2011, were characterized by uncertainty, bloodshed, and persistent violence. In July 2006, the war between Hezbollah and Israel established the party and the community on whose behalf it claimed to speak as a prominent regional force. Furthermore, Hezbollah's proclaimed victory was appropriated by Bashar al-Assad. The way he did so, however, reignited sectarian fires. In a speech before a conference of the Syrian

Journalists Union on 15 August 2006, Assad stated that he considered that among those on the losing side in the war were the Arab states that did not support Hezbollah, headed by what he referred to as "half-men,"[20] and the 14 March coalition in Lebanon, whose Sunni leaders he had once labeled servants of Saudi Arabia.

The situation would only get worse. More than a year later, in May 2008, Hezbollah, responding to a government decision it opposed, deployed gunmen in a coup of sorts in western Beirut's predominantly Sunni neighborhoods.[21] The party and its allies surrounded the residence of Saad Hariri, Rafik's son, obliging him to seek the protection of the Lebanese army, and ransacked his television station. To Beirutis this harked back to the Lebanon of the 1980s, when militias ruled the streets.[22] The Saudi ambassador fled the capital in a private yacht, having disguised himself to avoid the wrath of pro-Syrian, particularly Shia, militiamen.

This would be repeated a few years later when, in early 2011, Hezbollah withdrew from the government of then prime minister Saad Hariri because of the progress by the Special Tribunal for Lebanon and the likelihood—at the time—of it accusing Hezbollah of Rafik Hariri's assassination. This torpedoed the Saudi-Syrian deal and blew up Saad Hariri's government. Not long afterward, Hezbollah again sent threatening messages when it deployed unarmed men wearing black shirts in several locations of Beirut, as an implicit reminder of what had taken place in 2008. Furthermore, in the years after Rafik Hariri's killing, a long series of political assassinations occurred, paralyzing Lebanese political life. Politicians, journalists, and public intellectuals belonging to the same camp hostile to Damascus and its Lebanese allies were all targeted.

The Syrian bonfire and Lebanon's sectarian flames

By the time the Arab revolutions began in 2010–11, taking on acute sectarian dimensions throughout the Middle East, sectarian cleavages were already running deep in Lebanon. The stage was set, the actors were prepared, and the breakdown in Syria only exacerbated matters. Syria had long behaved as an arsonist-firefighter, provoking crises it would then be asked to resolve. By 2011 the arsonist may have been out of Lebanon, but the fire it had largely contributed to spreading was burning with heightened intensity. And Syria was out only in direct and visible ways. Its influence was still pervasive, in part because the conflict in Syria had widespread repercussions in Lebanon. For the Lebanese, calculations of gains and losses from the war in Syria were no longer restricted to their own country. They were now assessed in the larger Syrian-Lebanese sphere, as if the two countries, going back in time, were almost one again.

As for Hezbollah, the fall of Assad's regime would have represented a strategic setback to what was referred to as the resistance axis. It would have led to a disruption of Iran's supply line to the party and represented the first stage in a possible extension of Sunni power from Lebanon to Syria to, eventually, western Iraq. Paradoxically, the Shia perception of threat was not allayed by Hezbollah's military power, even as the party conducted itself with a mixture of hubris and arrogance. Hezbollah loudly trumpeted its military involvement in Syria, which was accompanied by an attitude of intolerance and a tendency to tight control of its social space and silencing dissent in Shia ranks.

On the opposing side, for Lebanon's Sunnis and their non-Sunni allies, Assad's fall would bring justice after a long series of grievances. It would also roll back Iran's hegemony in the Levant and reactivate the conditions for a free and viable Lebanon as had been envisaged in 2005. To Sunnis, recent years have been characterized by incessant humiliation and an accumulation of resentments, along with a sense of despair and impotence in confronting Hezbollah's superior military force.

Here a fascinating paradox was at play. Sunni political forces had come a long way since Lebanon's creation in accepting the state and integrating into it. The Taif Agreement had reconciled them with their country, and the long years of Harirism had given them a feeling of ownership of the venture, or at least a good part of it. It is this embrace of Lebanonism that now stands to be broken by the rivalry between the main Muslim sects, as Sunnis suspect Shia of seeking to redefine the state unilaterally to their advantage. The timidity, erosion, and, later, physical absence of the traditional Sunni leadership, and the fact that the ensuing vacuum was increasingly filled by radical Salafi factions empowered by the battle in Syria, reinforced this impression.

Squeezed between the two major Muslim sects, whose struggle expanded beyond Lebanon to Syria, Lebanon's other religious sects began feeling more endangered than ever and increasingly defined themselves as minorities.[23] Since the end of the war in 1990, Lebanon's Christians had internalized a feeling of marginalization and defeat, even coining a word for this: "disenchantment" (*ihbatt*), which became a political slogan at times. The turn of events in 2005 had brought on a new political posture, one no less self-marginalizing and potentially self-destructive. Polarized between the two Muslim sects fighting for their own legacy in Lebanon, Christians were then subjected to the frightening imagery of the decline and exile of the Syrian and Iraqi Christian communities.[24]

Here again the paradox was striking. More than a century earlier, Arab, particularly Levantine, Christians had been at the vanguard of the Arab Awakening that brought about a revival of classical literature and arts, as well as introducing ideas of nationalism, secularism, statehood, and other concepts that helped shape the Arab sense of modernity.[25] Now that the Arabs were rising up against their autocratic rulers under the banner of what Christians considered disturbing platforms and slogans—for instance, the key role of political Islam in the uprisings and the introduction of sharia law in several states' constitutions and legislation—the Christian mindset was reverting to self-preservation. For a large number of Christians, their fears were accompanied by an irresistible appeal to emigrate, as shown by the dramatic erosion in the number of Christians all across the Middle East over a period of decades.[26]

Faced with such existential questions, Lebanon's Christians have been divided over how to respond. One part of the community has called for alignment with other armed and bellicose minorities in the region in an alliance of minorities (*hilf al-aqalliyyat*). Both the Assad regime and Hezbollah have promoted this idea, albeit under the rubric of the protection of Christians, as a counterweight to rising radical Sunni Islamist groups in the region. Another part of the community has drawn from what remains of liberal Arab nationalism and moderate Islamist traditions in vowing never to divorce from the Arab majority, implicitly the Sunnis. Proponents of this view are betting on an Arab Awakening-like revival, a liberal and pluralistic venture that would ultimately bring Christians security, in line with the aspirations that spurred the Arab revolutions.

Among the Druze, the region's unraveling has engendered the same feelings of anxiety and fear. However, their response has been slightly different, due to the fact that the community is much more fragile, facing a demographic decline, and is concentrated in a triangular stretch of land between Lebanon, Syria, and Israel. The Druze have no doubt that the decades ahead will be filled with fierce infighting in the broader Muslim community and that they will have to deploy all their talents of survival to endure. In this regard, from the Lebanese mountains to Druze areas in Syria, the community has regularly entertained notions and fantasies of engaging in autonomous security while remaining neutral, or has yearned for the establishment of de facto buffer zones guaranteed by regional powers, in a quest for communal preservation and survival.

As the war in Syria has continued, sectarian cleavages in Lebanon have started to shift increasingly from an interest-based orientation to an identity-based orientation, and from one that is political to one that is much more symbolic. In other words, the mechanisms of political identification have taken on a more existential dimension, characterized by a zero-sum approach to politics that is incompatible with the more traditional means of pursuing interests, such as power games, negotiations, and other forms of transactions. The fear factor has come to supersede everything. Both levels were never mutually exclusive, intermingling with and reinforcing one another. However, while intersectarian competition was originally oriented toward political grievances and revolved around issues of prerogatives, representation, power-sharing, governance, and a say in decision-making, and while mobilization was made in a political, although very sectarian, context, the struggle has taken on a religious coloring, with individuals and groups defining themselves as endangered communities.

The violence in Syria, with its unbearable images and stories of political-sectarian aggression, has led to a vicious cycle of attacks and retaliation. As a consequence there has been an ever-greater resort to religious zeal and identification, encouraged by radicals providing funding. In their efforts to mobilize and recruit, parties on all sides of the sectarian divide in Syria have instrumentalized religious symbols and discourse. Apocalyptic legends have been revived, generating more extremism.

The lines between interest-based politics and identity politics have become fatally blurred. Under interest-based politics, all issues, small or large, remain negotiable, exchangeable, and transactional. Under identity politics, which now predominates, matters cannot be negotiated because everything is viewed as being linked in some way to communal survival. Extreme violence has highlighted the existential aspect of the issues. Negotiation and compromise are perceived as a first step to defeat, loss, surrender, and, ultimately, slaughter.

Conclusion

The sectarian resurgence across the Middle East and the violent dislocation of several of the region's states and their very uncertain futures have underscored the need for new formulas of power-sharing and sectarian accommodation. These could allow communities with subnational identities to coexist in larger entities, while at the same time contributing to their preservation. To many observers of crumbling nations such as Bahrain, Iraq, Syria,

Libya, and Yemen, the Lebanese model of political sectarianism may represent a framework for conflict resolution in shattered Arab political societies facing problems of inclusion and power-sharing and serve as an example for their political reconstruction.

However, as appealing as this idea may seem, it comes with several caveats. The first involves the background of the formation of the Lebanese system. Time and historical experience have largely rendered sectarianism commonplace in Lebanon's social and political culture, so that it is now deeply entrenched in the collective ethos and national behavior. This is completely lacking in other Arab countries where, on the contrary, models of very centralized Jacobin states (which rely on a unifying definition of national identity for state-building) are the rule and where the idea of pan-Arabism was always more attractive than that of states constructed around subnational identities. Lebanon has always been admired in Arab political culture and envied for its social and cultural liberalism and openness, but also very much vilified and denigrated for its system of governance that has undermined national identity, while generating crisis after crisis, interrupted by sporadic wars.

Lebanonism has also been tarnished by an original sin. The country was established on the ruins of the dream of Arab unity after 1920. The narrative of the National Pact sought to idealize the country's sectarian-based system, injecting it with an element of universalism—that of coexistence and dialogue between Christianity and Islam. What would be the grand narrative of other societies in the Arab world, one that could legitimize sectarian political systems in states that had once glorified Arab nationalism?

Another limitation to the adoption of a Lebanese formula in other Arab countries has to do with the fact that these are very different societies in terms of demographics and size, and in the way states are collapsing. Over time and despite crises and conflicts, Lebanon always emerged from its travails thanks to a desire to preserve what it had, rather than allow permanent breaks. Lebanon's sectarianism was largely perpetuated by a recurring formula to overcome crises—that there was no winner and no vanquished. Such an outlook was deeply rooted in society and the political elite, and was often imposed by outside intervention. This allowed for hegemony and pre-eminence to be better accepted, or at least more smoothly translated and imposed,[27] through governance mechanisms that accommodated those on the losing side as well. Lebanon's demographic make-up, originally defined by parity between Muslims and Christians and later by a division roughly of thirds among Sunnis, Shia, and Christians, was an additional helping factor in that regard, easing the implementation of a consociational culture by ignoring or concealing the true demographic weight of each sect.

This is definitely not the case in Arab countries where a consociational culture is missing. Nor is it likely in countries where cruelty, bloodshed, and population displacements have rendered reconciliation difficult. And it is particularly challenging in places where a demographic majority feels strong resentment toward a repressive minority in power, or where demographics are so imbalanced that the majority does not see why it has to make concessions to the smaller sects.

Another impediment to the adoption of a Lebanese-style sectarian solution has to do with regional sponsorship of any such system. It was clear that the Taif Agreement could function only because it had an external regulator, Syria, that could enforce decisions thanks to its domination. Which power or set of powers could ultimately emerge to guarantee peace in Syria? Or Iraq, Yemen, and Bahrain? To what extent would outside powers be accepted and respected, and for how long? Lebanon's crisis today is in large part due to the absence of a regulator, a reminder of the limitations of its endlessly patched-up system.

As far as Lebanon is concerned, today it is at a crossroads, facing three potential choices. For its first choice, the country could, once again, mend its system of political sectarianism in a way that addresses its imbalances and discrepancies, mainly those affecting the Sunni-Shia relationship. Yet such a possibility is not endlessly on offer. A revision of the political system needs to take into account the prevailing balance of power and reflect it as accurately as possible. Because the regional and domestic situations are in flux, it is almost impossible to conceive of engaging in such a process under present conditions. Moreover, a modified system is not likely to be sustainable for long before new variables intervene to alter again the way it functions. It is therefore probable that simply patching up Lebanon's consociational model will not bring about a lasting solution to the problem of balancing social diversity and political unity.

From gradualists to those advocating a radical and sharp abolition of political confessionalism, the main premise of the second choice is that Lebanon will always be doomed to lurch from crisis to crisis for as long as it is cursed with a system that creates dissatisfaction at home and invites permanent interference from outside. It is, ironically, the chaos in the region that tarnishes the achievement of such a project today. At a moment when strongly centralized states are disintegrating, the challenge would be to prove that Lebanon, the most kaleidoscopic of all Levantine societies, could produce a secular, tolerant state. The reality is that because of its political culture, political economy, and social make-up, Lebanon is shaped in such a way that its transformation into a centralized Jacobin system remains very difficult.

The third choice is to put in place a more diffuse political system—running the gamut from forms of decentralization all the way to federalism and even partition. Advocates of such efforts believe that it is necessary to face reality boldly and confront Lebanon's history of repeated conflicts in order to imagine something fundamentally new. For some Christians, an amicable divorce would be the last guarantee preventing the community's disappearance. For Sunnis, where such approaches are starting to make headway, it could be seen as the optimal way of keeping emboldened political Shiism at bay, until better times. As for the Shia community, the jury is still out. The community's main representative, Hezbollah, sometimes creates the impression that it would accept a more decentralized system, which would allow it greater autonomy to maintain its independent weapons arsenal; yet in its discourse, the party claims to seek a strong centralized state.

What the option fails to take into account is the balance of power that would come to define any discussion about establishing a more diffuse system. Most important is how this might affect the bargaining capacity of each community, which would allow it to enjoy a satisfactory share of an already small territory. Final outcomes will be defined by such a balance and who can impose what on others. Some communal representatives who believe that federalism or extensive decentralization would protect their share of power may come to realize that, if the present system is altered, they would retain much less than they initially expected. It is in this sense, for instance, that many have advised Christian advocates of a federal solution to stick to Taif, since it gives their community parity, instead of looking to replace it with a new system that might leave Christians further diminished because their bargaining power today is limited.

Whatever the answers, some points will have to be kept in mind. Since the formation of the Lebanese system, all changes, both gradual and profound, have followed episodes of violence of some sort. The challenge today is to negotiate a new system of governance without Beirut once again paying so heavy a price. At the same time, any attempt at revisiting Lebanon's political system could hardly fail to be affected by the Syrian crisis. What Syria's ordeal has highlighted is the paradoxical nexus between plurality and authoritarianism. The Lebanese model, despite all its shortcomings and the criticism of its neighbors, accommodated pluralism as much as possible, and exceptionally well when compared with an environment of authoritarian systems and dictatorial regimes. Now that Syria, and more particularly the centralized Syrian state, is imploding and Lebanon's system is collapsing under the weight of its own contradictions, the recourse to either model—the centralized state or the consociational state—should be raised only with caution.

Lebanon's system of political confessionalism is in crisis, and all other political models entail crippling costs and potential pitfalls. What the Lebanese should consider is that the entire Middle East is today in disarray, so that transformations of any sort, anywhere, are unlikely. They should, for now, seek consolation in the fact that while Lebanon is by many benchmarks a failed state, their society is stronger, more resilient, and more inventive than the state.

The Lebanese formula is far from being a road without bumps. On the contrary it is one where accidents occur all too frequently, and it is dangerously nearing a tipping point. The Lebanese should thus admit that theirs is a country of permanent precariousness, of endless instability, a country perpetually on the brink.

7

TWITTER WARS

SUNNI-SHIA CONFLICT AND COOPERATION IN THE DIGITAL AGE

Alexandra Siegel

Introduction

From fiery sermons disseminated by Salafi televangelists to gory videos circulated by the self-proclaimed Islamic State, sectarian narratives and hate speech are on the rise across the Arab world. As the conflicts in Iraq, Syria, and Yemen rage on, hostile messages and violent images circulate twenty-four hours a day through both traditional and social media channels.

While the use of sectarian language is hardly a new phenomenon, dehumanizing anti-Shia and anti-Sunni slurs are increasingly making their way into common discourse.[1] Qualitative studies and journalistic accounts suggest that the escalation of the Syrian civil war, rising sectarian violence in Iraq, and, more recently, the Saudi-led intervention in Yemen have been marked by a proliferation of intolerant rhetoric, especially anti-Shia hate speech.[2] As these conflicts have intensified and become battlefields in the regional power struggle between Iran and the Sunni Arab states, language that casts members of a religious out-group as "apostates" or false Muslims has become more widespread—among not only clerics and fighters on the ground but also average citizens.[3] This rise in sectarian language is particularly visible in the online sphere, where extremist voices are amplified, and viral videos can make their way across the globe in a matter of seconds.

At the same time, increased social media use has precipitated what has optimistically been referred to as the "democratization of communication" throughout the region, facilitating contact and cooperation across sectarian lines.[4] For example, in the early days of the Arab Spring, Sunni and Shia activists in Bahrain, Kuwait, and Saudi Arabia attempted, however unsuccessfully, to use Twitter and Facebook strategically to bridge divides and unite in opposition to their respective regimes.[5] More recently, online campaigns condemning sectarian violence have emerged, especially in the aftermath of attacks on Shia mosques in Saudi Arabia and Kuwait in May and June 2015.[6]

While the spread of hate speech or countersectarian messages alone may appear relatively inconsequential in the face of mounting battlefield casualties and terrorist attacks, mainstream acceptance or rejection of intolerant, divisive rhetoric can have substantive consequences on the ground. Sectarian narratives—in diverse flavors and forms—have long been exploited by ruling families, foreign occupiers, local politicians, religious leaders, and extremist groups to garner support while discrediting and dividing would-be opponents.

Today is no exception. The degree to which sectarian language and ideologies resonate with Arabs across the region may have key geopolitical ramifications. For example, as the Sunni Gulf ruling families and state-sanctioned clerics beat war drums, they rallied their populations behind the intervention in Yemen by casting it as a sectarian battle between their fellow Sunnis and the Iran-backed Zaydi Shia Houthi rebels. Despite the complexities of the conflict, fixating on sectarian divisions rather than strategic motivations for fighting enabled them to shore up much-needed domestic support while casting those who objected as treasonous and pro-Iranian. The more readily citizens embrace sectarian narratives, the more easily rulers can consolidate power and weaken political opposition. The spread of sectarian rhetoric therefore plays a key role in the ongoing battle for regional dominance between Iran and the Sunni Arab States. In a different vein, when the Islamic State produces Hollywood-inspired videos peppered with anti-Shia violence and hate speech, long-standing but often latent religious differences are portrayed as elements of a divinely backed battle for dominance.[7] When sectarian language and ideologies are more broadly accepted, violent conflicts can become more deeply entrenched and extremist groups become better able to recruit and maintain followers.

Despite these consequences for regional and global stability and security, little is known about how sectarian and countersectarian narratives spread and fluctuate over time. A unique Twitter data set collected at New York University's Social Media and Political Participation lab—an assortment that includes almost 7 million Arabic tweets containing anti-Shia, anti-Sunni, and countersectarian keywords sent between early February and mid-August 2015—allows for analysis of the roles that violent events and social networks play in the spread of intolerant language online.[8]

Given the challenges of systematically measuring shifting sectarian attitudes—a highly sensitive topic—with survey data or other more traditional research methods, Twitter data provide an unprecedented real-time view of changing discourses over time. Furthermore, Twitter's architecture allows for analysis of individuals' connections to political elites, well-known clerics, vocal militants, extremist groups, and other citizens on the same platform, giving valuable, detailed insight into the structure of communication networks and the sources through which people receive information.

The data provide suggestive evidence that the online volume of sectarian and countersectarian rhetoric fluctuates dramatically in response to regional episodes of violence—particularly reacting to the Saudi-led intervention in Yemen, clashes between Shia militias and the Islamic State in Iraq, and the bombings of Shia mosques in the Gulf. Furthermore, Twitter users expressing diverse and often conflicting views frequently engage with one another and are not isolated in ideologically homogeneous echo chambers. Finally, the online sectarian narrative is driven by a diverse combination of Twitter users including prominent clerics, Shia militia leaders, Islamic State supporters, influential Saudi businessmen, popular media outlets, and average Arab users. These findings offer real-time insight into the manner in which events on the ground influence expressions of religious tolerance and intolerance in the online sphere, as well as the role that political, religious, and extremist actors play in driving this conversation.

The vocabulary of online sectarianism and countersectarianism

In the years following the escalation of the Syrian civil war, six main derogatory terms have been frequently used to disparage Shia Muslims online:

Rafidha (rejectionist), *Hizb al-Shaytan* (party of the devil), *Hizb al-Lat* (party of Lat), *Majus* (Magianism or Zoroastrianism), *Nusayri* (followers of Nusayr), and *Safawi* (Safavid).[9] *Rafidha* refers to Twelver Shias, the largest of the Shia sects, and implies that they have rejected "true" Islam as they allegedly do not recognize Abu Bakr, the first caliph, and his successors as having been legitimate rulers after the death of the Prophet Muhammad. For example, Salafi cleric Abdulaziz al-Tarifi tweeted to his approximately 800,000 followers in February, "Jews and Christians did not used to collude with the rafidha as they do today in this country and every country."[10]

Similarly, *Hizb al-Shaytan* and *Hizb al-Lat* are both used in reference to the group Hezbollah and its Shia followers. Lat alludes to the pre-Islamic Arabian goddess al-Lat, who was believed to be a daughter of God. This brands Hezbollah and its supporters as a group of polytheist non-believers. These terms were illustrated in a tweet sent from a now-suspended Islamic State account in March 2015: "Hezbollah, Hizb al-Lat, Hizb al-Shaytan, party of Zionists, party of nonbelievers, there is no peace between you and between true Muslims."[11]

Nusayri is a reference to Abu Shuayb Muhammad Ibn Nusayr, the founder of the Alawite offshoot of Shia Islam during the eighth century. It implies that the Alawite religion is not divinely inspired as it follows a man, rather than God. Although it is used in diverse contexts, this term often highlights the sectarian nature of the Syrian conflict and serves to disparage Alawites. As a Sunni Iraqi woman tweeted in early August, "#Assad_crimes: a Nusayri soldier in [Syrian President Bashar al-Assad's] army tortured a Muslim Syrian man and his wife and took off her hijab in front of her husband and beat and tortured her."[12]

Along these same lines, *Majus* is a derogatory term that references the pre-Islamic religion Zoroastrianism, implying that Shia Islam is nothing more than a deviant religion of the past. Illustrating the common use of this term in the Arab Twittersphere, a Sunni Bahraini man tweeted to his approximately 6,000 followers, "After Operation Decisive Storm, America gave Tikrit as a gift to the rafidha Majus Iran! America is the mother of crimes in our Arab world and the supporter of the Safawi Majus project."[13]

Finally, *Safawi*, which recalls the Safavid dynasty that ruled Persia from 1501 to 1736, is used to depict Shia ties to Iran. Sometimes the term is also used in the neologism *Sahiyyu-Safawi* (Zionist-Safavid) to suggest that there is a conspiracy between Israel and Iran against Sunni Muslims.

At the same time, several slurs have become more common for characterizing Sunni Muslims in sectarian discourse: *Wahhabi* (a follower of Abd al-

Wahhab), *takfiri* (a Sunni Muslim who accuses another Muslim of apostasy), *Nasabi* (those who hate the family of Muhammad), and *Ummawi* (Umayyad).[14] The term *Wahhabi* is directly affiliated with those who follow the teachings of Sunni Salafi Muhammad Ibn Abd al-Wahhab, the primary theologian who developed the Saudi brand of Sunni Islam. While the term is not exclusively used in a sectarian manner, it has been used in the context of the conflicts in Iraq, Syria, and Yemen to brand Sunnis as ideological proxies of Saudi Arabia. For example, the "Electronic Mahdi Army," a Twitter account of an Iraqi Shia militia group, tweeted, "Praise God the Wahhabis surrendered and embraced the Shia doctrine of the people of the house of God's messenger. We ask God to give guidance to all the Wahhabi Jews."[15] Similarly, the term *takfiri* is used as a sectarian slur to depict Sunnis as Muslims who declare other Muslims infidels.

The term *Nasabi* (and its plural, *Nawasib*) describes Sunnis as those who hate the family of Muhammad and are considered non-Muslims. As a member of the Shia-aligned Popular Mobilization Forces identified on Twitter as "Ali the Babylonian" tweeted in early August, "Oh Ali, extend the humiliation of the Nawasib!"[16]

Finally, the term *Ummawi* references the seventh- and eighth-century Umayyad Empire and is used to insult Sunnis as those who committed historical injustices against the Shia. For Sunnis and Shia alike, these derogatory terms elucidate long-standing historical tensions and serve to paint one another as blasphemous infidels.

Regarding countersectarian rhetoric, phrases that have been commonly used to decry sectarianism online include: "no to sectarianism," "I am Sunni, I am Shia," "Islamic unity," and "neither Shia nor Sunni." These expressions, often presented in the form of hashtags, have been tweeted across the Arab world and are particularly common in condemning violence. For example, these terms often appeared alongside the viral spread of the hashtag "#Before_you_blow_yourself_up," used to mock suicide bombers and call for national unity in the aftermath of the bombing of the Kuwaiti Shia mosque on 26 June 2015.[17] Along these lines, a Kuwaiti businessman tweeted at the time, "I am Sunni, I am Shia, I am Kuwaiti. Those who make distinctions between us are cowards."[18]

As these descriptions and examples of common sectarian and countersectarian jargon in the Arab Twittersphere suggest, such language is used by diverse Twitter users, discussing everything from sectarian foreign policy grievances to calls to violence and general intergroup relations. The proliferation of these terms in a wide variety of tweets expressing sectarian sentiments makes them useful tools for building a data set of sectarian and countersectarian tweets.

In particular, the dynamics of sectarian and countersectarian online rhetoric can be analyzed using over 160 million Arabic tweets collected through New York University's (NYU's) Social Media and Political Participation lab from 3 February to 17 August 2015. These tweets contained a broad set of Arabic keywords related to social and political issues as well as ongoing violence, including the terms described above. The collection was then filtered such that each tweet in the data set contained at least one derogatory sectarian reference or countersectarian keyword.[19] The terms *Wahhabi* and *takfiri* were removed from the set of filters as the tweets containing these terms alone included a wide variety of content—particularly condemnation of Islamists in Egypt—that was not relevant to sectarianism. This resulted in a data set of approximately 7 million tweets, the vast majority of which contain anti-Shia rhetoric.

Demographics of the Arab Twittersphere

Since the outbreak of the Arab Spring protests, social media use among Arabs has grown exponentially, with the proportion of Arabic language tweets and tweets coming from the Middle East rising dramatically between 2011 and 2015.[20] Furthermore, the use of online social networks for political discussion has become increasingly common.

While social media users certainly do not form a representative sample of the Arab population, their demographic make-up has become progressively more diverse in recent years. The percentage of Arab social media users who report discussing politics, community issues, or religion online ranges from 60 to 81 percent across the region.[21] According to the 2014 Arab Social Media Report, a recurring series produced by the Mohammed Bin Rashid School of Government's Governance and Innovation Program that highlights and analyzes usage trends of online social networking across the Arab region, Kuwait has the highest Twitter penetration—or percentage of Twitter users in its overall population—in the Arab world, followed by Saudi Arabia, the United Arab Emirates, Qatar, and Bahrain. While second place in terms of penetration, Saudi Arabia boasts the largest total number of Twitter users in the region and is home to 40 percent of all active Twitter users in the Arab world. Of the Arab Twitter users 37 percent are female, and increasingly large percentages of social media users are now over thirty years old, although two-thirds of the Facebook-using population still fall in the fifteen to twenty-nine age bracket.[22]

These regional disparities in levels of Twitter popularity are clearly reflected in both the geolocation and location descriptions that Twitter users in the data set list on their profiles (see Figure 7.1). The geolocated tweets only make up a small sample of Twitter data, as it is relatively uncommon for users to enable geolocation services, but the top locations stated on the profiles of Twitter users in the data set follow a similar pattern. Of the collection of approximately 7 million tweets containing anti-Shia, anti-Sunni, or counter-sectarian rhetoric, the vast majority are from the Gulf and are especially concentrated in Saudi Arabia. For those tweeting anti-Shia content, Saudi Arabia, Kuwait, and "land of God" (a phrase often used by pro–Islamic State accounts) are the most commonly listed locations. For those tweeting anti-Sunni terms, the top locations are Iraq, Saudi Arabia, and Kuwait. Finally, countersectarian rhetoric was most frequently tweeted from Kuwait, Saudi Arabia, and Bahrain.

The dominance of Saudi Arabia is likely a reflection of the fact that a substantial percentage of active Arab Twitter users are Saudi. Additionally, Saudi Arabia has a long history of sectarian tensions and is home to many Salafi clerics who are known to tweet inflammatory sectarian rhetoric. It is therefore unsurprising that sectarian tweets might be more common in Saudi Arabia than in other parts of the region, particularly given the high levels of media coverage of the Saudi-led intervention in Yemen in this period.

Violent events and the spread of sectarian rhetoric online

Sectarian violence—whether it be perpetrated in war-torn Iraq, Syria, or Yemen, or shattering the usual calm of Kuwait or Saudi Arabia—appears to provoke a dramatic response online. Graphic videos and images circulate rapidly on Twitter, often accompanied by dehumanizing and divisive rhetoric. Emotions run high as conflicts are portrayed as existential battles between religious groups, heightening perceived threats and placing blame for atrocities committed by small minorities on all co-religionists. Visualizing fluctuations in anti-Shia, anti-Sunni, and countersectarian tweet volume over time can provide insight into the manner in which events on the ground influence expressions of religious tolerance and intolerance in the online sphere. This reinforces recent findings suggesting that sectarian violence both drives intolerance and can easily be exploited by elites to achieve sectarian aims.[23]

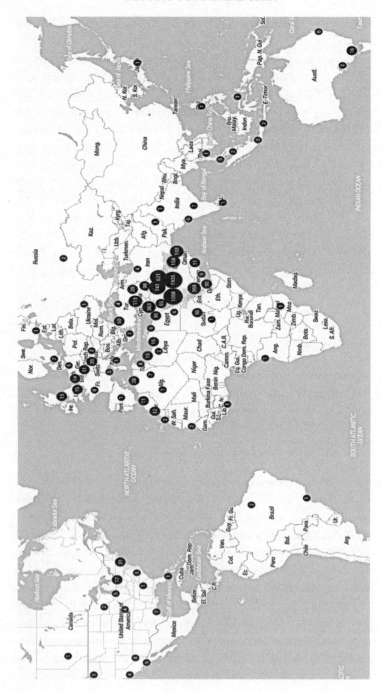

Figure 7.1: Geolocated Sectarian and Countersectarian Arabic Tweets

Anti-Shia spikes

The most dramatic spike in tweets containing anti-Shia terms in the period under study occurred following the first air strikes in Yemen in late March, as the Saudis launched Operation Decisive Storm against the Iran-backed Houthi rebels (see Figure 7.2).[24] While sectarian clashes in Iraq and Syria, the release of a viral Islamic State video showing the Camp Speicher massacre of Shia Iraqi Air Force cadets, and Shia mosque bombings in Kuwait, Saudi Arabia, and Yemen also produced small spikes, the Yemen intervention was by far the most influential event driving anti-Shia rhetoric on social media in this period. Further demonstrating the influence of Operation Decisive Storm on the volume of anti-Shia tweets, the most commonly used Arabic hashtags in tweets containing anti-Shia keywords between February and August 2015 included: #SaudiArabia, #DecisiveStorm, #Yemen, #Iran, and #Houthis. For a sense of scale, #SaudiArabia was tweeted 1.4 million times, and the other hashtags appeared over 500,000 times each.

As fighter jets from Bahrain, Egypt, Jordan, Kuwait, Morocco, Qatar, Sudan, and the United Arab Emirates joined the Saudi-led operation in Yemen, a kind of pan-Sunni zeal swept through the region. Portraying opposition to the military intervention as a treasonous threat to national unity, many Sunni Arab leaders framed the conflict in starkly sectarian terms, as a war against all Shia connected to Iran's "Safavid" empire, referring to one of the most powerful ruling dynasties of Persia that established Shia Islam as the state religion.[25] Houthi fighters in Yemen who belong to the Zaydi offshoot of Shia Islam may have little in common with the Alawite Shia in Syria or the Shia populations of Gulf countries that adhere to the most common Twelver sect of Islam. However, Gulf rulers and the Saudi state media in particular have continually fixated on the common thread of Shia Islam that loosely ties these groups to one another—as well as to Iran. By ignoring other local identities and strategic motivations that drive actions on the ground, rulers have worked to drum up support for the intervention in Yemen and to shore up national unity.[26]

In the Gulf, support and opposition to the intervention developed along religious lines, and criticism of the intervention was punished harshly. In Saudi Arabia, Shia-led protests in the Eastern Province against military involvement in Yemen were crushed by security forces sent to confront "terrorist elements," according to the Saudi Press Agency.[27] While Kuwait's parliament voted overwhelmingly to join the air strikes, the nine lawmakers who opposed participation were all Shia.[28] After condemning the intervention on

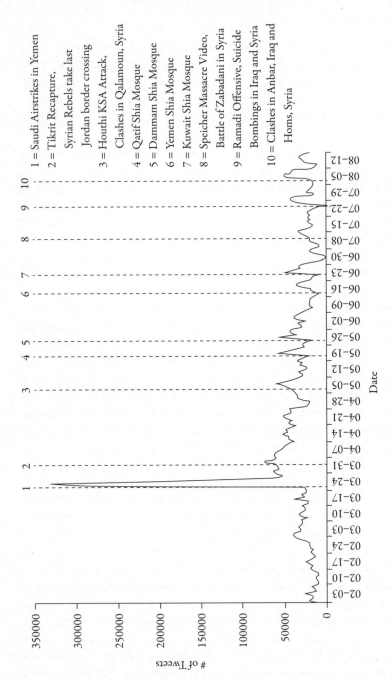

Figure 7.2: Daily Volume of Tweets Containin Anti-Shia Rhetoric

1 = Saudi Airstrikes in Yemen

2 = Tikrit Recapture,
    Syrian Rebels take last
    Jordan border crossing

3 = Houthi KSA Attack,
    Clashes in Qalamoun, Syria

4 = Qatif Shia Mosque

5 = Dammam Shia Mosque

6 = Yemen Shia Mosque

7 = Kuwait Shia Mosque

8 = Speicher Massacre Video,
    Battle of Zabadani in Syria

9 = Ramadi Offensive, Suicide
    Bombings in Iraq and Syria

10 = Clashes in Anbar, Iraq and
     Homs, Syria

his Twitter account, Khaled al-Shatti, a prominent Kuwaiti lawyer and former member of parliament, was arrested on charges of challenging the emir, demoralizing Kuwaiti soldiers, offending the Kingdom of Saudi Arabia, and threatening Saudi relations with Kuwait.[29] Similarly, in Bahrain, Shia activists were arrested for criticizing participation in Operation Decisive Storm, including prominent opposition leader and human rights activist Nabeel Rajab who was charged with spreading "false news and malicious rumors," as reported by the Arabic Network for Human Rights Information, after tweeting critically about Bahrain's involvement and sharing graphic photos of a burnt corpse and a child buried under rubble.[30]

Although the Saudi government and its coalition partners officially justified the intervention as a means of fighting for "legitimacy," "stability," "unity," and "security" in Yemen,[31] and preventing a Houthi incursion into Saudi Arabia, from the first days of the conflict the Saudi religious establishment portrayed the intervention in vitriolic sectarian terms. On 26 March, the kingdom's highest religious authority authorized the military operation as a war to defend religion. The Council of Senior Religious Scholars issued a fatwa, pronouncing any soldiers killed in the fighting martyrs, stating, "One of the greatest ways to draw closer to God almighty is to defend the sanctity of religion and Muslims."[32] Taking to the Twittersphere, clerics did not shy away from spewing rancorous rhetoric depicting the conflict in Yemen as a religious holy war. This was illustrated by a series of tweets sent by Saudi Sheikh Naser al-Omar to his 1.8 million Twitter followers: "It is the responsibility of every Muslim to take part in the Islamic world's battle to defeat the Safawis and their sins, and to prevent their corruption on earth."[33] In a video posted on his Twitter account in the same period, he told dozens of Saudi men seated in a mosque that their "brothers" in Afghanistan, Iraq, Syria, and Yemen were fighting a jihad, or holy war, against the "Safawis."[34] Similarly, immediately following the intervention, Saudi cleric Abdulaziz Toufayfe derided the Shia tradition of visiting family burial sites, calling the Shia "people of idols, worshippers of graves" in a message that was retweeted over 12,000 times by 8 April 2015.[35]

In this charged climate, with both Sunni leaders and the clerical establishment endorsing hostile sectarian narratives, the volume of anti-Shia tweets skyrocketed. This rise in anti-Shia rhetoric mixed with wartime Saudi nationalism stoked fears among the region's Shia minority. In Saudi Arabia's Eastern Province, Shia residents became concerned that the intervention in Yemen had heightened suspicion of the kingdom's Shia population and put increased pressure on King Salman to deal more harshly with future Shia unrest.[36]

Anti-Sunni spikes

Anti-Sunni tweets are significantly less common than those containing anti-Shia rhetoric in this data set (see Figure 7.3). This is partly driven by the fact that the only keywords used to gather these tweets were *Nasabi*, *Nawasib* (those who hate the family of Muhammad, singular and plural), and *Ummawi* (Umayyad), in order to avoid drawing in large numbers of irrelevant and non-sectarian tweets. Additionally, anti-Sunni tweets are much more likely to come from Twitter accounts with relatively few followers—including those of Shia militia groups and their supporters—which simply do not have the audience devoted to clerics, Islamic State accounts, and other influential users that drive anti-Shia rhetoric. Moreover, given the relatively disadvantaged and often precarious minority status that the Shia face across the region, it is unsurprising that anti-Sunni rhetoric is less common.

In the six-month period under study, several spikes in the quantity of tweets containing anti-Sunni terms also appear to correspond to violent events on the ground, despite the relatively low volume of messages. While ongoing violence in Syria contributes to these fluctuations, many of the tweets sent in these periods of elevated anti-Sunni tweet volume reference sectarian violence in Iraq. This may be influenced by the much larger Shia population in Iraq relative to Syria, as well as the fact that fighting against the Islamic State in Iraq—particularly the role of Shia militias backed by the Iraqi government and Iran—received a great deal of media attention in this period.

Increases in the volume of anti-Sunni hate speech on Twitter appear to be driven by a combination of pan-Shia pride and fear. On the one hand, pan-Shia nationalism, in which Shia populations in the Gulf states feel emboldened by the political ascendance of Iraqi Shia and the success of Shia militias in fighting the Islamic State, is on the rise. Yet on the other hand, Shia in Sunni-dominated Gulf states feel threatened by and fear reprisals for the violence perpetrated by Shia across the region, whether it be in Iraq, Syria, or Yemen.

The first two spikes in the number of tweets occurred during the intensification of the Tikrit offensive led by the Iraqi army and Shia militias against the Islamic State in mid-March and their recapture of Tikrit in late March.[37] The Tikrit offensive was seen as revenge for the Islamic State's massacre of 1,700 Shia soldiers at Camp Speicher in June 2014. Up to 30,000 pro-Iraqi government forces participated in the offensive, the majority of which belonged to Shia militia groups under the umbrella of the Popular Mobilization Forces.[38] Amid reports of atrocities carried out by Shia militia groups against Sunni civilians, it is unsurprising that the social media accounts of Shia militia

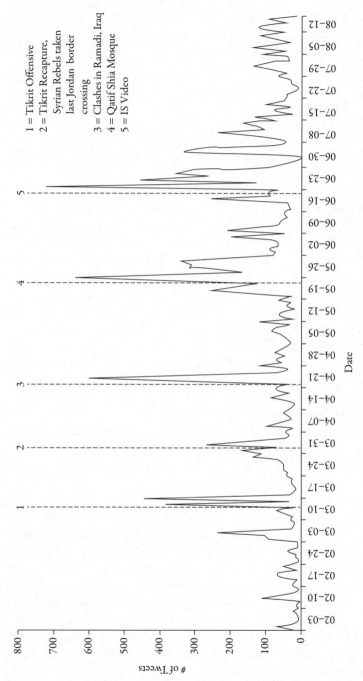

Figure 7.3: Daily Volume of Tweets Containing Anti-Sunni Rhetoric

groups were often peppered with violent sectarian rhetoric in this period.[39] Along these lines, an account affiliated with Ahul Bayt, a Shia Iraqi satellite channel, tweeted immediately following the build-up to the Tikrit offensive, "Oh Shia of Iraq, you defeated the Nawasib in Tikrit, so the Nawasib will take revenge on your brothers in Bahrain! Grant them victory over their enemies! #Free Tikrit."[40] While most of the tweets appeared to focus on the recapturing of Tikrit by Iraqi government forces and Shia militias, the second spike also coincided with the predominantly Sunni Syrian rebels' capture of a key Jordanian border crossing from Bashar al-Assad's armed forces and Iran-backed Hezbollah fighters.[41]

The third large fluctuation followed clashes between the Islamic State and Shia militias in Ramadi, Iraq, in late April;[42] and the fourth increase occurred in the aftermath of the Islamic State's attack on a Shia mosque in Qatif in the Eastern Province of Saudi Arabia in late May. Offline, hostile anti-Sunni language has also played a key role in sectarian fighting. For example, following the Islamic State's attack in Qatif, Shia militias in Iraq dubbed their campaign to take back Ramadi from the group's forces *Labbaik Ya Husayn* (Here I am, O Husayn).[43] Given that the mosque attack was carried out on the birthday of Imam Husayn—the martyred grandson of the Prophet Muhammad who is especially honored by Shias and whose death is commemorated annually through Ashura rituals—this name is particularly significant. Because hardline Salafists and the Saudi Wahhabi brand of Islam vehemently oppose Shia veneration of Husayn, the campaign's name was clearly designed as a sectarian provocation in response to the mosque bombing.

The final spike occurred following the release of a particularly gruesome Islamic State video, showing its fighters incinerating, drowning, and blowing up men—assumed to be Iraqi Shia—accused of helping the United States and its allies bomb Islamic State bases in Iraq and Syria.[44]

The most commonly used hashtags in the anti-Sunni tweets in this time period—#Kufar (non-believers), #Iraq, #Daesh (a derogatory term for the Islamic State), #Wahhabi, #Salafi, and #Popular Mobilization—also suggest the strong influence that opposition to the Islamic State had on these narratives. For example, numerous anti-Sunni tweets in this data set contain rhetoric similar to a tweet sent from a Shia militia's account proclaiming, "Oh Allah, grant victory to the Popular Mobilization Forces and our security forces in the fight against the Wahhabi Nasabi Daesh, God damn them."[45] These hashtags were tweeted between 95 and 270 times in the data set, reflecting the much smaller volume of tweets containing anti-Sunni rhetoric relative to anti-Shia rhetoric.

Countersectarian rhetoric

Like anti-Sunni and anti-Shia sectarian rhetoric, countersectarian rhetoric in this period also appears to correspond to violent events on the ground (see Figure 7.4). In particular, bombings of Shia mosques carried out by the Islamic State in the Eastern Province of Saudi Arabia, Yemen, and Kuwait were each met with online calls to stop sectarian violence and rhetoric as well as anger at the perpetrators of these attacks.

The first relatively modest spike occurred following a suicide bombing during Friday prayers on 22 May 2015, at the Shia Imam Ali Ibn Abi Talib mosque in the village of Qudeih in the Eastern Province.[46] A week later, the province was again wracked by violence when a car bomb went off at a Shia mosque in Dammam, and this saw a second fluctuation in tweet volume.[47] Following the attacks, the Saudi government pledged cross-sectarian national unity and offered compensation to Shia communities impacted by the attacks.[48] Though the gesture did little to assuage Saudi Shia fears of persecution in an increasingly charged sectarian climate, condemnations of the attacks and calls for an end to sectarianism were on the rise in the immediate aftermath of the violent events.

The third, more modest spike in tweets containing countersectarian rhetoric came following a series of Shia mosque bombings in Yemen carried out by the Islamic State that killed over 142 people.[49] The Islamic State's Yemen branch claimed responsibility for the attack online, calling Houthi rebels agents of Iran and stating that "infidel Houthis should know that the soldiers of the Islamic State will not rest until they eradicate them ... and cut off the arm of the Safawi plan in Yemen."[50] In response to these gory attacks, calls for Islamic unity and condemnations of violence again appeared on Twitter.

The most dramatic increase in the volume of countersectarian tweets occurred in the aftermath of the Islamic State attack on the Imam Sadiq Mosque in Kuwait—one of the largest Shia houses of worship in the country—on 26 June 2015.[51] Following the attack, Kuwait's ruler Sheikh Sabah al-Ahmad Al Sabah made a personal visit to the mosque. State television footage and photos on social media showed the emir navigating through large crowds in front of the mosque to enter the building and survey the damage. Government ministers, including Prime Minister Sheikh Jaber al-Mubarak Al Sabah, also made appearances to visit the wounded. Following the attack, the government suspended the Al Watan TV station, known for broadcasting anti-Shia rhetoric.[52] While sectarian tensions certainly persist, Shia citizens are relatively well integrated into the Kuwaiti state—especially compared to

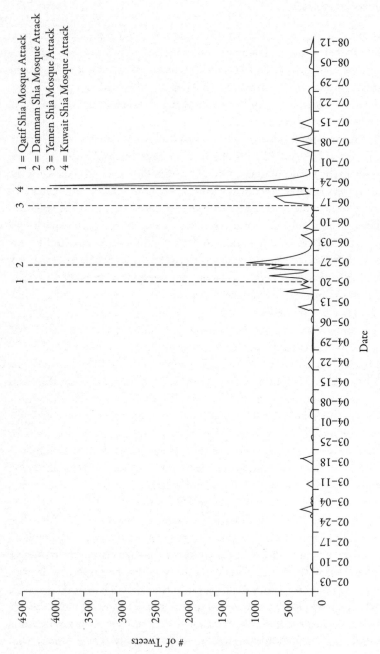

Figure 7.4: Daily Volume of Tweets Containing Countersectarian Rhetoric

Shia populations in Bahrain and Saudi Arabia. Kuwaiti Shia are given the rights of citizens: they are permitted to practice their religion, vote and run in elections, hold office, and use their own legal codes and traditions in personal status laws.[53] Against this backdrop, it is unsurprising that an attack on a Shia mosque in Kuwait would produce a particularly dramatic outcry and condemnations of sectarian rhetoric and violence.

Social networks and the dynamics of sectarian communication

In addition to facilitating the dynamic study of online sectarian rhetoric in response to events on the ground, Twitter's network structures provide insight into the mechanisms by which sectarian and countersectarian rhetoric is spread in the Arab Twittersphere. In particular, retweet networks offer detailed information regarding the users that drive sectarian conversations online, as well as the manner in which diverse actors communicate. When people tweet, they may get retweeted by other Twitter users, repeating the message for their followers to view. Each retweet is a one-way flow of information that links the first person to each person who retweets or forwards the original tweet to his or her own followers, thereby creating a retweet network. These networks (visualized in Figures 7.5, 7.6, and 7.7 below) demonstrate both the process by which diverse, influential Twitter users impact the spread of sectarian and countersectarian rhetoric, as well as the manner in which users espousing anti-Shia, anti-Sunni, and countersectarian messages engage with one another online.

The anti-Shia retweet network in Figure 7.5 shows Twitter users represented by dots of varying sizes, or nodes, and linked by thin gray lines, or edges, which represent unidirectional information flows in the form of retweets.[54] Node size is determined by the number of times a given user is retweeted. Users in the network who are more closely connected to one another pull closer to each other, while less connected users drift further apart due to the attraction of more strongly connected users.[55] Clusters of influential users and the people who are closely connected to them are surrounded by brackets and labeled in Figure 7.5.

As the anti-Shia retweet network diagram indicates, a sizable portion of the network is composed of retweets of messages sent by accounts affiliated with or supporting the Islamic State. While the large hub of the network consisting of retweets of pro-Islamic State accounts is extremely densely connected, other accounts retweeting the organization are diffused throughout the network.

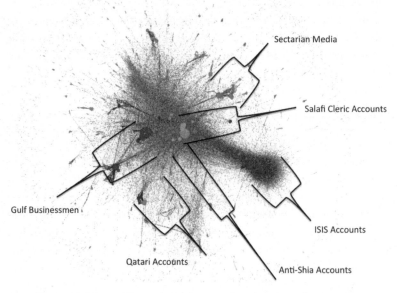

Figure 7.5: Twitter Network Connections Based on Anti-Shia Retweets

This densely connected cluster and wide reach throughout the network may be a reflection of the organization's expertly choreographed social media strategy. The Islamic State employs a well-documented online tactic of shock and gore, in which it produces Hollywood-quality videos and images detailing the brutal killings of hostages, terror attacks, and other violent events, which are then disseminated by official Islamic State social media users; by a large dedicated network of Islamic State "fanboys," as the authors of one report described them; and by regular Twitter users.[56] The group has also been known to reach large global audiences by hijacking trending hashtags and otherwise creatively taking advantage of the structure of social media platforms. The viral nature of this communication is reflected by the dense yet far-reaching structure of the Islamic State's anti-Shia retweets, as well as the high rates of retweets enjoyed by its accounts. On the one hand, communication generated by these accounts forms a tight-knit community in which like-minded users retweet one another's content; on the other hand, pro-Islamic State users also engage with and respond to content produced by diverse sources, from clerics to prominent Saudi businessmen and sectarian media outlets.

As the central cluster of Salafi Clerics in the network diagram suggests, a few Salafi clerics tweeted messages containing anti-Shia rhetoric, which were then retweeted in large numbers, forming the largest core of the network. In particular, the clerics with the highest rates of retweets in this network were Mohammed al-Arefe, Naser al-Omar, Saud al-Shureem, and Abdulaziz al-Tarifi. At the time these data were collected, these clerics had cultivated wide followings on Twitter with 12.7 million, 1.8 million, 1.25 million, and 800,000 followers, respectively.[57]

Sectarian media outlets, explicitly anti-Shia Twitter accounts, and influential Gulf Twitter accounts also play a key role in spreading anti-Shia rhetoric throughout the network. Sectarian media outlets, including the vehemently anti-Shia Wesal satellite network with almost 600,000 followers and Safa TV with approximately 340,000 followers, also produce widely retweeted anti-Shia content.[58] In addition, several Gulf businessmen play a key role in driving the sectarian narrative. Saudi businessman and academic Khalid al-Saud with 240,000 followers,[59] Saudi businessman Khaled al-Alkami with over 200,000 followers,[60] and Dubai-based businessman Bandar bin Mohammed al-Rajhi with over 60,000 followers are displayed in the "Gulf Businessmen" cluster of the retweet graph.[61] A few Twitter accounts devoted to anti-Shia content, in the "Anti-Shia Accounts" cluster, also have fairly high rates of retweets. These include accounts such as "Savifi Risks" and "Risks Iran," as well as an account called "Jaysh al-Sunna" (Sunni Army), which have approximately 20,000–90,000 followers and share frequent anti-Shia news updates and sectarian rhetoric.[62] Finally, the influence of a Qatari nationalist Twitter account with over 30,000 followers can be seen in the small yellow portion of the network.[63]

A visualization of the anti-Sunni retweet network in Figure 7.6 provides important insight into the different, and sometimes conflicting, manner in which derogatory anti-Sunni rhetoric is used in the Arab Twittersphere.

Unlike the anti-Shia retweet network, well-known elite actors whose accounts have hundreds of thousands of followers are not driving anti-Sunni rhetoric. The 'Anti-Sunni Tweets' cluster in the center of the network graph contains tweets expressing anti-Sunni sentiments sent by a variety of relatively small accounts, primarily based in Iraq. Many of these accounts are affiliated with Shia militia groups or contain pro-Shia militia identifiers in their Twitter biographies. An example of an anti-Sunni tweet in the blue cluster came from the account "Imam al-Mahdi," with over 6,000 followers, in mid-July: "#Victory_from_God: Conquering is near, the banner of #Imam_al-Mahdi is raised in the center of Fallujah despite the impure squalor of the Nawasib of the world."[64]

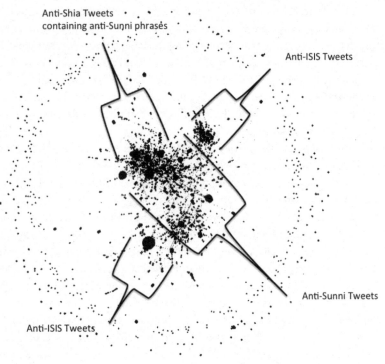

Anti-Shia Tweets
containing anti-Sunni phrases

Anti-ISIS Tweets

Anti-Sunni Tweets

Anti-ISIS Tweets

Figure 7.6: Twitter Network Connections Based on Anti-Sunni Retweets

As the two "Anti-Isis Tweets" clusters in the network graph show, some of the most retweeted messages containing anti-Sunni rhetoric are directed at the Islamic State. For example, a Baghdad-based pro-Shia militia account with almost 45,000 followers dedicated to identifying and suspending Islamic State Twitter accounts tweeted in the aftermath of the Qatif mosque bombing, "Stop Daesh Nasabi account, nonbelievers in the Shia God. Fight Daesh with all the power you have, oh Shia of Ali."[65] Similar types of anti-Islamic State messages that contain anti-Sunni rhetoric were sent by accounts represented by the smaller red dots, including the following tweet sent by the Bahrain-based account "hassansharif50" in mid-August: "You are Sunni, you are Wahhabi Nasabi, you are the son of one of the Jewish and American dogs, oh Nawasib, oh Dawash [the plural term for Daesh]."[66]

In addition to this anti-Sunni rhetoric, the data set of tweets containing anti-Sunni slurs also drew in tweets from users who objected to the use of anti-Sunni rhetoric. Depicted in the "Anti-Shia Tweets" cluster on the top left of the network graph, in general, these users expressed anti-Shia sentiments. For example, a Kuwaiti lawyer with over 12,000 followers tweeted, "To any Sunni subjected to any insult accusing him of being a takfiri, Nasabi, Wahhabi, Daeshi by any scum on Twitter, bring up the issue immediately!"[67] Articulating more explicitly anti-Shia sentiments, a Gulf-based user who calls himself Abo-Ahmed tweeted in early June, "The mother of one of the elements of the criminal #Halsh [a derogatory term for Hezbollah] boasts that her son killed seventeen Sunni Syria Nawasib. Shoot yourselves in the heart."[68] Similarly, Sheikh Adnan Aroor, a Sunni cleric from Hama in Syria, tweeted in May, "The behavior of the rafidha in #Iraq, #Syria, and #Yemen is the murder of the innocent, rape of women, and theft of property. It's the exact definition of Nasabi, a word they own and use in their writing."[69]

The majority of tweets from influential users in the countersectarian network are sent by relatively small accounts, similar to the anti-Sunni network in Figure 7.6. The light-colored nodes in Figure 7.7 represent users that express explicitly countersectarian sentiments. As the overlap between the light and dark clusters suggests, Sunni Twitter users respond and engage in conversation with users who tweet anti-Sunni rhetoric.

Many of the tweets driving the countersectarian conversation in this period were in fact messages that condemned promoting tolerance as Shia propa-

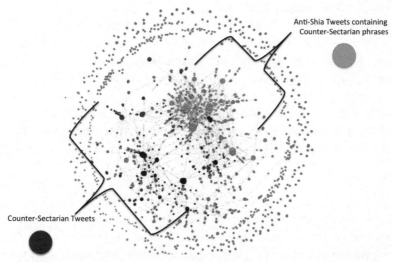

Figure 7.7: Twitter Network Connections Based on Countersectarian Retweets

ganda. Influential users expressing these views are represented by light colored dots. For example, an Iraq-based account known as "Liberal Parody Account" tweeted in late May to its 6,000 followers in the aftermath of the Saudi mosque bombings, "Iraq's Shia army #burns_Sunni_youth and tortures a Sunni sheikh and exposes Sunni corpses, and then the liberal comes and says 'no to sectarianism.'"[70] Another influential account, using the pseudonym "Abdullah al-Salafi," tweeted in early June to its 46,000 followers, "The rafidha in the Eastern Province raise banners with pictures of Hezbollah criminals and demand their release?! Then they say no to sectarianism!!"[71] Along these lines, another Saudi Twitter user, known as "Political Critic," tweeted in the same time period, "They burn and kill Sunnis in cold blood and then say 'no to sectarianism' ... tragedy. The systematic policy of the Majus #Shia_mobilization_burns_Saudi_Arabia."[72] As the countersectarian retweet network depicts, light-colored anti-Shia Twitter users are tightly clustered around these influential users, but they also engage directly with dark-colored users tweeting countersectarian content.

The majority of tweets expressing countersectarian sentiments were sent by Gulf Twitter users in the aftermath of the Kuwait mosque bombing on 26 June 2015 (as reflected in Figure 7.4). For example, one of the countersectarian users with a relatively high rate of retweets was Wafaa Ahmed, an Emirati academic, who wrote, "They blew up a Shia mosque to sow discord. But do you know where they mourn? In the Grand Mosque [a Sunni mosque]. #No_to_Sectarianism #With_Kuwait_Against_Terrorism."[73] Her tweet referenced a gathering of hundreds of Shia and Sunni Muslims who prayed for national unity at Kuwait's Grand Mosque a week after the attack.[74] Other users driving the spread of countersectarian rhetoric in this data set used similar language, such as a tweet sent by an account known as "Cinderella Kuwait" with over 6,000 followers who stated on the day of the mosque attack, "No to sectarianism, no to killing Muslims, there is no God but God, Muhammad is God's Messenger. We refuse to kill Shia or Sunni Muslims, retweet, retweet O nation of Muhammad."[75]

Conclusions

Four years after the outbreak of the Syrian civil war, as Shia militias confront the Islamic State in Iraq and Syria, the Sunni Arab states remain embroiled in the conflict in Yemen, and anti-Shia terrorist attacks have wracked the normally calm Gulf states, little is known about the extent to which these violent sectarian events systematically impact attitudes throughout the region. In primarily non-democratic Arab societies in which ruling families and religious leaders have often used sectarian narratives to weaken their political opponents and potential challengers, rising sectarian tensions can have significant consequences for authoritarian durability, political reform, and support for radical ideologies.

The data set of 7 million tweets provides suggestive evidence that the online volume of sectarian rhetoric increases sharply in response to violent events on the ground—particularly in reaction to the Saudi-led intervention in Yemen, clashes between Shia militias and the Islamic State in Iraq, and the bombings of Shia mosques in the Gulf. While these findings may seem to paint a bleak picture of the state of sectarian antagonisms in the Arab world today, the fact that levels of anti-Shia and anti-Sunni hate speech—at least in the short term—appear to fluctuate rapidly and generally return to equilibrium in the aftermath of violent events suggests that upticks in sectarian antagonisms may be short-lived.

Additionally, the data indicate that the online sectarian narrative is driven by a diverse combination of Twitter users, including prominent clerics, Shia militia leaders, Islamic State supporters, influential Saudi businessmen, popular media outlets, and average Arab users. The overlap between content disseminated by the Islamic State and its sympathizers and the sectarian vitriol spewed by influential clerics, business leaders, and Gulf media commentators is particularly troubling. When hate speech moves from the realm of terrorists and extremists to state and socially sanctioned actors, sectarian narratives take on even more power, breeding intolerance and further alienating marginalized populations across the region.

Despite this, while prominent actors may accelerate the spread of sectarian rhetoric, they can also use their online (and offline) influence to mitigate its effects. Although social media often amplify the most polarizing voices, they can also provide influential leaders with a valuable means of cross-sectarian communication. These opportunities are highlighted by the finding that Twitter users espousing diverse and frequently clashing messages often engage with one another and are not isolated in ideologically homogeneous echo chambers. Although countersectarian messages are sometimes seen as pro-Shia propaganda, recognizing the limitations of these narratives may provide new inspiration and insight for activists pursing Sunni-Shia cooperation across the region.

Recent research suggests that influential actors or institutions in the Gulf have recognized the power of these online political communication networks and are using automated bots, cyborgs, or professional trolls to spread sectarian rhetoric and other content on Twitter.[76] While simple bot detection methods provide little evidence of widespread bot activity in this particular data set, future studies should systematically investigate not only the role of everyday citizens, media outlets, and well-known state and non-state actors in producing sectarian content, but also the use of automated Twitter campaigns that may be deliberately designed to exacerbate sectarian tensions in the online sphere.

While social media data alone do not completely capture the state of sectarian tensions in the Arab world, they nonetheless paint a detailed empirical picture of the manner in which sectarian and countersectarian narratives gain short-term traction, as well as the actors that contribute to the spread of hate speech and tolerant dialogue across the region. By providing a real-time measure of shifting sectarian rhetoric in the Arab world, Twitter data offer unique insight into one of the most destabilizing sources of conflict and violent extremism facing the world today.

Anti-Sunni	Translation
ناصبي	Nasabi
نواصب	Nuwasib
الأموى	Umayyad

Anti-Shia	Translation
الرافضة	Rejectionist
الروافض	Rejectionists
حزب الشيطان	Party of the Devil
حزب اللات	Party of Laat
مجوس	Majous
نصيرية	Followers of Nusayr
صفوى	Safavid

Countersectarian	Translation
وحدة وطني	National Unity
انا سني انا شيعي	I'm Sunni, I'm Shia
وحدة اسلامية	Islamic Unity
لا سنية لا شيعية	Not Sunni, Not Shia
لا للطائفية	No to Sectarianism

8

THE POLITICAL ECONOMY OF SECTARIANISM

HOW GULF REGIMES EXPLOIT IDENTITY POLITICS AS A SURVIVAL STRATEGY

Justin Gengler

In the first days of 2016, authorities in Saudi Arabia unexpectedly and unceremoniously put to death dissident Shii cleric Shaykh Nimr Baqir al-Nimr, a perennial anti-government firebrand and rhetorical leader of Arab Spring protests in the kingdom's Shia-dominated Eastern Province. Executed alongside forty-six other individuals convicted mainly of association with al-Qaeda and its affiliates, al-Nimr was lumped together as just another "terrorist" threatening the nation's stability and security.[1] The public response was swift and predictable. While Western missions protested at the political nature of the charges against al-Nimr—which included "disobeying the ruler," "inciting sectarian strife," and "encouraging, leading, and participating in demonstrations"[2]—the move was cheered by many ordinary Saudi Sunnis, for whom the cleric's calls for greater Shia recognition and empowerment represented at once religious and political heresy. Further afield, the execution sparked popular protests in Iraq, in Bahrain, and in Iran, where demonstrators overran Saudi Arabia's consulate in Mashhad and set fire to its embassy in Tehran. The attacks prompted a formal severing of diplomatic ties between the two regional rivals, with the Iranian Supreme Leader Ayatollah Ali Khamenei warning that Saudi Arabia would face "divine revenge" for its killing of the "oppressed scholar" and "martyr."[3]

Yet, behind this latest outward manifestation of sectarian-based conflict between citizens and governments of the Middle East, most Gulf observers were quick to identify a more mundane cause. A week before al-Nimr's execution, Saudi Arabia had announced a 40 percent increase in the price of vehicle fuel as well as sweeping cuts to subsidies for electricity, water, and other goods on the back of an expected $98 billion budget shortfall (equal to 60 percent of projected state revenues) for 2016.[4] Amid depressed oil prices and expectations of a weak market for years to come, the Saudi state, like other members of the Gulf Cooperation Council (GCC), can no longer afford to underwrite the onerous social and economic benefits provided for decades to citizens, and faces the uphill battle of selling unwelcome and painful economic reforms without offering corresponding concessions in the political realm.[5] The surprise execution of Nimr al-Nimr, then, and the resulting escalation in domestic and regional tension were seen as affording a well-timed distraction from Saudi Arabia's new fiscal reality, and the dubious policies—including a costly, disastrous war in Yemen—that helped usher it in. It was, in the words of one commentator, "red meat to the sectarian radicals."[6]

Such is but one case in a larger pattern of political instrumentation of sectarian and other group divisions that has become a defining feature of the Middle East and to a lesser extent North Africa since the beginning of the Arab uprisings.[7] As non-democratic regimes have come under pressure for reform or wholesale abdication, rulers have hit back most often by positioning themselves as the defenders of a core group of (usually co-ethnic) constituents under ostensible threat from foreign actors or the illiberal demands of fellow citizens. The force of these appeals has been bolstered by a heightened sense of insecurity among Middle East publics in the light of widespread civil war and disorder, the increased capabilities and reach of terrorist organizations, shifting geopolitical alliances, concerns over Iran's nuclear program, and perceptions of American military and diplomatic withdrawal from the region. The result is that a substantial proportion of citizens who might agree in principle with the need for change are expected to choose nonetheless to abstain from opposition, or indeed even to orient *against* the opposition, for uncertainty over the eventual outcome of popular mobilization. In short, challenged rulers can capitalize on the fears of more risk-averse individuals and members of sectarian, ethnic, or other groups whose preferential political or economic status would likely be overturned in the event of revolution or fundamental reform.

This strategy of autocratic self-preservation, sometimes likened to "protection-racket politics," is not limited to the post-2011 period, nor again is it specific to the Arab world.[8] But the seeming ubiquity and success of its use in thwarting opposition movements in this context has begotten something of a conventional wisdom: that fear-mongering and timely activation of sectarian and other latent social divisions offers beleaguered Arab governments a critical pressure relief valve that enhances authoritarian durability. And, as in the case of al-Nimr's execution, such an observation may appear to find strong anecdotal support in current events. However, until now, the actual individual-level causal story underpinning this interpretation has not been interrogated empirically. Is it in fact true, in other words, that Arab citizens who prioritize stability over other aims tend to be more supportive of incumbent regimes as guarantors of the status quo? If so, does such a relationship hold universally, or only for some categories of citizens or countries? Moreover, how does the prioritization of stability mediate the normal relationship between the performance of and popular support for governments? Are status quo-oriented citizens more forgiving than others of poor economic and/or political performance, or are their expectations similar to those with different individual priorities?

This chapter investigates these and related questions using mostly original survey data collected in four Arab Gulf countries between 2013 and 2016 (see Appendix A). The diverse sample of cases includes societies that witnessed major political upheaval (Bahrain), limited protests (Kuwait and Oman), and virtually no popular reform demands (Qatar) during and after the Arab Spring. The aim is to discover whether and under what circumstances Gulf citizens prioritize stability and security over competing individual and societal goals; to what extent this prioritization influences individual orientations toward the prevailing political authority; and how it might work to attenuate the tacit social contract between citizens and rulers of non-democratic rentier societies. In exploring these relationships, the analysis sheds light on the political economy of sectarianism in the Middle East and especially the Arab Gulf region, revealing the strong incentives that rulers face to cultivate non-economic sources of legitimacy in order to maintain the necessary preponderance of political support while maximizing scarce resource revenues. The exploitation of latent social tensions affords one such source.

The logic and drivers of sectarianism

Writing in 1974, an economic advisor at Kuwait's state-run development fund helped launch a research program spanning multiple disciplines when he observed that the capacity to meet citizens' material needs without extracting taxes "helps to explain why the government of an oil-rich country ... can enjoy a degree of stability which is not explicable in terms of its domestic economic or political performance."[9] While the basic tenets of this rentier state[10] paradigm remain valid today, almost half a century on political scientists and other scholars have come to recognize the diverse non-material bases of authority and stability in the Arab world generally and in the Arab Gulf region particularly. These include the very institutions of monarchism, Islam, and the ruling family; traditional forms of political consultation rooted in tribal custom; stewardship of the arts, culture, and higher education; international prestige;[11] and, increasingly since 2011, the provision of security and order in the face of real and imagined "foreign" adversaries.

This final ingredient, which is the focus here, comprises in its current manifestation two distinct elements: the state's ability to protect citizens at a time when the sufferings of their Arab neighbors are on constant, conspicuous display; and the foreignness of the threat facing the nation, whether from a geographical or ideological standpoint. The former narrative exerts an attractive force, bolstering support for the status quo among more security-minded citizens. The latter acts as a reinforcing negative influence by encouraging rejection of what is branded as alien: alien countries (Iran, the West), alien political ideas (the Muslim Brotherhood, Western liberal democracy, the Islamic State), and alien religious interpretations (Shiism). Beyond their main effects of dampening popular appetite for dissent, these threat perceptions have also helped feed the rise of a previously unknown nationalism in those places where they have been most actively cultivated, namely Bahrain, Saudi Arabia, and the United Arab Emirates. In all countries of the Arab Gulf, however, leaders have benefited from a visceral sense of physical insecurity, inexplicable forces spurring regional change, and a future replete with unknowns.

This one might call the political economy of sectarianism, the latter understood broadly as the politicization of ascriptive group identities. Public uncertainty surrounding the interests and intentions of different groups in society earns leaders a political "subsidy" by decoupling support among certain factions and individuals from actual political and economic performance. For these supporters, the state's provision of stability—whether as a good per se, or as protection of entrenched interests—serves as an effective substitute for the public and private benefits otherwise expected of governments and duly expected by other, less status quo-oriented members of society. This dynamic is doubly enabling for regimes because, at the same time that it enhances legitimacy, it also frees up resources for deployment elsewhere that might otherwise have been spent buying support. By feeding inter-communal distrust, sowing fear of external threats, and emphasizing their unique ability to guarantee security, ruling elites can reinforce backing among loyalists and dampen incentives for protest among reformists more cheaply than through the standard provision of material benefits. A sectarian strategy thus carries the prospect of significant political as well as economic pay-offs compared to a traditional system of direct patronage. It is at once an allegiance-building and a cost-saving measure.

Although the origin and extent of sectarian and other social group competition varies widely across the six Arab Gulf countries, still one can identify a set of mechanisms that today contribute to polarization either directly or indirectly by heightening overall feelings of insecurity. Some purposeful and some less deliberate, these mechanisms include (1) electoral and legislative rules that institutionalize descent-based cleavages rather than cross-cutting programmatic coalitions; (2) exclusionary national narratives that highlight differences among citizens; (3) the securitization of opposition, especially among Gulf Arab Shia populations as presumed sympathizers with Iran; (4) an emboldened GCC foreign policy that has contributed directly to regional instability and promoted a militaristic nationalism in some Gulf states; and (5) the specter of radical economic reorganization in the face of dwindling oil and gas revenues.

Institutionalizing group conflict

Arab Gulf societies feature a natural tendency toward political groupings based on ascriptive affiliation. This owes first to the region's low-information political environment, largely devoid of open media, political parties, or an independent civil society that might transmit information about the attitudes and preferences of fellow citizens. At the same time, the rentier system privileges individual rather than group competition for private economic benefits conferred by the state, militating against programmatic or class-based coalitions. Together, the latter factor disincentivizes political action among citizens with shared economic or normative interests, while the former limits the ability of like-minded citizens to identify each other and coordinate politically even if they so desired.[12]

Rather than implement measures to counteract this predisposition for descent-based conflict, instead most Gulf states have actively sought to enhance sectarian, tribal, and other group cleavages in order to avoid the emergence of a more dangerous category of actor: socially cross-cutting factions with broad bases of support capable of exerting effective political pressure. A primary weapon in this battle is governments' design of formal representative institutions. Although Gulf legislatures wield no effective power outside Kuwait and to a lesser extent Bahrain, still the rules governing their election and function offer insight into states' larger strategies of structuring political competition in a manner conducive to preserving the status quo. And, universally, these institutions have had the intended consequence of deepening and indeed *institutionalizing* group competition behind the veneer of modern democratic politics.

In Bahrain, electoral districts gerrymandered utterly along sectarian lines undermine the electoral prospects of populist and secular candidates, begetting a lower house of parliament structurally divided among Sunni Islamists, loyalist tribal "independents," and, in times of its participation in elections, an opposition Shia bloc. The GCC's oldest and most influential legislature, the Kuwaiti National Assembly, is subject to an ever-changing set of rules governing voter eligibility, the number and shape of electoral districts, and the voting system that are crafted to suit the political circumstances of the day. To counter the strong influence of Arab nationalism in the decades after independence in 1961, Kuwait naturalized more than 200,000 Bedouin tribesmen to serve as a reliable pro-government bloc in parliament. When the Iranian Revolution later shifted focus to Kuwait's large Shia minority, the state redrew and expanded electoral districts from ten to twenty-five in time for the 1981 vote, with tribal areas and urban merchant elites disproportionately represented. More recently, a shift toward opposition among tribal factions necessitated yet another change. After four parliamentary dissolutions in four years, in 2012 Kuwait reverted to the five-district system while also doubling the number of candidates a voter can select, with the hope that larger districts and greater choice would hamper tribal coordination of voting via informal "primary" elections.[13]

Similar if less consequential manipulations can be observed even where elected deliberative bodies enjoy a purely advisory role. For its symbolic municipal council elections, Saudi Arabia employs an electoral system seen nowhere else in the world, in which voters are able to cast ballots in all districts of their municipality. This provision undercuts localized bases of support to ensure that, among other things, minority Shia candidates are unlikely to succeed outside the Shia-dominated Eastern Province. In the UAE, voter franchise is limited to a hand-picked electoral college that included less than 1 percent of Emirati citizens in the first Federal National Council elections of 2006. The electorate was later expanded to allow participation of around 12 percent of nationals in 2011, and then to roughly 225,000 eligible voters, or around 20 percent of citizens, in 2015. There, as in Qatar and Oman, electoral results tend to follow patterns of family and tribal settlement owing to districting and voting rules. For instance, a study of Qatar's 2015 municipal council elections found that the single greatest determinant of both voter registration and the act of voting itself was the number of candidates from the same family or tribe running in an individual's district.[14] In short, Gulf regimes have generally succeeded in structuring acceptable avenues of political participation around existing social fault lines, rather than in a way that encourages citizens to overcome narrow group identities.

Selective national narratives

A second direct contributor to the social fragmentation of Gulf citizenries is the explicit ascriptive-based distinctions between citizens that are engrained in the very images and histories propagated and celebrated by Gulf countries. Crafted in the images of ruling families, official narratives reflect the ideal of the Sunni Arab tribesman and even specific schools of Islamic jurisprudence: Hanbali in Saudi Arabia and Qatar, Maliki in Bahrain and Kuwait, Ibadi in Oman, and a more Sufi orientation in Dubai and Abu Dhabi. Necessarily excluded from this ostensibly national portrayal are citizens of non-tribal origin, non-Arabs including notably those of Persian ancestry, citizens who subscribe to a different Sunni tradition, and of course Shia Muslims. Additional distinctions, especially prominent in Bahrain, Kuwait, and Qatar, separate "native" citizens from "latecomers" who gained citizenship after some legally-defined temporal cut-off. Except in Bahrain, where new arrivals receive preferential treatment as an incentive to immigrate,[15] naturalized citizens are seen by more established families as dissipating state resources and thus the welfare benefits to which the latter are entitled by birth, and so are generally afforded fewer political and economic rights. There also remain substantial populations in Qatar and especially Kuwait that have been denied citizenship altogether despite the long-term residence of their families and tribes, again so as not to dilute the state benefits enjoyed by others.[16]

This pyramid of citizenship and belonging, codified both in law and in the public imagination through the media, school curricula, art and architecture, and everyday life, makes clear society's descent-based dividing lines—and also, critically, who stands to lose and gain from a fundamental change in political organization. The open differentiation of social groupings means not simply that some citizens have a greater personal interest in maintaining the prevailing system, but that the relative incentives of all groups to support the state as ultimate benefactor are understood by all—it is common knowledge. The Gulf state features in this way an inherent social tension whereby advantaged groups recognize the disproportionate propensity for opposition among disadvantaged groups, while second- and third-tier citizens understand similarly that members of advantaged groups are more likely to support the regime. And since the line between advantaged and disadvantaged is determined largely by ascriptive criteria, outward markers of group affiliation—accent, dress, skin color, given and family name, and so on—communicate information not simply about social affiliation, but about presumed *political* allegiances. Quotidian social interaction among Gulf citizens thus entails a constant sizing-up and interpretation of visible cues so as to allow cognitive placement of others on the pyramid of citizenship, and their evaluation as likely ally or rival.

The securitization of opposition

The securitization of opposition is a third source of group fractionalization in the Arab Gulf states that operates both directly and indirectly. This notion refers to the growing conception and treatment of dissent as a veritable national security threat, to be addressed within a law enforcement framework, rather than being an ordinary political challenge.[17] It is the delegitimization of political disagreement itself. Specific targets are dictated by domestic politics, but include Shia activists and societies, the Muslim Brotherhood, Salafist groups, and even individual online critics of Gulf regimes. The post-2011 trend toward securitization increases social polarization directly by promoting an "us" vs "them" dichotomy that paints fundamentally political actors, along with their real and imagined supporters, as threats to the general welfare. In publicly demonizing their opponents, Gulf states such as Bahrain, Saudi Arabia, and the United Arab Emirates have also linked domestic actors to transnational movements and rival governments, painting dissenters as foreign-inspired—even foreign-backed—traitors.

In addition to ostracizing major segments of Gulf populations, the redefinition of opposition as a state security problem also fosters group competition indirectly by raising society's overall threat perception level. Rather than view fellow citizens as competitors for resources within a normal political framework, individuals are encouraged instead to fear partisans of rival groups and ideologies as potential terrorists. The effect is to magnify existing apprehensions over widespread regional instability and civil strife and, moreover, to make external conflicts seem closer to home by linking them to groups and individuals operating domestically. In this way, even citizens of apparently stable Gulf countries may come to see themselves as but a few steps removed from a fateful breakdown in law and order, and ruling families as alone equipped to protect against such a possibility.

GCC activism and nationalism

A separate cause of heightened feelings of insecurity among Gulf publics is the new-found foreign policy activism of GCC governments themselves. Excepting Oman, which, to the annoyance of other Gulf leaders, maintains a stubborn neutrality, and to a large extent Kuwait, which has offered mostly token participation in GCC initiatives, the Gulf states have shown an unprecedented willingness to act militarily to counter perceived expansion of influence by challengers to their religious-cum-political authority, whether Iran, the Muslim Brotherhood, or the Islamic State. Beginning with the GCC's Peninsula Shield force dispatched to quell mass demonstrations in Bahrain in March 2011, the alliance has undertaken a string of interventions spanning the breadth of the Arab world. Led by Saudi Arabia and the UAE, it has carried out air strikes and armed fights in Libya and Syria, financed embattled governments in Egypt and Lebanon, and embarked on a full-scale invasion of Yemen. That Gulf citizens feel more vulnerable amid a neighborhood descended into chaos, then, owes in no small part to the deliberate foreign policy choices of their own leaders, whose involvement in what began as domestic political conflicts has likely increased the duration and, in the case of Yemen, also the brutality of these Arab civil wars.

Five years of participation in armed conflict have also given rise to what Madawi Al-Rasheed has called a "militarized hypernationalism" in those countries most heavily involved, especially Saudi Arabia and the United Arab Emirates.[18] There and elsewhere in the GCC, the need to protect the country in the face of aggressive Iranian and Shia expansionism has been transformed from the stuff of official news agencies into a general political mantra demanding action and sacrifice by ordinary citizens and rulers alike. Since 2014, Kuwait, Qatar, and the UAE have all introduced compulsory military service for male citizens, and the Grand Mufti of Saudi Arabia has called for his country to adopt a similar policy to help in the fight "against the enemies of religion and the nation."[19] At the same time, senior Gulf royals have also been active—and highly conspicuous—participants in the Yemen war, including numerous Saudi princes, the eldest son of Dubai's ruler, the son of Abu Dhabi's crown prince, two sons of the Bahraini king, and the son of the ruler of Ras Al Khaimah, who was seriously injured in a missile attack.[20]

More than simply drumming up popular support for a costly and largely unsuccessful military campaign, the GCC's engineered patriotism is intended, as Al-Rasheed writes, to "perform the miracle of homogenizing ... subjects and molding them into one entity."[21] But this larger instrumental value also means that Gulf rulers face the perverse incentive of sustaining rather than curbing their engagement in external conflicts, and indeed even the conflicts themselves, as a temporary antidote to social fragmentation and weak national belonging. Leaders in Saudi Arabia, Bahrain, the UAE, and elsewhere thus emerge as both a primary source of, and self-styled solution to, the sectarian-based insecurity facing their nations, drawing closer those citizens who accept the premise of the existential threat posed by Iran and other unsanctioned Islamic movements, while further alienating those domestic groups implicated as potential sympathizers.

The specter of economic upheaval

A final major source of uncertainty among Gulf publics is the process of fundamental economic transformation now being embarked upon to a greater or lesser extent by all GCC countries as a result of diminishing natural resource revenues. All Gulf governments have moved to shore up enormous budget deficits by curtailing expensive subsidies on fuel, electricity, and other commodities, while at the same time investigating new sources of revenue through once-unthinkable taxation and privatization of core state assets.[22] At the regional level, all six Gulf countries have agreed to implement a GCC-wide value-added tax of 5 percent by as early as 2018, and Saudi Arabia has publicly indicated a willingness to impose excise taxes as well.[23] Yet, rather than temporary measures to solve a short-term fiscal challenge, Gulf leaders have made clear to citizens that the changes presently being studied will herald a fundamental break with the traditional Gulf rentier model in place for generations. This message was aptly summarized in a November 2015 speech by Qatar's emir, steward of the region's most extensive welfare system, in which he warned Qataris in unusually blunt terms that the state can no longer afford "to provide for everything."[24]

Thus, at a time when political anarchy sits at the doorstep of the Gulf nations, and enemies seem intent on exploiting any weakness, GCC citizens face a simultaneous unraveling in the economic sphere of the one thing upon which they could always depend: the generous financial support of the state. Such timing, one expects, is not a coincidence. The extreme sense of anxiety permeating the Gulf region means that governments enjoy a reservoir of popular support and legitimacy simply for their provision of security in an insecure region, affording them the freedom to renegotiate their tacit social contract with citizens more or less unilaterally. In the end, a less generous but stable state is preferable to the state of nature. And, indeed, it is precisely this argument which is being articulated by Gulf rulers themselves, alongside their allies in global financial institutions,[25] that serious reforms are needed to avoid eventual economic collapse, and to guarantee the continued security and prosperity of Gulf societies.

Stability above all? How Gulf citizens' preferences enable Gulf regimes

Citizens from all four surveyed countries (see Appendix A) were asked to identify their first and second most important priorities from among competing national goals. These goals included "boosting economic development," "maintaining the country's security and stability," "giving people more say over important state decisions," and "preserving the identity and culture of the country."[26] (In the Bahrain survey, this final option appears instead as the standard WVS [World Values Survey] item "protecting freedom of opinion.") Notably, despite similar exposure to regional sources of insecurity, the data reveal wide cross-national variation in the prioritization of stability among Gulf nationals. Depicted in Figure 1, the resulting pattern suggests at first glance an unexpected relationship: prioritization of stability seems to be high-

Figure 8.1: Prioritization of stability above competing national aims

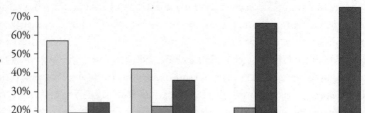

est in those places where stability already prevails. A full two-thirds of Qataris and three-quarters of Kuwaitis, for instance, identify stability as their top priority, compared to a mere quarter of Bahrainis. Indeed, a majority of citizens in Bahrain and a plurality of those in Oman do not rank stability even among the top two national goals.

One might speculate that this can be attributed to a selection effect whereby those societies that witnessed more substantial post-2011 unrest, such as Bahrain, experienced protests and violence precisely due to citizens' relative unconcern for stability compared with other political and economic objectives. However, this explanation cannot account for the divergent cases of Oman and Kuwait, which both saw low to moderate levels of protest in the post-2011 period, yet whose citizens possess very different priorities in regard to stability. After Bahrain and Saudi Arabia, Kuwait experienced the most widespread and sustained protest activity of any GCC country, with sporadic and at times sizable demonstrations continuing through 2014. By contrast, Oman's protests were short-lived and largely restricted to the geographic periphery. The mechanisms underlying popular preferences for stability seem therefore to defy easy explanation: it is neither true that Gulf citizens crave stability when they lack it, nor that they take it for granted when they enjoy it.

Formal examination of the individual-level determinants of stability preferences does little to elucidate the sources of variation across the surveyed populations. This result is summarized in Figure 8.2. In some countries, namely Qatar and Bahrain, individual prioritization of stability is almost entirely unrelated to basic demographic and socioeconomic variables that one might expect to predict political risk aversion and support for the status quo. On the other hand, in Oman and Kuwait, stability preferences are indeed linked statistically to individuals' age, gender, education, level of economic satisfaction, and income. Yet these results are inconsistent across the two countries, with female citizens more likely to cite stability as a top priority in Kuwait, but less likely in Oman; and vice versa for more educated individuals. The only consistent cross-country finding is the negative relationship between income and prioritization of stability seen in both Bahrain and Kuwait. This finding would seem to militate against another possible explanation for the observed cross-country variation, namely that desire for stability is highest in those societies where citizens have most to lose financially from any radical political transformation. Overall, then, the survey data reveal a more complicated story of why certain Gulf nationals prefer stability over potentially positive change, one deserving of more study than is possible here.

Figure 8.2: Demographic and socioeconomic correlates of stability preferences

Variable	*Country*			
	Bahrain	*Kuwait*	*Oman*	*Qatar*
Age	–	–	Positive	–
Education	–	Negative	Positive	–
Female	–	Positive	Negative	–
Economic satisfaction	–	Positive	–	–
Household income	Negative	Negative	–	–

Note: Based on results of multivariate ordered logistic regressions estimated separately for each country—symbol denotes no statistically significant relationship.

Political deference and the link to stability

To measure deference to political authority, respondents in Kuwait, Oman, and Qatar were asked the extent of their agreement or disagreement that "citizens should always support the decisions of the state, even if they disagree with those decisions." This item has been validated across four waves of the Arab Barometer survey conducted throughout the MENA region since 2006;[27] however, it is not included in the WVS. In Bahrain, therefore, we measure popular orientations toward the state more broadly using the item, "How much trust do you have in government institutions?" The distributions of responses to the former question are given in Figure 8.3. As with prefer-

Figure 8.3: Agreement that citizens should always support state decisions

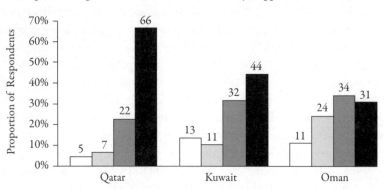

ences for stability, the survey data reveal considerable cross-societal differences in Gulf nationals' political deference, with Qataris demonstrating the highest levels and Omanis the lowest. The responses in the Bahrain survey are not directly comparable, but three-quarters of Bahraini citizens report either a "very high" (24 percent) or "high" (48 percent) level of trust, while only 7 percent say they have "no trust at all" in state institutions. (Results not shown.)

When we analyze the individual-level determinants of political orientations via multivariate regression, we encounter once again mostly inconsistent findings across the four countries surveyed. These results are summarized in Figure 8.4. In Oman, female citizens are associated with lower levels of political deference, while in Bahrain females are linked to more positive orientations toward the government. Age is a significant positive predictor of deference only in Oman, and education level a negative predictor only in Qatar. Regarding our independent variables of interest, the extent of one's prioritization of stability is a strong positive predictor of deference in Qatar, while in Bahrain those who cite stability as their top priority are, all else being equal, more *negatively* oriented toward the state. The sole common thread across three of the four societies is the positive link, especially strong in Kuwait, between economic satisfaction and political deference.

Based on these initial findings, therefore, one is tempted to conclude that the only compelling explanation of why individuals tend to support or oppose governments is the long-standing maxim of rentier state theory: that materially satisfied Gulf citizens make politically quiescent Gulf citizens. That is, nationals will remain loyal to the regime insofar as it lives up to its half of the implicit social contract governing state-society relations in the GCC. However, this story changes dramatically when one proceeds to examine the conditioning effect of stability preferences on the relationship between economic and political satisfaction. The results of this analysis (for Qatar) are depicted in Figure 8.5, which shows the link between economic satisfaction and political deference *conditional on* how a respondent prioritizes stability versus other national aims.

Figure 8.4: Estimating political deference by ordered logit

	(1) *Bahrain*	*(2)* *Kuwait*	*(3)* *Oman*	*(4)* *Qatar*
Female	0.281* (0.015)	−0.180 (0.144)	−0.403** (0.002)	0.221 (0.151)
Education	−0.0197 (0.654)	0.0137 (0.827)	0.0996 (0.158)	−0.166* (0.010)
Age	0.000284 (0.946)	0.00750 (0.127)	0.0127+ (0.074)	0.00777 (0.197)
Economic satisfaction	0.0758** (0.009)	0.135*** (0.000)	0.0122 (0.738)	0.0832* (0.026)
Stability				
2nd Priority	0.0772 (0.617)	0.249 (0.287)	−0.123 (0.521)	0.689** (0.009)
1st Priority	−0.359** (0.006)	−0.0757 (0.669)	−0.113 (0.422)	0.904*** (0.000)
Cut 1	−2.353*** (0.000)	−0.796* (0.035)	−1.634*** (0.000)	−1.768*** (0.000)
Cut 2	−0.677 (0.132)	−0.0839 (0.822)	−0.148 (0.672)	−0.739 (0.103)
Cut 3	1.410** (0.002)	1.317*** (0.001)	1.301*** (0.000)	0.661 (0.148)
N	1169	944	792	757
pseudo R^2	0.009	0.011	0.008	0.022

Note: All models estimated by ordered logistic regression with robust standard errors; *p*-values in parentheses; + $p < 0.10$, * $p < 0.05$, ** $p < 0.01$, *** $p < 0.001$.

Each line in the figure corresponds to a different group of citizens: the uppermost dotted line to those who cite stability as their top priority, the middle dashed line to those Qataris for whom it is a second priority, and the bottom solid line representing those who do not mention it at all. (The 95 percent confidence bars for the middle line are omitted for clarity.) Clearly, the extent to which economic satisfaction leads to political deference among Qatari nationals depends critically on how far an individual prioritizes security and stability. Among the most stability-conscious, there is no relationship at all between economic conditions and willingness to defer to government decisions. For this group, the predicted likelihood of complete political deference (i.e., "strong" agreement with the statement that citizens should always support the decisions of the government) is 64 percent among individuals with the lowest possible self-rated economy, compared to an estimated 75 percent among those whose satisfaction is rated at 10 out of 10. Neither this relationship, nor the relationship among Qataris who rank stability as a second priority, is statistically significant. By contrast, among citizens who prioritize national goals other than stability, economic satisfaction is a strong predictor of political deference, as indicated by the sharply upward sloping solid line. For this group, a person of "low" economic satisfaction (defined as one standard deviation below the mean) is 39 percent likely to report total political deference, compared to an estimated 62 percent among citizens of "high" satisfaction (i.e., one standard deviation above the mean).

What is more, this political subsidy enjoyed by the Qatari state due to public concerns over stability—the distance between the top line and the bottom line in Figure 8.5—increases as economic satisfaction declines. Less financially satisfied citizens, in other words, are much more likely to remain politically supportive if they are stability-oriented. A Qatari of average satisfaction, for instance, is an estimated 70 percent likely to be deferential if stability is his or her top priority, compared to only 50 percent among those who do not mention stability—a gap of 20 percent. But the corresponding proportions for a Qatari of low economic satisfaction are 68 percent and 38 percent respectively, this 30 percent gap being now twice as large. For a Qatari of the lowest possible satisfaction category, finally, this discrepancy grows even larger to an estimated 18 percent likelihood of total deference among those unconcerned about stability, compared to a 64 percent likelihood among stability-oriented citizens. This difference attributable to stability preferences is significant at a high level of statistical confidence for all but the top two categories of economic satisfaction (i.e., 9 and 10). In conclusion, save for those at the highest

Figure 8.5: The effect of economic satisfaction on political deference conditional on stability orientation (Qatar)

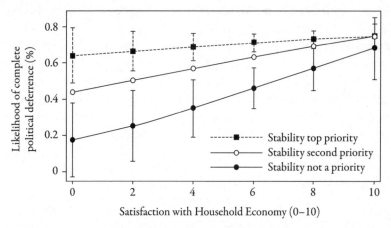

levels of economic satisfaction, concern for the maintenance of public order makes Qatari citizens willing to accept lower levels of economic benefits in return for the same level of political acquiescence.[28]

Summarized in Figure 8.6 are the corresponding results for Bahrain, Kuwait, and Oman. Rows report the boost in political deference owing to economic satisfaction conditional on stability preferences. To offer a real-world test of significance, marginal effects here are evaluated as the difference between an individual of lower than average versus higher than average satisfaction (as opposed to minimum versus maximum), operationalized as −1 and +1 standard deviations, respectively, from the country-specific means. The upper-left cells, for example, give the relationship between economy and deference for Bahrainis who cite stability as their top concern. In this case, there is no statistical link ($p = 0.600$) between these two variables when the stability condition is imposed. As in the case of Qatar, in Bahrain economic satisfaction relates to political orientations *only* among individuals who prioritize national aims other than stability. Specifically, being of high versus low economic satisfaction boosts the likelihood of political deference by 49 percent among this group of citizens, who, as per Figure 8.1, represent more than half of all Bahrainis.

The findings from Kuwait are somewhat different but substantively consistent with those from Bahrain and Qatar. Here the relationship between economic satisfaction and political deference is statistically significant across all stability preference groups; however, the *magnitude* of the effect is almost three times as large among citizens who do not prioritize stability (an estimated 80 percent increase in the likelihood of political deference) compared with those who do (less than a 30 percent increase). The former effect is also associated with a higher degree of statistical confidence. So, while the rentier link does operate among Kuwaitis independent of how they prioritize stability, the data show that this relationship is attenuated among more stability-concerned citizens. Even in Kuwait, therefore, the state earns a political discount due to popular risk aversion, being able to buy and preserve the political support of status quo-oriented citizens more cheaply than that of others.

Figure 8.6: The conditioning effect of stability preferences on the rentier link between economic satisfaction and political deference

Stability	Bahrain		Kuwait		Oman		Qatar	
	effect	p	effect	p	effect	p	effect	p
1st priority	–	0.600	+24%	0.005	–	0.628	–	0.327
2nd priority	–	0.953	+29%	0.072	–	0.376	–	0.154
Not a priority	+49%	0.000	+80%	0.000	–	0.404	+55%	0.027

Note: percentage changes calculated as differences in predicted likelihoods evaluated at country-specific "low" (−1 standard deviation) versus "high" (+1 standard deviation) economic satisfaction; predictions estimated by ordered logit with usual controls for age, gender, and education level; p-values report the significance of Wald tests carried out using Stata's post-estimation function margins.

We arrive finally at the deviant case of Oman, where an individual's satisfaction with his or her household financial situation is never a predictor of political acquiescence. Together with the results examined in Figure 8.4, this finding confirms that very little indeed—only gender and potentially age—seems to account for variation in Omanis' propensities to defer to political authority. Neither satisfaction, nor stability preferences, nor the interaction between the two can explain why some citizens reserve their right to dissent from government decisions while others feel that they must remain supportive of policies with which they personally disagree. One might speculate that in Oman deference to the state is inextricably tied to the person of Sultan Qaboos bin Said Al Said, ruler since 1970 and widely credited with modernizing the once underdeveloped and internationally isolated country. It might be that Omanis' orientations toward the prevailing regime are shaped above all by views of the larger social and economic progress spearheaded by the sultan over five decades, rather than individual outcomes in the areas of economic well-being and political efficacy. Whatever the case, it is clear that Oman does not follow the pattern observed in the three other Gulf countries considered here.

The benefits and risks of regimes' manipulations of identity threats

This chapter has sought to examine the micro-level foundations of the political economy of sectarianism in the Arab Gulf region. It has done so by studying the tangible political implications of popular feelings of insecurity, offering a more systematic and rigorous test of the oft-repeated idea that it is Gulf governments who ultimately benefit from the heightened politicization of sectarian and other group identities. By leveraging mass survey data collected recently in four diverse Gulf societies, the analysis presented a direct investigation of the empirical connection between threat perceptions and appetite for dissent among GCC citizens. And the findings tell a more complex story than the one usually articulated. Specifically, the results of the multivariate analysis show that concerns over stability do not impact political orientations directly by reducing willingness to adopt an oppositional position, but rather indirectly by severing or attenuating the normal link between the performance of Gulf governments and the support *for* Gulf governments.

Valuing order as a public good in itself, more stability-minded citizens are willing to accept lower levels of economic welfare in return for the same level of political deference toward the regime. For these individuals, the state's provision of security is in effect an economic substitute for the private financial benefits otherwise expected by Gulf citizens, an intangible benefit that enables states to purchase political loyalty at a subsidized cost compared to what they would spend through the direct patronage of citizens. In Qatar, for instance, political deference among security-oriented citizens at the lowest level of economic satisfaction remains *higher* than that among the economically most satisfied citizens who do not prioritize security. The positive boost from the state's safeguarding of law and order, in other words, utterly outweighs the negative impact of poor economic delivery for more stability-minded citizens.

The obvious upshot is that Gulf governments have a direct economic-cum-political incentive to augment as far as possible the share of the citizenry that prizes stability over other societal aims, including through the embellishment or wholesale manufacture of domestic and external threats to security, as well as the exacerbation of social tensions. In practice, however, this incentive is tempered by the countervailing concern of states that their stoking of public fear and distrust may yield a cure worse than the disease. Indeed, such was the experience of Bahrain's rulers in the aftermath of the Shia-led uprising of February 2011. To stymie the momentum of the protest movement, Bahrain used the specter of Shia empowerment and Iranian intervention to rouse ordinary Sunnis from their traditional political slumber, the latter soon organizing their own mass demonstrations in support of the ruling Al Khalifa family. Yet, having once convinced Sunnis of the existential threat posed by Iran and its Shia agents in Bahrain, authorities found it impossible to quiet their own supporters, who would begin pressing demands for an even harsher security response to continued protests, thus quickening the spiral of violence and repression that characterized the post-2011 period. Some activists even dared to criticize senior royals, including King Hamad himself, for their perceived weakness.[29] By the time of parliamentary elections in 2014, the new Sunni movements appeared poised to capitalize on their grass-roots appeal, and it was only through last-minute gerrymandering of electoral districts that Bahrain was able to stuff the proverbial genie back in the bottle.

There exists, then, a fine line between a regime emphasizing its protection of citizens against mostly hypothetical dangers, and the inadvertent creation of *actual* breakdowns in security and order through policies that incite social hatred and uncontrollable public hysteria. Still, on balance one is forced to conclude that the ruling strategy pursued by Bahrain and other Gulf governments remains, regrettably, highly successful.[30] Some indication of this can be gleaned by comparing public reactions to fiscal austerity measures taken or proposed by GCC countries since 2015. In principle, the retrenchment of state welfare benefits along with the promise of various forms of new taxation is an issue that should unite Gulf citizens from across the social spectrum, since reforms apply equally to, and are equally unwelcome to, members of all confessional, tribal, and other groupings. In actuality, however, one observes stark differences in popular response to announced economic changes that defy simple structural explanations, pointing instead to the power of some states' sectarian narratives.

Though distinguished by wealth, Kuwait and Bahrain share much in common: they feature the region's most robust and long-standing formal representative institutions; both have active and largely progressive civil societies; and they are not dissimilar in terms of social group composition and cleavages. Yet citizen reactions to fiscal austerity there could not be more divergent—

and in the opposite way to what one would have expected.[31] In Bahrain, where the curtailing of government subsidies and benefits entails real economic pain for a citizenry largely impoverished by Gulf standards, public protest was limited to complaints on social media. In Kuwait, by contrast, the state's repeated attempts at spending reductions and revenue generation have met with stiff resistance in parliament, and in April 2016 precipitated a three-day strike by oil workers, the first in twenty years. What is it that allows workers in Kuwait to come together for political action, while in Bahrain citizens remain politically quiescent despite being objectively more affected by state-imposed austerity?

In short, Bahrain remains stuck in the cycle of political stagnation and repression brought on by the 2011 uprising. Having spent the past five years fighting on either side of a conflict over the rightful division of political and economic resources, Bahrainis continue to view this newest policy question through the lens of communal interests, security, and regional politics, with the state as ultimate beneficiary. For Shia and other citizens inclined toward opposition, activism has proved both futile and dangerous, and the risks of detention, imprisonment, or wholesale revocation of citizenship far outweigh the expected impact on government policy. For Sunnis, the calculations are more complicated. On the one hand, as the ruling family's core support base, the group receives a disproportionate share of state largesse and thus stands to lose the most from cuts to public sector salaries and other benefits. Their voice is also potentially more influential, in that opposition among Sunnis would raise the possibility of cross-sectarian political coordination. But in the post-2011 landscape, dissent has been made synonymous with Shia activism and tantamount to treason, and Sunnis are loath to oppose even those policies that negatively affect them. Tellingly, rather than blame Bahrain's fiscal woes on economic mismanagement or corruption, many Sunnis have found ways of faulting the usual suspects in Bahraini Shia and even Iran. If not for the economic destruction and increased security spending necessitated by the uprising, one common reasoning goes, as well as Iran's deliberate flooding of the oil market, Bahrain would not find itself in its current financial predicament in the first place.[32]

Bahrainis' inability to overcome sectarian cleavages has meant that the state, far from offering political concessions in return for welfare reduction, in fact has taken the opportunity to consolidate further its grip on power. In January 2016, parliamentarians moved to quiz the finance minister after the government bypassed the legislature to enact a 60 percent hike in fuel prices with a mere nine hours' notice. Shortly before the vote to allow the questioning, Bahrain's minister of interior paid a visit to legislators expressing his astonishment that parliamentarians, keenly aware of the country's fiscal crisis, were nonetheless posing more of an obstacle to needed change than regular citizens.[33] Soon after, parliament altered its own rules to require a three-quarters majority in order to interrogate ministers, effectively forfeiting enhanced legislative oversight included in limited post-2011 reforms. At the same time, Bahrain has aggressively stamped out what remains of its opposition, including through the unprecedented disqualification of religious leaders from politics[34] and prosecution of critics of the ruling family, government institutions, and even Bahrain's military involvement in Yemen. The state's rationale in the latter instance is indeed an apt paraphrase of the security mantra that today dominates public discourse in the Gulf states. The official Bahrain News Agency reported:

> In light of the delicate situation in the region ... the Interior Ministry warned against any attempt to exploit the situation through division or sedition, or issuance of statements against the approach Bahrain has taken [in the Yemen conflict].

> The Interior Ministry said it would take appropriate steps against individuals that put the safety and security of the country at risk.

> The Ministry stressed that the situation required strong national unity, general order and stability.[35]

Conclusion

For most of the past half century, the states of the Arab Gulf have been defined by their unique combination of economic generosity and political parsimony, a system preserved by vast resource wealth and traditional institutions of rulership that have managed to retain a preponderance of legitimacy. Yet, some fifty years on one is tempted to say of the Arab Gulf monarchies that it is their adept management of social group cleavages and identities, rather than economic distribution per se, that powers their continued longevity. The GCC may be rich, but one does not remain rich by spending all of one's money. Instead, both out of fiscal necessity and a desire to maximize private consumption, Gulf rulers seek to buy popular loyalty as cheaply as possible, deploying resources strategically while also cultivating intangible sources of legitimacy so as to lessen the need for financial patronage.

This chapter has demonstrated the present-day efficacy of such a strategy. In elucidating the empirical link between political loyalty and individual preferences for stability, it lends substance to the notion, frequently articulated but never systematically tested, that Gulf governments can effectively scare their populations into acceptance of the political status quo. Under conditions of insecurity, the majority of Gulf Arabs prefer a known situation that is less than ideal to a potentially better situation, the transition to which carries some non-trivial risk of going very wrong. Fortunately for Gulf rulers and unfortunately for Gulf nationals, the post-2011 Middle East and North Africa offer plenty of examples of the latter, but few, if any, success stories.

9

THE ROOTS OF SECTARIAN LAW
AND ORDER IN THE GULF

BAHRAIN, THE EASTERN PROVINCE OF SAUDI ARABIA,
AND THE TWO HISTORICAL DISRUPTIONS

Staci Strobl

Introduction

Criminal justice agencies (police, courts, and corrections) in Arabian Gulf
countries have been increasingly under pressure from internal social movements and human rights organizations to counter sectarian-based abuses and
discrimination within their institutions. The Arab Spring and events thereafter have shed a light on institutional violence and discrimination, in particular,
in Saudi Arabia and Bahrain where the governments are at odds with Shia
social and political movements. Some of the more concerning abuses include
the state execution of Shia opposition leader Sheikh Nimr al-Nimr in Saudi
Arabia, and the citizenship revocations of opposition activists in Bahrain.
Contemporary Sunni and Shia leaders use sectarian-based political speech and
behavior for the purpose of maintaining their political roles and prestige.

However, far from being merely a problem of the political elite, sectarianism has been part of the working routine of institutions and institutional actors within these countries for at least two hundred years, since the historical expansion of Sunni interior tribes into the Gulf coastal region. By taking a long historical view of the development of sectarianism in cultural and political discourse in the region, the current anti-Shia tendencies of Saudi and Bahraini national criminal justice institutions come into better focus as the product of a particular pathway of historical events that shaped contemporary institutions into discriminatory entities.

Underpinning this argument is the theoretical notion that national criminal justice institutions are one of the primary carriers of dominant notions of social order in the contemporary age. They are tasked with the very practical job of maintaining order in the streets, detecting and adjudicating wrongdoing, and administering punishments. They also contribute to the more abstract function of preserving national security. Police, for example, must be on call to respond to who is dangerous and what "ought not to be happening about which something ought to be done [now]."[1] Within police studies, Robert Reiner has argued that in the day-to-day activities of police, they are rarely the crime-fighters of popular media depictions, and more often keepers of social order through the seemingly neutral and routine activities of patrol and other forms of community contact and outreach.[2]

Criminal law bounds criminal justice practice (though law, of course, reflects the cultural notions of order as well). Further, criminal justice practice is rife with discretionary moments in which actors draw from the larger social dispositions and reflect the value systems of the societies in which they are embedded. Reiner argues that police, therefore, are susceptible to the problematic demands of social and political systems that suffer from the policies and politics of inequality. In other words, if inequality is a feature of the social order, then as maintainers of order, police will be active maintainers of social inequality.[3]

How criminal justice authorities describe public security decisions, deployments, punishments, and applications of law provide insight into the vantage point of the powerful in ruling governments themselves, particularly in less than democratic contexts where decision-making is not transparent nor publicly participatory. Meanwhile, expressions of social support and/or opposition to decision-making offer important viewpoints that can reveal popular cultural notions of order. Together, notions of order have official and popular variants, related to each other, often dialectically, forming the operant discursive frame.

Notions of order maintenance in the Arabian Gulf context, and in particular in Bahrain and the Eastern Province of Saudi Arabia, have been operating in a sectarian discursive framework for at least two hundred years. In contemporary times, the subordination of Shia groups in these countries economically and politically has been well-documented[4] as well as their denigration in popular discourse.[5] Mainstream Sunni society continues to construe Shia as dangerous and the countries' criminal justice systems have consistently been called out for differential and brutal treatment of Shia.[6] Further, the criminalization of anti-government political speech[7] and the execution of Sheikh Nimr Al-Nimr point to official order maintenance regimes that find an internal enemy in Shia and their allies who would seek to include them fully in political life.[8] Shia constitute a strong majority of the population in Bahrain, and approximately 15 percent of the Saudi state, where they are concentrated in the Eastern Province.

By drawing briefly on recent ground-breaking historical scholarship which brings Gulf history into better focus in a regional sense, and more extensively on the development of the order maintenance function during the era of British colonial influence, sectarian motivations emerge within the very foundations of modern Bahrain and Saudi Arabia, finding particularly stark expression in their criminal justice apparatuses.

Gulf sectarianism and the two historical disruptions

Sectarianism in the Arabian Gulf is a transnational phenomenon in that sect identity crosses national boundaries. As such, scholarship has emphasized international causes and effects in their explanations. More recently, however, scholars are beginning to see that sectarianism plays out in particular national contexts in important ways and that domestic politics and national institutions contribute greatly to the perpetuation of sectarian strife. Frederic Wehrey's *Sectarian Politics in the Gulf* is one example of research that brings the issue back into domestic focus. He argues that by solving social and political problems in the national context, the use of sectarian politics as a strategic tactic by power-players will no longer be as salient, demonstrated through his analysis of post-invasion Iraq politics in the region.[9] The notion that domestic problems play into the rise of sectarian-based politics is sensible and a welcome relief from past analyses that insufficiently considered local milieux. However, taking a longer historical view reveals that the regimes in the Gulf today were established with sectarian agendas in mind, because of the symbolic identification of groups competing for power and control. The argument here is that the use of sectarian-based political strategies and the development of sectarian institutions is not merely the product of elite political actors choosing a strategy that best maintains their power (though it may be an effective strategy). Rather, it is a deeper interplay of more socially and culturally embedded notions of identity that have developed in Arabian Gulf history, and shaped the nation-state as sectarian. In fact, seeing the world through a sectarian lens (even if one is tolerant of other sects) is part of the cultural language and practice of Gulf people, elite or otherwise.

To unpack how sectarianism cuts deeper into the social fabric of Saudi Arabia and Bahrain, two major historical disruptions are analyzed here: the pushing of Sunni tribes from the interior into the Gulf Coast in the eighteenth century, and the British colonial project in the twentieth century (which shored up Wahhabi expansionism to the Eastern Province in Saudi Arabia and invented a modern Bahrain). Both of these political regimes had particular notions of how to achieve social and political order and who should have control of the legitimate means of violence; however, these notions were not inevitable or intrinsic to the region, but rather the result of power struggles and cultural contestations that ushered in new, hybrid eras. Together, the results of the two disruptions form the basis of today's nation-states and their sectarian-based criminal justice systems. In essence, the first disruption becomes institutionalized, in part, into the second, and so broadly speaking the problem can be defined as one of post-coloniality. The nation-state and its institutions act as a forced overlay in a milieu that—although often claimed by external and imperial powers over the centuries—was never fully brought into the rational-bureaucratic fold of nation-ness until the early twentieth century.

Building a nation-state involves the centralization of the chief concentrated means of violence.[10] The nation-state emerges only after it has wrested control over those internal groups who have previously held the authority for legitimate violence. Taming local, tribal, or clan-based violence is the necessary precursor to a modern criminal justice system, so that local communities become subordinate to the government's security apparatus rather than to their traditional patrons. In the first disruption, the Sunni tribes competed for control over port cities and enclaves in the Gulf, usurping the previous proto-capitalist, seafaring, and mercantile order. During the second upheaval, Saudi Arabia, underwritten by the British, used violence to detribalize and gain control of wider swaths of the Arabian Peninsula in the early twentieth century. And in Bahrain, the imperial British political agents and the ruler's

British advisor established a modern policing and court system, delegitimizing other forms of justice or modifying them into hybrid forms.

William Sewell in *Logics of History* (1996)[11] understood major historical disruptions as important theoretical categories. Such events are transformative of the larger social structure when they are imbued with heavy symbolic significance for contemporaries; the interpretation of the event is as important as the event itself. Disruptive events are moments when competing conceptions clash, many outcomes are possible, and the result of the competition sets the stage for authority, legitimacy, and security going forward. This idea can be linked to post-colonial theorists describing colonial disruptions more generally in the sense that they are both devastating and agenda-defining well beyond the initial action.[12] Post-colonialist theorists also provide an important reminder that reading history against the grain is necessary because many of the primary sources brought to bear on a subject are written by colonial elites and in languages of conquest; this does not destroy the enterprise of trying to make sense of colonial narrative, but it does require a critical reading that looks for points of fissure and pays attention to the shadows of those who have been potentially silenced.

Sewell sees the game-changing event as one that is the result of a fundamental upheaval that cannot be contained in the previous social order; it links two or more modes of activity in a new way, evidenced by the discursive contestations in which the event occurred. As such, structure-changing events are also cultural transformations, shaped by particular local conditions and characterized by heightened emotion and collective creativity in overcoming profound insecurities within everyday life. The new world that the event births has an "authoritative order" that sets the stage until the next major upheaval. As such, the ability to use symbols in the highly charged event, and the outcome of which symbols are more utilitarian, inform the power relations in subsequent moments by establishing a repertoire of operant cultural symbols and practices. Sectarianism in the Gulf context is one such operant cultural symbol, which has utility precisely because it is part of a deeper discursive repertoire.

Taking the long view of sectarian competition in the Gulf

In the Gulf, the sectarian cultural milieu resulted from the insufficient resolution of the effects of the two aforementioned historical events or disruptions (the conquest of Sunni tribes and the British colonial project). Before that, other external entities that claimed whole or parts of Bahrain and the Saudi

Gulf coastline, such as the Ottomans, the Persians, or the Portuguese, never invested in deep social or political reform. Without overly reducing the importance of their influences, the Ottomans, for example ruled Al-Hasa (on the Saudi Gulf coast, now the Eastern Province) by under-resourced military garrisons,[13] largely relying on Sunni tribes and coastal mercantile communities to police themselves, permitting much of the locals' way of life and sense of social and political order to carry on as it had been.

Imperial neglect of the region ended in the eighteenth century when two major strains of cultural order were competing for local authority: an indigenous proto-capitalist society which historians have referred to as part of a larger Arabian Gulf/Indian Ocean common seafaring culture; and the Sunni tribal groups who arrived in force in the eighteenth century as interior peoples moved into the coastal regions. The Sunni tribes (King Abdul Aziz Ibn Saud's allies and the Al-Khalifah) controlled Bahrain and the Gulf coast of Saudi Arabia when the second disruption occurred. The British in the twentieth century, unlike other imperial powers who occupied the region, engaged in very deep social and political reform, mediating between the insufficiently resolved contest between indigenous and Sunni tribal notions of power, authority, and order, while adding an additional disruption in the form of the imposition of the nation-state. Each disrupting group, first the Sunni tribes and then the British, engaged in political maneuvering to take the legitimate means of violence from the one preceding. The ways in which the British regime mediated and controlled the competing authorities became the foundations of the modern nation-states and their maintenance of social and political order going forward. Emphasizing and de-emphasizing the Sunni hegemonic projects of the ruling families in certain ways served a colonial imperial agenda of allegedly maintaining maritime security, and later stabilizing the region for the exploitation of oil.

The notion of hybridized forces is a mainstay of post-colonial theory, and suggests that observations in a particular context must be disaggregated in order to wrestle with the complexity operating in a given environment.[14] Here, individuals and institutions are liminal, between forms, between languages, between symbols, and ultimately exhibiting creolity.[15] It also suggests a discursive approach. In words, symbols, and other cultural expressions, the tensions inherent in a particular milieu can be deconstructed: in this case as the seemingly contradictory ideas of national unity and sectarian pride coexist and compete within both Saudi Arabia and Bahrain. Nowhere are these complicated signs and symbols more evident than in the discourse around criminal justice in Bahrain and Gulf coastal Saudi Arabia, so far as what they represent and how they should be deployed. Cloaked in the symbols of nation-states and public protection, these forces also exhibit Sunni hegemonic intentions and practice routine sectarian discrimination, a tack they have taken since their institutional inception.

Of course, an exploration of the roots of sectarianism in cultural conceptions of order could extend back to the original conflicts within Muslim societies around the caliphate's leadership, which gave rise to the fundamental split between the Sunni and Shia branches in the first place. Indeed, the original upheaval by definition is an important historical antecedent to the topic at hand, but the focus here is how that split factored into symbolic identity during competitions for power and control in the Gulf Coast in later centuries. Further, notions that "Islam" may be an important factor in the Gulf region while simultaneously discounting the variable "sect" cannot hold water. Islam is almost never practiced in the Gulf region outside one of these broad-based traditions, nor has any major pan-Islamic ideology ever taken hold in the Gulf; in other words, the day-to-day practice of Islam in the region is within a sectarian framework and returns to Muslim piety in recent decades involve sect-adherences. These points should, however, not lead to essentializing the split as setting up an inevitable path to sectarian conflict, nor to asserting erroneously that any sectarian conflict is necessarily a theological argument, but rather that the historical importance of previous events related to sectarianism factor into the forms that social life takes locally, and the identities of social groups in competition for power and authority, even today. Moreover, such an original ripple could not continue to have present-day viability but for its eventual institutionalization into the modern nation-state, and by extension regional alliances like the Gulf Cooperation Council (GCC).

An Indian Ocean culture: the Arabian Gulf as a safe(r) space to be Shia

The coastal areas of the Arabian Gulf had for many centuries been part of a larger Indian Ocean culture characterized as one that valued free trade and religious tolerance. The Gulf's people, as late as the early twentieth century, moved freely and migrated frequently among small port cities, which were more connected to each other than to their hinterlands. The difficulty in traveling between the coast and the interior partly contributed to the development of a unique Gulf (*Khaliji*) culture. There was enduring exchange and cross-settlement between the people of the Arabian and Persian shores of the

Gulf, with the water, not the land, being the center of things.[16] Compared to other parts of the Middle East, Khalijis were less urbanized and less settled. Large populations were semi-nomadic, moving with the trade winds and by season among different parts of the Gulf coast and into the Indian Ocean.

Both sides of the Arabian Gulf saw the rise and fall of classic Muslim empires which claimed its shores, such as the Abbasid, Seljuk, and Safavid. In reality, these empires had little control over the daily lives of the Gulf people, aside from their relatively fleeting military pass-throughs and tax collections. As a practical matter, Gulf society before the seventeenth century was governed by a series of loose political frameworks that permitted the Indian Ocean culture to flourish as a seafaring network of small businesses, trade by dhow, pearling and fishing operations, and some agriculture.[17]

The common culture of the Indian Ocean can be considered one that had a relatively elastic sense of social order. Cohesion around mutually beneficial trade found a wide variety of ethnic, religious, and racial groups cooperating, intermarrying, and sharing a common folkloric tradition with hybridized elements taken from the coasts of East Africa and South India (e.g. musical styles, traditional foods). In important cultural and material artifacts that point to a Gulf/Indian Ocean common identity, the society had been self-labeled the "people of the dhow,"[18] the *ahl-i-hava* ("people of the wind" in Farsi)[19] and the "people of the sea."[20] The cross-cultural cohesion may have cemented itself among the religious and ethnic diversity of the crews of the dhows, many of whom were slaves to their maritime masters, but cooperated amongst themselves on long pearling journeys over the course of a diving season.

Historians have noted that the Gulf coast (as well as the Swahili coast) was a safe space for divergent religious sects to settle, driven out by less tolerant Sunni imperial masters and tribes in the interior.[21] Shia religious and cultural life was free to develop in the Gulf into the eighteenth century. Of course, when claimed by the Safavid empire, Shia theological and cultural development on the littoral was most pronounced (in Bahrain; Saudi Arabia at this time was controlled by the Ottomans).[22]

The most important customary law at the time revolved around commercial interests. Reportedly, divers and other workers were not paid in wages, but shared in profits; as such, the livelihood of the labor force was subject to the ebb and flow of volatile market conditions. Colonial administrators indicated that by the late nineteenth and early twentieth century, the system was rife with exorbitant interest being charged for profit-sharing advances, corrupt bookkeeping, unpaid labor, and other exploitative conditions bordering on slavery. Although sources are scant on the details, a highly evolved method of commercial arbitration developed with disputes heard and resolved at the *majlis-al-urf* (customary council)[23] or in the municipal *majlis* within port cities. *Na'turs* (port watchmen) enforced customary law in the ports and pearl markets. *Na'turs* reported to either private merchant fleets or port municipalities, and later, with the coming of more industrialized colonial trading operations, were hired by corporations, such as the Mesopotamian-Persian Trading Corporation (MESPERS).[24] One colonial advisor, Sir Charles Belgrave, later became interested in recording these customs as the pearling industry was collapsing in the 1930s, claiming to have written down the traditional pearl diving laws—known only orally to the pearling community itself.[25] Unfortunately, no such documents could be found in his preserved papers at the University of Exeter.

Meanwhile, non-commercial matters were the domain of the *qadis*, Muslim legal scholars who heard disputes related to social behavior and wrongdoing and ruled from a combination of legal tradition and local custom. The *qadis* were literate and learned within their sect-based religious traditions (mostly Shia at this time, but there were also Sunni *qadis* for Sunni groups). They adjudicated orally, often outdoors and in a variety of roving venues, and did not write down information about cases. It is important to note here that within the Gulf seafaring community, the two broad-based traditions of sharia-based adjudication were separate, but coexisted.

The first disruption: people of the sea occupied by the people of the land

The encroachment of the Sunni tribes, or the people of the land, onto the Gulf littoral—perhaps motivated by drought and famine conditions further in the interior[26]—represented a major rupture in the social order of the Gulf, determined as they were to establish their presence and enforce a new political order in the region. The Sunni tribes brought with them a system of honor and loyalty to a patriarchal and hereditary social structure,[27] divergent from the exchange-based networks of the Gulf. Their customs included the *dakhalah* system of protector-protégé relationships.[28] Interacting with the indigenous people in a hierarchical manner, the Sunni tribes demanded the paying of tolls for protection (*khuwa* or *zakat*), competing with each other and thus transferring interior tribal conflicts to the sea. The Sunni tribes operated in a semi-nomadic way, moving among certain broadly defined and fluid spheres of control on land (*dirah*) that often overlapped as tribes negotiated safe passages through others' *dirah*.[29] Although in their conquests of the ports they also sometimes took to the sea, their sense of territorial expansion was land-based. Warfare, often described in colonial accounts as mere "raids," was common as the Sunni tribes competed against each other for control over the littoral. The indigenous settled merchant communities were drawn into this competition for control, coerced into paying *zakat* or *khuwa* to a conquering tribe. The merchants, however, had some bargaining power. With multiple tribes competing for the tributes of coastal merchant communities, disgruntled communities could change their allegiances or move their operations to another *dirah*.[30]

The tribal alliances were inherently unstable (considered from a Western perspective). For example, the Dawasir tribe were at some moments allies of the Al-Khalifah in Bahrain, and at other times, and in subsequent branchings-off, enemies, raiding Bahrain from the sea. Similarly, the Al-Khalifah paid tribute to Ibn Saud in the eighteenth and nineteenth centuries, and were likely only holding back its territorial expansion and potential subjugation through the protection of the British in the relevant treaties of the nineteenth century. Meanwhile, the Persians claimed Bahrain throughout this period as well, after having lost the territory in the post-Safavid period. Peter Lienhardt, a Gulf ethnographer, interprets the anthropological evidence in the region as suggesting that before the formal nation-state system took hold, people were used to wide variations in power and influence, which were negotiated and renegotiated again and again.[31]

The nature of rule within the tribes and how they administered justice starkly differed from the more indigenous, maritime communities. For the people of the land, the tribal leader was a sheikh among sheikhs, and subject to acceptance among a group of leading males (though not a hereditary system). Competition among sheikhs often led to unresolved disputes that then resulted in new branches of the tribe being born. Conflicts within tribes were handled by an all-male council (*majlis*) of tribal leaders (*sheikhs*) who would hear the grievances of people wronged and administer a resolution. Sanctions for wrongdoing were enforced by the *majlis* as the chief protectors of the safety of their people. Routine consultation on decision-making with other adult males in the tribe maintained the legitimacy of the *sheikhs* within the *majlis*.[32] Interestingly, in Bahrain and Saudi Arabia, there remains among ruling families an enduring preference for consultative councils (*shura*) and other *majlis*-like governance bodies. Assuredly, ruling families make overtures to, and have intellectual agreement with, parliamentary democracy at some level of government (for Saudi Arabia, on the municipal level; for Bahrain, on the national level when not suspended). Yet, the reliance on appointed groups of mostly closed-door decision-makers is a mainstay, and in fact could be argued to be a more legitimate governance body in the eyes of contemporary tribal traditionalists.

Conflicts related to Muslim law (*sharia*) were handled in consultation with the local *qadi* (customary judge) and his circle of *ulema*, or learned elite.[33] Self-appointed third-party mediators often emerged to solve conflicts before they were brought to the *majlis* and *ulema*.[34] Traditional conflict resolution practices involved notions of sensitive symbolics."[35] Quranic injunctions instruct Muslims to keep the peace among themselves, hence the need for *hall wasat* (solution as middle way). Because of the Arab cultural primacy of honor (*sharaf*) to one's reputation, and the interconnectedness of the individual's reputation with the larger family, clan, or tribe, face-saving techniques are preferred to overt conflict. Helping the parties in "saving face" (*dakhilah*) is a major part of the role of a Sunni Arab mediator.

In Saudi Arabia, when Ibn Saud conquered Qatif in 1913, the Shia merchants in the town negotiated a hands-off policy from the Saudi regime: they could practice their religion unfettered as long as the population was politically docile.[36] However, over the ensuing years the official state discourse constructed by Wahhabi clerics labeled Shia as rejectionists (*rafidha*). Sectarian intolerance, rather than tolerance, became deeply embedded in the identity of the ruling Sunni elite and the Saudi state, eventually codified in law and reinforced in state schools. Since the state's inception, the Shia in the Eastern Province (formerly Al-Hasa) have been treated as a security threat rather than a community to be integrated. As a result of their underclass status, Shia were never included in proto-police (*fedawiyyah*) forces in the Gulf region.

Among the tribes, the above cultural systems of order operated among themselves, but the tribes' relationship to previously existing populations in the Gulf was one of subjugation. In Saudi Arabia, the Ottomans ruled the Gulf littoral after 1871, but their political representatives in Al-Hasa and Qatif (both now the Eastern Province) were Sunni tribal sheikhs from the Banu Khalid tribe, charged with keeping control over the Shia coastal communities. The Banu Khalid had been the overlords of the coastal region in decades previous to the coming of the Ottomans, and according to one source, most branches of the tribe subjected local Shia to mistreatment and repression, including crippling taxes and theft of their possessions.[37] As Al-Rasheed notes, a proper micro-history of pre-Saudi tribal subjugation in the Eastern Province has not been completed and so the details of the exact enforcement regime are scarce. However, given that most of the Banu Khalid tribes had similar cultural notions of anti-Shia order maintenance as other non-Wahhabi interior tribes, the more detailed historical record on Sunni hegemonic trends in neighboring Bahrain is a reasonable approximation.

In Bahrain, the people known colloquially as *Baharna* (indigenous Shia agriculturists) were enslaved and a feudal order was established by the Al-Khalifah tribe, an offshoot of the Bani 'Utab.[38] Baharna who previously had operated within local spheres of power and influence in cooperation with maritime communities suddenly had tribal overlords and were an underclass. Meanwhile, merchants in their communities operating in the ports were coerced into paying tribute; over time, some Shia families managed to win over the trust of the royal family and rise to elite status. However, the Al-Khalifah's *fedawiyyah*, or tribal militias, actively enforced Shia subordinate relations. Essentially, towns and enclaves of the Bahrain *dirah* were divided among the royal sheikhs and each of them directed their personal *fedawiyyah* to maintain order in that locale. In addition, customs also suggest that *jama'a* (male followers) of the sheikh were obligated to take up arms in defense of the tribe in a crisis.[39] *Fedawiyyah* demanded bribes and violently treated accused wrongdoers. They were known for their "repeated excess earn[ing] them the animosity of the people."[40]

Under the Al-Khalifah control of Bahrain, the two sect-based systems of dispute resolution continued, one for the Sunni tribe and its Sunni allies and another for Shia; the Shia *qadis* followed the Jafari legal school, and the Sunni adopted the Maliki school. A third system was maintained around the existing pearling industry and its customs for the arbitration of disputes. Although small disputes were handled separately, the court of last resort was the royal one in Muharraq, subject to the customs and whims of Sunni tribes rather than sharia or other written law. Another proto-judicial venue in the nineteenth century was the *lawhah al-aqfal* (council of chains) in Manama, where offenders of sharia or customary law were subjected to public scrutiny by a roundtable of municipal notables.[41]

In the early twentieth century (before the second disruption), colonial administrators noted the draconian nature of the Al-Khalifah approach to justice, particular related to issues involving Shia. They cite "years of oppression by the ruling family" that are "far too numerous to quote, but details are on record... [of] illegal seizure of property, wrongful imprisonment with cruelty, and political murders, for which no one has been brought to trial, and no [effort] made to enforce justice."[42] To make matters worse, one of Sheikh Salman's wives, unspecified, held her own trials of local peasants and meted out harsh punishments.[43] Other members of the royal family also reportedly held courts for criminal wrongdoing, with colonial administrators marveling at the allegedly inconsistent results. The overall system of justice prior to colonial reforms was contributing to "bitter relations between the Sunni and the [Shia]... deliberately encouraged by the rulers for years."[44]

The details of the historical entrance of the predecessors of today's Gulf rulers have long been suppressed in official narratives. Although rulers acknowledge having arrived in the regions in the eighteenth century, their violent conquest, warring resource competition, and virtual enslavement of local populations goes un-emphasized and mostly forgotten. This glossing over the disruptive nature of the Sunni tribes to the way of life of the indigenous people of the Gulf becomes reified in colonial discourse as official colonial policies around "preserving Sunni influence."[45] It also "demonstrat[ed] that an Arab state can advance on Western lines under British protection and still retain its Arab character,"[46] as took hold in the 1920s.

"It's (still) not safe to be Shia here": British colonialism and the arrival of the nation-state

In a general sense, British influence in the Gulf, formalized in the nineteenth century, protected the coastal sheikhdoms from absorption into either the Saudi state, expanding from the interior, or Persia. The British took it upon themselves to curtail the ebb and flow of other tribal conflicts and sea piracy, which from their perspective hobbled the further development of trade in the region.[47] James Onley notes that it is likely that in cooperating with the British, the Gulf tribal regimes operated within their own cultural frameworks of alliance and negotiations of control, treating the British as if they, too, were a Gulf tribe, albeit one with more military and economic might.

In the 1920s, without disrupting the basic sectarian framework and instead incorporating it, both the Bahraini and Saudi Arabian regimes involved themselves in the invention of nation-states and the creation of national criminal justice systems. They did so in different ways: one within the direct control of the British, and the other with indirect financial and political backing (including a "regular subsidy" from Britain to Saudi Arabia).[48] But British influence in the region was a major force in the development of both Saudi Arabia and Bahrain as nations.

Although some historians have characterized the development of the nation-state of Saudi Arabia as being one of unique tribal consolidation,

Madawi Al-Rasheed has convincingly argued that the country's modern foundations are not an indigenous invention. Rather, the role of the British is "paramount ... [as] the main external player."[49] From another perspective, the British (and French) encircled the Saudi state in the late colonial period; therefore, the British, in signing treaties and demarcating boundaries with the Saudis, effectively brought the territory into the world nation-state system; the effects are clear in the British-style administrative structures that become incorporated into the Saudi state. What is notable is that Bahrain and Saudi Arabia arrived at the institutionalization of their ongoing sectarian anxieties, and found ways to build the existing Sunni hegemony and anti-Shia order maintenance traditions into the new national foundations, an example of post-colonial hybridization. The previous subjugation of the people of the land by the people of the sea is absorbed into the nation-state, with what emerges anew being a curious combination of colonial administration and Sunni tribal hegemony. For Bahrain, the imposition of the Order-in-Council (OiC) colonial laws and the immediate social and political consequences represent the second upheaval that forever changed law and order. For Saudi Arabia, the second upheaval involved the effect of Britain's deep colonizing endeavor in the Gulf trucial states on Saudi state-building vis-à-vis its own Shia population.

Many sources state that Bahrain was merely a protectorate[50] or part of "informal empire,"[51] and not extensively colonized. However, historical evidence garnered by James Onley convincingly shows otherwise in his apt comparison of a fully colonized Indian princely state as being almost identical in administrative features to the post-OiC Bahrain regime. Despite nineteenth-century treaties that limited the British to external protection of Bahrain, the OiC laws represent very deliberate internal meddling, a deep administrative takeover from the loosely connected "native agents" of the nineteenth century to the professional political agents charged with the task of state-building in the early twentieth century. The OiC laws granted administrative powers to a British political agent (who reported to the political resident in Bushehr, who reported to the Viceroy's office in New Delhi), reorganized customs administration, created a state treasury and land registry, and established courts and a state police force. All this was accomplished after a series of intrigues that effectively forced Sheikh Isa bin Ali Al-Khalifah to abdicate in favor of his son Sheikh Hamad bin Isa Al-Khalifah.[52] (Another aspirant to the throne and son of the ruler, Sheikh Abdullah bin Isa Al-Khalifah, led a politically problematic opposition campaign for several years thereafter.)[53] Sheikh Hamad was installed because of his willingness to permit the British to undertake the OiC endeavor—though to be fair, the full extent of the reforms intended were never presented to him; many "secret" political agent memos went to and fro between the Political Agency, Political Residency, New Delhi, and London as to how to make such comprehensive restructuring of Bahraini society palatable to him after ascension. The British took a gradual approach and although the OiC was drafted in 1913, the reforms, encompassing education, criminal justice, land use, taxation, and more, were rolled out one at a time[54] from 1919 to 1927. Indeed, the OiC laws were a major source of tension between the political agent and Sheikh Hamad throughout the 1920s.[55] Perhaps to assuage tensions, Sheikh Hamad was encouraged to take on a British special advisor who would be in his employ but assist in state-building, a role first imagined by Political Agent Major Clive Daly and then famously occupied by Sir Charles Belgrave for a period of thirty-one years.

The British had a liberalizing effect on some of the worst degradations the Al-Khalifah performed on the indigenous population, such as the feudal enslavement (*sakhra*) of the Baharna, which the British opposed and rolled into their long-standing, empire-wide crusade against slavery. However, much of the other sectarian behaviors of the Sunni tribal leadership were built into the structure of the new Bahraini state, most evident in the new criminal justice system. The British institutionalized the existing separate Sunni and Shia court systems, but regulated the *qadi*s as salaried, governmental posts. Where once *qadi*s emerged organically from the two communities of learned Muslim scholars, the reforms rendered them subject to contractual obligations with defined job descriptions and relegated them to personal status cases (divorce, custody, etc.).[56] Their jurisdictions were taken completely out of criminal matters and many civil ones as well, but were kept separate as Shia or Sunni. The *qadi*s were selected after a rigorous interview process orchestrated by Belgrave, allegedly to overcome the many complaints from the two sect-constituencies over corruption. Further, an appointed council was developed to provide a check on the administration of justice by the new *qadi*s.[57] After uncovering bribery by a particularly corrupt Shia *qadi*, "Sheikh Khalaf," a very sectarian punishment was administered: "He was ultimately told by the Government of Bahrain to go to the [h]oly places in Iraq and he went away in May 1927. His existence in Bahrain was deemed undesirable."[58] The government then received correspondence noting Khalaf's good behavior from Iraq's King Faisal, whose security sector monitored him while abroad.[59] What should be highlighted about the institutionalization of the *qadi* is that the

British never entertained the notion of de-sectarianizing the Muslim adjudicators. Although much ink was spilled attempting to break the corruption in both *qadi* communities, it was inconceivable in this cultural context that the two sects could ever fuse their legal traditions, or accept one over the other. Reading against the grain, this shows how deeply embedded sectarianism was in the notions of social order operating across the society.

Meanwhile, colonial criminal law officially absorbed customary law. The political resident in Bushehr was authorized to establish the Political Agent's Court (PA Court). The political agent sat on the court as a District Magistrate,[60] its main purpose the trying of criminal and civil cases involving non-Bahraini citizens as defendants. In practical terms, the category of non-Bahraini included British citizens, citizens of British colonies and protectorates, and people from other countries not in the British Empire. The source of law for this court was the Indian Penal Code and Criminal Procedure Code of 1861. Appeals to the PA Court's decisions were sent to Bushehr and decided by the political resident. A final appeal went to the "Full Court for the Persian Gulf," also centered in Bushehr, but with two or three additionally appointed judges often pulled from colonial courts in Kenya or Cyprus, or from England.[61] For the local population, the Bahrain Court was established for criminal and civil cases not applicable to the *qadi* courts or the PA Court. It was essentially the invention of Belgrave. Judges included Belgrave, who had only minimal legal training in a previous role in the Colonial Service, and members of the Sunni royal family whom he deemed competent in legal adjudication; thus, criminal matters were shifted entirely to British and Sunni adjudicators. The source of law for the Bahrain Court was a patchwork of English laws in translation, the Indian Penal Code and Criminal Procedure Code of 1861, and "common sense alone."[62]

Regarding policing, Indian sepoys had been on hand earlier to protect imperial interests as part of the Levy Corps. In 1926, the Levies had 200 officers, mostly Baluchis recruited from Muscat.[63] However, during this period a Bahraini police force (albeit with many Indian officers) was deputized as part of the municipal administration of Manama, eclipsing the *fedawiyyah* system, leaving only a few token protectors for the emir himself. According to colonial records, Sheikh Hamad characterized his *fidawi* as being opposed to the new colonial style justice of police and trial courts because it effectively criminalized their "squeezing" of local people.[64] Perhaps as a result, the Levies were not envisioned as so different from the *fedawiyyah* system in the sense that they were "to support [Sheikh Hamad's] prestige [and] enable him to exert some authority,"[65] ostensibly over forces that did not support his emirship in the forced abdication of his father as well as Shia. Therefore, this first colonial force, from which the contemporary force is born, was primarily directed toward preservation of the Sunni ruler and largely manned by foreigners, something that can also be said about the Bahraini police today.

Far from being in a state of passive acceptance, Shia critics allied with Sunni sympathizers to counter the institutionalization of a Sunni-dominated criminal justice system. The importance of this moment is that in such a comprehensive reform of the nature of order maintenance in the country, there could hypothetically have been a break from the sectarian discursive frame. In fact, many proposed responses to reform that could have addressed these inequalities were selected *against* by the colonial administrators and the Al-Khalifah rulers. Zoe Holman notes that there was a balancing act between the marginal population and the monarchy, but the OiC reforms did little to curb the divisiveness emanating from the royal family.[66] Just two years after the reforms began, a petition was submitted to the political agent calling for the abolition of *sakhra*, sudden arrests without warrants, the unfair trying of criminal cases in the Bahrain Court by members of the ruling family, and unsanitary prison conditions. Even Sheikh Hamad's camels were apparently causing the Shia harm by being let loose to graze over Shia lands, disrupting cultivation efforts. After little response to the emerging pleas, an incident perceived as anti-*Baharna* flared into an unrest and began a Shia social movement. In late 1921 or early 1922, one of the Emir's *fidawi* had badly beaten a *bahraini* man during an arrest in Manama. In retaliation, a group of Baharna attacked a *fidawi*. By February 1922, Baharna "demonstrations"[67] wracked the Manama *Suq* after the Baharna led a strike, refusing to work at their agricultural and shopkeeping jobs and collecting in protest in the *suq*. Posing a serious challenge to Al-Khalifah authority and having economic consequences, the Baharna, accompanied by a few Sunni notables, were invited to a meeting with Sheikh Hamad where they repeated their demands. At the meeting, the deputy ruler (at that time) capitulated to the demands, but in reality did not move on any of them. He did lament with the political agent, however, that the difficulty with the Shia was rearing its head due to "past misrule."[68]

Subsequently, further complaints were received by Sheik Hamad that Dawasir tribes were attacking Shia villages and plundering them while the Al-Khalifah were doing nothing to protect them. It was also in this period that Sheikh Khalid Al-Khalifah led a group of Dawasir in a series of "murderous onslaughts" against Shia in Sitra.[69] And rumors circulated that a spate of missing young girls in Muharraq had been kidnapped for Sheikh Abdulla bin Isa Al-Khalifa's pleasures.[70] Among the only responses noted was that Political Resident Arthur Trevor rebuked Sheikh Isa for the allegations of *sakhra*.[71]

The overall lack of response to Shia demands may have been complicated by the continued Persian claims to the archipelago. In 1922, Persia was building a case that Bahrain still belonged to it and hoped to take the case to the League of Nations. Having it be widely known that the Shia were oppressed in Bahrain may have given Persia a sympathetic case. In any case, we know that calls to protect Shia from Dawasir violence fell on deaf ears. The following year Dawasir raided the Shia village of 'Ali, killing and wounding several people, forcing the colonial authorities to provide a means of justice. They put the offending Dawasir Chief, Abdulla al-Doassari, on trial in the PA Court. He was convicted and fined 15,000 rupees, 13,000 of which went to compensate victims—considered light punishment by the political resident at the time. Unfortunately, the matter was far from settled.

Two Shia were murdered on the road between Budaiyah and Diraz later in the year, reportedly as payback for testifying against the Dawasir chief at trial,[72] pointing to the very deep sectarian layers operating in Bahrain at the time. Complicating matters further, Sheikh Ibrahim bin Khalid al-Khalifah led the Dawasir on the aforementioned murderous anti-Shia raid on Sitra in 1923, without any recorded meaningful consequences to him or his family.[73] By 1923, the political agent in Bahrain was reporting that his office routinely received complaints by Shia against the royal family for a customs service that contributed to Sunni wealth by seizing Baharna property. Sunni allies of the royal family were accused of being immune from the taxation charged to Shia people. For example, the Baharna stated that they were the only group being charged the date-garden and fish taxes, despite technical applicability to people of a variety of identities; the *raqibiah* (neck-tax or poll tax), collected arbitrarily from Shia males; and a special tax for Shia for Muharram festivities.[74] Another petition from the Baharna and their allies surfaces again in 1923, calling for equal consideration of Shia in relation to taxes, and protection from marauders.

On 10 May 1923, the sectarian crisis fully unfurled with riots between "Persian" (Shia) and "Nejdi" (Sunni tribal) elements leading to eight dead and numerous wounded. Some of those killed were slain by police responding to the crisis.[75] Telegrams from Bahrain to the political resident anxiously begged for a "gunboat [to] visit here as soon as possible and stay till the end of Ramazan [*sic*] it would have a steadying effect."[76] Construed as being started by foreign elements loyal to Persia and Ibn Saud respectively, the local nature of the conflict is without question two days later: "Yesterday sunnis [*sic*] of Budaiyeh and Raffah attacked Shiahs [sic] of Ali, houses burnt and several casualties. To-day [*sic*] situation improving believed to be in hand, though religious feeling still running high."[77]

It was later determined that the immediate cause for the violence was a conflict over a stolen watch. A young boy in the *suq* had taken it from a Nejdi man (identified as "Qusaibi") and sold it to a Persian man in a jewelry shop. When Qusaibi demanded its return, the Persian shop-owner refused unless he was paid 3 rupees for it. Unable to come to an agreement, both men reportedly went together to consult a mediator. Subsequently, the Persian and a friend arrived at the mediator's abode staggering from dagger wounds, along with a growing group of Nejdis. The mediator attempted to call for help from the political agency, but in doing so inadvertently inflamed a riot between Qusaibi's group and a gathering of Persians, igniting sectarian tensions. Further, although the political agent wanted Qusaibi to be prosecuted for his role in instigating the violence, the royal family would not do it for fear of Saudi retaliation, and the political agency would not do it for fear of arousing further criticisms of British interference in local affairs already triggered by the Order-in-Council reforms just being enacted.[78] The agent had been recently criticized in many editorials in Egyptian newspapers, read in the Gulf, for implementing the reforms.[79] Also underscoring tensions was the forced abdication that provoked many loyalists to Sheikh Isa to call for an end to the British in Bahrain.[80]

The stalemate in responding to the violence that Qusaibi likely incited characterizes the state disposition toward sectarian upheavals for years to come. Importantly, critiques of modern criminal justice transgressions are extensions of a long line of mostly verifiable complaints that the state does not punish crimes involving Shia victims, nor does it protect them from violence in the first place. The British, far from being unaware of the sectarian system they were perpetrating, did so for the larger political reasons of securing and stabilizing the region for trade, and later specifically for oil. Drawing attention to the consequences of this policy, Political Resident Cyril Barrett wrote: "[The policy] means administering the islands for sake of the Chief of the tribes, exploiting the people for the rulers, and treating the Shi'ah [*sic*] as people of an unprivileged class... The family—the Al-Khalifah [are] uneducated savages with the veneer of town manners."[81]

The rule of law set up in the 1920s and continuing to this day is insufficient to contain sectarian anxieties precisely because they are almost always interpreted from the point of view of a royal family whose enduring disposition is to see the granting of Shia rights as a threat to its very legitimacy.

Turning to the eastern regions of Saudi Arabia, the development of Saudi administration in the Al-Hasa and Qatif regions is less documented. Interestingly, in some colonial records, the British political agent in Bahrain was considered by the British to be an active consultant or ambassador to the Ottoman and then Saudi administrators of Al-Hasa. Though not a formal protectorate of Britain, Saudi Arabia had a special relationship with the British who actively supported Ibn Saud's capture of Al-Hasa from the Ottomans, and provided financial support for the regime until at least 1924. Britain entered into a treaty relationship with the Saudi state in 1927, recognizing Abdul Aziz Ibn Saud as king of the Saudi state and that the state was an independent entity from British protectorates.[82]

There were two main effects of British colonialization on eastern Saudi Arabia. First, as the details of Bahrain's emergence as a modern nation-state were negotiated internally, the Saudis became increasingly anxious about the potential for Shia ascension in the Bahraini territory and the effect this would have on its own Shia population. Secondly, the British project in a general sense in the region, later reinforced by the discovery of oil, propelled Saudi Arabia to enter more fully the system of nation-states, working out border disputes and de-tribalizing in favor of a nationalist identity. Despite a new focus on a nationalist identity, the king adopted a *majlis*-based (tribal), consultative style of government that remained behind closed doors. Local rulers' councils were subordinate to the edicts emanating from the national one in Riyadh. Most of the new state's revenue came from *zakat* (based on landholdings, livestock, and other property) as well as tax collection.

Although historical records on order maintenance and the Shia of Al-Hasa and Qatif in the early twentieth century are difficult to come by, we do know that one motivation for Abdul Aziz taking the Eastern Province in the first place rested in a capitulation to the extreme anti-Shia ideology of Wahhabi enthusiasts from the interior. The *ikhwan*, Wahhabi Bedouin tribesmen, became agents of de-tribalization and a means of building a national identity distinct from the myriad tribal identities within the territory. United instead by their Wahhabi ideology, the *ikhwan* became warriors for the new Saudi nation-state. After solidifying interior areas for the Al-Saud, they demanded a jihad against the Shia in Al-Hasa and Qatif.[83]

Inspired by the *ikhwan*, a sedentary Nejdi community took to fighting perceived infidels in Al-Hasa and Qatif. Once having conquered Al-Hasa, the newly established local Sunni leadership prohibited many Shia religious services from being held, using the *mutawwa'a* as enforcers.[84] The local leaders were reportedly consultative, drawing on tribal tradition, but did not regularly include Shia in consultation.[85] For example, the governor of Al-Hasa at this time, Abdulla ibn Juluwi, was a member of a branch of the Al-Saud and was given the authority to use violence against its Shia population (and any competing Sunni tribes) in order to maintain Saudi hegemony.[86] Only a handful of Shia, who made deals with the ruling elites, were able to avoid oppression in the new Saudi state.[87] *Mutawwa'a* routinely extracted a heavy tax from Shia and non-Muslims (*jizyah*). Many of the tax collectors worked on a commission basis. Any opposition to the taxation was treated with violence, including collective punishment for individual incidents of resistance. In the early days of the Saudi administration of Al-Ahsa, Shia courts were allowed to operate, primarily for personal status issues. However, many Shia were slowly replaced along the way and the Shia judges' jurisdictions narrowed, as Sunni administrators took on more state-administered tasks.[88]

It was also at this time that loyal Sunni families in the region were enlisted to begin to collect customs duties and to enforce visa requirements (functions necessitated by the modern bureaucratic systems being brought by the British to the region), particularly important for administering coastal Al-Hasa and Qatif. These notable families were initially established under Ottoman rule, administratively weak in peripheral regions such as the Arabian Gulf.[89] Further, members of these families were sent to neighboring sheikhdoms to represent the Saudi state abroad. In Bahrain, they enjoyed the company of the new bureaucratic elite at dinner parties with the royal family, regional notables, and colonial agents.[90] According to Al-Rasheed, these families became part of the Saudi civil service that formally would develop in the next decade.[91]

In critical histories of Saudi Arabia from a Shia perspective, the capture of Al-Hasa is not described as a time of unification as in state-sponsored textbooks, but rather as an era of occupation. One critical historian argues that the Saudi *ikhwan* engaged in two major solidarity-building efforts in order to build the Saudi state: they sought solidarity through the spreading of a Nejdi (interior) cultural hegemony, as well as sectarian (Sunni) solidarity (*asabiyya madhhabiyya*).[92] Whereas state sources indicate that the Shia of Al-Hasa welcomed the Saudis as a relief from Ottoman rule, Al-Hasan deeply contests this.

After the two disruptions: the persistence of sectarian conflict

Gulf activists and scholars have observed that every generation has its sectarian upheaval, with post-OiC sectarian crisis points cropping up again in the late 1930s, the 1950s, the 1980s, and 1990s (after the Iranian Revolution), and yet again during the events of the Arab Spring. Although each of these events is complex and has its immediate sparks, this analysis suggests that these subsequent crises are the aftershocks of an insufficiently resolved sectarian competition at the administrative births of these states. When colonial administrators were engaged in inventing the Bahraini state, the Shia underclass attempted many times to make the case that they should be written more fully into the civil life of their country. Years of subjugation meant that as a group, though significant in numbers, they were less educated and less organized than the royal family and its allies (notably, the following clans: Jalahima, Manai, Dossari, and Naim). Once the OiC laws began to be implemented in the mid-1920s, at times the Shia managed to convince particular actors of the political establishment of the need to address the sectarian problem. As Political Agent Cyril Barrett wrote in 1929: "The real Bahraini, though an Arab, is a Shi'a not a Sunni; and the history of the islands shows that for long periods it was subject to Persia. This, although not leading to any desire for Persian rule, must modify the tribal outlook."[93]

Or it must not. In this case, the Sunni tribes were able to master more effectively the political and social changes wrought by the British encroachment; the Sunni view of social order would dominate, even as new institutions were developing. Royal families in Bahrain and Saudi Arabia collaborated better with British interests, appearing as they did as the self-proclaimed rulers. They were also more recognizable as a proto-government than other local possibilities: the royal families' down-trodden serfs, the Baharna, or the seafaring merchants with ties to distant ports. The colonial period did not shift the fundamental status quo of tribal elites composing the ruling core. In its hybridized form, the colonial period managed only to lay down the superficial trappings of the modern nation-state and ended the most egregious parts of a feudal-tribal system while leaving behind long-standing social and political problems, notably sectarian-based inequalities.

Contemporary criminal justice: not very different from the 1920s

The colonial shoring up of Sunni monarchies cemented an anti-Shia law enforcement and order maintenance tradition that continues to today.

Although neither force releases official data based on sect-identities of its employees nor its arrestees, information gleaned from sporadic official data on other measures, human rights reports, and other sources provides evidence of the sectarian nature of these forces once all pieces of the picture are considered together. Both the Saudi Arabian and Bahraini police forces are highly centralized under ministries of the interior, answerable to kings. Defense and internal security have always formed a significant chunk of these countries' overall budgets: between 20 and 48 percent of Bahrain's total expenditure from 1974 to 1983.[94] More recent figures suggest that the military (external security, not policing) is 4 percent of Bahrain's GDP while it is approximately 10 percent of Saudi Arabian spending.[95] Despite the end of the colonial era, both Saudi Arabia and Bahrain continue to send criminal justice personnel (police, judges, and lawyers) to Britain for education and training: the colonial experience lives on in post-colonial modes of professional development.[96] In policing and the military, both Bahrain and Saudi Arabia have virtually no Shia officers among their ranks; they had a few more before the Arab Spring, but most were dismissed as collective punishment for unrest and were treated as potential traitors despite their service records. Certainly, Shia have not risen to positions of leadership, except in the Women's Police Directorate in Bahrain.

In Bahrain, independence from Britain in 1971 hardly changed the main administrative structure nor the criminal justice system, though the name of the police force changed to Bahrain Public Security. Overall, the system is one in which the criminal code, though no longer utilizing the Indian Penal Code, is similar to it, founded on common law principles with some borrowing from the civil law tradition. As in colonial times, only the personal status courts employ the sharia. Sunni sharia derives primarily from the Maliki school of legal thought, while Shia judges rule from the perspective of the Jafari school.[97] Despite independence, key British advisors remained in play in the criminal justice system long after independence. For example, Colonel Ian Henderson's leadership of the Security and Intelligence Service (SIS) and other sensitive security posts lasted for over thirty years. Called the "Butcher of Bahrain," Henderson helped to orchestrate a number of heavy-handed criminal justice responses to Shia political opposition.[98] Examples include subjecting them to detainment without trial, and torture.[99]

Particularly problematic from the Shia perspective has been the importation of Sunnis from other countries, such as Yemen, Jordan, Syria, and Pakistan, to fill police officer positions. In 2005, the police numbered approximately 9,500 to 11,000 officers, with only a handful of Shia male police officers (representation of Shia is slightly higher for female police). Throughout the 1990s, the Bahrain government discouraged Shia from applying for positions in the Bahrain Defense Forces (BDF) and the Ministry of the Interior, by requiring them to show a certificate of good behavior and conduct (*shihadah husin al-saluk wa al-sirah*). This certificate could only be acquired from the police themselves and was issued to Shia who were without any arrest record, including any arrests for political demonstration or speech violations.[100] According to the Ministry of the Interior, in 2005 14 percent of the police force were Arab expatriates and an additional 38 percent were non-Arab expatriates, making the Sunni expatriate foreign penetration into policing a sizable 52 percent, or over half of all officers. It is this make-up of the police that has led many critics to go so far as to label the national force as virtually foreign mercenaries. Also in 2005, among police occupying the top thirty positions of the Ministry of the Interior, all were Sunni and fifteen of them were members of the royal family.[101]

The early part of the 2000s saw an opening up of the possibilities for less rigid sectarian restrictions on employment in the force, as part of a liberalization program implemented by King Hamad bin Isa Al-Khalifa (later virtually rescinded with the suspension of the Bahraini Constitution). Bahraini police officers began to participate more robustly in international police professional organizations, and the Ministry of the Interior hosted an International Police Executive Forum conference on community policing in Manama in 2003. The Ministry of the Interior inaugurated their own community police force two years later, reportedly following the model of those in Japan, Finland, and the US. Drawing on the police studies mantra that democratic policing necessarily involves forces that resemble the populations they serve in terms of racial, ethnic, religious, and gender composition, Bahrain also sought to follow this trend ostensibly in order to obtain a modicum of democratic legitimacy in the eyes of foreign observers. In 2005, half of the twenty female community police officers hired identified as Shia. According to one police colonel, a similar ratio applied to the group of nearly 200 male officers hired, though he declined to provide more specific numbers.[102] The events of the Arab Spring in Bahrain in 2011 have led to a rolling back of any inroads to Shia participation in policing, protection of Shia populations from political detention and torture, and inclusion of Shia into the life of the country. By almost all measures, including the Bahrain Independent Commission of Inquiry (BICI) report of 2012, anti-Shia behavior on the part of criminal justice system actors has only worsened. Reforms promised by the government have been primarily seen as window-dressing by international observers, whether journalists, human rights organizations, or academics. Most male Shia officers have been fired from police posts, and an unofficial ban on Shia hiring has been reported.

Meanwhile, dozens of Shia opposition leaders, activists, and their Sunni allies remain imprisoned for behavior related to speech and political organizing.[103] According to Americans for Democracy and Human Rights in Bahrain, in 2015 Bahrain revoked the citizenship of 208 Bahrainis, 72 of whom had theirs stripped by ministerial order in one quick court procedure. Those who lost their citizenship included Sayed Ahmed Alwadaei, Director of Advocacy at the Bahrain Institute for Rights and Democracy; Abbas Busafwan, a journalist; and Shaikh Hasan Sultan, a former opposition member of the National Assembly (the national legislature). Dubious terrorism charges were used to revoke the citizenship of thirteen additional individuals, such as photojournalist Sayed Ahmed al-Mousawi, who was sentenced to a term of imprisonment for ten years. Also the same year, the number of detainees on death row in Bahrain increased by more than 75 percent. Eight individuals were on death row in 2016; in the 1990s and early 2000s, capital punishment was involved in zero to two cases a year.[104]

In Saudi Arabia, most of the daily law enforcement duties fall on the Department of Public Safety, which is divided between a regular police force and the *mabahith*, a secret police for matters of national security. The country is divided into fourteen provinces, one of which is the Eastern Province containing Al-Hasa and Qatif. A province's police are under the control of a provincial general manager; however, key appointments to the force are handled by the national-level Public Safety Directorate. There are no women in the role of sworn police officers, although women work in female prisons and female-support services within the criminal justice system. In addition to the Department of Public Safety, a religious police force (*mutawa*) comprises the Commission for the Promotion of Virtue and Prevention of Vice, which enforces Wahhabi standards of behavior and dress.[105] Drawn from the self-professed vigilantes of local mosques, the *mutawa* are hired by the government when funds are available. They direct their energies overwhelmingly on women who violate dress codes, marriage tradition, or otherwise deviate from the Wahhabi social norms; women are considered legal minors under Saudi law. The court system in the country relies on Judicial Council's interpretation of the sharia from the Hanbali school of law. Appeal courts exist at the regional level, but the king acts as the final appeal in all criminal cases. Trials and other proceedings are not public, and the accused must often act in their own defense.

Because of their underclass status, Shia are nearly unrepresented among the leadership, rank and file of either country's national police force. In essence, Shia participation in civic life is expected to be confined to their own segregated communities. In Saudi Arabia's case, only a handful of Shia have been appointed to the national *shura* council. In fact, the main task for the police, rather than public security, is to protect the monarchy from dissent and behavior that would threaten its control of its territory—particularly likely to occur in the Eastern Province where most of the Shia minority reside. In addition, since the 1970s, the *mutawa* has also concerned itself with anti-government speech and behavior from the point of view that political dissent is anti-Wahhabi as well. The *mutawa* was particularly active in maintaining bans on public Shia religious festivals. A 1965 national security law went so far as to prohibit criticism of the government; and since the 1970s, the Ministry of the Interior has included censors who vet publications and revoke licenses for anti-government media. Interestingly, media that exhibit hate speech toward Shia populations are not censored—even many official religious publications by the state have hate speech against Shia within them.[106] In 1993 there was an easing of anti-Shia attitude by the Saudi government, with a relaxing of bans on Shia celebrating 'ashura, the publication of important Shia texts on family law, and a public dialogue around religious identity; however, long-term reforms never materialized and many believe that the reforms ultimately failed to address the larger problem of Shia marginality.

The police in the Eastern Province regularly continue to arrest and mistreat Shia individuals for activities and speech related to their oppressed status; the military has reportedly also contributed forces to the effort. In May 2010, dozens of protesters were arrested by public safety department police officers and military forces during anti-government protests in the Eastern Province. In the same year, Munir Al-Jassas, a Saudi-Shii activist who often writes about human rights issues, was imprisoned for over a year without charges. The events of the Arab Spring have spawned a cycle of demonstrations and government crackdowns in reaction, culminating in the execution of Sheikh Nimr al-Nimr. In one particularly telling moment, after the 22 May 2015 attack on a Shia mosque in Qudeih, Eastern Province, members of a local Shia neighborhood assembled a neighborhood watch. They were arrested by the Saudi police on the grounds that solely the state is allowed to keep order,[107] a tragic paradox for Shia who go unprotected by the state and targeted by it as a criminal class.

The persistence of sectarianism in criminal justice discourse

In exploring the discourse of police and other Sunni security officials—whether in official publications or news media quotations—the notion that Shia populations are categorically different from Sunnis and threaten the state still characterizes justifications for contemporary anti-Shia police crackdowns. Reading narratives of the 1920s around sectarian violence is not so different in theme and tone from that of today's equivalent descriptions. Abuses against Shia persist, but they still go ultimately unpunished and uncorrected in the name of larger political goals. Sheikh Nimr Al-Nimr's execution in Saudi Arabia in 2016 was punishment for a comment in a Friday sermon: "our dignity is more precious than the unity of this land." In this phrase, Al-Nimr is reflecting the Sunni monarchy's notion of "unity" being exclusive,[108] coexisting problematically with discrimination and abuse. With an apartheid mentality on the part of the state, it is difficult to see why Shia separatism, however improbable to achieve, would be desired.

In Bahrain, even after the BICI report, the public relations arm of the national police apparently saw no problem with thinly disguised sectarian tracts in their *Al-Amn* magazine, constructing Gulf nations as (only) their Arab (Sunni) regimes, with threats against them (in particular) equated to attacks against the countries (at large): "The threat to Arab regimes in the Gulf remains our main concern ... any quarter that thinks of jeopardizing the sovereignty and integrity of our countries should not expect that we accept that."[109] Similarly, an editorial blamed the country's unrest on "the parties claiming to call for freedom and democracy" who have a "selfish mindset."[110] And all this for the sake of the "homeland and not for a certain sect or narrow interests," even as the equation of the homeland with the regime arguably makes its interests quite narrow. A subsequent editorial calls for the criminalization of "the abusers of the social media who sing out of tune," even as it is titled "Our Belief in Dialogue Remains Firm"[111]—apparently as long as those dialoguing toe the party line.

What is difficult to admit for many is that dialogue in this context is infused with hierarchies (related to notions of saving face and honor), acting as an important cultural disposition that must be considered. There is a lack of cultural support from traditional power bases, whether religious or secular, for dialogue that flattens hierarchies and includes all comers. In the Gulf context, public dialogues have traditionally acted as performances of the status quo hierarchies, performances that are deeply embedded in the region's social relations. Therefore, the mere presence of dialogue alone is not necessarily evidence of liberalization or democratization, as is often assumed by Western observers.

Moreover, the recent implementation of a Gulf Cooperation Council (GCC) police force threatens to make Sunni hegemony even more institutionalized than it already is. The official mission of the new force is described as fighting all domestic attempts that would shake national security and stability. We again see a thinly disguised mission to preserve Sunni hegemony. The mainstream opposition in both countries is secular in nature, even as many local Shia institutions participate. The political and discursive frame in a global media-saturated sense has shifted from national and constitutional rights to one of human rights and international law. The secular approach, interestingly, is one that must be constantly reinforced, as a call for Shia rights is often misconstrued as a call for Shia theocracy, or annexation by Iran. One of the main opposition rallying cries since long before the events of the Arab Spring is *la shi'a wa la sunni bus Bahraini* (not Shia and not Sunni, just Bahraini). This inherently acknowledges that one of the main obstacles to a new way forward is a sectarian discursive frame. Hypothetically, the slogan could have been not man or woman, or not Arab or Persian, or not rich or poor, or any number of identities, and yet the popular call for an inclusive Bahrain acts as an interrogation of sect-identity. Further, nationalism "divorced from the Sunni-dominated Arab identity of old [is] a convenient way of breaking apart the old order,"[112] as it can appeal to allies within the state as well as make sense to people from beyond the region who can act as key allies in solving problems of sectarianism and human rights.

Sectarianism and criminal justice: What should be done?

The first step toward policy solutions is for major Western allies in the region to attach meaningful consequences to sectarian divisiveness on the part of Sunni regimes, such as significant military and economic sanctions. Without consequences, regimes only pay lip-service to reform efforts. In Bahrain, after the release of the BICI report, the government promised security sector reform, but made only superficial changes without fully acknowledging past abuses. Several years on from the report, little has altered in the level of violence and political tensions, and in fact the criminalization of anti-government protesters has increased, not decreased. In essence, the government responded cynically to its evaluators and the resulting international pressure to change, such as it was, hoping to slide through with a weak performance without making any substantive changes. The US, despite acknowledging a poor record of reform, maintains arms sales to Bahrain. And Bahrain's friendly relationship with the United Kingdom has never been friendlier, with the building of a new British base in the country and effusive comments of moral support between the two governments. Without Western demands for transitional justice—and true consequences if it is not forthcoming—nothing will change.

Any solutions must wrestle with culturally and institutionally-embedded sectarianism in a direct way through a comprehensive program of transitional justice conceived of as a targeted program of de-sectarianization. Unfortunately, sect-silent solutions around building general capacities for democracy, equality, and economic participation—though helpful and welcome—will not allow the necessary collective healing from past traumas that must occur for sustainable and healthy states to emerge from their fractured foundations. The Shia of Bahrain and the Eastern Province of Saudi Arabia have been subjected to state violence for generations, and yet this violence has never been fully admitted by either Sunni regime.

The de-sectarianization program should allow victims of past sectarian criminal justice discrimination and abuse to have the opportunity to voice their experiences and for evidence of the institutionalized sectarianism within police and security forces to be aired publicly, bringing a variety of witnesses, experts, and informants to bear. As in South Africa, Morocco, and more recently in Tunisia, such processes should aim primarily toward truth-seeking rather than punishment and revenge. It should seek out international organizers and broad support to maintain a legitimate neutrality capable of containing what will be emotional, controversial, but hopefully transformative testimony. Relevant documents that support (or refute) the testimony should be provided by the governments in an additional show of transparency. Further, since this study has pointed to the importance of the operant discursive framework, deliberate attempts to eradicate state-sponsored texts and speech of anti-Shia language will be important (while not necessarily stifling non-governmental public discourse that may be sectarian—in an effort to support candid dialogue and airing of grievances).

Were these countries to take security sector reform seriously, they would also need to implement a lustration process in a manner that allows for a thorough and impartial vetting. The truth and reconciliation model advocated here does not hold anyone criminally responsible for past abuses, but it does permit states to ban individuals, whether permanently or for a period of time, from further government employment. If the vetting process finds individuals who have had leadership positions in a criminal justice agency and they have used those positions to commit serious human rights abuses or directed others to do so, they should be sanctioned through disbarment from civil service.

Once these large processes of truth and reconciliation and lustration begin, reforms along the lines of the blueprint proposed by Human Rights First should be implemented.[113] Criminal justice employees must be drawn from historically under-represented groups, those jailed as the result of unfair criminal prosecutions should be released, and criminalization of political speech should be overturned. Reform would include best practices from state responses to inter-ethnic conflict in post-independent Slovenia.[114] Police human rights training there takes a "joint" approach in which historically marginalized community leaders act as co-instructors with police authorities in frank discussions about cultural differences, police powers, and human rights. Language training is also included and has been found to have a profound effect on softening chauvinisms. Having Bahraini and Saudi officers learn Persian, which some Shia in their territories speak, could have a similar effect. This type of co-produced institutional change with difference-yet-unity in mind, in which the historically marginalized are invited to set the agenda in a formal way, is arguably more sustainable than approaches that are less inclusive, less transparent, and less interactive with the people being protected, policed, adjudicated, or punished.

Regrettably, in Saudi Arabia, a truth and reconciliation process appears much more of a distant prospect given the degree to which the state is officially and overtly committed to its Wahhabi identity and Shia exclusion. Although some inroads have been made to include more Shia in local governments, the result is a kind of Shia tokenism. Further, the execution of Sheikh Nimr Al-Nimr for anti-government speech only shows how even small attempts at Shia empowerment threaten the state, and how little reform can be expected. Saudi Arabia jumps in on opportunities to act as a self-appointed bulwark against perceived Iranian expansionism, and although this avenue may exaggerate Iranian threats, it falls squarely within the erroneous discursive framework operating in the West. If there is no political opening for a comprehensive program of de-sectarianization in Saudi Arabia, then at the very least the US and the UK should refrain from buying into overblown Iranian threats. A first step would be to foster a more sensible and less reactionary approach though an inter-agency review in the US, seeking to refine the official understanding of the nature of the threat. Another place to start, short of a program of de-sectarianization, would be to call for reform of the official edicts, state-sponsored publications, and official discourse that disenfranchise and dehumanize the Shia minority group. This will potentially spark some movement toward envisioning the potential for a Wahhabi state that does not define itself so centrally through the construction of an internal enemy.[115] This may involve the Saudi government's clerics emphasizing different aspects of their doctrine than they have in the past, and could be positively construed as an important intellectual and theocratic review for the kingdom.

In any case, direct approaches, as outlined here, toward a new future despite a sectarian history of violence will be gut-wrenching for many. Years and generations of collective trauma for victims have made the issue highly emotional. Meanwhile, there remain those who, bound by their own traditions, would defend Sunni hegemony—even in a global, human-rights-developing age that places such chauvinistic dispositions more and more in the margins. It will be important for those working on this transnational justice to understand that it is a long and winding process, perhaps as complicated as was the path to the present difficulty. Ultimately, all groups within Gulf societies have to find a place in civic life that mutually and meaningfully offers safety, dignity, and respect—on their own terms.

PART III

DOCTRINAL AND CLERICAL SOURCES
OF SECTARIANISM

10

THE KINGDOM AND THE CALIPHATE

SAUDI ARABIA AND THE ISLAMIC STATE

Cole Bunzel

Introduction

For Osama bin Laden, the United States was the "head of the snake"—the primary target of al-Qaeda's jihad. "Its many tails," the authoritarian regimes of the Middle East, were deemed of secondary importance.[1]

For Abu Bakr al-Baghdadi, however, it is the regime in Saudi Arabia that is the "head of the snake," as he has said in a metaphorical revision worthy of note.[2] This revision by the leader of the Islamic State marks a significant change in the priorities of the global jihadi movement now spearheaded by that group. Notwithstanding the deadly terrorist attacks in Paris in November 2015, this group's focus is on the Middle East before the West. Its slogan, "remaining and expanding," is indicative of its foremost aims: entrenching itself in its Syrian and Iraqi territories and conquering new ones. One of those territories increasingly in its sights is Saudi Arabia, home to Islam's holiest places and one-quarter of the world's known oil reserves.

The competition between the jihadi statelet and the Gulf monarchy is playing out on two levels, one ideological and one material.

Ideologically, the Islamic State presents itself as the true guardian of the particular version of Islam native to Saudi Arabia—that is, Wahhabism, a variant of Salafism.[3] Over the past two decades the jihadi-Salafi movement, which encompasses both al-Qaeda and the Islamic State, has become more Wahhabi in orientation, its leaders and thinkers rooting their radical ideas in the Wahhabi tradition.[4] Wahhabism has thus emerged as the most prominent feature of the Islamic State's ideology. It follows that the conflict between Saudi Arabia and the Islamic State can be understood as one between competing models of the same idea, namely an Islamic state. Both are self-professed Islamic polities claiming to represent Wahhabi Islam.

Materially, the Islamic State has launched a string of attacks on Saudi soil, targeting Shia civilians and Saudi security forces, and has made its presence official with the establishment of three declared provinces. The latter are, of course, provinces in name only. The Islamic State does not administer or oversee territory in Saudi Arabia; it carries out terrorist attacks in the name of an administrative fiction that it hopes one day to make reality. While for the foreseeable future the provinces will remain fictional, the terrorism intended to realize them is likely to continue.

Throughout 2015, several authors offered rather unfavorable comparisons of Saudi Arabia and the Islamic State, some drawing a direct line from one to the other. They pointed out the similar educational curricula used by the two and the shared practice of beheading, among other things.[5] Kamel Daoud, in a November 2015 *New York Times* op-ed, argued that "Saudi Arabia is a Daesh that has made it," referring to the group by the Arabic acronym for its former name—a "dressed up" form of the same thing.[6] But for the most part these comparisons are wide of the mark, as Saudi Arabia seeks partnership with the West and does not aspire to global conquest.

The comparison worth noting is the one in the minds of the Islamic State's jihadi thinkers, the idea that Saudi Arabia is a failed version of the Islamic State. As they see it, Saudi Arabia started out, way back in the mid-eighteenth century, as something much like the Islamic State but gradually lost its way, abandoning its expansionist tendencies and sacrificing the aggressive spirit of early Wahhabism at the altar of modernity. This worldview is the starting point for understanding the contest between the kingdom and the caliphate, two very different versions of Islamic states competing over a shared religious heritage and territory.

The Islamic State and Wahhabism

"Wahhabism" is historically a pejorative term, so its adherents generally do not identify as such. But certain words and phrases serve to indicate affiliation. Thus the Islamic State addresses its supporters in Saudi Arabia, the historical heartland of Wahhabism, as "the people of *tawhid*" (God's unity) and "the people of *al-wala wal-bara*" (association and dissociation), appealing to them via the most prominent Wahhabi theological concepts. In doing so, it emphasizes the historical position of the Saudi people as the keepers of the Wahhabi creed. The Al Saud, the royal family, in the Islamic State's telling, has failed to live up to expectations, selling out the creed. In the group's imagery, the royal family has become the Al Salul, a designation referring to Abdallah ibn Ubayy ibn Salul, a leader of the so-called "hypocrites" of early Islam, who are repeatedly denounced in the Quran.

Competing models

Historically, Saudi Arabia has pinned its legitimacy on the support it gives to Wahhabism, a theologically exclusivist form of Sunni Islam that arose in central Arabia in the mid-eighteenth century. The government has conferred on the Wahhabi religious establishment the privilege of regulating social order, granting the religious scholars a large degree of control over the judicial and educational systems, and allowing them to run a religious police force. In return, the rulers earn the approval of a deeply conservative Wahhabi populace.

By these means, the kingdom's rulers have long portrayed theirs as an Islamic state, and King Salman bin Abdulaziz Al Saud, who acceded to the throne in January 2015, is no different. The new king has described Saudi Arabia as the purest model of an Islamic state, saying it is modeled on the example of the Prophet Muhammad's state in seventh-century Arabia. "The first Islamic state rose upon the Quran, the prophetic *sunna* [that is, the Prophet's normative practice], and Islamic principles of justice, security, and equality," he stated in a lecture in 2011. "The Saudi state was established on the very same principles, following the model of that first Islamic state." What is more, the Saudi state is faithful to the *dawa* (mission) of Muhammad ibn Abd al-Wahhab, meaning Wahhabism, upholding the "banner of *tawhid*" and "calling to the pure faith—pure of innovation and practices having no basis in the Quran, *sunna*, and statements of the Pious Forbears."[7]

The Islamic State makes the same claims for itself. It, too, models itself on the first Islamic state, as its early leadership stated upon its founding in October 2006: "We announce the establishment of this state, relying on the example of the Prophet when he left Mecca for Medina and established the Islamic state there, notwithstanding the alliance of the idolaters and the People of the Book against him."[8] Another early statement appealed to the Wahhabi mission, claiming that the Islamic State would "restore the excellence of *tawhid* to the land" and "purify the land of idolatry [*shirk*]."[9]

The Islamic State, like jihadi groups before it, declares the kingdom's rulers apostates, unbelievers who have abandoned the religion and must be killed. The judgment derives from their perceived failure to rule in accordance with God's law, their alliance with the West, and their tolerance of Saudi Arabia's Shia minority, among other things. The Islamic State presents itself not only as the one true Islamic polity on earth, but also as the only one faithful to the Wahhabi mission. As early as 2007, the Islamic State claimed to have assumed the role of the "political authority that protects and spreads *tawhid*."[10] In contrast to modern Saudi Arabia, it seeks to do so via military expansion, as "Islam recognizes no borders."[11]

Which state, it might be asked, has the better claim to this heritage? A review of the relevant history suggests a rather mixed answer.

The first Saudi-Wahhabi state

The history of Saudi Arabia is widely understood as the history of three successive Saudi-Wahhabi states: the first 1744–1818, the second 1824–1891, and the third 1902–present. Unbeknownst to most observers, the Islamic State holds up the first of these as a model to be emulated: an example of an Islamic state that spread *tawhid* via military conquest, killed the heretics standing in its way, and posited no boundaries to its expansion. The Islamic State is not wrong to see much of itself in the historical first Saudi-Wahhabi state, a radical, expansionary state whose interpretation of Islam was condemned as a fanatical heresy by nearly the entire Muslim world.[12] Here, for example, is a typical description of the founder of Wahhabism by an anonymous contemporary: "He has appointed himself leader and requires that the Muslim community obey him and adhere to his sect. And he compels them to do this by the force of the sword, believing that those who oppose him are unbelievers and deeming it licit to take their blood and property even if they demonstrate the pillars of Islam."[13]

This first Saudi-Wahhabi state was the product of an agreement reached between the chieftain Muhammad ibn Saud and the preacher Muhammad ibn Abd al-Wahhab in the small desert oasis of Diriyah in central Arabia. The two leaders agreed to support each other, the Al Saud supporting the Wahhabi mission and the Wahhabi missionaries supporting Saudi political authority.

Gradually, the Saudi-Wahhabi state came to encompass most of the Arabian Peninsula, including by 1805 the holy sites of Mecca and Medina. Its expansion was predicated on jihad, understood as offensive religious war against all manifestations of *shirk*. As the Wahhabis saw it, most of the world's Muslims had fallen into *shirk*, and the Wahhabis' duty was to eliminate and replace it with true Islam.

In numerous letters, Ibn Abd al-Wahhab explained the basis of his expansionary jihad, arguing that he and his followers were calling people to turn away from idolatry. "For this we are fighting them," he wrote. "As God Almighty said, 'And fight them till there is no persecution,' that is, *shirk*, 'and the religion is God's entirely' [Quran 8:39]."[14] A son of his explained the Wahhabis' right and duty to conquer all who had learned of the mission and rejected it. "Whoever has received our mission," he said, "and refused it, remaining upon *shirk* ... him we excommunicate and fight... Everyone we have fought has been made aware of our mission... The people of Yemen, Tihama, the Hijaz, greater Syria, and Iraq have been made aware of our mission."[15]

Wahhabis mostly fought fellow Sunni Muslims, but the Shia also came under attack. Ibn Abd al-Wahhab had written that the Shia—"the accursed Rejectionists [*al-Rafida*]—were the first to bring *shirk* into this Muslim community."[16] In 1791, the Wahhabis attacked the Shia areas of eastern Arabia, pillaging towns and killing some 1,500 people. The court historian of the first Saudi-Wahhabi state justified the attack as a proper response to the Shia heresy—"they had raised a lighthouse for Rejectionism"—and lauded the destruction of Shia mosques—"temples of Rejectionism" (*kanais al-rafd*).[17]

Another massacre of the Shia came in 1802, when the Wahhabis invaded the Shia shrine city of Karbala in Iraq. The Wahhabi armies, according to the court historian of the second Saudi-Wahhabi state, "entered [the city] forcibly, killing most of its people in the markets and in [their] homes... Nearly 2,000 of its men were killed."[18] The city was pillaged and objects of Shia devotion were destroyed. The commander of the expedition, a grandson of Muhammad ibn Saud, wrote to the Ottoman governor in Iraq to explain his actions: "As for your statement that we seized Karbala, slaughtered its people, and took their possessions—praise belongs to God, Lord of the Worlds! We make no apology for that, and we say: 'And like catastrophes await the unbelievers' [Quran 47:10]."[19]

In 1818, the first Saudi-Wahhabi state finally met its demise when the Egyptian army of Muhammad Ali, at the direction of the Ottomans in Istanbul, overran Diriyah after a seven-year campaign. The Saudi capital was razed and its political and religious leaders were exiled or executed. The fanatical heresy of Wahhabism seemed to meet its end.

The second and third Saudi-Wahhabi states

Soon after, however, the Saudi-Wahhabi alliance resurfaced in a second state formed in 1824. Growing in fits and starts, the second Saudi-Wahhabi state never attained the power and size of the first, and its political leaders were less ideologically charged. It collapsed in 1891 during a long civil war.

The third and final Saudi-Wahhabi state emerged in 1902 when Abdulaziz ibn Saud, a member of the Saudi family living in Kuwait, took Riyadh and conquered the rest of Arabia in about two decades. In 1932, Abdulaziz renamed his state the Kingdom of Saudi Arabia.

At first, the third Saudi-Wahhabi state looked much like the first. The basis of its expansion, as before, was jihad to spread *tawhid* and eliminate *shirk*. It took up arms against fellow Sunni Muslims on the grounds that they had apostatized from Islam. As one of the leading Wahhabi scholars in Riyadh, Sulayman ibn Sihman, wrote in a poem to Abdulaziz in 1921 about the opposition in Hail in northern Arabia: "Fight them for God's sake, for they are an army of unbelief."[20]

Ibn Sihman and his colleagues also urged the king to purge the Arabian Peninsula of the Shia. In 1927, they called on him to convert or expel the Shia of the Eastern Province.[21] Much to the scholars' chagrin, however, the king allowed the Shia to remain. As the kingdom ceased waging expansionary jihad and began tolerating the Shia, it resembled less and less the first Saudi-Wahhabi state. They may not have liked it, but the official Wahhabi scholars of the kingdom acknowledged that the king was acting in accordance with his prerogative as ruler in calling off armed jihad.

Yet despite this acknowledgment, the Wahhabi scholars of the third Saudi-Wahhabi state held to the radical mold of their forebears for decades to come. They continued to fashion an intolerant and sectarian version of their faith. Thus the jihadis of al-Qaeda and the Islamic State, though viewing King Abdulaziz as having betrayed Islam, often quote the scholars who served him, and even those who came after. For example, Turki al-Binali, the thirty-one-year-old Bahraini presumed to be the mufti of the Islamic State, begins one of his books with a poem by Ibn Sihman.[22]

Generally, the last scholarly authority from the Wahhabi religious establishment accepted by jihadis is Muhammad ibn Ibrahim, Saudi Arabia's former grand mufti who died in 1969. Yet some jihadi scholars have viewed certain hardline members of the present Saudi religious establishment with favor, even studying with them. Binali, for example, is proud to have studied with the hardliner Abdallah ibn Jibreen. They spent much time together in what Binali called Riyadh's "Tora Bora quarter," the al-Suwaidi district, in the mid-2000s.[23] In 2004, Ibn Jibreen wrote Binali a recommendation for the Islamic University of Medina, praising the future mufti's "commitment to learning."[24]

Yet as a general principle, jihadis view the first Saudi-Wahhabi state as a political experiment worth emulating and the third Saudi-Wahhabi state as a betrayal. In a 2013 lecture, Binali reminded his audience that one must differentiate among the Saudi states. "The first is not like the second, and the second is not like the third. The third is the last in sequence and the last in worth."[25]

The fourth Wahhabi state

Indeed, the Islamic State is a kind of fourth Wahhabi state, given its clear adoption and promotion of Wahhabi teachings. In an essay in early 2014, Binali highlighted the resemblance between the first Saudi-Wahhabi state and the Islamic State.[26] After "implementing Islamic sharia in Diriyah," he said, the first Saudi-Wahhabi state "expanded to numerous cities and villages ... fought people identifying with Islam ... and was stormed by a mass of accusations and confronted with a flood of lies." With the Islamic State, he continued, "history is repeating itself in identical fashion."

Many of the Islamic State's official publications are classic works of the Wahhabi canon, including some by Ibn Abd al-Wahhab himself. One of these is a lengthy treatise on the requirement of excommunicating fellow Muslims deemed somehow wayward. In the preface, the editor praises Ibn Abd al-Wahhab for "waging war against *shirk* ... in all its forms, inside Arabia and beyond, and waging jihad against all those standing in the way of the mission of *tawhid*." He boasts that the Islamic State promotes the very same *aqida* (creed) that "Sheikh Ibn Abd al-Wahhab adopted, called to, and fought for."[27]

Two more official publications of Wahhabi texts include *The Four Principles* and *The Nullifiers of Islam*, both also by Ibn Abd al-Wahhab. The first of these teaches that "the idolaters of our time" (that is, the opponents of the Wahhabis) are "more severe in idolatry" than the idolaters whom the Prophet Muhammad fought in the seventh century.[28] The second is a list of ten things that can nullify one's Islam, in effect rendering one an unbeliever.[29] Particularly significant is nullifier number eight, "supporting the idolaters against the believers"—a violation of *al-wala wal-bara* (association and dissociation). In mid-2015, a video from Deir Ezzor province in eastern Syria showed a classroom of supposedly penitent Syrians studying the nullifiers with a Saudi teacher and admitting guilt in the matter of nullifier number eight, since they had supported the regime of Syrian President Bashar al-Assad.[30] Beyond these original texts,[31] the Islamic State promotes Wahhabism in many other publications. For example, the most important text at Islamic State training camps is a lengthy explication of Wahhabi creed, apparently written by Binali.[32]

Online supporters of the Islamic State, who universally embrace Wahhabi theology, have similarly likened the group to the first Saudi-Wahhabi state. The most representative publication in this regard, from mid-2014, is titled "Sheikh Baghdadi in the Footsteps of Imam Muhammad ibn Abd al-Wahhab: The Resemblance Between the Wahhabi and Baghdadi States." Distributed online by pro-Islamic State media outlets, this highly detailed comparison of the two state-building projects concludes that "the Islamic State is an extension of Muhammad ibn Abd al-Wahhab's mission [*dawa*] and state [*dawla*]—the first Saudi state." The mainstay of the resemblance, according to the pseudonymous author, is both states' determination "to fight *shirk* in all its forms" and to "implement Islamic law immediately upon seizing territory."[33]

A similar article, distributed by the Islamic State's semi-official al-Battar Media Agency, described the Islamic State's mission as "an extension of Sheikh [Muhammad ibn Abd al-Wahhab's] mission." The author, who goes by the pseudonym Abu Hamid al-Barqawi, drew attention to the similar accusations made against the two states by their respective enemies, namely accusations of excess in the *takfir* (excommunication) and killing of fellow Muslims. He noted that both states were denounced as Kharijites, an early radical Muslim sect.[34]

These online supporters of the Islamic State also find in the example of the first Saudi-Wahhabi state a model for the group's current campaign of violence in Saudi Arabia, particularly its atrocities against the Shia. One of the most prominent online jihadi writers, who goes by the pseudonym Gharib al-Sururiyya, cited the first Saudi-Wahhabi state's raids on the Eastern Province and Karbala to illustrate the continuity between those attacks and the current campaign. Quoting at length the works of the court historians mentioned

THE KINGDOM AND THE CALIPHATE

above, he concluded that the Islamic State's actions are an extension of the first state's. "The men of *tawhid* were attacking and destroying the temples of the idolatrous Rejectionists, unhindered by borders," he wrote. "And now the Islamic State, may God support it, has broken down borders and attacked the temples of the Rejectionists in the Gulf and elsewhere." He went on to quote several Wahhabi scholars' condemnations of the Shia.[35]

Departures from Wahhabism

The religious character of the Islamic State is, without doubt, overwhelmingly Wahhabi, but the group does depart from Wahhabi tradition in four critical respects: dynastic alliance, the caliphate, violence, and apocalyptic fervor.

The Islamic State did not follow the pattern of the first three Saudi-Wahhabi states in allying the religious mission of Wahhabism with the family dynasty of the Al Saud. It is the fourth in this succession of states only in its Wahhabi component, viewing alliance with the current members of the Al Saud as impossible on account of their impiety. The official poetess of the Islamic State, Ahlam al-Nasr (Dreams of Victory), summed up the group's position on the matter in a January 2016 essay: "The Al Salul today sanctify themselves by appeal to the mission of the Sheikh [Muhammad ibn Abd al-Wahhab]," but in fact "the sheikh and his mission have nothing to do with these apostates [that is, the Al Saud]."[36]

The aspiration to the caliphate is another departure from Wahhabism. The caliphate, understood in Islamic law as the ideal Islamic polity uniting all Muslim territories, does not figure much in traditional Wahhabi writings. The Wahhabis could have held up their state as a counter-caliphate to the Ottoman caliphate, which they declared a state of *kufr* (unbelief) until its demise in 1924. But they never did. And in fact it is somewhat ironic that Wahhabism, which began as an anti-caliphate movement, should become the instrument of a pro-caliphate movement.

Violence was by no means absent from the first Saudi-Wahhabi state, as has been seen. But the Islamic State's gut-wrenching displays of beheading, immolation, and other forms of extreme violence aimed at inspiring fear are no throwback to Wahhabi practices. They were introduced by Abu Musab al-Zarqawi, the now-deceased former leader of al-Qaeda in Iraq, who had been introduced to them by a certain Egyptian scholar in Afghanistan named Abu Abdallah al-Muhajir. It is the latter's legal manual on violence, popularly known as *Fiqh al-dima* (The Jurisprudence of Blood), that is the Islamic State's standard reference for justifying its extraordinary acts of violence.[37]

The Islamic State's apocalyptic dimension also lacks a mainstream Wahhabi precedent.[38] As William McCants, a scholar of jihadism at the Brookings Institution, has set out in detail in a book on the subject, the group views itself as fulfilling a prophecy in which the caliphate will be restored shortly before the end of the world.[39] While the Saudi Wahhabis and the Islamic State Wahhabis share an understanding of end times, only the latter view themselves as living in them.

The Islamic State is, therefore, by no means the inevitable expression of historical Wahhabism. It does bear greater resemblance to the first Saudi-Wahhabi state in its commitment to fighting jihad against perceived heretics, particularly the Shia, than does the modern Saudi kingdom. Indeed, the Islamic State has wantonly killed Shia in the same places in Saudi Arabia where its Wahhabi forebears wantonly killed Shia. But in spurning the traditional alliance with the Al Saud, it has adopted certain ideas about politics, violence, and the apocalypse that the three Saudi-Wahhabi states never did. Nonetheless, those nostalgic for the more aggressive Wahhabism of old could be forgiven for seeing more of this in the Islamic State than in modern Saudi Arabia.

The Islamic State in Saudi Arabia

The Islamic State is divided into different *wilayat* (provinces), some more real than others. In November 2014, after receiving pledges of *bayat* (singular *baya*: fealty) from individuals in Algeria, Libya, Egypt's Sinai Peninsula, Yemen, and Saudi Arabia, Abu Bakr al-Baghdadi heralded these territories as new "provinces." Baghdadi was laying claim to Saudi territory and was encouraging his supporters there to join together. Whereas Baghdadi had previously ordered all the world's Muslims to make *hijra* (to emigrate) to Iraq and Syria, Saudis were now no longer obliged to join the thousands of their brethren who had gone there to fight. They could fulfill their duty of *hijra* by building up the Islamic State at home.

First the Shia

Since the November announcement, the Islamic State has indeed been active in Saudi Arabia. Administratively, the group has carved the country into three provinces: Najd province in central Arabia, Hijaz province in western Arabia, and Bahrain province in eastern Arabia ("Bahrain" being an old term for eastern Arabia, excluding the modern country of that name). On a popular website run by Islamic State supporters, the three are grouped together as "the

Provinces of the Land of the Two Holy Places."[40] The provinces have taken responsibility for a variety of attacks in pursuit of a strategy focused on the kingdom's minority Shia population and Saudi security forces. Seventeen separate security incidents related to the Islamic State were reported between November 2014 and November 2015, including one carried out in Kuwait (see Figure 10.1).

Figure 10.1: Islamic State-Related Security Incidents in Saudi Arabia

November 3, 2014	Shooting at a Shia mosque in al-Dalwa near Holul in the Eastern Province kills seven, injures seven
November 22, 2014	Shooting of a Danish citizen by Islamic State supporters in Riyadh
January 5, 2015	Attack on Judaydat Arar border post near Iraq kills three, including a Saudi general; four militants also killed
March 29, 2015	Attack on security patrol in western Riyadh injures two
April 8, 2015	Attack on security patrol in eastern Riyadh kills two
May 8, 2015	Attack on security patrol in south of Riyadh kills one
May 22, 2015	Suicide bombing at a Shia mosque in al-Quay in the Eastern Province kills 21, injures more than 100
May 29, 2015	Suicide bombing at a Shia mosque in al-Dammam in the Eastern Province kills three, injures four
June 26, 2015	Suicide bombing at a Shia mosque in Kuwait city, Kuwait, kills 27, injures more than 200
July 4, 2015	Shootout during a raid in Tail kills one officer and one militant; three others arrested
July 14, 2015	Shootout during a raid in Khamis Mushay near Abha kills one militant and his father, injures two
July 16, 2015	Militant murders a relative in the security forces, then detonates suicide bomb at checkpoint at al-Hair Prison in Riyadh, injuring two
August 6, 2015	Suicide bombing at a mosque of the Saudi Emergency Force in Asir kills 15, injures 33
September 23, 2015	Two militants kill a relative in the security forces in filmed shooting, also kill two civilians and one police officer outside police stations near Hail
October 15, 2015	Shooting attack at a Shia mosque in the Eastern Province kills five, injures nine
October 15, 2015	Suicide bombing at a Shia (Ismaili) mosque in Dahda, Najran Region, kills one injures 19

The strategy in place was outlined by Baghdadi in his November 2014 announcement (see Appendix B). Addressing the Saudi people, he said: "Unsheathe your swords! First, go after the Rejectionists [*al-Rafida*, that is, the Shia] wherever you find them, then the Al Salul [that is, the Al Saud family] and their soldiers, before the Crusaders and their bases." In Saudi Arabia, the Islamic State has acted accordingly, with suicide bombers targeting Shia mosques yielding the most casualties. While there have been more security incidents involving Saudi security forces (nine) than Shia (six), the group has managed to kill more Shia (64) than security forces (25). One attack has been reported against a Western target, a Danish citizen.

The last time jihadis registered this much activity in Saudi Arabia was in 2003–6, when al-Qaeda in the Arabian Peninsula (AQAP) waged a low-scale insurgency that killed some 300 people. Over several years, the Al Saud family managed to destroy AQAP, which then reconstituted itself in Yemen.

It is interesting to observe that the Islamic State's strategic priorities in Saudi Arabia contrast sharply with those of AQAP. AQAP's priorities in Saudi Arabia were, first, Westerners and Western interests; and, second, the Saudi security forces and the regime.[41] It did not go after the Shia at all. With its anti-Shia strategy, the Islamic State is trying something quite different. Playing to the inherent anti-Shiism of Wahhabi religious doctrine, and to the widespread fears of creeping Shia domination of the region, it is presenting itself as the champion of Sunni Islam at a time when the Shia are seen to be taking over the Middle East.

The leaders of Najd province, in two audio statements released in May and October 2015, have described and justified this anti-Shia strategy at length.[42] Both statements are diatribes against Shiism. The first (translated in full in the Appendix B) accuses the Saudis of failing to carry out their Islamic duty of expelling the Shia from the Arabian Peninsula and by contrast cites Baghdadi's order to "kill the Rejectionists wherever they are found." "The Al Salul," it says, "will never protect you from the Rejectionists. Indeed, they have been unable to protect their artificial borders from the Houthi scum, so how will they protect you from the Rejectionists if they join together against you?"

The second statement presents an overview of the Shia threat, which can be summarized as follows: The Sunnis are under a regionwide attack by an Iranian-led Shia conspiracy (witness Iraq, Syria, and Yemen, where the Shia are taking power with Iranian support). The Shia aspire to a massive state in the shape of a crescent, stretching from Syria through Iraq, down through eastern Arabia to Oman and Yemen, ultimately encompassing Islam's holy places in the Hijaz. The Shia of the Eastern Province are secretly loyal to Tehran and are readying to free themselves of the Sunni yoke when the time is right. Meanwhile, members of the Al Saud family are complicit in this plot to the extent that they care only about their power, wealth, and survival.

The two statements emanating from Najd province appeal to Wahhabi theology to demonstrate the Shia's abiding enmity for the true Muslims. For example, the first statement describes the Shia as a group of idolaters and applies to them the alleged statement of the Prophet Muhammad, "Expel the idolaters from the Arabian Peninsula." Dipping into the Wahhabi heritage, it quotes Sulayman ibn Sihman—one of the scholars who urged King Abdulaziz to expel the Shia back in 1927—to the effect that civil war is preferable to a ruler who fails to rule in accordance with God's law.

Hypocrisy allegations

Indeed, it is common practice for the Islamic State and its supporters to assert that their actions against the Shia are in accord with Wahhabi theology. They even maintain that their actions find sanction in the official teachings of the Saudi religious establishment. Thus the second statement from the leaders of Najd province argues that "the mujahideen in the Arabian Peninsula ... have killed only those against whom the clerics of the Al Salul theorized a judgment of excommunication and death." Abu Musab al-Zarqawi may have been the first to argue along these lines when, in a lecture on Shiism in 2006, he quoted a fatwa from Saudi Arabia's Permanent Committee for Islamic Research and Fatwa Issuing that clearly excommunicated the Shia.[43]

Islamic State supporters online frequently quote official Saudi scholars to justify anti-Shia attacks. For instance, after a shooting at a Shia mosque in the Eastern Province in mid-October 2015, a supporter tweeted the following quote from Ibn Jibreen, the scholar with whom Turki al-Binali studied: "The Rejectionists are in the main idolaters ... theirs being greater idolatry [*shirk akbar*] and apostasy from Islam, for which they are deserving of death."[44]

The intrinsic anti-Shiism of Wahhabism poses a problem for Saudi religious scholars when it comes to condemning the Islamic State's attacks in the kingdom. The group and its online supporters accuse these Saudi scholars, sometimes rightly, of backsliding and hypocrisy.

These accusations can be rhetorically powerful. For example, a lengthy Islamic State video from July 2015 features Saudi fighters in Aleppo pointing out contradictions in the scholars' statements. "A short time ago," one of the

Saudis in the video says, "the scholars of the Al Salul were excommunicating the Rejectionists, indeed excommunicating the generality of them... They excommunicated them, but when the caliphate fought them ... they issued condemnations."[45] The video then shows statements (mostly tweets) by Saudi scholars before and after the Islamic State attacks in the Eastern Province. In one sequence, Muhammad al-Arifi, the most popular Saudi preacher in the country with more than 14 million followers, is shown in a scene before the Islamic State attacks scolding "the Rejectionists" for transgressing the bounds of Islam and making war against "the Muslims." In a scene following the attacks, he is shown expressing profound sympathy for the people of the Eastern Province, who are mostly Shia.

The same video further accuses these scholars of holding the Islamic State to a double standard, since these men, while criticizing the Islamic State's targeting of the Shia in Saudi Arabia, still condemn the Shia in Yemen and urge the Saudi government to wage jihad against them as "idolaters." Numerous tweets to this effect are presented. A Saudi then remarks to the camera: "They excommunicate the Rejectionists in Yemen and proclaim them Muslims in the Eastern Province!"

Scholarly outreach

In late 2014, rumors began circulating that the Islamic State was trying to recruit more of the world's jihadi scholars to its cause, as most of them had sided with al-Qaeda's Ayman al-Zawahiri over Baghdadi.[46] The recruitment effort, spearheaded by Binali, fared rather poorly, with the biggest names doubling down on their opposition to Baghdadi and reiterating their support for al-Qaeda. But in Saudi Arabia it seemed to yield a measure of success.

In the early 2000s, Saudis were some of the chief ideologues of the jihadi-Salafi movement, contributing large numbers of fatwas, essays, and books to a growing corpus of online literature. Unlike most jihadi thinkers, these men were trained Muslim scholars with advanced degrees and, in some cases, university positions. They gave the movement greater legitimacy and theological depth. A cohort of these men was known as the Shuaybi school, named for the late Saudi Humud al-Uqla al-Shuaybi, a former university professor in Riyadh and al-Qasim. Its other leaders were Nasir al-Fahd, a professor of theology at Imam Muhammad ibn Saud Islamic University in Riyadh, and Ali al-Khudayr, a mosque leader who taught theology and law in al-Qasim.[47] In 2003, they were arrested for supporting AQAP. This was a major blow that, according to

Thomas Hegghammer, an academic specializing in jihadism and the author of a book on AQAP deprived the organization of "a crucial legitimising resource."[48] Since 2003, little has been heard of these jihadi scholars, whom the Saudis have kept under lock and key.

Fahd and Khudayr are among more than 4,000 Saudis being held in Saudi Arabia as "security prisoners," which is Saudi parlance for supporters of jihadism as advocated by al-Qaeda and the Islamic State.[49] According to a senior prison official quoted in the Saudi press, there has been a major ideological split among the prisoners, who have smuggled out messages in support of either the Islamic State or al-Qaeda.[50] One of these messages from early 2014, recorded by the jihadi scholar Sulayman al-Ulwan, decried Baghdadi and his claim to statehood.[51] However, most of what has been leaked is supportive of the Islamic State, suggesting that Saudi Arabia's jihadi prison population has gravitated in its direction.[52] One former AQAP ideologue, Hamad al-Humaydi, authored several pro-Islamic State works from his cell that were published online between 2014 and 2015; and another, Faris al-Zahrani (also known as Abu Jandal al-Azdi), allegedly gave *baya* to Baghdadi from prison.[53] Both were executed by Saudi authorities on 2 January 2016, in a group of more than forty condemned for what the state deemed terrorism.[54]

In a mid-May 2015 audio address, Abu Bakr al-Baghdadi appealed directly to Saudi Arabia's imprisoned jihadi religious scholars (*talabat al-ilm*) for their support, saying "we have not forgotten you, nor will we ever forget you," and promising to fight for their freedom.[55] Three months later, in August 2015, the Islamic State won its biggest prison victory when a handwritten letter of *baya* from Nasir al-Fahd was leaked from al-Hair prison; it called on all mujahideen to join the Islamic State. The Islamic State's semi-official media agencies online proclaimed and circulated Fahd's statement, which did not address Saudis in particular but did express the hope that the Islamic State would eliminate all the illegitimate regimes ruling the region. Significantly, he attempted to pre-empt criticism by noting that while the Islamic State had caused excessive shedding of blood, this was an excusable error in light of trying circumstances.[56]

With Fahd on board, the Islamic State is clearly hoping for Khudayr's endorsement as well. The video featuring Saudis in Aleppo, discussed above, shows some of the Saudis seated before a well-placed copy of one of Khudayr's books.[57]

Just how influential the *baya* from Fahd—and a potential one from Khudayr—will be on the Saudi scene is hard to say. In October, a prominent jihadi writer online who uses the pseudonym Abu l-Maali Aqil al-Ahmad trumpeted "Fahd's call" as a major victory.[58] But thus far, the *baya* has not energized the Islamic State's campaign in Saudi Arabia, perhaps because Fahd did not specifically encourage the Islamic State's attacks in Saudi Arabia. He may have been unaware of them. The greatest effect of the *baya* has probably been in persuading those already harboring jihadi sympathies to support the Islamic State over al-Qaeda. For the moment, that is an invisible victory. But over the long term, Saudi Arabia has to worry about the contagion effects of having thousands of citizens behind bars who are loyal to the caliph in Raqqa.

A range of supporters

As of March 2015, more than 2,000 Saudis had gone to join jihadi groups in Syria and Iraq, according to the Saudi Interior Ministry. But far more remained back home. Between November 2013 and July 2015, the number of Saudi security prisoners had nearly doubled as Saudi security forces arrested those attempting to leave for Syria and Iraq and disrupted the Islamic State's networks in Arabia.[59]

Saudi supporters of the Islamic State do not fit a single profile but are a mixed bag, ranging in age from teenagers to septuagenarians. Scattered, anecdotal information in the media suggests that the majority of this group consists of young men, most of them hailing from central Saudi Arabia in the Riyadh area or the conservative al-Qasim area some 200 miles to the northwest. The six Saudis who carried out suicide bombings in the name of the Islamic State's Arabian provinces in 2015 seem to have been mostly from central Arabia, ranging in age from fifteen to thirty-five. The largest networks that Saudi security forces claim to have broken up were in Riyadh and al-Qasim. None of this is surprising given past experience, but more data would be required for a more significant demographic comparison between Islamic State supporters and earlier groups of Saudi jihadis.

The support network's upper ranks also encompass a range of people. The reputed religious leader of the al-Qasim network, for example, was the blind, septuagenarian scholar Hamad al-Rayyis, who has links to the Shuaybi school and is now in prison.[60] Other minor religious scholars of different ages have emerged as Islamic State supporters as well. Faris al-Zahrani was in his mid-forties and Hamad al-Humaydi was in his late fifties when they were executed in January 2016. Nasir al-Fahd is in his late forties.

Then there are the Islamic State's generally younger Saudi logisticians, themselves a diverse group. They include Abd al-Rahman al-Mujil, a former employee of the Ministry of Health, and Abdallah al-Fayiz, who previously fought with al-Qaeda in Iraq. Both are believed to have coordinated extensively with Islamic State leaders in Syria and Iraq.[61]

Be patient, do not rush

The Islamic State's military campaign in Saudi Arabia has failed to gain traction in the year since its launch.

Several reasons seem to account for the slow pace of the Islamic State's campaign in the country. The first is the regime's effective counterterrorism infrastructure, which was put in place as a result of the AQAP insurgency in the mid-2000s. It combines elite policing with advanced surveillance, intelligence, and special forces training, and a certain restraint in repression, offering rehabilitation and mediation programs and eschewing torture.[62] The government announced in July 2015 that multiple raids over the preceding year had prevented attacks and led to the arrest of more than 400.[63] The crackdown seems to have severely damaged the network of Islamic State militants and sympathizers, particularly in the al-Qasim region, which was home to the largest and best-organized network in the country.[64]

Another reason is the apparent lack of charismatic leadership, apart from those in prison, supporting the Islamic State in Saudi Arabia. In its campaign, AQAP encountered a significant setback with the loss of its leader Yusuf al-Uyayri, who had been a key recruiter and fundraiser and was the link between the militants and the Shuaybi school; he was killed by Saudi security forces during a shoot-out in 2003. The Islamic State has no comparable figure in what it considers its Arabian provinces, and it is uncertain whether it has many competent people at all. The first statement from Najd province has several errors, suggesting a mediocre standard of learning and poor accuracy on the part of its leadership.

Yet another reason for the campaign's slow pace is the historical tendency of Saudi jihadis to prefer jihad abroad to jihad at home. Saudi Arabia has been a major contributor of fighters to foreign jihad theaters, from Afghanistan in the 1980s to Iraq in the mid-2000s, and to Syria and Iraq today.[65] But stirring unrest at home has proven difficult, probably for reasons to do with the religious character of the state and the wealth of average Saudis relative to their neighbors. Altering this tendency will be a challenge for the Islamic State. Because the Saudi regime is playing only a minor role in the fight against the group in Iraq and Syria, it has inspired little resentment. Meanwhile, the Saudi people, surveying the regional upheaval, are keenly aware of the destructive consequences of a rebellion at home.

Nonetheless, the Islamic State's attacks in the kingdom are likely to continue for some time for two reasons. The first is that with its attacks on the Shia in outlying areas, the group is not disrupting the lives of most Saudis, some of whom sympathize with attacks on the Shia as idolaters. This is in contrast to the reaction to AQAP's attacks on Western civilians in downtown areas. The second reason is that the campaign's external stimulus, namely the Islamic State's inspiring presence in Iraq and Syria, is by no means on the verge of receding. The AQAP campaign failed in part because it got going only with a massive influx of veteran jihadis, whose depletion spelled its ruin. With a more enduring external stimulus, the Islamic State's campaign in Saudi Arabia is likely to hold up longer than AQAP's.

But as of January 2016, the Islamic State had gone three months without pulling off a major attack in the kingdom. Whether the current dry spell marks the decline of the Islamic State in Saudi Arabia or is merely the eye of the campaign's storm is too early to tell. But the group's leaders in Syria and Iraq seem to be running out of patience.

In November 2014, Baghdadi had counseled his supporters in Saudi Arabia, "Be patient, do not rush."[66] But in mid-December 2015, the group launched a full-scale propaganda campaign calling for attacks in Arabia. In the space of just a few days, the Islamic State put out fifteen official videos from its provinces, from Syria and Iraq to Yemen and the Sinai, all concerning Saudi Arabia, many of them calling on the group's supporters there to step up their efforts. At the same time, the Islamic State's unofficial media agencies released 26 essays in the same vein.[67] The Islamic State, as Baghdadi's earlier statement would suggest, seems to be playing the long game in Arabia. But it is also clearly disappointed in its progress there.

Saudi scholars and the Islamic State

With jihadis openly laying claim to the Saudi religious heritage, the Saudi religious establishment might be expected to engage this threat in serious intellectual combat. Yet nothing of the sort has taken place. Instead, the kingdom's scholars have reluctantly addressed the issue of the Islamic State by issuing only blanket condemnations. There is little sense of urgency in their words and actions, and absolutely no recognition of the Islamic State's Wahhabi character. Meanwhile, Saudi liberals who are clear-eyed about the

Islamic State's Wahhabi character, along with at least one dissident religious scholar, have reignited a debate over Wahhabism in the kingdom. They want the religious establishment to lead an effort to reform Wahhabi doctrine, but many of them view the institution as too weak to handle the task.

The scholars reprimanded

In mid-2014, the late King Abdullah castigated the Saudi religious establishment for its silence in the face of the jihadi threat. In August 2014, a month after the Islamic State declared itself the caliphate, Abdullah fumed at the establishment scholars during a public gathering at his palace in Jeddah. Earlier that day he had given a speech warning about the dangers of Islamic extremism and calling on "the scholars of the Islamic community to carry out their duty before God and confront those trying to hijack Islam and present it to the world as the religion of extremism, hate, and terror." Muslim scholars, he suggested, needed to do more. Those who "have hesitated or are hesitating to carry out their historical responsibilities against terrorism for the sake of worldly benefits or hidden objectives, tomorrow they shall be its first victims," he said.[68] At the reception at his palace, the king made clear that those he had in mind were his own court scholars.

Discussing the "deviants" of the Islamic State, the king decried "how a person could take hold of another person and slaughter him like a sheep." Then, raising his voice, he motioned reproachfully at the scholars seated beside him. "Your scholars, all of them are listening. I am asking them to expel the laziness that is around them," he said, turning to face the men concerned. "They see laziness in you, and silence in you. And you have a duty. You have a duty [to defend] your world and your religion, your religion, your religion!" The several dozen scholars sat stone-faced during the king's condemnation.[69]

The reluctance of the scholars to address the Islamic State was partly because of their support for the revolution in Syria, which they have cast as a legitimate jihad. Though adapting their views to suit government policy, the scholars have remained unwavering supporters of the Syrian jihad.[70] In 2012, the Council of Senior Religious Scholars, which was created by royal decree in 1971 and is the country's highest religious authority, issued a fatwa prohibiting non-official donations pursuant to a government order. But in line with their innate sectarianism, the scholars have been much more vocal in denouncing the crimes of the Assad regime and Iran than in condemning the Islamic State or al-Qaeda.

King Abdullah's 2014 outburst directed at the religious scholars was not his first. Known as a moderate reformer, he had had prior public disputes with the religious establishment when he was the crown prince. In November 2001, after the terrorist attacks on 11 September brought Wahhabism to the world's attention, Abdullah addressed the scholars in a public statement, warning against indulging "extremism" (*al-ghuluww fi l-din*) at this "critical" phase, suggesting that some official scholars were given to extremist opinions.[71] The Saudi intelligentsia saw in this a clear message to the scholars to revise the religious discourse of the country in a more tolerant direction.[72] Accordingly, the educational curricula, for example, began putting more stress on the concepts of moderation and justice in Islam and less on exclusivist notions like *al-wala wal-bara*.[73] But these were minor changes.

Questioning Wahhabism during the AQAP campaign

Calls for revising the religious discourse of the country would continue after May 2003, when al-Qaeda began a bombing campaign in Saudi Arabia which would last several years, targeting Western expatriates and Saudi security forces. The attacks prompted some Saudis to question the bases of Wahhabism in unprecedented public fashion. But the state only let them go so far.

Two of the most prominent critics were Saudi liberals Jamal Khashoggi and Mansour al-Nogaidan. Khashoggi, a US-educated journalist, was removed from his post as editor of the semi-official Saudi newspaper *al-Watan* for publishing articles critical of Wahhabism. In one article, Khashoggi blamed the May 2003 bombings on the broader religious culture in the kingdom. In response, a group of official scholars met with Crown Prince Abdullah to complain, leading to Khashoggi being fired. Though reinstated in 2007, Khashoggi was again forced to step down in 2010 for publishing yet more articles hostile to Wahhabism.[74]

In similar fashion, Nogaidan, a Saudi Islamist-turned-liberal commentator, launched an assault on Wahhabism in newspaper op-eds in the wake of the 2003 bombings. Sentenced to 75 lashings for his outspokenness, he took his story to the *New York Times* where he declared that "many [Saudi] religious leaders sympathize with the criminals" of al-Qaeda. He accused Saudi Arabia's "educational and religious institutions" of being "breeding grounds for terrorists" and called for reforms to "our extremist religious culture."[75] After Nogaidan's article appeared in the *New York Times*, he was imprisoned for five days.[76]

Among the religious class, however, few dissenters emerged in the post-2003 period. Several members of the Sahwa, the country's broad-based Islamist movement, called for re-examining the more exclusivist and violent parts of the Wahhabi religious heritage, but they soon ceased to speak up.[77] Only one man with scholarly pretensions, Hasan bin Farhan al-Maliki, a historian holding rather eccentric views by Saudi standards, wrote critically of the Saudi religious tradition.[78] In *Preacher, Not a Prophet*, published in 2004 in Jordan, Maliki called Saudi Arabia's official religious class extremists (*ghulat*) and blamed them for fostering a religious culture conducive to jihadi violence. It was futile for the religious establishment to counter al-Qaeda's jihadi ideology, he wrote, for the jihadis were merely doing what the religious establishment had taught them.[79] Maliki's views were naturally not well-received in Riyadh, where scholars rushed to dismiss his work. He lost his job at the Ministry of Education.

The limited revision of Wahhabism that took place in the wake of the AQAP campaign of 2003–7 was largely superficial. National Dialogue conferences were held to discuss Islamic extremism, and the religious curriculum of primary education was updated to accommodate a "tone of tolerance," as David Commins, a scholar of Saudi and Wahhabi history, characterized it. In one textbook, for example, according to Commins, "sections about bearing enmity to infidels were removed altogether."[80] Yet there was no serious re-evaluation of basic Wahhabi principles.

Questioning Wahhabism during the Islamic State campaign

The rise of the Islamic State beginning in 2013 has revived the internal Saudi debate over Wahhabism, and once again Saudi liberals are at its forefront. The opening shot in this period was fired by Saudi economist Hamza ibn Muhammad al-Salim in a very provocative newspaper article, "Salafism on Its Deathbed," in September 2013. Salim declared that Wahhabism was now "only a burden on the Saudi state," with international charges against it accumulating daily. Many Saudis, he said, just wanted "to dispense with it" altogether.[81]

The king's 2014 reprimanding of the scholars brought yet more anti-Wahhabi voices to the surface. In marked contrast with the preceding period of debate, the most prominent voice has been that of a dissident religious scholar, Hatim al-Awni, a professor of *hadith*, the statements attributed to the Prophet Muhammad, at Umm al-Qura University in Mecca. Awni is a marginal figure in the Saudi religious landscape because of his background. Born in Taif in the western Hijaz province of Saudi Arabia, Awni is related to the Sharif family that ruled the Hijaz prior to the Saudi conquest of the region in the 1920s. Be that as it may, his positions are worth relating as representative of liberal Saudi criticism of Wahhabism and the increased openness of the debate.

On 3 August 2014, just two days after King Abdullah's public rebuke of the scholars, Awni published a fiery essay on his website entitled "The Lazy Scholars," a clear reference to the king's remarks. Taking aim at the very scholars who were the target of the king's wrath, Awni claimed that they had criticized the Islamic State "only lazily" because they did so "without conviction." In reality, "the bases of their thought and their *takfir* [excommunication of other Muslims] are in agreement with those of [the Islamic State]," he wrote. Their difference with the Islamic State is only a matter of "political loyalty." They and the Islamic State shared the "same principles of *takfir*," namely *takfir* of "those providing assistance to unbelievers against Muslims," of those who rule "by other than what God has revealed," of those who engage in impermissible acts when visiting graves, of those who adhere to rival theological schools of Sunni Islam, of those who are simply ignorant of the fundamentals of the religion, of the Shia, and so on.[82]

At the end of the month, Awni brought his critique to the pages of one of the country's leading semi-official newspapers, *al-Hayat*, calling for a campaign to correct the extremist views in the standard compendium of Wahhabi writings, *al-Durar al-saniyya fi l-ajwiba al-Najdiyya* (The Glistening Pearls of Najdi Responsa). According to Awni, this book—sixteen volumes of Wahhabi essays, fatwas, and correspondence from the time of Ibn Abd al-Wahhab to the mid-twentieth century—was the fount of extremism. (Indeed, Turki al-Binali, the Islamic State's mufti, has frequent recourse to the book, even quoting it without notes by volume and page number in his lectures.)[83] But Saudi Arabia's religious scholars refused to acknowledge the relationship between the ideas on display in *al-Durar al-saniyya* and the ideas of jihadi-Salafism as represented by the Islamic State. Their denial, in Awni's words, amounted to a "betrayal of the Islamic community and the country." There were three kinds of Saudi religious scholars, according to Awni: the ignorant who simply do not understand what is in the book; the opportunists who defend it to advance their own careers; and the crypto-jihadis, the largest group of all, who wish Saudi Arabia would be more like the Islamic State.[84]

In May 2015, in response to the Islamic State's attacks on Shia mosques, Awni again accused the religious establishment of ideological complicity. The official scholars' condemnations of the attacks, he argued, were insufficient. They needed to "clarify their position with respect to the Shia: Are they Muslims? And if so, how do we reconcile classifying them as Muslims with the statements in *al-Durar al-saniyya* that clearly affirm their unbelief?"[85]

Significantly, Awni has called not for ditching Wahhabism altogether but for reforming it. In a televised interview, he described an envisioned "correctionist movement" (*harakat al-tashih*), to be led by the Al al-Sheikh (the descendants of Ibn Abd al-Wahhab) and the Council of Senior Religious Scholars. It would be, in his view, a continuation of certain revisions made by Abd al-Aziz ibn Baz, the former grand mufti who famously gave opinions on *takfir* at odds with the bulk of the Wahhabi tradition.[86]

Like Awni, the Saudi liberals critical of Wahhabism generally argue for reforming, not dumping, Wahhabism. Some of them have praised Awni for his outspokenness and hailed him as their leader.[87] But Saudi Arabia's scholars have not been interested in participating in this debate.

The scholars respond

As King Abdullah suggested, the official Wahhabi scholars had said little about the Islamic State prior to August 2014.[88] After the king's reprimand, they had no choice but to speak up. Since then, their condemnations have appeared in the semi-official Saudi press almost weekly.

Three themes recur in these routine statements: name-calling and conspiracy-mongering, exonerating the Wahhabi tradition, and announcing plans to combat terrorist ideology. On 19 August 2014, Abd al-Aziz Al al-Sheikh, the grand mufti of the kingdom and head of the Council of Senior Religious Scholars, introduced these themes in the establishment's first statement on the Islamic State.[89]

Al al-Sheikh characterized the Islamic State, along with al-Qaeda, as "an extension of the Kharijites, who were the first group to leave the religion." The association of jihadis with the Kharijites, an early Islamic sect known for its violence and eagerness in *takfir*, is of course not new. Mainstream Muslims have branded extremist rivals as Kharijities for decades. For Saudi scholars, it is the term of abuse of first resort.

It is important to note that in Islamic theology the designation "Kharijite" does not necessarily amount to a charge of unbelief and apostasy. Perhaps only one establishment scholar, Sa'd al-Shathri, a professor and former member of the Council of Senior Religious Scholars, has gone that extra step to declare the Islamic State to be not only Kharijites but "unbelievers"—"more disbeliev-ing," indeed, "than Jews and Christians and idol-worshippers."[90] But this posi-tion is rare.

The corollary of such name-calling is conspiracy-mongering. The two often appear together, as when the Council of Senior Religious Scholars described the Islamic State's "client, Kharijite thought," alleging that the group had been fashioned by "hidden hands" with the aim of "sowing division" and "sullying the pure Islamic religion."[91] Shathri described the Islamic State as "an exten-sion of the former Baath Party,"[92] while another establishment scholar, Abd al-Latif Al al-Sheikh, said it "was conceived and developed in the womb of the Muslim Brotherhood," its actions showing evidence of a "foreign agenda."[93] Yet another, Salih ibn Humayd, said it is "the creation of international intel-ligence agencies."[94] The list of conspirators is long. In December 2015, the kingdom's mufti described the Islamic State as "soldiers for Israel," but also added that they are Kharijites.[95]

Indeed, the scholars seem willing to attribute any source to the Islamic State but Wahhabism and hope to stifle any discussion of the Wahhabi connection. This was the message of Abd al-Aziz Al al-Sheikh's early statement calling for "elevated discussion that does not call people traitors and does not accuse." Soon after, the Council of Senior Religious Scholars stated that it "rejects what some writers have said in connecting terrorist ideas to educational meth-ods or to the esteemed writings of the scholars."[96] This was intended to dismiss all that Hatim al-Awni had said. Shathri said of the Islamic State: "The truth of this organization is that it has no connection to the mission of Sheikh Muhammad ibn Abd al-Wahhab."[97]

Yet the religious establishment has not denied that the Islamic State exerts a certain attraction on Saudi youth. "The Council of Senior Religious Scholars is following with great concern the development of Daeshi thought" in the kingdom, the *al-Watan* newspaper reported in October 2015.[98] In his August 2015 statement, Abd al-Aziz Al al-Sheikh announced that he would put for-ward "a comprehensive plan" to strengthen the moderation (*al-wasatiyya wal-itidal*) of true Islam and deter Saudis from joining the "Kharijite groups." "The overarching objective of Islamic sharia," he said, "was protecting the order of coexistence." In October the scholars unveiled their eight-point plan, which focused on holding conferences, reaching out to vulnerable youth to refute their errors, and increasing the public presence of the establishment scholars, including on social media. The implementation of this plan, if forthcoming at all, is certainly lethargic.

The persistence of unreconstructed Wahhabism

In short, official Saudi scholars are not interested in countering the Islamic State by reforming Wahhabi doctrine. Their plan, as Saudi liberals have pointed out, does not differ from previous efforts of cosmetic reform. There is no bold re-examination of the Wahhabi heritage, only self-vindication.[99] As Saudi liberals, including Hatim al-Awni, see it, the scholars are simply unwilling to look in the mirror. The scholars believe that the liberals are taking advantage of the present situation to bring down Wahhabism.

But even if the religious establishment wanted to embark on bold religious reform, some of the leading liberal voices have questioned whether it is capable of doing so. A weakness, they have observed, has set in since the death of the establishment's two most revered scholars in 1999 and 2000, and the establishment is no longer a strong historical force and trendsetter.[100] The non-official scholars, who may have more clout in society, seem for their part just as hesitant to discuss reform as their official peers.

The climate is one that ensures the persistence of what Awni called "al-Durar al-saniyya Salafism," meaning unreconstructed Wahhabism that enshrines a hostile and confrontational approach to non-Wahhabi Muslims and non-Muslims alike. Beyond the religious establishment's nice talk of coexistence and moderation, the core Wahhabi teachings and the textual heritage of Wahhabi militancy remain. The teachings do not inevitably lead to something like the Islamic State but are certainly compatible with it, and the heritage is no doubt one that the Islamic State looks to for inspiration.

What is positive about the present climate in Saudi Arabia is that critical voices are no longer being smothered. In addition to social media, the official press has become an approved outlet for Awni and liberal critics of Wahhabism since the rise of the Islamic State. The religious establishment would like the government to intervene and put an end to this conversation, as the government did in 2003 and after, but so far this has not happened. Awni has not lost his university position, nor have journalists been fired. This time around, it has become publicly acceptable to speak ill of Wahhabism, a dramatic change from a decade ago and an astounding change from a century before, when in the early 1920s King Abdulaziz assured the scholars that anyone criticizing Wahhabism would be "exposed to danger."[101]

The problem is that the religious scholars have not been pressured to engage with the criticism. With the ascension of King Salman, busy consolidating his rule and winning allies among the scholars, they are unlikely to be prodded in a reformist direction.[102]

Conclusion

The contest between Saudi Arabia and the Islamic State is not a close one. There is no sense of alarm in Saudi Arabia itself, where the Islamic State's violent campaign focusing on Shia and government targets has gained only limited ground. The ruling Saudi family seems to regard the Islamic State as only a nuisance, not a fundamental threat. Only in a future where the Islamic State has gained enormous new resources and territorial holdings would the threat be considered more severe.

But the struggle between Saudi Arabia and the Islamic State is also a contest for the soul of Wahhabism, and on this front the jihadis have made strides. Over the past few decades, the jihadi-Salafi movement has increasingly billed itself as the rightful heir to the Wahhabi tradition and has appropriated its textual resources. The Islamic State in some sense represents the culmination of this effort—a Wahhabi state as radical and sectarian as the original Saudi-Wahhabi state, though departing from it in certain ways. It is thus truer today than ever, as Western analysts have argued for years, that the Wahhabi form of Islam is a crucial component of jihadism.

Yet, though Wahhabism and jihadism are intimately linked, it is not necessarily prudent to think in terms of fighting jihadism by fighting Wahhabism. Indeed, Wahhabism (or Salafism, as most Wahhabis would prefer it to be called) has become a global movement not dependent on the support of one state, no matter how great its oil reserves. Saudi backing is not the only or even the main cause of the movement's spread throughout the Islamic world.[103] And the vast majority of Wahhabis, or Salafis, reject the violence and the political project of the Islamic State.

It is also worth considering that the Al Saud's support for Wahhabism is what gives the kingdom's rulers their legitimacy. Should the royal family's ties to the movement be sundered, chaos in the Arabian Peninsula would almost certainly result. This is not to mention that a Saudi divorce from Wahhabism would automatically confer on the jihadis the status of protectors of the Wahhabi mission.

But a less hostile, if not less intolerant, form of Wahhabism is a possibility. Dissidents such as Hatim al-Awni want the official religious scholars to tone down the *takfir* and disavow the more aggressive episodes of Wahhabi history. That is probably the most that can reasonably be hoped for. But such reform, if it is happening at all, is coming very, very slowly.

11

RELIGIOUS SECTARIANISM
AND POLITICAL PRAGMATISM

THE PARADOX OF EGYPT'S AL-NOUR SALAFIS

Stéphane Lacroix

Introduction

Salafis are known for their doctrinal intransigence and strong condemnations of any group or movement that does not share their religious views. Before the Arab Spring, with a few minor exceptions such as in Kuwait, Salafis limited their presence to the social sphere and refused to join the political game. This trend was reversed in the wake of the Arab Spring, when Salafi political parties started to be established in various Arab countries, most successfully in Egypt. So, how did this politicization of Salafism affect the movement's religious stances and its relationship to other social and political forces?

One of the biggest surprises of the post-revolutionary period in Egypt was not the electoral victory of the Muslim Brotherhood, which many had predicted, but the emergence of Hizb al-Nour (the party of light), a Salafi party founded in June 2011, as a strong contender to the Brotherhood and the second-largest party in the parliament.[1] The political behavior that Hizb al-Nour adopted from the start puzzled most observers, who had expected it to become an Islamist party on the far right of the Muslim Brotherhood and therefore much more politically intransigent. It is true that the Salafi sheikhs behind Hizb al-Nour, belonging to a religious organization called the Salafi Da'wa, were repeatedly taking virulent religious stances against non-Salafi religious groups, such as Sufis, Shia, or Christians, as well as against competing political forces, including liberals and the Brotherhood. Yet, the party adopted an extremely pragmatic attitude toward politics, allying itself with groups and parties that shared little of its religious ideology. Following the 3 July 2013 coup, Egyptian pro-army liberals commonly praised Hizb al-Nour, which had backed the coup, labeling the party as moderate while describing the Brotherhood as intractable radicals. However, many liberals reconsidered their view once it became clear that the party's political pragmatism did not entail the renouncement of its religious views, despite apparent attempts at backtracking on some of its more controversial positions.

Hizb al-Nour offers the rare example of a party that has been both extremely pragmatic in its political positions and strongly sectarian and intransigent in its religious stances. The balance between those two sides of Hizb al-Nour's discourse has depended on power shifts within the party. Initially, the party's founders made a genuine attempt to resolve some of the contradictions between its political and religious stances by arguing that politics was by nature a distinct domain from religion and entailed separate rules. But in late 2012, the sheikhs took control of the party, leading to a different, and purely instrumental, approach to politics based on what was perceived to be in the interest of the Salafi Da'wa. The party's recent stances can thus be better explained by analyzing Hizb al-Nour not as an Islamist party, but as the lobbying arm of a religious organization whose goal fundamentally remains to change society from below, not from above.

The Roots of Hizb al-Nour: the Salafi Da'wa

The origins of Hizb al-Nour lie in a powerful religious organization called *al-da'wa al-salafiyya* (the Salafi Da'wa, or the Salafi Call). First called *al-madrasa al-salafiyya* (the Salafi school), the Da'wa was established in 1977 by Alexandrian former members of the Islamist student groups known as *gama'at islamiyya*, who refused the decision of the *gama'at's* leadership to join the Muslim Brotherhood. Those members had embraced Salafism and saw the

Brotherhood's understanding of Islam as fundamentally unorthodox. Besides, the Da'wa's priority was not to strive for political change, but to spread its Salafi conceptions to society. For that purpose, although comprising all doctors and engineers by training, Da'wa members established themselves as sheikhs, whose main activity would be to preach in Alexandria's mosques.[2]

In their sermons, they preached "Sunni orthodoxy" against the beliefs and practices of Sufis, Shia, Christians, and liberal Muslims;[3] they called for ultra-conservative social practices inspired by the Prophet's *sunna* (tradition), producing fatwas and books prohibiting *ikhtilat* (gender-mixing) and men shaking hands with women, and encouraging Muslim men to grow beards;[4] but they largely avoided discussing hot political topics, and when they did discuss issues of governance, they stuck to theoretical statements. For instance, they considered democracy, and all kinds of political systems claiming their legitimacy from the people and not from God, to be contrary to Islam,[5] but they avoided publicly denouncing the Egyptian regime. They also refused to participate in elections, arguing that change would only come from below by spreading their message to create *al-ta'ifa al-mu'mina* (the community of the believers).[6]

The peculiar circumstances of its creation thus made the Salafi Da'wa different from previous Salafi organizations in Egypt, such as Ansar al-Sunna al-Muhammadiyya (the supporters of the Prophet's tradition), which was founded in 1926. The Da'wa's founders had all been student activists in the 1970s, so they decided to apply the principles of organized activism to Salafism. Their project was, in a sense, to borrow from the Muslim Brotherhood's organizational playbook, while replacing the Brotherhood's message with Salafism. Though the Da'wa has not reached the degree of institutional sophistication that characterizes the Brotherhood, it nevertheless has developed its own organizational pyramid headed by a *qayyim*[7]—the functional equivalent of the Brotherhood's supreme guide—although no formal *bay'a* (pledge of allegiance) was required in the case of the *qayyim*. Numerous branches and sections were established, and a council of scholars including the Da'wa's founders was tasked with running the organization. The "activist Salafism" of the Da'wa was justified through Salafi fatwas, notably by Kuwaiti-naturalized, Egyptian Salafi sheikh Abd al-Rahman Abd al-Khaliq, about the religious legality of collective action.[8]

The Da'wa's influence grew from the 1980s onward, not only because of its organizational structure and resulting power to mobilize but also due to favorable political circumstances. Because of its apparent lack of interest in politics, the Egyptian security apparatus generally considered the Da'wa as more benign than most Islamist groups. For instance, only a few Da'wa members were detained after former president Anwar Sadat's assassination in 1981, when Islamists from all factions, including those unconnected to the event, were thrown in jail. In the decades that followed, the Da'wa was generally subjected to less pressure than the Muslim Brotherhood and jihadi groups—at times, the government even saw the Da'wa as a useful counterforce. Although the Da'wa was sometimes forced to dismantle some of its sections and its leaders were repeatedly arrested—a sign that the security apparatus lacked confidence in the Da'wa's commitment to the status quo—its affiliates were generally released more promptly than other Islamists. Despite the restrictions it faced, the Da'wa was able to expand considerably, establishing a presence across Egypt (especially in the north), far from its original stronghold in Alexandria. Although this is impossible to prove, a widespread belief is that generous donations from associations and individuals in the Gulf may have helped provide the Da'wa with the financial means to grow.

The growth of Salafism in Egypt was particularly quick in the 2000s. From 2006 onward, the government gave broadcasting licenses to Salafi channels, starting with Qanat al-Nas and later Qanat al-Rahma. Again, the government likely saw them as politically useful, because it assumed they drove conservative Muslims away from the politicized discourse of the Muslim Brotherhood and jihadi groups. By the end of the decade, those channels had become among the most widely watched in Egypt. Most of the sheikhs preaching on those channels were not officially affiliated with the Da'wa—they were "independent sheikhs" such as Mohammed Husayn Ya'qub, Abu Ishaq al-Huwayni, or Mohammed Hassan—but since the Da'wa was by now the biggest Salafi group active in Egypt, the increasing appeal of Salafism helped to attract thousands of new members and increase its outreach.

Entering the political sphere

The revolution of 25 January 2011 against former president Hosni Mubarak took the Salafi Da'wa by surprise. The sheikhs had never believed that any genuine change could come through politics, so they first reacted by denouncing the event as a *fitna* (chaos, sedition) and advising their members not to participate in the protests.[9] It was only a few days before the fall of Mubarak that the Da'wa finally joined the demands for change. Just as the Muslim Brotherhood's initial lack of commitment to the revolution prompted internal criticisms against the leadership, the Da'wa was also internally criticized. Among the critical voices was Imad Abd al-Ghaffour, a medical doctor who had played a crucial role in establishing the Da'wa in the late 1970s. While his ties with the organization declined over time—especially while abroad, including in Turkey where he had spent most of the 2000s—Abd al-Ghaffour still carried a lot of weight among the sheikhs. A few days after Mubarak's official resignation on 11 February, Abd al-Ghaffour, who claimed to be an early supporter of the revolution, decided that in the new revolutionary era that was emerging, Salafis needed their own political party to have a say in the transition. He went to see the sheikhs one by one, eventually convincing them to allow the creation of Hizb al-Nour, which he would head.[10]

The relationship between the party and the Da'wa was quite strained from the beginning. Interviewed in April 2011, Yasir Burhami—who had officially become the Da'wa's number two after the *qayyim* Abu Idris but was in reality the organization's strongman[11]—acknowledged the relationship between the Da'wa and Hizb al-Nour but refused to describe Hizb al-Nour as the Da'wa's political arm.[12] The sheikhs either did not believe that Abd al-Ghaffour's project could be successful, or were afraid that the party's stances could harm the Da'wa.

The relationship between Abd al-Ghaffour and Burhami would continue to deteriorate steadily, although for different reasons. By late 2011, it was clear that Hizb al-Nour was becoming a success. The party's membership had grown exponentially, and it was now fielding candidates in all districts for the parliamentary elections. Its electoral posters were seen everywhere, and it had received the support of many prominent independent Salafi sheikhs. Hizb al-Nour went on to gain—as part of an "Islamic coalition" in which it was the senior partner—about 25 percent of the votes in the parliamentary elections, making it the second-largest political party in Egypt after the Muslim Brotherhood's Freedom and Justice Party.

To achieve that, Abd al-Ghaffour had endorsed moving away from the contentious religious discussions that were so prominent in the Salafi Da'wa. He constructed a political discourse that in many ways was quite unexpected, leading the party to (1) pledge respect to the procedures and rules of democracy;[13] (2) put forward young men as spokesmen, both as a way of presenting itself as harboring the aspirations of the youth and of insisting that its officials were new (or clean) players; and (3) portray itself as favorable to the revolution and open to other political players both domestically and internationally.[14] Its discourse even had almost leftist undertones, especially when the

Salafis were trying to cast themselves as the real representatives of the poor, implicitly accusing the Muslim Brotherhood of being the candidates of the conservative bourgeoisie.[15] The party proudly retained its Islamic identity and continued calling for the implementation of sharia (Islamic law), but it insisted on a gradual and benign process, and Abd al-Ghaffour was adamant about focusing on politics, not theology. He even rejected the label "Salafi" for the party, arguing that it is a "party for all Egyptians."[16]

Debating the purpose of Hizb al-Nour

The party's huge electoral gains awoke the interest of Yasir Burhami, who had not initially believed in the project. He was now convinced that Hizb al-Nour could be a powerful tool in the hands of the Da'wa. All he needed was to gain control of the party. For him, it was merely justice, since he believed the party's achievements had only been possible because of the strengths of Da'wa networks and not, as Abd al-Ghaffour proclaimed, because of the appeal of the party's political discourse.[17] Thus, in 2012, the party split into two factions: those loyal to party president Abd al-Ghaffour and those loyal to Da'wa strongman Burhami.

The split did not simply revolve around the power dispute between Abd al-Ghaffour and Burhami; there was a more profound issue at stake. For Abd al-Ghaffour and his associates, Hizb al-Nour was to be a political party like all others,[18] meaning that it would fully embrace the rules of the political game. It still saw itself as a religious party, but it was open to myriad alliances to advance its goals and be a government party with an applicable political program.[19] To draft that program, Abd al-Ghaffour even put together a team of mostly non-Salafi academics.[20]

Abd al-Ghaffour believed that his goal could only be achieved by making the party fully separate from the Da'wa. As one close aide of Abd al-Ghaffour argued, "We may consult the Da'wa sheikhs, whom we deeply respect, if we need a fatwa from them on a specific issue, but we don't want them to meddle with the party's daily business because this is politics and politics is not their specialty."[21] Many who had been involved in the party since the beginning agreed with Abd al-Ghaffour. This was partly because—as a result of the Da'wa's initial reluctance toward Hizb al-Nour—many of them had not been closely tied to the Da'wa and few were even religious scholars per se.[22] After becoming an active part of the political game, many members of Hizb al-Nour saw themselves more and more as politicians and understood how different this was from being a sheikh.[23]

Burhami had a different plan for the party. He believed that the party's gains should benefit the Da'wa and *maslahat al-da'wa* (the interest of the Da'wa) should be the party's main consideration in determining its positions.[24] Burhami was, of course, happy with the idea of Hizb al-Nour pushing for sharia-based legislation when possible, but he believed this should never be at the expense of the Da'wa. Thus, Burhami was unwilling to see Hizb al-Nour as a regular political party; he considered it, above all, the lobbying arm of the Da'wa in the political sphere. One could argue that Burhami's position had not really changed since the pre-2011 period. He still did not consider politics a vehicle for change per se—at least not before society was religiously ready; as the Da'wa had argued many times, reform would only come through preaching Salafi Islam to society, and protecting the body that did this was the only worthy goal.

Despite the huge differences between the Salafi Da'wa and the Muslim Brotherhood, this quarrel somehow mirrored the debate that had existed since the mid-1990s between the Brotherhood's "reformists"—who were willing to engage fully in politics and make the necessary compromises, including the separation between the *gama'a* (the religious organization) and its political activities—and the "conservatives," otherwise referred to as *tanzimiyyun* (organizationists), who believed that real change could only come through the *gama'a*.[25] As in Hizb al-Nour, this was both an intellectual and organizational debate. From 2009, the organizationists, led by Khayrat al-Shater, had taken control of the Brotherhood, leading to a new wave of reformist criticism in the wake of the revolution. Alluding to that comparison, Yusri Hammad, a former spokesman and dissident of Hizb al-Nour, declared, "Burhami wanted us to make the same mistakes the Brotherhood leadership was criticized for!"[26]

To challenge Abd al-Ghaffour and question his independence, Burhami targeted the party's excessive pragmatism by reminding his audience of the religious red lines that Salafis are not allowed to cross. This was done through a series of fatwas published on Burhami's website from January 2012. In one of those fatwas, he criticized Abd al-Ghaffour for saying on a talk show that Hizb al-Nour is open to people of all religious backgrounds and that he wishes Christians would run on Hizb al-Nour's lists in the future;[27] this, Burhami argued, is forbidden because Christians should not be allowed in the parliament since this would give them *wilaya* (authority) over Muslims. Burhami also targeted Abd al-Ghaffour's statement that Hizb al-Nour is open to alliances with all political parties, not just Islamist ones, including the Free Egyptians Party founded by Christian businessman Naguib Sawiris; Burhami responded by proclaiming that "any alliance with groups that oppose God's Law is absolutely forbidden."[28] Later, in 2012, one of Abd al-Ghaffour's aides, party spokesman Mohammed Nour, was temporarily suspended from the party after Da'wa sheikhs publicly criticized his attendance at an event at the Iranian embassy.[29] Burhami also attacked Abd al-Ghaffour for attending the national day celebrations at the Turkish embassy, arguing that those are nothing more than a "celebration of the end of the Ottoman caliphate."[30] According to an associate of Burhami, Abd al-Ghaffour's pragmatic behavior meant that he was trying to implement the "Turkish paradigm" of political Islam within Hizb al-Nour, and that was unacceptable.[31]

The last time the two factions in Hizb al-Nour found common ground was during the presidential elections, when they jointly decided not to present a candidate and to back Abd al-Mun'im Abu al-Futuh, a reformist dissident of the Muslim Brotherhood who portrayed himself as a liberal Islamist and was trying to form a large coalition uniting parties and individuals from both sides of the political spectrum. Yet, each faction had a different rationale. The supporters of Abd al-Ghaffour saw Abu al-Futuh as an acceptable choice, because he was a consensual Islamist and his election would be the most likely to guarantee the continuation of the political process and prevent the return of the security state. Muslim Brotherhood candidate Mohammed Morsi was also quite popular among this group.[32]

Burhami and his allies saw things quite differently. Their main objective was to prevent the election of Morsi, because of both the long-time rivalry between the two organizations and the belief that giving the Brotherhood such power would harm the Da'wa. In their view, the political hegemony of the Muslim Brotherhood was eventually going to result in the movement's religious hegemony. To protect their religious presence, keeping Morsi out of power was thus a necessity. However, Burhami and his allies still believed that they needed to back an Islamist candidate (especially after Burhami's fatwa criticizing Abd al-Ghaffour's openness to liberals), so this left three possible choices. The first was Hazim Salah Abu Isma'il, a proclaimed revolutionary Salafi who had no ties to the Da'wa and was seen as much too politically uncontrollable.[33] The second was Mohammed Salim al-'Awwa, who had barely any chance of winning and was known (and denounced by Salafis) for having good relations with Iran.[34] The third was Abu al-Futuh, whom Burhami and his allies disliked on a religious account, but was seen as the lesser evil.[35]

Since Abu al-Futuh lost in the first round (partly because grass-roots Salafis were not enthusiastic about supporting such a liberal candidate), Hizb al-

Nour leaders were faced with another dilemma for the second round: Mohammed Morsi or Ahmad Shafiq, Mubarak's last prime minister. Here, they reluctantly decided to back the "Islamic candidate" Morsi, although they did not really support his campaign. Just before the announcement of the results, Burhami paid a cordial visit to Shafiq to negotiate favorable conditions if he were to prevail.[36]

During the second half of 2012, Hizb al-Nour's divisions became more visible. Proponents of Abd al-Ghaffour started accusing Burhami of meddling with the party's affairs by pushing for the appointment of Da'wa loyalists to key administrative positions. Since Hizb al-Nour had internal elections scheduled for the fall, the purpose was allegedly to assure the dismissal of Abd al-Ghaffour and his team and their replacement by pro-Da'wa figures.[37] To voice their protest, Abd al-Ghaffour's proponents established a "reform front" within the party, calling for the Da'wa and party to fully separate—something they had been insisting on, but not publicly, for a year.[38] Tensions continued to escalate, with an attempt by pro-Burhami figures to pronounce Abd al-Ghaffour's dismissal in September 2012. In December 2012, Abd al-Ghaffour and his allies announced that they were leaving Hizb al-Nour to establish their own political party, Hizb al-Watan (the party of the homeland), whose main slogans would be "the separation of politics and preaching (*da'wa*)" and "the preference for competence over loyalty to the sheikhs."[39]

This meant that the Da'wa, and Burhami, had finally won. On 9 January 2013, a close associate of Burhami, Yunis Makhyoun, was elected unchallenged as president of the party. Abd al-Ghaffour's line had been defeated and, after almost two years of ambiguity, Hizb al-Nour had finally become the political arm of the Salafi Da'wa.

A different kind of Salafi pragmatism

Hizb al-Nour's takeover by Burhami and the Salafi Da'wa did not put an end to the party's pragmatism, however. Its pragmatism just changed in nature, driven by different considerations.

Hizb al-Nour's half-hearted support for Morsi during the second round of the presidential election had not done much to fix the relationship between the Da'wa and the Brotherhood. Hizb al-Nour had apparently hoped that Morsi would make it part of the national unity government he had promised his backers between the two rounds. But, just like most other political factions that had bet on Morsi, Hizb al-Nour was deeply disappointed. Despite being the country's second biggest political force and a fellow Islamic party, all it was granted were three appointments within Morsi's presidential team. Two Hizb al-Nour officials, Khaled 'Alam al-Din and Bassam al-Zarqa, were appointed to a large and merely symbolic presidential advisory body, while then Hizb al-Nour president Abd al-Ghaffour was offered the position of presidential aide for social dialogue.[40] Giving the most senior position of the three to Abd al-Ghaffour made matters worse with the Da'wa, who saw this as a Brotherhood move to play on Hizb al-Nour's divisions.

Despite this view, Hizb al-Nour initially tried to adapt to the new political reality and avoided criticizing Morsi. An issue that brought the Muslim Brotherhood and Hizb al-Nour together was the constitution. A constitutional assembly was appointed by the parliament in early June 2012, a couple of weeks before the latter's dissolution by the constitutional court. That assembly included Brotherhood and Salafi sympathizers in more or less the same proportion as in the parliament (about two-thirds). The two factions shared an interest in reinforcing the influence of Islam in the constitution, which was strongly opposed by the remaining members of the assembly (especially the liberals and Christians). Their objective alliance eventually produced the December 2012 constitution, which kept article 2 of the 1980 constitution ("The principles of *shari'a* are the main source of legislation") unchanged but added article 219 ("The principles of *shari'a* include its general proofs, its fundamental and legal rules, and its recognized sources within the Sunni schools") to ensure that article 2 would now be legally binding.

In January 2013, Hizb al-Nour's public position on Morsi markedly shifted, with increasingly critical statements emanating from the party's spokesmen. There were three reasons for this change. First, now that the constitution had been adopted (both by the constitutional assembly and by a referendum where it received 63 percent of the votes), Salafis and the Brotherhood had lost the last shared interest they had. Second, the political tide was shifting against Morsi in the wake of the constitutional declaration he had issued in late November 2012 granting judicial immunity to the decisions of the presidency, which had resulted in demonstrations and bloody clashes in front of the presidential palace. Though Hizb al-Nour had opposed the initial protests in the name of "stability and order," it now started voicing criticisms. Third, and maybe most importantly, the changes and appointments that Morsi was making in the ministries were starting to worry the Da'wa, which by then had taken over Hizb al-Nour. As Patrick Haenni has shown, the Brotherhood adopted different attitudes toward state institutions depending on whether they were seen as strong or weak.[41] In strong institutions, like the army or the interior ministry, Morsi never appointed Brotherhood or explicitly pro-Brotherhood figures and only tried to promote second-rank officials, after having made a deal with them to ensure their loyalty (ironically, this is how then general Abd Fattah al-Sisi was chosen to become the new minister of defense). In weak institutions, the Brotherhood's involvement reached much further. One of those weak institutions was the Ministry of Religious Affairs, where Morsi replaced most of the previous team with Brotherhood loyalists. Not long after, Morsi proposed the creation of a preachers' syndicate, a move that the Da'wa—which includes many sheikhs without formal religious degrees—saw as another attempt to marginalize them.[42] The Da'wa viewed these actions as the start of a Brotherhood takeover of the religious sphere, and that was an existential threat.

From early 2013 onward, Hizb al-Nour started turning into an opposition party, joining other political groups in denouncing *akhwanat al-dawla* (the Brotherhoodization of the state). The term had become a motto used by anti-Brotherhood activists, but it first appeared in a speech by Hizb al-Nour spokesman Nadir Bakkar in late January 2013.[43] Not long after, Hizb al-Nour even claimed it possessed a record of all cases of Brotherhoodization and threatened to make it public.[44] In early February 2013, Hizb al-Nour figures vocally criticized the state visit of then Iranian president Mahmoud Ahmadinejad, whom Morsi had invited, accusing him of Shia proselytism.[45] With this move, Hizb al-Nour accomplished two things simultaneously: it reaffirmed its doctrinal intransigence toward the Shia, while attacking the Brotherhood.

The Brotherhood reacted by accusing Khaled 'Alam al-Din, one of the two Salafi members of the presidential advisory team, of corruption and dismissing him. 'Alam al-Din denied those accusations in a press conference, and Bassem al-Zarqa resigned in support of his colleague. This meant that there were no Hizb al-Nour representatives left in Morsi's presidential team (Abd al-Ghaffour remained in place, but he was now the president of Hizb al-Watan). This only reinforced Hizb al-Nour's resolve to join ranks with the opposition. The Brotherhood continued its retributive strategy, and in May 2013 Burhami was detained for a few hours at Alexandria airport as he was coming back from Saudi Arabia, where he had performed Umrah.[46] Although he was quickly released, the Salafis perceived this action as a declaration of war. The amount of contact Hizb al-Nour had with other players involved in Morsi's fall, especially the army, remains unclear, although the newspapers reported joint meetings between Hizb al-Nour members and liberals to form a common front in the name of "national unity," which never really materialized.[47] However, it is clear that, with the Tamarrod campaign gaining strength and the 30 June 2013 protests approaching, Burhami was aware that the balance of power did not favor the Brotherhood and he was perfectly happy with that.

Although Burhami did not call for Hizb al-Nour members to join the anti-Morsi protests, he clarified that "if millions of protesters take the streets on June 30th, [he] will demand Morsi's resignation."[48] On 3 July 2013, when then defense minister Sisi announced that Morsi was no longer Egypt's president and that the army would supervise the implementation of a new roadmap, Galal Murra, a senior representative of Hizb al-Nour, was one of the few leaders sitting behind him—next to liberal figure Mohammed al-Baradei; Tamarrod leader Mahmoud Badr; the sheikh of al-Azhar, Ahmad al-Tayyib; and Pope Tawadros II of Alexandria. To justify Hizb al-Nour's position, Burhami explained that it was the only way to "protect the Islamic identity in the constitution and to guarantee the presence of an Islamic party able to preserve the gains of the Islamic current as a whole."[49]

At the time, this seemed to be a smart move. The group the Da'wa considered its main contender and historical rival in the religious sphere—the Brotherhood—was now out of the game. And with Hizb al-Nour being the only Islamic party to support the roadmap, the army would have no choice but to rely on it to regain control of the mosques. On paper, not only had the Da'wa preserved its social presence, it now had huge opportunities to expand. Some in Hizb al-Nour may have envisioned a scenario similar to those seen in Sudan and Pakistan. In Sudan, a faction within the army had relied on the Islamist National Salvation Front (NSF) to seize power in 1989. While the military governed, the NSF was in charge of social and religious affairs. In Pakistan in the 1980s, under Zia ul-Haq, a similar deal between the army and Islamist groups, especially the Jamaat-e-Islami, was made. For the Da'wa, the idea of relinquishing power to the army, or even to a purportedly secular government, was not an issue in itself. It was still arguably far better than a Brotherhood government because secular or military actors supposedly have no claim over what constitutes the Da'wa's primary domain: the religious sphere.

Salafis under Sisi: trapped between the security state and a restive Islamist base

More than three years after the army's takeover, Hizb al-Nour has many reasons to feel dissatisfied. It quickly became clear that the new regime had no intention of giving the Salafis the kind of prominence they were hoping for. The Salafis were given no representation in the transitional government and were granted only one seat out of fifty in the constitutional assembly that was appointed during summer 2013. Thus, they had no way to influence the content of the new constitution. Acknowledging that, Bassam al-Zarqa, who had first been appointed, stopped attending and was replaced by another Hizb al-Nour member, Mohammed Mansour.[50] At the time, though, Salafis blamed their marginalization on the liberals, who still retained a significant influence over public affairs. Yet, the gradual exclusion of the liberals and the monopolization of power by the military did not radically change the situation for the Salafis. It is true that while some of the more radical secularists had openly called for the dissolution of Hizb al-Nour—based on it being a "religious party," which is forbidden by the new constitution[51]—the army apparently never thought of banning the party. The generals seemed convinced that Hizb al-Nour could still be useful to their strategy. However, while they allowed the Da'wa to retain most of its social presence, they made sure the movement would feel the heavy pressure of the state.

What Hizb al-Nour had apparently not sufficiently considered was that, with the Brotherhood gone as a contender, there was another player that could claim control over the mosques: al-Azhar. The leadership of al-Azhar, which largely adheres to a traditional form of Islam with Sufi leanings, had always been strongly opposed to the Salafis. Because of its former pro-Mubarak stance, al-Azhar's social influence had declined significantly over the last few decades—and even more in the wake of the revolution—but it still carried enormous symbolic and institutional weight. The sheikh of al-Azhar, Ahmad al-Tayyib, himself a Sufi by training, saw the military takeover (which he had backed from the start) as an opportunity to regain his authority. And the new regime saw al-Azhar, a state institution, as a much more trustworthy partner than the Salafis.

The new regime therefore chose to rely on al-Azhar to regain the social and religious terrain lost to the Islamists. And it chose to do so through its religious arm, the Ministry of Religious Affairs, headed by an Azhari who had previously worked with al-Tayyib, Mohammed Mukhtar Gum'a. Starting in March 2014, the ministry adopted several laws and decrees to put all of Egypt's mosques under the control of the state. Imams now had to be al-Azhar graduates; and for those who were not, which was the case with many Da'wa preachers, they needed to obtain a *tarkhis* (license) to preach after passing an exam. In addition, it was announced that all of Egypt's

Friday preachers now had to pronounce the same sermon sent to them in advance by the ministry.[52]

This represented a major theoretical threat to Salafis, but because the regime neither had the human resources to fully take control of the religious domain nor wanted to declare an all-out war on the Salafis, exceptions were made for most Da'wa preachers. Still, this was enough to prevent further expansion of the Da'wa and to keep Salafis under close watch.[53]

The post-Morsi era also had other consequences for the Da'wa. One core claim of Hizb al-Nour after the Da'wa's takeover of the party was that it was "intransigent with issues of doctrine, but flexible with political issues."[54] The first stance was fundamental to maintaining its religious legitimacy: yes, it could make alliances—which was already a shift from Burhami's 2011 position when he had attacked Abd al-Ghaffour for saying precisely that—but it could never compromise on key doctrinal issues. Yet, in the new era, with an unprecedentedly repressive political environment for Islamists, Hizb al-Nour would be forced to make more concessions than it had probably ever imagined.

Once Hizb al-Nour had backed the military takeover, it had no choice but to support all the political developments that followed: the violent repression of the Muslim Brotherhood and the massacres of hundreds of their followers at Rabaa al-'Adawiya and al-Nahda on 14 August 2013—despite statements criticizing the police's brutality;[55] the adoption of the new constitution, for which Hizb al-Nour campaigned (although it was much less Islamic than the previous one); and the election of Sisi to the presidency, which it supported. One major debate between Burhami and Abd al-Ghaffour in 2011 had centered on the possibility of Hizb al-Nour offering positions to Christians on its electoral lists. In that debate, Burhami took a firm stand, arguing that Salafi doctrine prohibited this. Yet, in the first parliamentary elections after the coup, in 2015, the electoral law required that each list include a percentage of Christian candidates in order for it to be valid. Hizb al-Nour accepted and fielded Christian candidates. When confronted with the contradiction between that decision and the Da'wa's position back in 2011, party president Yunis Makhyoun said that they had made it because "(they) were forced to"—which prompted a huge campaign against Hizb al-Nour in the national media.[56] In internal circles, Da'wa figures justified their reversal by referring to the Islamic legal principle of weighing *al-masalih wa-l-mafasid* (benefits and harms).[57]

Hizb al-Nour's stances led to strong reactions among Salafis abroad. Tens of Saudi Salafi sheikhs close to the Sahwa movement signed a joint letter criticizing Hizb al-Nour in the most virulent terms,[58] and Egyptian-Kuwaiti sheikh Abd al-Rahman Abd al-Khaliq, who had been among the Da'wa's early influences in the 1980s, wrote the following to Burhami: "You were one of Satan's soldiers, but you have advanced in evil, and you are now his teacher."[59] This also led to a relative decrease in Hizb al-Nour's following. During summer 2013, it was not uncommon to see Hizb al-Nour members or sympathizers demonstrating with the Brotherhood against the coup.[60] There were numerous public defections from Hizb al-Nour and the Da'wa, including from the top leadership. Sa'id Abd al-Azim, one of the Da'wa's co-founders and foremost sheikhs, took a pro-Morsi stance and ended up leaving the country in December 2013.[61] Mohammed Ismail al-Muqaddim, another major name in the Da'wa and probably its most widely respected sheikh, retreated from public life after the coup to avoid having to take a stance. Both Abd al-Azim and al-Muqaddim have now been officially removed from the Da'wa's administrative council.[62] As for Burhami, there were reports that he sometimes had to preach under armed protection, after receiving numerous threats from anti-regime Islamists.[63]

The final blow took place during the 2015 elections, in which Hizb al-Nour was the sole religious party to compete. Some in Hizb al-Nour speculated that the party could do really well, since it was now the only electoral option for religious conservatives. The results showed quite the opposite, however, with the party only gaining twelve seats out of 596, merely 2 percent of the total and more than ten times less than in 2011. There were objective reasons for that defeat, starting with the electoral system that had been designed to favor state-supported candidates. A ratio of 80 percent of the members of parliament were to be chosen through individual elections (known to favor local notables with strong clientelistic networks and state connections), and for the 20 percent of seats reserved for electoral lists, a majority-vote system was adopted, meaning that the list with more than 50 percent would take all the seats in the district. Also, Hizb al-Nour was running alone, against electoral lists comprising several parties (sometimes tens of parties, like in the fervently pro-Sisi list, "For the love of Egypt"), and it presented candidates in less than half of the districts.[64] Finally, the media, dominated by liberal pro-state figures, adopted an anti-Hizb al-Nour tone in its coverage of the elections.

In places where the Da'wa had a limited presence historically, Hizb al-Nour performed badly. In Da'wa strongholds, Hizb al-Nour lists did much better, obtaining as much as 30 percent of the votes in the West Delta District—yet not enough to get a single seat. The few Hizb al-Nour members of parliament who made it were elected on individual seats after the second round in places like Alexandria or Kafr al-Sheikh. Although Hizb al-Nour tried to highlight those few successes, it was not enough to counter the impression of a major defeat.[65]

The debate that ensued renewed demands from within the Da'wa to abandon politics once and for all and return to preaching. Similar demands had been voiced in the wake of the military takeover, and entire sections of Hizb al-Nour had apparently seceded to return to purely religious activities.[66] At this stage, the Da'wa appeared to be losing much more through its political involvement than it was gaining. Why then did Burhami and his allies refuse to back down? One possible explanation is that Burhami believed that Hizb al-Nour's strategy would eventually pay off. Hizb al-Nour figures have argued that the 2015 elections actually demonstrated the party's resilience, in particular in its strongholds, and claimed that they would do much better in the forthcoming local elections. A more probable explanation is that it would be simply impossible for the Da'wa to go back to where it was before 2011. A Hizb al-Nour decision to withdraw from politics would be seen by the regime and public opinion as a disavowal of the current political system. In a context where Islamists are being heavily repressed, with more than 50,000 of them in prison, this could unleash state repression against the Da'wa. Hizb al-Nour stays in the game mostly to ensure the survival of the religious organization behind it. The interest of the Da'wa continues to dictate the policies of Hizb al-Nour.

Why Hizb al-Nour is not an Islamist party

Hizb al-Nour has been recurrently characterized by journalists and academics as an Islamist party somehow comparable to the Muslim Brotherhood but with a Salafi understanding of Islam. Yet, if an Islamist movement believes that Islam serves as a blueprint for politics, and aims at governing a country according to its conception of what an Islamic state should be, then Hizb al-Nour—at least in its post-2013 form—can hardly be described as Islamist. There are key differences between the Muslim Brotherhood and Hizb al-Nour beyond the two groups' distinct political choices during the last five years. Those differences stem from fundamentally distinct approaches to politics.

The Muslim Brotherhood is the archetype of an Islamist movement. Its final aim is to seize power to implement its Islamic political vision. Yet, it does not care much about theological disputes within Islam: it preaches a conservative message, but one that allows for some plurality of interpretation. In contrast, the Salafi Da'wa—in line with other Salafi movements elsewhere—was established to restore the theological purity of Islam and preach that purity to fellow Muslims. Politics were always peripheral to that vision.

One major reason for the clash within Hizb al-Nour in 2011 and 2012 was that Abd al-Ghaffour seemed to be taking politics too seriously. He believed that Hizb al-Nour was more than the political arm of a religious movement— rather, a party with a political message that it was willing to implement in government. Had his faction succeeded, Hizb al-Nour could have become an Islamist movement. The party Abd al-Ghaffour and his allies founded in December 2012, Hizb al-Watan, confirmed this by siding with the Brotherhood throughout 2013 and after the coup, as part of a larger coalition of Islamist parties opposed to the new regime.

When Da'wa sheikhs seized control of Hizb al-Nour in late 2012, they acted according to their traditional vision of politics. For them, the party was, above all, a means to preserve or reinforce the social influence of their religious movement. Islamicization (or Salafization), they believed, would happen from below, not from above. The interest of the Da'wa would therefore dictate which decisions should be made. Hizb al-Nour would thus be devoid of an ideological vision, at least in the common sense of the term—and this is precisely what makes it something very different from an Islamist party.

One could argue that this derives from the fact that Hizb al-Nour is a party run by sheikhs, which is a rare occurrence in the Middle East. The leaders of the Muslim Brotherhood, for instance, have mostly been secular figures, and the organization has always maintained an ambiguous relationship with the religious establishment. Yet, sheikhs tend to harbor a world view more centered on what remains their primary function: preaching both to ensure people's salvation and to reform society from below. As Ashraf Thabit, a senior Da'wa figure and one of Burhami's main associates in Hizb al-Nour, argued in early 2012:

> The parliament is not, has never been, and will not be the solution for us. We believe change will only come from below, not by simply changing the laws. The parliament is only a means to help us practice what is the basis for us, *da'wa*. This is our *manhaj* [methodology]. What matters most is purifying the *umma*'s creed.[67]

Hizb al-Nour's pragmatism: continuity and change

Pragmatism has been a constant in Hizb al-Nour since its creation, and it has translated both into the group's practical acceptance of non-Salafis as political partners and into its adoption of political stances that apparently contradicted its religious sectarianism. Yet, the rationale for that pragmatism changed in late 2012. From 2011 to 2012, Hizb al-Nour's pragmatism was comparable to that found among mainstream Islamist parties elsewhere—in that they revised (or put aside) some of their doctrinal conceptions as they adapted to the political game. This evolution is related to what some scholars have termed the "inclusion-moderation" hypothesis.[68] Though this short episode did not produce any genuine doctrinal revisions on the part of Salafis, it nevertheless gave birth to a secular discourse that was carried by a new type of actor, the Salafi politician, who felt he did not need to justify all his positions systematically in religious terms because politics was by nature a relatively separate domain.[69] That the proponents of this line ended up forming a party called Hizb al-Watan (the party of the homeland) is in itself quite telling.

Since 2013, Hizb al-Nour's pragmatism has derived from a different source: the party's largely instrumental approach to politics. This puts into question the two common explanations usually given to explain Hizb al-Nour's support for the military takeover on 3 July 2013. The first supposes that Saudi Arabia is the main backer of Hizb al-Nour and that Hizb al-Nour acted on Saudi orders; but the Da'wa was never particularly close to the Saudi regime, and the Saudi strategy toward Egypt mainly consisted in backing the remnants of the Mubarak state and the army, not the Salafis. According to the second explanation, the Salafi Da'wa's allegedly close ties with the security apparatus under Mubarak explain Hizb al-Nour's stance; but while those ties were real (just as they were for most religious movements operating under the Mubarak regime), they were never as strong as many presume. Those explanations may be one small part of the story, but they are far from being the whole story. The party's stances were not merely opportunistic or driven by external interests; there was a clear logic behind them, defending what was perceived as being in the interest of the Da'wa as a preaching movement, whatever the political cost.

This again forced Salafis to adopt political stances that contradicted their doctrinal beliefs. This time, however, those were justified through arguments of necessity, as when Hizb al-Nour's president argued that the party was forced by the electoral system to have Christians on its lists or that it had to weigh benefits and harms. Although those justifications have caused some discomfort among grass-roots Salafis, the Da'wa's base largely accepted them. One can assume that this passive pragmatism is unlikely (and certainly not meant) to produce doctrinal revisions, despite all the political concessions that Hizb al-Nour has been willing, and will probably continue, to make. The paradox between the party's extreme political pragmatism and its rigidity and sectarianism at the doctrinal level thus seems perfectly sustainable and will likely remain.

12

RELIGIOUS AUTHORITY
AND SECTARIANISM IN LEBANON

Alexander D.M. Henley

Introduction: the paradoxes of Lebanon's religious leaders

In Lebanon, as in many Middle Eastern countries, common myths surrounding religious leadership and sectarianism appear to be the bases for policy by Middle Eastern officials and Western diplomats alike. These myths may stem partly from a lingering stereotype of Islam as having no clergy and being, therefore, less institutionalized than many Christian churches. Yet that stereotype is less true than ever after a century or more of state-driven modernization. Institutional contexts are key to understanding the roles of Islamic and other religious leaders in Lebanon today.

Moreover, the influence of the state system in the Middle East has been pervasive, restructuring every facet of social life including the religious lives of the region's numerous sects.[1] One must be wary of imagining the modern state to be the binary opposite of sectarianism and religious leaders, as if it has not been deeply implicated in their development for a century or more.

The case of Lebanon shows how senior religious leaders are generally more representative of an array of clerical and political elites than of a community of ordinary believers. These individuals are also likely to be shaped by the culture of the state and of the national public before which they are supposed to represent their community. One result of these particular institutional and cultural contexts is that Lebanese religious leaders have repeatedly demonstrated both the ability and the will to combat sectarian antagonisms through their public rhetoric and posturing.

Still, the societal function of Lebanon's religious leaders and their relationship to the issue of sectarianism raise core questions of representation, such as 'Can these leaders be taken to represent religious communities legitimately, as both custom and Lebanese law expect them to do?' Such questions have become acute in the Middle East more generally, where sectarianism is an ever-growing concern. Like Lebanon, countries such as Iraq and Syria are viewed by many as deeply divided societies, most saliently along religious or sectarian lines.

Yet since the country's establishment, Lebanon—alone among Middle Eastern countries—has had a political system based on the representation of sects. The Lebanese state recognizes eighteen sects, the formal representatives of which have a variety of powers by virtue of their relationship with the state. This includes five Islamic sects (Sunni, Shia, Druze, Alawite, and Ismaili); the Maronites and eleven other Christian sects; and the Jewish community.[2] Within their communities, religious leaders are legally responsible for managing religious affairs, sitting atop nationwide hierarchies of clerics who run places of worship, schools, and personal-status courts that adjudicate many aspects of the daily lives of Lebanese citizens, including marriage, divorce, and inheritance. Outside their communities, they function as spokesmen in their communities' interactions with public authorities.

Lebanon's long history with formal religious representation makes it a valuable prism through which to study the many dimensions of state engagement with religious leaders, as well as the realities and myths of religious leaders' connection to sectarianism. Are they truly representative of Lebanese society's sectarian diversity? As leaders, are they implicated in the problem of sectarianism?

Lebanon's religious leaders tend to reflect a series of paradoxes that greatly complicate any facile interpretation of their roles. While they are religious representatives, their leadership is not organic. Rather, they are products of elite clerical hierarchies, and so represent particular institutions before their communities at large.

Religious leaders also have to manage an inherent ambiguity in their roles, whereby they must navigate a gray zone between their strictly religious roles and their broader duties as communal representatives. While the former demands qualities tied to their standing as members of an institutional religious elite, communal representativeness tends to require a broader popular mandate.

And while religious representatives are not politicians, they are also not apolitical. As their recognition as representatives is normalized, these religious leaders often find themselves caught up in an interplay of local, national, and regional political interests.

Perhaps the most singular paradox is that, although Lebanese religious leaders have not incited sectarian hatred and may, in fact, be well-placed to defuse sectarian tensions, at the same time they embody a system of separate confessional regimes for family law and education that keeps communities separate and rigidly defined.

This complex reality casts doubt on the benefits of assuming that states' engagement of religious leaders implies engagement of their communities at large. One cannot take for granted that they are spokesmen for sectarian diversity, and should consider carefully the implications of further entrenching their positions as such. While it is an advantage that Lebanese religious leaders, or indeed religious leaders in other Arab countries, can help deradicalize sectarian tensions, the normalization of their roles as interlocutors also empowers institutions that divide populations and exclude nonconformists.

In other words, in seeking out allegedly authentic representatives through contacts with religious leaders, outside interlocutors may, in fact, be contributing to a system that only undermines broad representation. Effectively, this reinforces a confessional framework from which not a few Lebanese seek to break out. Lebanon's rigid system of religious representation and its highly problematic political order based on confessional power-sharing among elites have created a crisis of representation in the country. The consequences for stability and national cohesion have become more apparent as the state has failed to meet popular expectations.

Religious leaders as imperfect representatives

Top religious leaders in Lebanon are regular interlocutors on the rounds made by foreign emissaries seeking to negotiate a solution to the latest political crisis or stand-off. French President François Hollande's visit to Beirut in April 2016 was a case in point. It included meetings with the religious heads of the six largest communities as part of a two-day whirlwind tour.[3] The root rationale for such visits is generally understood to be addressing a problem that follows from some aspect of sectarian tension—today, this is usually between Sunni and Shia Muslims, whereas until the 1980s it was usually between Christians and Muslims.

On the assumption that sectarianism is the deeper social problem of which bickering politicians are just a symptom, it can seem like common sense to go to the source by speaking to the heads of the sects concerned. After all, who better to approach when trying to understand what makes religious communities tick than their official leaders who have recognized authority over their flocks? So who are these religious leaders in Lebanon, and what do they represent?

Religious leaders as unrepresentative elites

Religious leaders are often perceived as more natural representatives of sectarian diversity than politicians. Influential political blogger Mustapha Hamoui, who regards Lebanon's collective religious leaders as "a sort of defacto [*sic*] Senate," explains that this is because they "traditionally get up in arms and mobilize the faithful whenever an issue is perceived to threaten the influence of their faith."[4] Whereas the parliament is electorally engineered to be, in one scholar's words, "a body of generally moderate views," religious leaders are more in tune with their sects' divergent identities and aspirations.[5]

The religious institutions that religious leaders occupy have an aura of permanence that makes them appear essential to the traditional character of their respective communities. Kamal Salibi, a well-known historian in Lebanon, once called a given sect's religious institution "a repository for its historical experience" that by implication embodies all that makes its community different from its neighbors.[6] Indeed, press photographs of Hollande with assorted clerics in Beirut in 2016 were eerily similar to images of their clerical predecessors going all the way back to 1920.[7] This was when another Frenchman, General Henri Gouraud, recognized "the spiritual leaders of all confessions and rites" in his declaration of Lebanese statehood.[8] There is a long precedent in Lebanon for engaging religious leaders as interlocutors within a sectarian society. This precedent helped legitimize the practice of dealing with sectarian representatives in Lebanon.

These religious leaders, however, are not nearly as representative of the faithful as tends to be assumed. Being products of particular institutional politics, they have no more natural, or organic, connection to their communities than any politician does—indeed, potentially far less so. Even the term "leader" is in many cases a misnomer, as it implies a popular following that many prominent clerics do not necessarily enjoy. Indeed, by assuming the contrary, one may be reinforcing, rather than simply recognizing, religious leaders and institutions of sectarianism in the region.

The heads of religious institutions are chosen from among their respective clerical classes—Sunni *ulama*, Druze *uqqal*, Maronite clergymen, and so on. While all of them may be "men of religion" (*rijal din*), the term embraces a vast diversity in terms of functions, education, and motivations, between different sects and even within them. Clerics are often imagined to be believers par excellence, but people may enter the clergy for many reasons, and they often express a tremendous variety of interpretations of their faiths.

Moreover, the specialized education and sometimes rarified lives of clerics arguably set their religious experience far apart from that of the broader population. Particular institutional hierarchies have their own self-perpetuating cultures and norms, often including quite specific views on religious orthodoxy, which distance them from popular religion. Leaders are chosen from among this class of professional religious practitioners, but generally not simply according to strictly religious criteria. Indeed, virtually no head of a Lebanese community in the past century has been widely recognized for his excellence in theological learning, spiritual wisdom, or purity of faith.

Each Lebanese religious community has an electoral process through which its official leader is chosen, usually by a very limited and male-dominated elite, from an even more exclusive group of men. Elected candidates are almost always middle- or upper-level bureaucrats in a given sect's central clerical administration. They are very rarely charismatic individuals with a popular following, and frequently the opposite is true. Religious leaders are usually uncontroversial compromise candidates who have gained a modest name for themselves through their reliable services as judges or administrators in their religious establishments' Beirut headquarters.

A notable exception is the late Shia cleric Musa al-Sadr, who lacked the clerical or scholarly distinction of an Ayatollah, but was dubbed 'Imam' by his supporters, tens of thousands of whom rallied to his progressive reform movement in the 1960s and 1970s. Sadr leveraged this popularity to create his own institution of religious leadership for Lebanon's Shia, the Higher Islamic Shiite Council, for which he gained official recognition from the government. By contrast, his successors have been products of the institution rather than inheritors of his magnetism.

Electoral systems for the spiritual heads of Lebanese sects have evolved over the past several decades. The original model may be that of the Maronite church—its council is not only an electoral body but also a legislative one, governing the church in conjunction with the patriarch. This council of bishops is appointed by the patriarch and, in turn, elects a new patriarch from among its members when the old one dies (or retires, as the last two have done).[9]

Many of Lebanon's other major religious communities have adopted roughly equivalent models of unitary elected leadership, combined with corporate governance by a council of some kind. Under the Ottoman regime (from about 1516 to 1918), Sunni muftis of Beirut and other cities were elected by an informal gathering of salaried judges, preachers, and imams of that given city, albeit with the final decision going to the sheikh al-Islam, the empire's highest-ranking religious official in Istanbul.

After Lebanese independence, as the Sunni, Shia, and Druze communities sought to formalize the structures of their religious leaderships within a Lebanese state framework, successive laws were passed to define and redefine the workings of their leadership structures. These were shaped to a significant extent by political interests. Since Islamic institutions depend on state recognition, such laws had to be passed through the parliament, which gave politicians, not clerics, the final say on their content. Not surprisingly, then, the Muslim communities all developed legislative councils with ex officio seats for all current and former parliamentarians and ministers.

Unlike many Middle Eastern countries such as Egypt, Saudi Arabia, and Syria—in which the governments either directly or indirectly appoint senior religious leaders—Lebanon's communal power-sharing system makes its state structure considerably looser. This also means that the Lebanese state is not identified with any particular sect. The Lebanese government, therefore, does not appoint religious officials.

However, government recognition in Lebanon is still crucial to the exercise of privileges and powers granted to religious leaders by law or protocol. That is why, at times, factions with enough seats in government have been able to withhold recognition from a given religious official, opening the way for his replacement with a more favorable candidate.[10] This kind of situation has arisen with regard to the highest-ranking Druze religious figure, the sheikh al-aql, as well as with regard to the Sunni Higher Islamic Council and its appointments to regional offices.[11]

Religious leaders may present themselves as authentically representative of religious communities on the basis of tradition or cultural ownership of their sect's identity. However, giving such individuals a privileged place in policy consultations to help deal with the problem of sectarianism means that their claims and status must be scrutinized and not simply taken at face value.

Religious leaders are not necessarily popular

Because high-level religious leaders in Lebanon are generally drawn from elites and emerge from institutional apparatuses, and in a number of cases are dependent on the state, there is no cultural expectation that they be followed blindly—or at all. They are not "of the people," nor are they necessarily regarded as being "for the people."

In the vast majority of Islamic traditions, religious leaders are conceived not as binding authorities but as more or less educated religious specialists with specific functions in society.[12] These include preaching, leading prayers, offering spiritual guidance, or interpreting Islamic law, or sharia.

Sunni Muslims would generally not regard themselves as followers of any religious leader other than the Prophet Muhammad himself.[13] Sunni notions of religious authority are based on the rather fluid notion of consensus (*ijmaa*), allowing even the most pious to pick and choose quite legitimately between the opinions of different *ulama*, be they grand muftis or independent individuals.

Shiism does have a tradition of religious leadership and followership, with the convention that the Shia ought to subscribe to a single living "source of emulation" (*marjaa taqlid*), among a number of recognized senior scholars.[14] Yet even this system is highly fluid, belying the cliché that the Shia are religiously obligated to obey their religious leader. One may follow a *marjaa* anywhere in the world, and switch from one to another.

In Lebanon's case, for example, there was until recently one Lebanese *marjaa*, Ayatollah Muhammad Hussein Fadlallah, who died in 2010. He was undoubtedly popular among the Shia of Lebanon; however, even those who decided to follow a particular *marjaa* were under no obligation to choose Fadlallah, being free to pick any one among dozens of others in Iraq, Iran, and elsewhere. Many of his committed followers, moreover, would have distinguished his authority on religious matters from any discussion of politics, as such questions are the subject of open debate among Shia.

To complicate the picture further, Fadlallah was never recognized as the official head of the Lebanese Shia community, a position occupied since 2000 by Sheikh Abdel-Amir Qabalan, a cleric of lesser scholarly standing, but a long-serving member of the Higher Islamic Shiite Council, which was created to represent and organize the community in 1967.[15] Hezbollah's turbaned secretary general, Hassan Nasrallah, arguably the most powerful of Lebanon's Shia clerics, also competes with his more conventional counterparts for the ear of the community, despite his low standing as a religious expert.

Asking whether any one of the three is the broader Lebanese Shia community's real religious leader, more authentic than the others, is to miss the point. All three emerged from the community, although all of them in that process required some kind of support from outside the community or the country—whether foreign clerics and religious institutions, Lebanese politicians, or state sponsors.

Leadership in this context does not imply authority—let alone exclusive authority—over a pre-existing following. However, that is not to say that formal offices of religious leadership do not have enormous potential to reach a public audience and gain a following. Lebanese examples include Sunni grand mufti Hassan Khaled, who was assassinated in 1989,[16] and the late Druze sheikh al-aql at the time, Muhammad Abou Shaqra, both of whom became focal points for their communities during Lebanon's civil war (1975–90). In difficult times, with state services and patron networks of distribution disrupted, these figures were able to bring their influence and institutional resources to bear, arguably adopting from the political class the function of *zaim* (patron).

Former Maronite patriarch Nasrallah Sfeir, who retired in 2011,[17] could also be said to have earned popularity by stepping in to fill a leadership vacuum in the 1990s, when the defeated Christian political elite was in exile or suppressed. Just as Hassan Khaled had rallied the leaderless Sunnis during the war and held coordination meetings for what remained of their political leadership during the 1980s, Sfeir did so for the Maronites during their post-war nadir. He launched a Maronite revival movement to boost morale during the time of the Syrian presence (in the 1990s and 2000s) and combat the problem of mass emigration. He used the national and global resources of the Maronite church to instill a new faith in Lebanon among a generation of young Christians that had known only war, underlining that Lebanon was a sacred homeland for Christians.

Maronites belong to the wider Catholic church, and so a major patron of this Maronite revival effort was Pope John Paul II himself, with his superstar personality, who visited Lebanon in 1997 to promote the slogan that "Lebanon is more than a country, it is a message."[18] This was immortalized in a papal document titled "A New Hope for Lebanon."[19] The document helped raise global awareness of the combined Syrian and Israeli occupations of Lebanon, culminating in Sfeir's sponsorship of the Qornet Shehwan gathering, a broad coalition of Christian politicians and intellectuals that began speaking out against Syrian hegemony from 2001 onward.[20]

But as these diverse examples suggest, religious commitment among the Lebanese does not necessarily translate into commitment to religious leaders. In each case of a Lebanese religious leader gaining a large popular following, it has been due to a favorable combination of sociopolitical circumstances on the one hand, and the execution of a winning public relations strategy on the other. That is to say, broad popularity cannot be taken for granted, but must, to a significant extent, be earned once in office.

One need only ask around in Beirut to discover the cynicism with which religious leaders are commonly regarded, even among the most pious of any sect.[21] Attitudes toward religious leaders have little to do with levels of religious commitment, and Lebanon is hardly exceptional in this regard. Just as religiosity is comparatively high across the Middle East, polls conducted by political scientist Theodor Hanf confirmed that "the Lebanese are a nation of believers."[22] A full 90 percent of those polled in 2006 stated that they tried to live according to the teachings of their religion, with very little variation by sect. Perhaps more surprisingly, this proportion of committed believers has been increasing steadily in recent decades, up from 75 percent in 1987 and 80 percent in 2002, with strong showings among the country's youth. Hanf concluded, "In short, the Lebanese clergy of all religions have little reason to doubt the religiousness of the youngest generation."[23]

However, various Lebanese religious leaders have been met with vocal or even violent disapproval from their own believers. The most famous such incident took place during Lebanon's civil war. There was a mass protest by many Maronites against Sfeir on 5 November 1989, denouncing his support for the Taif Accord, which brought Lebanon's civil war to an end the next year under Syrian supervision.[24] Outraged supporters of Michel Aoun, a populist anti-Syrian general (and the current Lebanese president, elected in October 2016) who opposed the accord, burned tires outside several churches and stormed the patriarchal residence, assaulting Sfeir and forcing him to kiss Aoun's picture.

Taking the fifteen years of Lebanon's civil war as a whole, it is significant that while no senior Lebanese cleric came under physical attack from the militias of other sects, a number were killed, kidnapped, or roughed up by members of their own sect for their perceived wrongs.[25] Generally, public demonstrations against, or criticisms of, religious leaders are not uncommon. The Maronite patriarch since March 2011, Bishara al-Rai, has been widely denounced for certain actions, including engaging in a dialogue with Hezbollah and visiting Syria and Israel.[26] Former mufti Muhammad Rashid

Qabbani was disliked and distrusted by many Sunnis for his political stances and alleged corruption, having to be rescued from an angry mob surrounding a Beirut mosque in December 2013.[27] Among the Druze, both the current sheikh al-aql, Naim Hassan, and his late predecessor, Bahjat Ghaith, faced smaller protests on the steps of the Druze religious headquarters in Beirut over alleged corruption and their perceived failure to use funds from religious endowments for the good of the community.[28]

The ire or scorn of the faithful is often a reaction to specific actions or stances—in other words to the way religious leaders perform or abuse their leadership. But not all religious leaders are given the chance to disappoint, instead being written off from the moment of their accession to office. Hassan Khaled (who only became popular later), Qabbani, and successive Maronite patriarchs Antonios Khoreich and Nasrallah Sfeir initially received lukewarm welcomes from communities that regarded them as poor compromise candidates—uninspiring bureaucrats launched into leadership through no particular merits of their own.

Despite these ups and downs and the numerous factors that may contribute to the success or failure of a sitting religious official to attract a popular following, these offices do have an established place in public life. Religious leaderships are consistently listed among the most influential groups in Lebanon, alongside patrons, party chiefs, and ministers.[29] However, in polling carried out by Theodor Hanf over a period between 1981 and 2006, perceptions of their degree of influence fluctuated wildly, with between 3 percent and 23 percent of respondents identifying them as "most influential," depending on the timing of the poll.[30]

What the religious leaders generally have in their favor is a public platform and institutional resources that they can leverage to reach a wide audience. In a country such as Lebanon, whose government grants formal recognition to the religious heads of sects, these figures occupy a consistently high-profile place in the protocol of state matters and other public affairs. Religious feasts—especially those given the status of national holidays—provide near-guaranteed airtime on a regular basis for these representatives to address the public. Because of this platform, as well as whatever institutional capacities they have to disseminate messages to their flocks, Lebanese religious leaders have a powerful potential to influence, even if a positive reception by the public is far from guaranteed.

Religious leadership is inherently ambiguous

At the heart of religious leadership is an inherent ambiguity. Religious leaders are, of course, expected to possess characteristics such as religious expertise, piety, moral standing, and independence from political concerns. But they are also communal representatives, acknowledgment of which requires a broad electoral mandate and popular accountability.

Among all of Lebanon's Islamic sects there have been attempts to make religious leaderships more representative, as increasing national influence and even legal "immunities, rights, and privileges" for religious leaders have brought traditional modes of appointment under scrutiny for corruption.[31] Indeed, at times Lebanon's communities have competed—especially during the golden era of Lebanese state-building in the 1950s and 1960s—over the modernization of their religious leaderships. The processes by which religious representatives of sects were chosen sat uneasily alongside the democratic values being applied to the same communities' political representatives.

Since 1955, for example, the Lebanese mufti of the republic has been elected not only by clerics, but also by lay Sunni representatives from various sectors of society, including government, the civil service, professional associations, trade syndicates, and labor unions.[32] The law defining the Shia community's jurisdiction, passed in 1967 by parliament and serving as a constitution, sought to adopt similar principles.[33] It widened the pool of voters to elect a council, which, in turn, would elect the head of the Higher Islamic Shiite Council.

In 1962, the Druze community took the principle of democratic mandate the furthest, extending the vote for the sheikh al-aql to all Druze males above the age of twenty-one.[34] The community also took on the matter of candidacy, seeking to address the paradox of widening the number of electors while continuing to choose candidates from a tiny elite of qualified clerics. It did so by allowing anyone to stand for election as sheikh al-aql. Yet when this heightened concern that those competing for the post were laymen unfit to represent the Druze or hold such a religiously significant position, the elections were cancelled.

Who or what exactly does a religious leader represent? That is the fundamental question with which Lebanon's sects have struggled ever since the country's first attempts at democratization over half a century ago. Religious leaders are recognized by governments as legitimate interlocutors on the basis that they are authorized as leaders to speak on behalf of their co-religionists and that as men of religion they speak the language that represents that group's distinctive religious identity.

Unfortunately, these two principles conflict with each other when put into practice. Speaking in the name of a religious belief system demands the independent, moral judgment of a religious specialist, who may only be properly recognized as such by other religious specialists. Speaking as a communal leader, in turn, requires accountability to a larger group of constituents.

This reality has been starkly illustrated by Lebanese attempts to make the system of official religious leadership less ambiguous and more transparent. The Druze experiment with opening nominations to laymen was a fiasco, and both the Druze and Sunni communities have rewritten their constitutions in recent decades to avoid ever having to hold broad-based elections. Anything but a small electoral college could introduce the need for clerics or their supporters to engage in unseemly public campaigning.

On the question of tenure, as well, the paradox of religious representation has reared its head. While religious leaderships were conceived as lifelong positions, there have been more recent moves to limit their terms of office and make these officials more answerable to the electorate. Such efforts have been met with the argument that life tenure is necessary to give religious leaders the freedom to follow their conscience.[35] Clearly, there are two conflicting conceptions of religious leadership at work here, and they cannot be reconciled through a coherent system of religious representation that can satisfy modern democratic impulses.

Religious leaders do not exist in isolation from politics

Powerful interests inevitably play a role in shaping electoral outcomes, even within religious institutions. In countries such as Lebanon, where many religious institutions are legally recognized and integrated into the framework of the state, politicians in the parliament and other government posts also have considerable influence over defining the electoral processes for religious offices. As these offices receive greater recognition as representatives of sectarian diversity, the stakes grow higher.

The interests in play are not only internal to the communities but are equally likely to be national or international. Foreign stakeholders in Lebanese Sunni politics, for instance, have been decisive in the elections of the last three grand muftis of the republic at least, going back to the 1960s. The three were all elected with near or total unanimity following foreign interventions of some kind: Hassan Khaled, after a visit to Egypt in 1966 to gain then president Gamal Abdel Nasser's approval; Muhammad Rashid Qabbani, after a visit to Syria in 1996 to gain then president Hafez al-Assad's approval; and Abdel Latif Derian, after an agreement was reached between Egypt and Saudi Arabia in 2014.[36]

Where a particular political faction has had sufficient weight in parliament, they have sometimes been able to amend electoral laws to engineer overwhelmingly unanimous electoral outcomes in favor of particular religious leaders. The election of the grand mufti in 1996 is a case in point, with an amendment passed by parliament on the very morning that Qabbani was anointed.[37] That amendment reduced the number of electors from over 1,000 to 96.

A similar move was visible in the Druze community in 2006, enabled by the landslide victory of a single political bloc—led by Walid Joumblatt—in parliamentary elections the previous year.[38] The Syrian regime had up until then used an ambitious sheikh al-aql to act as a counterweight to the predominance of Joumblatt. However, Syria's waning influence from 2005 on allowed Joumblatt to win all the Druze seats in parliament and use them to bring to office a more compliant confessional council and religious leader.

Even the trajectory of the Shia cleric Musa al-Sadr, who did not fit the mold of most religious leaderships, was not immune to political machinations. The spectacular rise of this young, Iranian-accented cleric to national fame—even adulation—owes a great deal to his personal charisma and vision. He did not rise through the ranks of a party, as did Hezbollah's Secretary General Hassan Nasrallah, or through the Islamic scholarly milieu, as did Ayatollah Mohammed Hussein Fadlallah. However, even Sadr could not simply ride the wave of popular support into the office representing Lebanon's Shia. In order to overcome opposition from establishment politicians and clerics, he sided with then Lebanese president Fouad Shihab's government and its secret service, the Deuxième Bureau,[39] and later with Hafez al-Assad.

Religious leaders are only symbolically set apart from politics. Scratch the surface of these leaderships' inner workings, and they are inevitably bound up with the realities of local, national, and international power plays. In this way they are no different from any other institution in a region where the shortcomings of states have so often been filled by networks of patronage that erode any distinction between politics and society at large. It is naïve, therefore, to look to religious leaders as individuals who allow the bypassing of political representatives and to see them as more direct interlocutors with sects. Nor are the influences on religious leadership by any means restricted to stakeholders within their own communities. As valuable power bases, religious institutions invite intervention from other interested compatriots and foreigners alike.

Religious leaders and the problem of sectarianism

The link between religious leaders and divisive religious identities seems self-evident. The "persistence" of strong religious leadership almost a century after the establishment of modern nation states in the Middle East is said to indicate these states' failure to overcome sectarian identities.[40]

At the same time, secularist critics tend to accuse religious leaders of promoting sectarianism as a cynical means of self-preservation or through sheer narrow-minded fanaticism. Therefore, many civil society activists in the Middle East regard religious institutions, which might elsewhere be considered a valuable part of civil society, with intense suspicion.[41] There is, in short, a widespread view of religious leaders as somehow both products and perpetuators of sectarianism, creating preconceptions that obscure much of their actual relationship with sectarianism.

Because top-level religious leaders do not simply arise through popular acclamation, whether religious or sectarian, their status is far more dependent upon the culture and politics of elites at various levels of the clerical hierarchy, the community, the nation, and the region. What this means is that the factors shaping their behavior are complex and cannot be reduced to a few conventional motivations. While religious leaders may well personify Lebanon's sectarian system, they generally do not promote sectarian hatred as a means of reinforcing their authority. In fact, often the contrary is true.

Religious leaders tend not to incite sectarian hatred

None of the religious heads of Lebanon's sects indulges in overt sectarian rhetoric. Nor, generally, have any of them since independence in 1943.[42] This may surprise some Lebanese, who recall images of finger-wagging clerics perhaps standing with militia leaders responsible for wartime atrocities or using political language associated with a particular sectarian bloc.

However, the reality is that religious leaders often have to walk a fine line in terms of rhetoric and behavior among their own community, the political elite, and other communities. In order to avoid being ostracized and isolated, they usually take pains to remain in favor with the elite, in that way maximizing their own influence through their ability to engage in gentle persuasion or soft negotiation. At the same time, they avoid straying too far from the dominant political values of their own community, let alone the values of coexistence that are a part of Lebanese political life.[43]

So, for example, during the civil war, then Grand Mufti Hassan Khaled held regular meetings with leaders of the Muslim-Leftist coalition, including the Palestinian leader Yasser Arafat. Similarly, Maronite patriarchs Antonios Khoreich and Nasrallah Sfeir hosted summits with Christian politicians-cum-warlords.[44] These efforts to remain in the loop—that is, to maintain their influence within their communities—sometimes looked to outsiders like oppositional sectarian stances. Hence former members of Christian militias recall that when Hassan Khaled gave a speech, "it was an occasion for us to spit on the television."[45] However, when compared, the core agenda of the grand mufti was very similar to that of the patriarchs: limited reform of the political system to ensure equal participation, negotiated through constitutional channels between fellow Lebanese.

The rhetoric of Lebanon's various top religious leaders has been remarkably consistent throughout the years of war and peace.[46] These leaders valorize common ideals of citizenship, civility, and self-sacrifice for the nation, which they explain in terms of their religious traditions. The virtues of patience and the denial of one's own desires or private interests are themes often sounded during Ramadan, Lent, and Easter. Religious vocabulary is translated into political language: faith in Lebanon as a final homeland for all believers; peace and national salvation as the fruit of moral values, moderation, and obedience to the law; and even surrender of the material interests of the sect for the greater good of the nation.

In this context, it is worth remembering that high-profile religious leaders in Middle Eastern countries including Lebanon head institutions that are integrated into, or at least heavily invested in, the modern state order. They may supervise personal-status courts, run publicly owned mosques, receive salaries from the state budget, benefit from government funding of Islamic religious colleges, and so on. That is why they must, in some regard, adhere to the prevailing ideology of the state, which, in Lebanon at least, is heavily reliant on an ideal of cohabitation between the communities, no matter how divided communal life may be in practice.

In Lebanon as elsewhere, religious leaders not only benefit profoundly from state recognition and inclusion in national public life but also are particularly vulnerable when politics gives way to violence—both in terms of how it might affect their material resources and the fact that their precarious capacity for soft power is diminished during periods of conflict. "Their privileged role," as one scholar of Lebanon puts it, is "mainly due to the fact that there is a balance to maintain between the many religious communities."[47] It is the principle of confessional coexistence that helps keep these individuals in the limelight of public affairs as the doyens of dialogue. In Lebanon—and in many other cases—it is their diplomatic skills and record of sectarian political correctness that make them appropriate candidates for public religious offices in the first place.

Religious leaders' potential role in defusing sectarian tension

Cynical observers sometimes suggest that the sectarian political correctness of top religious leaders is simply a form of doublespeak.[48] Certainly sectarian politics in Lebanon and other countries in the region often incentivize politicians to present bland platitudes to national or regional publics, while reserving more divisive rhetoric for audiences within their own communities. Most religious leaders, however, are not generally driven by the electoral concerns that make this an attractive or a necessary strategy for politicians. Nor do they have the means available to politicians for pushing a sectarian agenda: direct involvement in government or legislative policy-making, or in certain cases even sponsorship of sectarian militias.

For religious leaders, words are their most effective weapon, and doublespeak would only blunt that weapon. On this basis, these religious leaders can be taken at their word as genuine opponents of a divisive, conflictual sectarianism. Much of their power lies in using—or threatening to use—their platform to sway the public for or against the policies of politicians. In practice they tend to avoid rocking the boat too much for fear of being excluded from the political elite's decision-making. Unlike politicians, however, they can choose to take that risk. They can rock the boat without sinking it completely, because religious leaders are not depending on re-election, are difficult to depose, and their institutions do not fall with their reputation as political parties might. This gives religious leaders a unique edge, and one that Lebanon's official heads of sects have successfully used as a last resort in defusing sectarian tensions.

Indeed, a striking pattern has emerged in Lebanon: whenever sectarian conflict looms, religious leaders have frequently offset sectarian polarization by siding against the dominant forces and majority opinion within their own communities.

For example, Maronite patriarch Bishara al-Rai caused stirs in March 2011 and again in May 2016 by staging dialogues with Hezbollah, alienating in the process many of his predecessor's staunchest supporters and allies.[49] After

2012, the then Sunni grand mufti, Muhammad Rashid Qabbani, was left even more dramatically out in the cold after meeting with Hezbollah representatives and the Iranian ambassador against the will of Saad Hariri's Future Movement, the largest political force in the Sunni community.[50] Qabbani's Shia counterpart, Abdel-Amir Qabalan, used his Eid al-Adha sermon in October 2013 to call on Hezbollah to surrender its weapons to the state and to stop sending fighters to Syria.[51] Each of these figures was lambasted for reneging on his responsibility to his own community, but they clearly regarded the reinforcement of national unity as a preferred means of preserving the higher interests of all communities.

Similar moves were made by predecessors to neutralize the sectarian overtones of conflict during the 1975–90 civil war, and even earlier crises. Most famously, then Maronite patriarch Boulos al-Meouchi joined the Muslim majority in opposition to then Maronite president Camille Chamoun to de-escalate an armed crisis in 1958.[52]

The primary concern of Lebanon's official religious leaders has long appeared to be prevention of the collapse of the state and its constitutional institutions and to be countering the sectarian dimension of polarization. These attitudes are possible, ultimately, because official religious leaders are not answerable to sectarian constituencies in the same way that politicians are.

How do religious leaders inhibit social integration?

Even as religious leaders generally defuse sectarian tensions, they also function as the keepers of social boundaries between sects. The sectarian personal-status courts and school systems that fall under these leaders' legal remit were initially intended to provide for freedom of religion, but they have ended up severely restricting people's freedom to live outside a confessional framework. In particular, the fact that the religious communities retain control over personal-status issues makes it extremely difficult for many Lebanese to marry outside their sect. Whatever exceptions and loopholes exist, religious institutions lay the tracks for members of their sect to conduct lives surrounded by co-religionists and punctuated by life events—birth, marriage, divorce, death, and inheritance—legally administered by a religious body. Subtly trapped by this pervasive reality, members of sects have their perceptions of society and citizenship shaped accordingly. Potentially, this can reproduce the social basis for sectarianism and create conditions ripe for sectarian mobilization.

These separate personal-status systems are popularly assumed to be relics of a pre-modern era, vestiges left intact as the modern state was built up around them. Lebanese advocates of secularism thus lay the blame at the feet of religious leaders as prime culprits in the preservation of an essentially sectarian society, arguing that civil authorities need to take over from them.

The truth, however, is quite different. It was, in fact, state recognition and the legislation of sects and their institutions in the twentieth century that led to the codification of personal-status law for legally binding courts in every community.[53] Various precedents existed in informal adjudication on the basis of customary local practice, but these were very different affairs from the unforgivingly enforced black-and-white rulings of an all-embracing modern legal system. Translating custom into legal code, for instance, meant that divorce became impossible for members of Lebanon's Catholic communities—including Maronites—for the first time, as did mixed marriages for the Druze.[54] Such principles could previously have been more easily fudged than they are today by a favorable cleric working in an informal and personalized system, avoided by opting to see an Ottoman judge in the nearest town, or simply ignored. State-driven centralization and rationalization have made many Lebanese sects what they are at present: rigidly circumscribed and clearly differentiated communities whose social lives are governed by monolithic religious hierarchies.

The dangers in the empowerment of religious leaderships

Lebanon's century-long experiment with religious representation shows us where state policies of confessional recognition lead in the long term. It also serves as a cautionary tale for statesmen considering dealing with religious leaders. When governments choose to recognize such individuals as spokespeople, the long-term consequences for the communities represented in this way can be profound and difficult to foresee.

For all the good intentions of Lebanon's official religious leaders in promoting peaceful coexistence, the empowerment of these institutions has contributed to the demarcation and practical separation of communal groups. Large numbers of Lebanese citizens do not feel properly represented by these religious leaders, who promote, and indeed enforce, their own visions of religious orthodoxy and social propriety.[55] Whereas Lebanon's confessional political system is designed—at least theoretically—to promote multi-party cooperation, the state has sponsored religious leaders to guarantee the basic interests of their various sects. The Lebanese system attributes primary sectarian identities to a population that does not always wish to be represented in those terms.[56] Within this restrictive context, popular aspirations have been frustrated by the confessional system's entrenchment of both political and religious elites.

Even among those integrated into the confessional system, official religious institutions have created a sense of marginalization. Take the Sunni community, which has as its religious leader the mufti of the republic. As a Beirut-based institution, the office of the mufti of the republic has always been occupied by the son of one of Beirut's established clerical families, which enjoy privileged access to high-ranking jobs in the city's personal-status courts, mosques, and religious schools, as well as connections with the political elite.[57] The mufti can impose his religious and political orthodoxy while claiming to represent all Sunnis on the national stage. This, combined with the consistent failure of Sunni politicians to secure equal state investment in Sunni communities outside Beirut,[58] explains why many Sunnis in Tripoli, Sidon, and the Beqaa Valley feel disenfranchised. As a result, there are those who have increasingly used Islamist organizations as an alternative means of expressing their religious identity. The monopolistic claims of the central hierarchy have heightened tensions between official and unofficial Sunni representatives, who have sometimes fought for control over local mosques, pushing preachers to conform to very different visions of Islam.

Meanwhile, Sunni secularists, indeed secularists in general, may protest against their religious leaders' power for different reasons, but are similarly disenfranchised and even more restricted by the religious representatives' hold over personal-status law. Not only have the religious leaders used their influence to block proposals for an optional civil personal-status code, but the previous Sunni grand mufti, Muhammad Rashid Qabbani, issued a fatwa declaring its proponents apostates.[59] The mufti's enforcement of a single vision of what it is to be a Sunni Muslim thus marginalizes a range of people in the community, contributing to their resentment of the system as a whole.

When it comes to Lebanon's crisis of representation, the inadequacy of imposing a religious form of representation contributes to widespread political alienation, the rise of activism against the political system and incidences of civil unrest across Lebanon today. The social impact may transcend hot-button political issues but ought to be seen as one of the common underlying causes behind protests by civil society groups in Beirut, Salafi militancy in Tripoli or Sidon, lawlessness in the Beqaa Valley, and support for ISIS and other Syrian-affiliated rebel groups in the north-eastern town of Arsal. State recognition of religious leaders has not improved the representation of diversity in Lebanon; on the contrary, it has served to suppress it.

Conclusion: how the state has restructured religious life

This leaves an essentially ethical question of whether and how such figures belong as religious representatives of sects as a supplement to democratic representation. Should states grant recognition to particular religious leaders and institutions for their value as allies in countering sectarian radicalization, when to do so misrepresents society, empowers those it recognizes, marginalizes many others, and ultimately helps create the social conditions for sectarianism?

It makes little sense to speak of religious leaders as representing sectarian diversity. On the other hand, they are certainly implicated in the socialization of citizens into communally bounded lives, inhibiting full social cohesion. It has not always been so. Lebanese clerics have never had so much political influence, nor power over their co-religionists, as they have been given since the twentieth century. Ironically, it has been secular state officials—whether French colonial administrators, Lebanese government ministers, or foreign diplomats—who have enabled and encouraged the monopolization of religious life through their recognition of certain clerics as interlocutors with confessional communities. Because senior clerics are often assumed to be natural religious leaders and representatives, state officials may not realize the transformation wrought by their dealings with such clerics. The Lebanese experience should stand as a warning that policies conceived with the best of intentions—to promote inclusive government and religious freedom—may have contrary effects in the longer term.

APPENDIX A

METHODOLOGY AND DATA FOR CHAPTER 8,
JUSTIN GENGLER

Hypotheses on threat perception and popular loyalty

From the preceding, one can formulate several testable hypotheses about the relationship prevailing today between popular threat perceptions and orientations toward governments in the Arab Gulf states. A first posits that Gulf citizens are more likely to be supportive of incumbent regimes when they prioritize security and order over competing national goals such as economic development, democratization, preserving local culture and tradition, environmental protection, and so on. Thus Hypothesis 1:

H1. Preferences for stability are associated with greater deference toward state authority.

In addition to following from the foregoing discussion about the Gulf context specifically, this hypothesis also accords with the general prediction of modernization theory that individuals more concerned over basic survival are less likely to expend time and energy on political involvement.[1]

A separate set of hypotheses summarizes the expected indirect effects of stability preferences—that is, how public concern over stability impacts other mechanisms that link government performance to individual political orientations in the GCC. Here we revisit the notion of the political "subsidy": a baseline level of popular support enjoyed by governments irrespective of their objective performance, simply in return for their protection of citizens against perceived foreign and domestic threats. The term subsidy refers then to the discrepancy between actual political support and the level of political support that would be expected to exist in the absence of public preoccupation with stability. To operationalize this argument, we consider the most obvious mechanism tying regime performance to citizens' political orientations in the rentier Gulf region: satisfaction with personal economic circumstances, this taken as a proxy for private benefit distribution. This gives Hypotheses 2A and 2B, which together predict that economic satisfaction will determine political deference toward the state *only among citizens who do not prioritize stability* above competing national concerns.

H2A. Among citizens who do not prioritize stability, greater economic satisfaction is associated with greater political deference.

H2B. Among citizens who do prioritize stability, the relationship between economic satisfaction and political deference is weak or non-existent.

Data and methods

Here we test these theoretical expectations using recent mass survey data from Bahrain, Kuwait, Oman, and Qatar. The Bahrain data come from the widely used World Values Survey[2] (WVS, conducted in 2013), while the data for the latter three countries were collected in an original survey of GCC nationals (2015) designed and implemented by the Social and Economic Survey Research Institute (SESRI) at Qatar University.[3] All surveys consist of large and nationally representative samples of adult citizens interviewed in person at their places of residence. The data include a total of 1,200 interviews conducted in Bahrain, 1,022 in Kuwait, 852 in Oman, and 793 in Qatar.

The aim of the analysis is to understand how popular preferences for stability shape political attitudes and behavior among individual Gulf citizens, and how this link varies across different Gulf societies. We begin by investigating the direct relationship between stability preferences and political deference, evaluating to what extent the data support the notion that more stability-oriented citizens are also more likely to remain supportive of Gulf governments even when they disagree with their policies. Next we proceed one step further to assess the *conditioning* effect of individual preferences for stability on other important processes through which citizens might come to assume a more oppositional or deferential political stance. Specifically, we analyze the moderating effect of stability preferences on the expected link between economic satisfaction and political satisfaction. If we find that this basic rentier relationship operates more weakly or not at all among those citizens who emphasize stability over other societal aims, then we will have evidence of the hypothesized political subsidy enjoyed by Gulf rulers as a result of popular concerns over security. Alternatively, if the data show that economically less satisfied nationals tend to exhibit less deference toward the state irrespective of their security orientation, then we will have strong evidence against this hypothesis.

To study these empirical relationships, we rely on a standard ordered logistic regression model estimated separately for each of the four countries. The model tests the effects of our independent variables of interest—economic satisfaction and concern for stability—while holding constant a number of potentially confounding social and economic factors.[4] These control variables include a respondent's gender (coded 1 for females); years of age; and education level (primary or below, high school graduate, some technical/college, university graduate). Economic satisfaction is measured by a respondent's self-reported satisfaction with the "economic situation" of his or her household (rated on an ascending 0 to 10 scale). Prioritization of stability is coded categorically (not a priority, second priority, first priority). To reduce the number of parameters in the model, age and education are estimated as continuous measures, while stability is estimated as a factor variable. Due to a relatively high rate of missing data, household income is not included as a control. Finally, to test the conditioning influence of stability preferences on the relationship between economic satisfaction and political deference (Hypothesis 2), we add a multiplicative interaction term between the *stability* and *economic satisfaction* variables. All models utilize robust standard errors and, where available, sampling weights to account for survey design effects.

APPENDIX B

COLE BUNZEL

The following are original translations of official Islamic State statements concerning Saudi Arabia. The first is an excerpt from Abu Bakr al-Baghdadi's November 2014 address, in which he declared the establishment of an official presence on the Arabian Peninsula and outlined a strategy there. The second is the first audio statement from Najd province, one of the Islamic State's three declared provinces in Saudi Arabia, released at the end of May 2015. It is both a statement of the Islamic State's intentions and motives in Saudi Arabia and a tribute to the suicide bomber who killed 21 Shia civilians at a mosque in the Eastern Province on 22 May 2015.

Excerpt from "Though the Unbelievers Be Averse," Abu Bakr al-Baghdadi, 13 November 2014[1]

O sons of the Lands of the Two Holy Places, O people of God's unity [*tawhid*], O people of association and dissociation [*al-wala wal-bara*]. Among you is the head of the snake, the stronghold of the disease. So unsheathe your swords, break your scabbards into pieces, forsake this lower world! There shall be no safety for the House of Salul, no relief from this day forward. There is no place for the idolaters on the Peninsula of Muhammad—may God bless and preserve him. Unsheathe your swords! First, go after the Rejectionists [*al-Rafida*, that is, the Shia] wherever you find them, then the Al Salul [that is, the Al Saud family] and their soldiers, before the Crusaders and their bases. Go after the Rejectionists and the Al Salul and their soldiers! Tear them to pieces! Seize them as groups and as individuals! Make life loathsome for them. Keep them busy with themselves, not us. And be patient, do not rush. Before long, God willing, you will see portents of the Islamic State.

"Expel the Rejectionist Idolaters from the Peninsula of Muhammad,"
Najd province, 29 May 2015[2]

Praise belongs to God, Empowerer of Islam by His support, Humbler of idolatry [*shirk*] by His power. And prayers and peace be upon the Chosen Prophet, and upon his family and his companions altogether.

God the Exalted said: "And when the sacred months are past, slay the idolaters wherever you find them, and take them, and confine them, and lie in wait for them at every place of ambush" [Quran 9:5].[3]

And God the Exalted said: "And fight the unbelievers totally as they fight you totally" [Quran 9:36].

And on the authority of Ibn Abbas,[4] may God have mercy on him, who said: The Messenger of God, may God bless and preserve him, said: "Whoso changes his religion, kill him."

Now, these Rejectionists [*al-Rawafid*, a variant of *al-Rafida*] are apostates from Islam, belligerent enemies of the Religion of God. The scholars [*ulama*] have agreed upon their unbelief, as Ibn al-Samani,[5] may God have mercy on him, stated. He said: "The Muslim community has agreed on the excommunication [*takfir*] of the Shia [*al-Imamiyya*]." The imams Abu Zura and Abu Hayyan,[6] both from Rayy, said: "We have met scholars in Iraq and Sham and the Hijaz, and all of them say that the Rejectionists have rejected Islam." The author of the book *al-Mughni*, may God have mercy on him, recorded the scholars' consensus that whoever accuses Aisha,[7] may God have mercy on her, of a sin, he is an unbelieving apostate—and this is the religion of the Rejectionists.

And the scholars have agreed that whoever rejects the *sunna* [that is, the traditions of the Prophet] is an unbeliever—and this is the religion of the Rejectionists.

And the scholars have agreed that whoever claims that the Quran is faulty is an unbeliever, for he repudiates the statement of God the Exalted: "We have surely sent down the Quran; and We will certainly preserve the same from corruption" [Quran 15:9].

And the scholars have agreed that whoever takes with God another god is an unbeliever—and this is the religion of the Rejectionists.

And the scholars have been in consensus that whoever seeks the aid of the dead for the fulfillment of needs and the relief of troubles is an apostate unbeliever—and this is the religion of the Rejectionists.

And whoever excommunicates the Companions [of the Prophet] has committed unbelief, for he repudiates the statement of God the Exalted: "God was well pleased with the believers when they were swearing fealty [*baya*] to thee under the tree, and He knew what was in their hearts, so He sent down tranquility upon them, and rewarded them with a nigh victory" [Quran 48:18]. And he repudiates the statement of the Prophet, may God bless and preserve him: "The Prophet is in Heaven, and Abu Bakr is in Heaven, and Umar is in Heaven, and Uthman is in Heaven, and Ali is in Heaven."

This is the religion of the Rejectionists. They are apostate unbelievers, whose blood and property it is licit to take. And it is obligatory for us to kill them, to fight them, and to drive them away, nay but to cleanse the land of their filth.

It is well-known to the observer of Rejectionist beliefs that the Rejectionists are of three kinds, Usulis [*Ilmiyya*], Akhbaris [*Khabariyya*], and Shaykhis [*Shaykhiyya*], and the most severe of these in unbelief are the Shaykhis, the followers of Ahmad al-Ahsai,[8] who are the Rejectionists of the Gulf. They view Ali, may God have mercy on him, as a lord who creates and sustains—far is God above that they say!—and they claim that the Power is Ali's, that he directs matters and relieves troubles—far is God above that, they say! They are the most severe of the factions of the Rejectionists in unbelief and apostasy, and thus killing them and fighting them wherever we find them are a duty incumbent on us.

Indeed, our state [that is, the Islamic State], may God strengthen it and grant it victory, has answered the command of God, who said: "Fight them till there is no persecution and the religion is God's entirely" [Quran 8:39]. It ordered its soldiers in all places to kill the enemies of the religion, and especially the Rejectionists, on account of the severity of their unbelief and their remoteness [from Islam]. Then what if, in addition to their unbelief, they are living in the Peninsula of Muhammad, may God bless and preserve him?

The Prophet, may God bless and preserve him, said: "Two religions shall not dwell together on the Arabian Peninsula."

And he, may God bless and preserve him, said: "Expel the idolaters from the Arabian Peninsula."

And what idolatry is worse than the idolatry of the Rejectionists? And what is more dangerous to Islam than the danger of the Rejectionists?

Did not the Sheikh of Islam Ibn Taymiyya al-Harrani say, "The Rejectionists are worse for the Muslims than the Jews and the Christians"?[9]

And so, answering the command of God the Exalted, then the command of the caliph of the Muslims, to kill the Rejectionists wherever they are found, one of the lions of the Islamic State, the worthy man—worthy we deem him and we vouch none above God—Abu Amir al-Najdi, the lion's claw, set out, carrying on his pure body instant death and terrible poison, to explode the belt of death among the masses of the idolaters in the temple of pagan idolatry, the place that God the Exalted detests. The flesh of the idolaters scattered, and the lives of the idolaters slipped away, by the act of this righteous monothe-ist—as we deem him, and may God deem him so. Their lives descended to hell, an evil homecoming. And although the Muslim community has lost this courageous lion, God has by him indeed purified the land of the filth of the idolaters. We deem him a martyr, and may God deem him so. And we hope for him the highest station among the martyrs, for verily he has delighted the hearts of the believers and enraged the hearts of the idolaters and hypocrites. So blessed be he whose departure from this lower world brings strength to this religion and degradation to unbelief and the unbelievers, delight to the believ-ers and rage to the unbelievers, idolaters, apostates, and hypocrites.

To God belongs your achievement, O mighty state of mine. The unbelievers have joined together against you, and yet you still await the purification of the Land of the Two Holy Places from the filth of the idolaters and the apostates.

I say to our people in the Land of the Two Holy Places: by God, the Al Salul will not benefit you, and they will never protect you from the Rejectionists. Indeed, they have been unable to protect their artificial borders from the Houthi scum, so how will they protect you from the Rejectionists if they join together against you?

O people of ours. Do you not remember in 1411 [1990/1991], when the Iraqi army penetrated the borders of the Al Salul, how they had more than forty civilian aircraft at the airport ready to bring the whole family of the Al Salul to the lands of unbelief, leaving the Sunnis unarmed to meet their fate?

O people of ours in the Land of the Two Holy Places. By God apart from Whom there is no god, only the Islamic State will protect you after God the Exalted. So come to your state. Come to the place of strength and power. Come to the Land of Islam, O young men of the Land of the Two Holy Places. O young men of the Land of the Two Holy Places, the spark has been lit. So come light a fire to burn the faces of the Rejectionists and the apostates. Come set fire to the thrones of the idolatrous rulers.

Come! For [the Prophet,] may God bless and preserve him, said, according to Tirmidhi in the *hadith* of Abu Hurayra:[10] "The martyr will not feel the pain of death but as one of you feels the pain of a pinch." Indeed, the martyrdom-seeker, though his parts become pieces and his limbs are torn apart, finds no pain in death. And when he is called forth on the Day of Resurrection, his wound will flow with blood, all of him being a wound. He will flow with blood from the top of his head to the soles of his feet. The martyrdom-seeker supports the religion with his blood, flesh, bones, veins, and arteries. So good for him! Good for him, since when he meets God the Exalted, God will say to him: "My servant, what carried you to do what you have done?" He will say: "I did this on your behalf, O Lord." God will say to him: "Right you are."

Come, O young men of the Land of the Two Holy Places. Come purify the captive land of the peninsula of the filth of the idolatrous rulers and the Rejectionists. Come, O you who seek the freedom of your prisoners. Heal your breasts! How often do they fill with rage and oppression, on account of the oppression of the idolatrous rulers and their followers? Come, O you who seek the application of God's law in the Land of the Two Holy Places. The law will not be applied but by jihad in the path of God. The law will not be applied but by jihad and martyrdom, but by blood and limbs—"until … the religion is God's entirely" [Quran 8:39]. Come, O people of *al-wala wal-bara*. There is only one death, so let it be in the path of God.

Sheikh Sulayman ibn Sihman,[11] may God have mercy on him, said: "If the people of the city and the desert fought each other until all of them perished, it would be better than if they erected an idol being worshiped apart from God."[12]

And what idol? The idol [*taghut*] of the peninsula, the best of lands and the cradle of revelation. It is ruled by an idol who is a vile servant of the Jews and the Christians. There the believer is degraded and humiliated, while the apostates, hypocrites, and secularists are strong and in charge. There God is blasphemed. There the Messenger of God, may God bless and preserve him, is blasphemed. The blasphemer is elevated in status, while the devoted [to God] who defends the honor of Muhammad, may God bless and preserve him, is imprisoned. Indeed, the peninsula has been worn thin to the point that its wear has been made manifest, to the point that women dare to blaspheme against and abuse the laws of the religion, blaspheme against God the Exalted, and blaspheme against the Prophet, may God bless and preserve him. You will not see a man zealous about God's religion rousing the inactive, following the practice of Islam, and killing him who blasphemes against the Prophet, may

God bless and preserve him, and ridicules the religion of God. And "surely we belong to God, and to Him we return" [Quran 2:156]. "And may the eyes of the cowards never sleep."[13]

O Lord, if the time of my death has come, let it not be upon a bier overlaid with green garments. Rather make my day as a martyr in a band, under assault and fearing in a broad valley path.[14] For truly we are a people admitting of no mediation; we are out front, above the worlds or below the grave.[15]

And you, O prisoners of the Land of the Two Holy Places. O men of audacity and honor. O you who have supported the religion of God. By God, we have not forgotten you and will not forget you. For the Messenger of God, may God bless and preserve him, said: "Set free the captive." We ask God the Exalted that He achieve your freedom by our hands—by God, even if our blood must flow and our limbs be torn apart at the gates of your prisons. God's setting you free by our hands is more desirable than this lower world and what is in it. So await relief from God by our hands, God willing.

And there is no might nor power save in God, the High, the Mighty. "And God prevails in His purpose, but most men know not" [Quran 12:21]. And peace and prayers be upon our Prophet Muhammad, and upon his family and his companions altogether.

NOTES

INTRODUCTION

1. Author's observation, 'Isa Town, Bahrain, November 2006.
2. See, for example, Tariq al-Jamil, *Power and Knowledge in Medieval Islam: Shi'i and Sunni Encounters in Baghdad* (London: I. B. Tauris, 2017). Across the centuries, there have been successive efforts at ecumenical rapprochement, to include attempts by some Sunni and Shia clerics to reconfigure and unify doctrines. For an overview, see Rainer Brunner, *Islamic Ecumenism in the 20th Century: The Azhar and Shiism Between Rapprochement and Restraint* (Leiden: Brill, 2004).
3. Werner Ende, "Sunni Polemical Writings on the Shi'a and the Iranian Revolution," in David Menashri, ed., *The Iranian Revolution and the Muslim World* (Boulder, CO: 1990), pp. 219–32.
4. Morten Valbjorn and Andre Bank, "Signs of a New Arab Cold War: The 2006 Lebanon War and the Sunni-Shi'i Divide," *MERIP Middle East Report* 37(242), March 2007, pp. 6–11.
5. Frederic Wehrey, "Uprisings Jolt the Saudi Iranian Rivalry," *Current History* (December 2011), pp. 352–7; F. Gregory Gause III, "Beyond Sectarianism: The New Middle East Cold War," Brookings Doha Center Analysis Paper no. 11, July 2014, https://www.brookings.edu/wp-content/uploads/2016/06/English-PDF-1.pdf; Raymond Hinnebusch, "The Sectarianization of the Middle East: Transnational Identity Wars and Competitive Interference," *Project of Middle East Political Science*, 4 August 2016, http://pomeps.org/2016/08/04/the-sectarianization-of-the-middle-east-transnational-identity-wars-and-competitive-interference/
6. Bassel F. Salloukh, "Sect Supreme: The End of Realist Politics in the Middle East," *Foreign Affairs Snapshots*, 14 July 2014, https://www.foreignaffairs.com/articles/middle-east/2014-07-14/sect-supreme#/cid=soc-twitter-at-snapshot-sect_supreme-000000
7. Examples include the conflict between establishment and quietist Salafi strands and more activist currents with roots in the Muslim Brotherhood. It has also manifested

itself as tensions between Salafi/Wahhabi traditions and other currents. See for example the August 2016 conference on defining Sunni Islam in the Chechen capital of Grozyny, which included Sufis and the four jurisprudential schools of Sunnism (Hanafi, Maliki, ShafiʾI, and Hanbali), but excluded Salafism/Wahhabism. Yaroslav Trofimov, "Excommunicating Saudis? A New Fracture Emerges in Islam," *Wall Street Journal*, 22 September 2016. Here again, however, geopolitics mixed with doctrine: the conference reflected splits between Russia and Saudi Arabia, with many Saudi observers decrying a Sufi-Russian-Iranian-Shia axis, along with what Saudis saw as turncoat participation by Egypt and the UAE.

8. For a discussion of the interplay between Saudi Arabia's clerical establishment and ruling family, see Raihan Ismail, *Saudi Clerics and Shia Islam* (Oxford: Oxford University Press, 2016).

9. The most influential treatise from this school was Robert Kaplan, *Balkan Ghosts: A Journey Through History* (New York: Picador, 2014).

10. David Remnick, "Going the Distance: On and Off the Road with Barack Obama," *New Yorker*, 27 January 2014, http://www.newyorker.com/reporting/2014/01/27/140127fa_fact_remnick?currentPage=all

11. Ibid.

12. Robert F. Worth, "Jihadist Groups Gain in Turmoil Across the Middle East," *New York Times*, 13 December 2013.

13. For example, Frederic Wehrey, *Sectarian Politics in the Gulf: From the Iraq War to the Arab Uprisings* (New York: Columbia University Press, 2013); Fanar Haddad, *Sectarianism in Iraq: Antagonistic Visions of Unity* (London: Hurst & Co., 2011); Tobias Matthiesen, *Sectarian Gulf: Saudi Arabia, Bahrain and the Arab Spring that Wasn't* (Stanford, CA: Stanford University Press, 2013); Lawrence Potter, ed., *Sectarian Politics in the Persian Gulf* (London: Hurst & Co., 2014); Brigette Marechal and Sami Zemni, *The Dynamics of Sunni-Shia Relationships: Doctrine, Transnationalism, Intellectuals and the Media* (London: Hurst & Co., 2013). For an academic study on sectarianism by Arab authors, see Hazim, Saghiyah, ed., *Nawasib wa Rawafidh: Munazaʿat al-Sunna wa al-Shiʿa fi al-ʿAlam al-Islami al-Yawm (Nawasib and Rawafidh: The Sunni-Shiʿa Confrontation in the Islamic World Today)* (Beirut: Dar al-Saqi, 2009).

14. For identity politics in domestic and foreign policies, Marc Lynch, *State Interests and Public Spheres: The International Politics of Jordan's Identity* (New York: Columbia University Press, 1999); and Lawrence Rubin, *Islam in the Balance: Ideational Threats in Arab Politics* (Stanford, CA: Stanford University Press, 2014). For sectarianism as a by-product of authoritarianism and weak states, Nader Hashemi, "Toward a Political Theory of Sectarianism in the Middle East: The Salience of Authoritarianism over Theology," *Middle East Institute*, 27 October 2015.

15. The book's framing of intra-sect conflict is broad. We deal primarily with the Imami

branch of Shiism, but also the Isma'ilis, the Zaydis, and the Alewis. The book also addresses intra-Sunni sectarianism, between Salafism and Sunni political Islam like the Muslim Brotherhood, more apolitical currents like Sufis, and even intra-Salafi competition. The chapters on Lebanon focus on that country's diverse sects.

16. With the exception of Chapter 1, the comparative and theoretical overview, and Chapter 9 on Bahrain and Saudi Arabia, all the chapters appeared previously as research papers published by the Carnegie Endowment for Peace; they appear here in a slightly modified form.

1. BEYOND SECTARIANISM IN THE MIDDLE EAST? COMPARATIVE PERSPECTIVES ON GROUP CONFLICT

1. Arun Khudnani, *The Muslims are Coming: Islamophobia, Extremism, and the Domestic War on Terror* (London: Verso, 2014).
2. Thomas L. Friedman, "Same War, Different Country," *New York Times*, 7 September 2013.
3. Rogers Brubaker, *Ethnicity without Groups* (Cambridge, MA: Harvard University Press, 2004).
4. See for example Richard Jackson, 'Constructing Enemies: "Islamic Terrorism" in Political and Academic Discourse', *Government and Opposition*, vol. 42, no. 3 (2007).
5. Richard Jenkins, *Rethinking Ethnicity* (London: Sage, 1997), 44.
6. Stephen Van Evera, 'Primordialism Lives!', *Comparative Politics*, vol. 12, no. 1 (Winter 2001), p. 20.
7. Mahmood Mamdani, *Good Muslim, Bad Muslim: America, the Cold War, and the Roots of Terror* (New York: Pantheon Books, 2004), pp. 17–18.
8. Fanar Haddad, *Sectarianism in Iraq: Antagonistic Visions of Unity* (New York: Columbia University Press, 2011).
9. Brendan O'Leary, *How to get out of Iraq with Integrity* (Philadelphia, PA: Pennsylvania University Press, 2009), pp. 19, 81.
10. Frank Wright, *Northern Ireland: A Comparative Analysis* (Dublin: Gill and Macmillan, 1992).
11. Jonathan Steele, *Defeat; Why they lost Iraq* (London: I. B. Tauris, 2009), p. 226.
12. Peter W. Galbraith, *The End of Iraq* (London: Simon & Schuster, 2006), pp. 97–101.
13. Gareth Stansfield, "Iraq: Divide or Die," *openDemocracy*, 22 November 2006.
14. Amin Maalouf, *On Identity* (London, Harvill Press, 2000), p. 21.
15. Arend Lijphart, "Cultural Diversity and Theories of Political Integration," *Canadian Journal of Political Science*, vol. 4, no. 1 (March 1971), p. 11.
16. Paul Dixon, "Is Consociational Theory the Answer to Global Conflict? From the Netherlands to Northern Ireland and Iraq," *Political Studies Review*, vol. 9, no. 3 (2011).

17. Arend Lijphart, *Democracy in Plural Societies* (New Haven, CT: Yale University Press, 1977), pp. 147–50.
18. Marie-Joelle Zahar, "Power Sharing in Lebanon: Foreign Protectors, Domestic Peace, and Democratic Failure," in P. G. Roeder and Donal Rothchild, eds, *Sustainable Peace: Power and Democracy After Civil Wars* (Utica, NY: Cornell University Press, 2005), p. 238.
19. Simon Haddad, "Lebanon: From Consociationalism to Conciliation," *Nationalism and Ethnic Politics*, vol. 15 (2009), p. 414.
20. Joshua Landis, "The Great Sorting Out: Ethnicity and the Future of the Levant," 18 December 2013, https://qifanabki.com/2013/12/18/landis-ethnicity/, downloaded 29 November 2016.
21. Christopher Phillips, "Sectarianism and Conflict in Syria," *Third World Quarterly*, vol. 36, no. 2 (2015), p. 370.
22. Michael Bell, "How Lebanon offers a model for a post-IS Middle East," *Globe and Mail*, 14 October 2014.
23. Fanar Haddad, *Sectarianism in Iraq*.
24. Eric Hobsbawm and Terence Ranger, *The Invention of Tradition* (Cambridge: Canto, 1983).
25. Steele, *Defeat*, p. 198.
26. Steele, *Defeat*, p. 199.
27. Eric Herring and Glen Rangwala, *Iraq in Fragments: The Occupation and its Legacy* (London: Hurst & Co., 2006), pp. 147–60.
28. Christopher Phillips, *The Battle for Syria: International Rivalry in the New Middle East* (London: Yale University Press, 2016), p. 54.
29. Steele, *Defeat*, p. 228.
30. Elizabeth Shakman Hurd, "Stop Trying to Make Syria's War into a Sectarian Conflict," *The Atlantic*, 15 March 2013.
31. Phillips, 'Sectarianism and Conflict in Syria', p. 358.
32. Phillips, "Sectarianism and Conflict in Syria," p. 366.
33. Heiko Wimmen, "Syria's Path from Civic Uprising to Civil War" (Washington, DC: Carnegie Endowment for International Peace, 2016), p. 5.
34. Cynthia Brown, *Playing the Communal Card* (New York: Human Rights Watch, 1996).
35. Donald L. Horowitz, *Ethnic Groups in Conflict* (Berkeley, CA: University of California Press, 2001).
36. Haddad, *Sectarianism in Iraq*, pp. 2, 3, 35–9.
37. Steele, *Defeat*, pp. 172–3.
38. Paul Dixon, "The 'real' and 'dirty' politics of the Northern Ireland peace process: A constructivist realist critique of idealism and conservative realism," in Timothy White, ed., *Theories of International Relations and Northern Ireland* (Manchester: Manchester University Press, 2017); Paul Dixon, "The Politics of Conflict: A

Constructivist Critique of Consociational and Civil Society Theories," *Nations and Nationalism*, vol. 17, no. 4 (2011).

39. See Richard M. Price, *Moral Limit and Possibility in World Politics* (Cambridge: Cambridge University Press, 2008) for an excellent discussion of these issues.

40. Duncan Bell, "Political realism and the limits of ethics," in Duncan Bell, ed., *Ethics and World Politics* (Oxford: Oxford University Press, 2010), pp. 104–5.

41. C. A. J. Coady, *Messy Morality: The Challenge of Politics* (Oxford: Oxford University Press).

42. Rogers Brubaker, *Ethnicity without Groups*.

43. C. Hay, *Political Analysis* (Basingstoke: Palgrave, 2002), p. 35. On Syria, see Phillips, *The Battle for Syria*, pp. 77–8, 80.

44. M. Billig, *Banal Nationalism* (London: Sage, 1995).

45. Haddad, *Sectarianism in Iraq*.

46. Dixon, "The 'real' and 'dirty' politics of the Northern Ireland peace process."

47. Jonathan Steele, "Most Syrians back President Assad, but you'd never know from Western media," *Guardian*, 17 January 2012. See also Musa al-Gharbi, "Syria Contextualized: The Numbers Game," *Middle East Policy*, vol. 20, no. 1 (2013).

48. Phillips, *The Battle for Syria*, pp. 78–9.

49. Paul Dixon, "Political skills or lying and manipulation? The choreography of the Northern Ireland peace process," *Political Studies*, vol. 50, no. 3 (2002), pp. 725–41.

50. Anonymous, "Human Rights in Peace Negotiations," *Human Rights Quarterly*, vol. 18, no. 249 (1996).

51. Roy Licklider, "Ethical Advice: Conflict Management vs. Human Rights in Ending Civil Wars," *Journal of Human Rights*, vol. 7, no. 4 (2008).

52. Rogers Brubaker, "Myths and misconceptions in the study of nationalism," in J. A. Hall, ed., *The State of the Nation* (Cambridge: Cambridge University Press, 1998), p. 273.

53. Peter Harris and Ben Reilly, *Democracy and Deep-rooted Conflict: Options for Negotiators* (Stockholm: International Institute for Democracy and Electoral Assistance, 1998), pp. 2–3.

54. Uri Savir, *The Process: 1,100 Days that Changed the Middle East* (New York: Random House), p. 93.

55. Steve Smith, "Positivism and beyond," in Steve Smith et al., eds, *International Theory: Positivism and Beyond* (Cambridge: Cambridge University Press, 1996), p. 13.

2. THE SECTARIANISM OF THE ISLAMIC STATE: IDEOLOGICAL ROOTS AND POLITICAL CONTEXT

1. Roula Khalaf, "Rise of ISIS Shakes Arab World from Long State of Denial," *Financial Times*, 16 July 2014, http://www.ft.com/intl/cms/s/0/9d802a64-0cde-11e4-bf1e-00144feabdc0.html

2. See Isabel Coles, "Islamic State Seeks to Justify Enslaving Yazidi Women and Girls in Iraq," Reuters, 13 October 2014, http://www.reuters.com/article/2014/10/13/us-mideast-crisis-iraq-yazidis-idUSKCN0I21H620141013; Tim Arango, "Escaping Death in Northern Iraq," *New York Times*, 3 September 2014, http://www.nytimes.com/2014/09/04/world/middleeast/surviving-isis-massacre-iraq-video.html?_r=0; and "Islamic State 'Executes 70 Sunni Tribesmen in Iraq,'" BBC, 5 October 2015, http://www.bbc.co.uk/news/world-middle-east-34446066; Liz Sly, "Syrian Tribal Revolt Against Islamic State Ignored, Fueling Resentment," *Washington Post*, 20 October 2014, http://www.washingtonpost.com/world/syria-tribal-revolt-against-islamic-state-ignored-fueling-resentment/2014/10/20/25401beb-8de8-49f2-8e64-c1cfbee45232_story.html

3. Ibrahim al-Shaalan, Twitter post, 5 July 2014, 7:07 p.m., https://twitter.com/ialshaalan/status/485605935688065024; and Hassan Hassan, "Now a Caliphate Has Been Declared, the Debate Begins," *National*, 9 July 2014, http://www.the-national.ae/opinion/comment/now-a-caliphate-has-been-declared-the-debate-begins

4. Eric Schmitt, "In Battle to Defang ISIS, U.S. Targets its Psychology," *New York Times*, 28 December 2014, http://www.nytimes.com/2014/12/29/us/politics/in-battle-to-defang-isis-us-targets-its-psychology-.html

5. Alastair Crooke, "You Can't Understand ISIS If You Don't Know the History of Wahhabism in Saudi Arabia," *Huffington Post*, 27 August 2014, last updated 27 October 2014, http://www.huffingtonpost.com/alastair-crooke/isis-wah-habism-saudi-arabia_b_5717157.html

6. For the first point of view, see Nasim Ahmed, "To Defeat ISIS We Need to Stop Shooting in the Dark and Understand Political Islam," *Middle East Monitor*, 8 October 2014, https://www.middleeastmonitor.com/articles/middle-east/14552-to-defeat-isis-we-need-to-stop-shooting-in-the-dark-and-understand-polit-ical-islam; for the second point of view, see William Dalrymple, "The ISIS Demand for a Caliphate is About Power, Not Religion," *Guardian*, 13 July 2014, http://www.theguardian.com/commentisfree/2014/jul/13/isis-caliphate-abu-bakr-al-baghdadi-jihadi-islam

7. This chapter refers to political Islam in its broad sense, because Islamist ideas since the 1960s, specifically, influenced new movements that did not necessarily identify with the Muslim Brotherhood. In some cases, as is argued, such movements were influenced by the Muslim Brotherhood and Salafism, but became critical of the two.

8. Jonathan Brown, "Salafis and Sufis in Egypt," Carnegie Endowment for International Peace, 20 December 2011, http://carnegieendowment.org/files/salafis_sufis.pdf

9. Ali Jumuah, "Wasila, Circumambulating Graves and Accusing Others of Shirk and Kufr," trans. Mahdi Lock, Marifah, last updated 20 December 2012, http://www.marifah.net/articles/Al-Watan_Ali%20Jumuah.pdf

10. Devin R. Springer, James L. Regens, and David N. Edger, *Islamic Radicalism and Global Jihad* (Washington, DC: Georgetown University Press, 2009), p. 50.
11. Mohammed bin Saeed al-Qahtani, *Min mafaheem aqidat al-salaf al-salih, al-wala wal baraa fil Islam* [The Islamic concept of allegiance and disavowal as preached by the early noble generations of Muslims] (Mecca, Saudi Arabia: Tayba Publishers, 2014), http://islamhouse.com/ar/books/468544/
12. Suhaib Webb, "Ibn Taymiyyah and the Division of Tawhid into Three Parts: A Call for Insaf and Taqwa," Virtual Mosque, 8 December 2007, http://www.virtualmosque.com/islam-studies/ibn-taymiyyah-and-the-division-of-tawhid-into-three-parts-a-call-for-insaf-and-taqwa
13. Stéphane Lacroix, *Awakening Islam: The Politics of Religious Dissent in Contemporary Saudi Arabia* (Cambridge, MA: Harvard University Press, 2011).
14. Hossam Tammam, "Tassaluf al-ikhwan: taakul al-utruha al-ikhwaniyyah wa su'ud al-salafiyyah fi jama'at al-ikhwan al-muslimeen" [The Salafization of the Muslim Brothers: The Erosion of the Fundamental Hypothesis and the Rising of Salafism Within the Muslim Brotherhood]; *The Paths and the Repercussions of Change* (Alexandria, Egypt: Bibliotheca Alexandrina, 2011).
15. Sujata Ashwarya Cheema, "Sayyid Qutb's Concept of Jahiliyya as Metaphor for Modern Society," in Nadeem Hasnain, ed., *Beyond Textual Islam* (New Delhi: Serials Publications, 2008). The chapter is available online as a draft paper at http://www.academia.edu/3222569/Sayyid_Qutbs_Concept_of_Jahiliyya_as_Metaphor_for_Modern_Society
16. John Calvert, *Sayyid Qutb and the Origins of Radical Islam* (New York: Columbia University Press, 2010).
17. Tammam, "The Salafization of the Muslim Brothers."
18. Ibid.
19. This attitude can be discerned during conversations with Islamic State members. They believe that the local population is ignorant of and resistant to true Islam.
20. Interview by the author, cited in Michael Weiss and Hassan Hassan, *ISIS: Inside the Army of Terror* (New York: Regan Arts, 2015), p. 222.
21. "Al-Salafiyya takhtariq jamaat al-Ikhwan al-Muslimin fi akbar hazza tandhimiya" [Salafism infiltrates the Muslim Brotherhood in the largest organizational shake-up], *Al Arabiya*, 28 November 2010, http://www.alarabiya.net/articles/2010/11/27/127653.html
22. Hassan Hassan, "New Syrian Islamic Council Repeats the Patterns of Old," *National*, 22 April 2014, http://www.thenational.ae/thenationalconversation/comment/new-syrian-islamic-council-repeats-the-patterns-of-old
23. "Sheikh al-Sururiyyah Mohammed Surur Zein al-Abidine li *al-Quds al-Arabi*" [Sheikh of the Sururiyyah Mohammed Surur Zein al-Abidine speaks to *al-Quds al-Arabi*], *al-Quds al-Arabi*, 20 January 2013, http://alqudsalarabi.info/index.asp?fname=data%5C2013%5C01%5C01-20%5C20z495.htm
24. Ben Kesling and Suha Ma'ayeh, "Jordan Releases Zarqawi's Spiritual Mentor from

Prison," *Wall Street Journal*, 16 June 2014, http://www.wsj.com/articles/jordan-releases-zarqawis-spiritual-mentor-from-prison-1402960962

25. CNN Arabic's interview with Abu Muhammad al-Maqdisi, "Al-Maqdisi li CNN bil arabi: Ibn Baz sabab tarki li jamiyat al-Mosul ... araftu al-Zawahiri wa al-Zarqawi bi Afghanistan wa lam ubayie al-Qaeda" [Al-Maqdisi to CNN Arabic: Ibn Baz was the reason why I left the University of Mosul ... I knew al-Zawahiri and al-Zarqawi in Afghanistan and did not pledge allegiance to al-Qaeda], 24 May 2015, http://arabic.cnn.com/middleeast/2015/05/24/me-240515-maqdisi-intv-p1. In the interview, al-Maqdisi stated that in his youth he was influenced by "activist Salafism, a blend of the Muslim Brotherhood and Salafism." He said that Salafi jihadism emerged later during the jihad in Afghanistan, where "different currents merged under so-called Salafi jihadism."

26. Michael Scheuer, *Osama bin Laden* (New York: Oxford University Press, 2011), p. 178.

27. Lacroix, *Awakening Islam*, p. 54.

28. Abu Muhammad al-Maqdisi, "Democracy: A Religion!" trans. Abu Muhammad al-Maleki, ed. Abu Sayf Muwahhid, Jihadology, uploaded 30 August 2010, https://azelin.files.wordpress.com/2010/08/democracy-a-relegoin.pdf; and Michael Weiss and Hassan Hassan, "Everything We Knew About This ISIS Mastermind Was Wrong," *Daily Beast*, 15 April 2015, http://www.thedailybeast.com/articles/2016/04/15/everything-we-knew-about-this-isis-mastermind-was-wrong.html

29. Zoltan Pall, "Kuwaiti Salafism and its Growing Influence in the Levant," Carnegie Endowment for International Peace, May 2014, http://carnegieendowment.org/files/kuwaiti_salafists.pdf

30. Ibid.

31. "Al-Qutbiyyah al-ikhwaniyyah wa al-Sururiyyah qaedat manahij al-Salafiyyah al-takfiriyyah" [Qutbism and Sururism: the foundations of Salafi takfiri ideology], al-Arab Online, 19 August 2014, http://www.alarab.co.uk/?id=30798

32. Lacroix, *Awakening Islam*, p. 52.

33. Ideas such as *wala wal bara* have roots in early Islamic thought and are held by the majority of Muslim clerics today, albeit in much mellower forms. Anti-Islamic State clerics from Syria, such as Ratib al-Nabulsi, Osama al-Rifai, and Moaz al-Khatib, advised Syrians against permanent residency in the West based on the *wala wal bara* principle. See Abdulsattar al-Sayid, "Hiwar hadi bain talameeth al-madrasah al-wahida houl fatwa al-sheikhayn al-fadhilayn al-Nabulsi wa al-Rifai fi mawdhoui hijrat wa iqamat al-Muslimeen fi diyar ghayr al-Muslimin" [A quiet dialogue among the disciples of the same school about the fatwa issued by the two sheikhs al-Nabulsi and al-Rifai about the migration of Muslims to non-Muslim lands], Islam Syria, 26 December 2014, http://www.islamsyria.com/portal/consult/show/792, for example, in which the participants said that no Muslim should

live permanently in the West and that Muslims who wish to study in the West can stay there temporarily as long as they have a wife and children who are too young to be influenced by the decadent Western lifestyle.

34. Ayman al-Zawahiri, "English Translation of Ayman al-Zawahiri's Letter to Abu Musab al-Zarqawi," *Weekly Standard*, 11 October 2005, http://www.weeklystandard.com/english-translation-of-ayman-al-zawahiris-letter-to-abu-musab-al-zarqawi/article/7397

35. Peter Bergen, "Strange Bedfellows—Iran and al Qaeda," CNN, 10 March 2013, http://www.cnn.com/2013/03/10/opinion/bergen-iran-al-qaeda/

36. Abu Musab al-Zarqawi, "Zarqawi Letter," US Department of State Archive, 12 February 2004, http://2001–2009.state.gov/p/nea/rls/31694.htm; see also Emily Hunt, "Zarqawi's 'Total War' on Iraqi Shiites Exposes a Divide Among Sunni Jihadists," Policy Watch no. 1049, Washington Institute for Near East Policy, 15 November 2005, http://www.washingtoninstitute.org/policy-analysis/view/zarqawis-total-war-on-iraqi-shiites-exposes-a-divide-among-sunni-jihadists

37. Bill Roggio, "'Iran Owes al Qaeda Invaluably,' ISIS Spokesman Says," *Threat Matrix* (blog), *Long War Journal*, 12 May 2014, http://www.longwarjournal.org/archives/2014/05/iran_owes_al_qaeda_invaluably.php

38. Ayman al-Zawahiri's letter to Zarqawi.

39. Shiv Malik, Ali Younes, Spencer Ackerman, and Mustafa Khalili, "The Race to Save Peter Kassig," *Guardian*, 18 December 2014,

40. "Al-Manarah al-Baydah lil intaj al-ialami, manhajuna wa aqidatuna, muqabala maa al-daktour Sami al-Aridi" [Al-Manara al-Baydah for media production's interview with Dr Sami al-Aridi, our methodology and doctrine], Internet Archive video, 29:45, posted by Abu Qudamah al-Muhajir, 21 October 2013, https://archive.org/details/Moqabla

41. The four main Sunni schools of jurisprudence are Hanafi, Hanbali, Maliki, and Shafii.

42. "Al-Manarah al-Baydah lil intaj al-ialami," Internet Archive.

43. Former Islamic State leader Abu Omar al-Baghdadi said: "Since the legislations that govern all Muslim lands today are falsehood rules and legislations, we consider all rulers and armies of these countries and that fighting them is more of a priority than fighting the crusader occupier." See "Aqidat al-dawla al-islamiyyah li amiraha Abu Omar al-Baghdadi" [The doctrine of the Islamic State, by its leader Abu Omar al-Baghdadi], goostmmb.wordpress.com, 23 January 2014, https://goostmmb.wordpress.com/2014/01/23/%D8%B9%D9%82%D9%8A%D8%AF%D8%A9-%D8%A7%D9%84%D8%AF%D9%88%D9%84%D8%A9-%D8%A7%D9%84%D8%A5%D8%B3%D9%84%D8%A7%D9%85%D9%8A%D8%A9-%D9%84%D8%A3%D9%85%D9%8A%D8%B1%D9%87%D8%A7-%D8%A3%D8%A8%D9%88%D8%B9

44. Interviews with Islamic State members in Turkey via the internet and telephone, over several months in 2014.

45. Abu Muhammad al-Maqdisi speaks about the Mecca incident and the Juhayman al-Utaybi movement: "Al-haqeeqa al-mughayabah Juhayman al-Utaybi wa hadithat al-haram" [The suppressed truth, Juhayman al-Utaybi and the Mecca incident], YouTube video, 15:01, posted by Ali al-Yafai, 3 September 2012, https://www.youtube.com/watch?v=0_zwh8_NDO0

46. Interviews with Islamic State members via the internet, January 2015.

47. Interviews with Islamic State members who are critical of the organization's campaign against what one member referred to as *muwahidin*, or true monotheists, via the internet, May 2015.

48. Abu Abdullah Imad Abdullah al-Tunisi, "Taeqeebat ala al-taeleeqat wa naqdh al-fatwa al-tunisiya lil sheikh al–hazeemi ... taqdeem al sheikh abi muhammad al maqdisi" [Responses to the comments and refutation of the Tunisian fatwa by Sheikh al-Hazimi ... introduction by Sheikh Abu Muhammad al-Maqdisi], Tawhid and Jihad Forum, 10 December 2014, http://www.ilmway.com/site/maqdis/MS_4872.html. In the introduction, al-Maqdisi wrote: "Many brothers have corresponded with me asking me to respond to al-Hazimi regarding his confusion and excessiveness, whose evil has spread among the youth until it infiltrated the jihadi arena in Syria, and his [fatwa] had a huge effect on bloodshed and violation of honor."

49. Interview with Hassan al-Dagheem via Facebook and telephone, December 2014.

50. Ari Soffer, "ISIS Executes 'Extremist' Members Plotting Rebellion," *Arutz Sheva*, 23 December 2014, http://www.israelnationalnews.com/News/News.aspx/189017#.Vm9edYuorHg

51. The list, which is not exhaustive, is based on discussions with two Islamic State-affiliated clerics and another Islamic State member, who provided the names and in one case pictures of a book disseminated by the Islamic State. The book in question, *Clarification About the Unbelief of He Who Assists the Americans*, is authored by Nasir al-Fahd.

52. Thomas Hegghammer, *Jihad in Saudi Arabia: Violence and Pan-Islamism Since 1979* (Cambridge: Cambridge University Press, 2010).

53. Interview with Thomas Hegghammer via e-mail, 23 December 2014.

54. Murad Batal al-Shishani, "Saudi Arabia's Jihadi Jailbird: A Portrait of al-Shu'aybi Ideologue Nasir al-Fahd," *Intelligence Quarterly*, 27 December 2010, http://www.intelligencequarterly.com/2010/12/saudi-arabia's-jihadi-jailbird-a-portrait-of-al-shuaybi-ideologue-nasir-al-fahd/

55. Robert Spencer, "Muslim Cleric who Issued Fatwa Permitting WMD Pledges Allegiance to Islamic State," *Jihad Watch* (blog), 25 August 2015, http://www.jihadwatch.org/2015/08/muslim-cleric-who-issued-fatwa-permitting-wmd-pledges-allegiance-to-islamic-state

56. Nasir al-Fahd, "Risalat mashrouiyat al-ighladh ala al-rafidha" [Permissibility of

excessiveness against al-rafidha], Quraa al-Arab, posted in 2001, accessed on 18 May 2016, http://arareaders.com/books/details/7096

57. Abulzahraa al-Athari, "Risalat nusuh wa irshad Abu Muhammad al-Maqdisi" [A message of advice and guidance from Abu Muhammad al-Maqdisi], Islamion.com, 10 May 2015, http://www.islamion.com/news/show/20391

58. Interviews with an Islamic State associate from Deir Ezzor via the internet, October 2015.

59. Interview with Ahmed Abazaid via the internet, December 2015.

60. Abu Muhammad al-Maqdisi, Twitter post, 19 March 2016, 1:34 a.m.: "Everyone who fights Muslims, whoever they are, with the help of the coalition, he becomes an apostate if he is a Muslim, and an enemy combatant if he is non-Muslim," https://twitter.com/lmaqdese/status/711108543739502592

61. "Hukum dukhoul al-intikhabat binyyat tahqeeq al-maslaha al-shariyya" [The rule about running for election to achieve sharia's interests], Islamweb, 10 April 2001, http://fatwa.islamweb.net/fatwa/index.php?page=showfatwa&Option=Fatwa Id&Id=5141

62. According to audio lectures by Abu Ali al-Anbari recorded in Iraq after the Islamic State's 2014 takeover of Mosul and obtained by the author.

63. Ibrahim al-Fares, Twitter post, 14 June 2015, 11:42 a.m., https://twitter.com/ibrahim_alfares/status/610155392820064256

64. Turki al-Binali, "Al-tarjama al-ilmiyyah lil sheikh al-mujahid Turki al-Binali" [The curricula vitae of the Mujahid Sheikh Turki al-Binali], Internet Archive document, posted by "sun1278," 4 March 2014, https://archive.org/details/s_shykh_bin3li

65. Abdul-Aziz al-Tarifi, Twitter post, 24 April 2016, 12:42 a.m., https://twitter.com/Altarefe_En/status/724141439744118784

66. Abdulsattar Hatita, "Al-Binali yadhghat li tawsee nufudh Daesh fi Libya rughm tazayud al-araqeel ala al-ardh" [Al-Binali seeks to expand the influence of the Islamic State in Libya despite growing setbacks on the ground], *Asharq al-Awsat*, 11 May 2015, http://aawsat.com/node/357561

67. Aymenn Jawad al-Tamimi, "Islamic State Training Camp Textbook: Course in Fiqh [Islamic Jurisprudence]" (brackets in the original), *Aymenn Jawad al-Tamimi's Blog*, 6 July 2015, http://www.aymennjawad.org/2015/07/islamic-state-training-camp-textbook-course-in

68. Sharia training organized by the Islamic State varies in length: two weeks, one month, forty-five days, six months, or up to one year.

69. List obtained by author in January 2015.

70. Lacroix, *Awakening Islam*, p. 56.

71. "Top Sunni Muslim Cleric al-Qaradawi Does About-Face, Opposes Suicide Bombings," *Jerusalem Post*, 29 July 2015, http://www.jpost.com/Middle-East/Top-Sunni-Muslim-cleric-al-Qaradawi-does-about-face-opposes-suicide-bombings-410483

72. This is the English title used by William McCants of the Brookings Institution,

who translated the book. See Abu Bakr Naji, *The Management of Savagery: The Most Critical Stage Through Which the Umma Will Pass*, trans. William McCants (Boston: John M. Olin Institute for Strategic Studies, 2006). *Tawahush* literally means savagery, and also connotes a power vacuum and chaos; it can also be translated as lawlessness. The term was coined by Abu Qatada al-Filistini, a Palestinian ideologue, who has denied he wrote the book. The author was first to reveal that the Islamic State uses the book as part of its curriculum.

73. The translation used is original and directly taken from the Arabic, *Idarat al-Tawahush*, by Abu Bakr Naji. The Islamic State used the word *tashreed*, or deterrence, as a title for the massacre carried out by its al-Battar squad, a special forces unit, against the Shaitat tribe in eastern Syria in August 2014. It was described at the time as the bloodiest single atrocity committed by the Islamic State in Syria, and featured graphic pictures of Islamic State members beheading tribesmen. See Liz Sly, "Syria Tribal Revolt Against Islamic State Ignored, Fueling Resentment," *Washington Post*, 20 October 2014, http://www.washingtonpost.com/world/syria-tribal-revolt-against-islamic-state-ignored-fueling-resentment/2014/10/20/25401beb-8de8-49f2-8e64-c1cfbee45232_story.html

74. Moataz al-Khatib, "Tandheem al-dawla al-islamiyyah: al-bunya al-fikriyyah wa taqeedat al-waqe" [The Islamic State: the intellectual structure and the complications of reality], Al Jazeera Center for Studies, 23 November 2014, http://studies.aljazeera.net/files/isil/2014/11/2014112355523312655.htm

75. Ibid.

76. *The Management of Savagery* provides advice to jihadists, including how to teach people religion; gradually plant eyes and ears everywhere; construct an intelligence apparatus; deter "hypocrites" and force them to suppress their hypocritical, demoralizing views and tolerate the influential among them to halt their harm; ally with those permissible to work with other than those who are already aligned with the movement; and keep attacking the enemy to make it seek peace. See the McCants translation, https://archive.org/details/TheManagementOfBarbarismAbuBakrNaji

77. See *Encyclopaedia Britannica*, "Battle of the Ditch," last updated 21 February 2016, http://www.britannica.com/event/Battle-of-the-Ditch

78. The battle took place in the seventh century between Muslims and the Persian army in Anbar, in modern-day Iraq.

79. James Kirchick, "ISIS Goes Medieval on Gays," *Daily Beast*, 19 January 2015, http://www.thedailybeast.com/articles/2015/01/19/isis-goes-medieval-on-gays.html

80. Interview by the author, published in Weiss and Hassan, *ISIS: Inside the Army of Terror*.

81. Abdelelah Haider Shaye, "Haqaeq fi taghreedat an dawlat al-khilafa al-Islamiyyah wa Ikhtilaf al-Qaeda" [In Tweets, Facts About the Islamic State and Its Differences

With al–Qaeda], Abdelelah Haider Shaye's blog, 4 August 2014, https://abdulela.
wordpress.com/2014/08/04/%D8%AD%D9%82%D8%A7%D8%A6%D9%82-
%D9%81%D9%8A-%D8%AA%D8%BA%D8%B1%D9%8A%D8%AF%D8%
A7%D8%AA-%D8%B9%D9%86-%D8%AF%D9%88%D9%84%D8%A9-%
D8%A7%D9%84%D8%AE%D9%84%D8%A7%D9%81%D8%A9-%D8%A7
%D9%84%D8%A5%D8%B3%D9%84-2/

3. THE SECTARIANIZATION OF THE SYRIAN WAR

1. See, for instance, Fouad Ajami, *The Syrian Rebellion* (Stanford, CA: Hoover
Institution Press, 2012).
2. Karla Adam, "Obama Ridiculed for Saying Conflicts in the Middle East 'Date Back
Millennia' (Some Don't Date Back a Decade)," *Washington Post*, 13 January 2016.
3. Dara Conduit, "The Patterns of Syrian Uprising: Comparing Hama in 1980–1982
and Homs in 2011," *British Journal of Middle Eastern Studies*, 13 May 2016, doi:
10.1080/13530194.2016.1182421; Christopher Phillips, "Sectarianism and
Conflict in Syria," *Third World Quarterly*, vol. 36, no. 2 (2015), pp. 357–76.
4. Steven Heydeman, "Syria's Uprising: Sectarianism, Regionalisation, and State Order
in the Levant," FRIDE and HIVOS, May 2013, p. 17.
5. Government spokeswoman Buthaina Shaaban on 26 March 2011; see "Assad
Adviser Warns of Sectarian Strife in Syria," Reuters, 26 March 2011; Bashar al-Assad
in his televised speech in parliament on 30 March 2011, available at: http://www.
presidentassad.net/index.php?option=com_content&view=category&id=303&
Itemid=469. The address included seventeen evocations of the Arabic term *fitna*,
which carries a strongly religious connotation and is often used to refer to sectarian (Sunni-Shia) conflict, thus prompting the audience to imagine a scenario of sectarian strife.
6. Kheder Khaddour, "The Alawite Dilemma (Homs 2013)," in Friederike Stolleis,
ed., *Playing the Sectarian Card: Identities and Affiliations of Local Communities in
Syria* (Beirut: Friedrich Ebert Stiftung, 2015), pp. 11–26. An earlier version of this
article was published in 2013 under the adopted name Aziz Nakkash. See also Aron
Lund, "Chasing Ghosts: The Shabiha Phenomenon," in Michael Kerr and Craig
Larkin, eds, *The Alawis of Syria: War, Faith and Politics in the Levant* (Oxford:
Oxford University Press), pp. 79–106.
7. Phil Sands, Justin Vela, and Suha Maayeh, "Assad Regime Set Free Extremists From
Prison to Fire Up Trouble During Peaceful Uprising," *National*, 21 January 2014.
8. See, for instance, the accounts about events in Latakia and Homs provided in Azmi
Bishara, *Syria: The Painful Path to Freedom* (Doha: Arab Center for Research and
Policy Studies, 2013). While clearly supportive of the uprising and based mainly
on interviews with Syrian activists, this account of the early phase of the uprising
has a balanced narrative that also exposes the shortcomings of the movement and
abuses committed by its supporters. For a similar narrative with more detail and

historical background, see Mohammed Jamal Barout, *The Last Decade of Syrian History: The Dialectics of Stagnation and Reform* (Doha: Arab Center for Research and Policy Studies, 2011).

9. Phillips, "Sectarianism and Conflict in Syria," 365.

10. According to Thomas Pierret, foreign actors relied on sectarian mobilization only reluctantly and mostly for lack of alternatives; see Thomas Pierret, "The Reluctant Sectarianism of Foreign States in the Syrian Conflict," PEACEBRIEF 162, US Institute of Peace, 18 November 2013.

11. See, for example, Elizabeth Shakman Hurd, "Stop Trying to Make Syria's War Into a Sectarian Conflict," *Atlantic*, 15 March 2013; or the spokesperson of the Syrian National Council, Basma Kodmani, in a televised debate on France 24, available at "Guerre en Syria: un mini-Etat Alaouite serait-il viable? (Partie 2)" [War in Syria: Would an Alawite mini-state be viable? (Part 2)], France 24, 24 July 2012, http://www.france24.com/fr/07-24-fr-syrie-armee-syrienne-libre-bachar-el-assad-etat-alaouite-debat-partie-2

12. Oliver Holmes, "Assad's Devious, Cruel Plan to Stay in Power by Dividing Syria—and Why It's Working," *New Republic*, 15 August 2011.

13. Rafif Jouejati, "What Do Syrians Want?", *New Internationalist*, 1 September 2015.

14. Nikolaos Van Dam, *The Struggle for Power in Syria: Politics and Society Under Asad and the Ba'th Party*, 4th edn (New York: I. B. Tauris, 2011).

15. Fabrice Balanche, "'Go to Damascus, My Son': Alawi Demographic Shifts under Ba'ath Party Rule," in Kerr and Larkin, eds, *The Alawis of Syria*, p. 92. The narrative of the rural outsiders who capture the city and subjugate or sideline the urban elites through tight community solidarity (*asabiyya*) has invited interpretations that draw on the work of the fourteenth-century historian Ibn Khaldun, who conceptualized dynastic turnovers in North Africa (contemporary Morocco) in similar terms. Also see, for instance, Leon Goldsmith, "Syria's Alawites and the Politics of Sectarian Insecurity: A Khaldunian Perspective," *Ortadoğu Etütleri*, vol. 3, no. 1 (July 2011), pp. 33–60; Emile Hokayem, "'Assad or We Burn the Country': Misreading Sectarianism and the Regime in Syria," *War on the Rocks*, 24 August 2016, http://warontherocks.com/2016/08/assad-or-we-burn-the-country-misreading-sectarianism-and-the-regime-in-syria/. In the author's opinion, the emphasis on the importance of structural factors for the (trans)formation of such communities that characterizes these neo-Khaldounian approaches offers a helpful corrective to interpretations that assume that religious or sectarian groups are immutable historical subjects with autonomous and cohesive agency. However, such interpretations still tend to overestimate communal solidarity as being a natural and resilient behavioral pattern and a key consideration of those who conquered the heights of power. Yet as Phillips notes, "[W]hile leading Ba'ath Alawis such as Saleh Jadid and Hafez al-Assad utilised sect-based networks to gain power,

they were opportunists, not sectarian chauvinists." (Phillips, "Sectarianism and Conflict in Syria," p. 364).

16. Khaddour, "The Alawite Dilemma," p. 19.

17. Hicham Bou Nassif, "'Second-Class': The Grievances of Sunni Officers in the Syrian Armed Forces," *Journal of Strategic Studies*, vol. 38, no. 5 (August 2015), pp. 626–49.

18. See, for instance, Donald L. Horowitz, *Ethnic Groups in Conflict* (Berkeley, CA: University of California Press, 1985), pp. 141–228.

19. Fabrice Balanche, "Géographie de la révolte syrienne" [Geography of the Syrian revolt], *Outre-Terre*, vol. 29, no. 3 (2011), p. 445; Balanche, "Damascus," p. 86.

20. Ibid.; see also Khaddour, "The Alawite Dilemma," p. 11. While the massive influx turned the Alawite quarters of the coastal cities into integral parts of enlarged urban areas, migration to Damascus was accommodated to a significant extent at the periphery of the city. For a portrayal of one of these new neighborhoods erected for security personnel, see Kheder Khaddour, "Assad's Officer Ghetto: Why the Syrian Army Remains Loyal," Carnegie Middle East Center, 4 November 2015.

21. Ratib Shaabo, "Communal Relations on the Syrian Coast," in Rustum Mahmoud, ed., *Myths and Realities of Community Relations in Syria: Peaceful Past and Unknown Future* (Le Hague: HIVOS, 2013), p. 14.

22. Khalid Abu-Ismail, Ali Abdel-Gadir, and Heba El-Laithy, "Poverty and Inequality in Syria (1997–2007)," Arab Development Challenges Report Background Paper 2011/15, United Nations Development Program, 2011. The report found that around one-third of the Syrian population was living below the poverty line and around 10 percent were living in extreme poverty in 2007, which is before the social effects of the massive three-year drought that hit Syria in 2006 became apparent. See Colin P. Kelley et al., "Climate Change in the Fertile Crescent and Implications of the Recent Syrian Drought," *Proceedings of the National Academy of Sciences of the United States of America*, vol. 112, no. 11 (17 March 2015), pp. 3241–6.

23. Bishara quotes a listing of Syria's one hundred most important businessmen published in 2010 by the Syrian business magazine *Al-Iqtisad wan-Naql* [Economy and transport], which included a relatively small number of Alawites (16 percent), who nevertheless controlled the overwhelming majority of large businesses (*Syria: The Painful Path to Freedom*, pp. 311f). See also Alan George, "Patronage and Clientelism in Bashar's Market Economy," in Kerr and Larkin, eds, *The Alawis of Syria*, pp. 159–79.

24. Hassan Abbas, "Governance of Diversity in Syria," Arab Reform Initiative, 20 June 2012, p. 13.

25. Thomas Pierret, "La Syrie d'un soulèvement à l'autre. Exacerbation du confessionnalisme, déséquilibres socio-économiques et ambiguïtés géopolitiques" [Syria, from one uprising to the next: Exacerbation of confessionalism, economic imbal-

ances, and geopolitical ambiguities], in M'hamed Oualdi, Delphine Pagès-El Karoui, and Chantal Verdeil, eds, *Les ondes de choc des révolutions arabes* (Beirut: Presses de l'Ifpo, 2014), pp. 221–34.

26. Laura Ruiz de Elvira and Tina Zintl, "The End of the Ba'thist Social Contract in Bashar al-Asad's Syria," *International Journal of Middle East Studies*, vol. 46, no. 2 (2014), p. 335.

27. Panagiotis Geros, "Doing Fieldwork Within Fear and Silences," in Heidi Armbruster and Anna Lærke, eds, *Taking Sides: Ethics, Politics, and Fieldwork in Anthropology* (New York: Berghahn Books, 2008), p. 98.

28. Torstein Schiøtz Worren, "Fear and Resistance: The Construction of Alawi Identity in Syria," Master's thesis, University of Oslo Department of Sociology and Human Geography, 2007.

29. By presidential decree, intelligence agents are accountable only to the army's chief of staff, not the courts. This decree was renewed and broadened by Bashar al-Assad in 2008. See Leïla Vignal, "Syrie, anatomie d'une révolution" [Syria: Anatomy of a revolution], *la Vie des Idées*, 27 July 2012, http://www.laviedesidees.fr/IMG/pdf/20120727_syrie.pdf, 4

30. Author's personal conversations.

31. This particular rumor might have been a case of perceived, communal power differentials, reflected through a narrative that highlights the inability of males to protect females in their group from the aggression of males in another group.

32. This erroneous belief was reproduced, for instance, in the otherwise helpful graphic of the Syrian military-economic elite provided by the Washington Institute for Near East Policy. See "Syria Regime Chart," Washington Institute for Near East Policy, 26 May 2015, http://www.washingtoninstitute.org/uploads/Documents/infographics/SyriaRegimeChart20150526v2.pdf

33. For a portrayal of Ali, and an insightful narrative on how Syrian intellectuals and artists negotiated the limited and ambiguous margins of dissent that slowly started to open in the second half of the 1990s, see Miriam Cooke, *Dissident Syria: Making Oppositional Art Official* (Durham, NC: Duke University Press, 2007), p. 69.

34. For an anthropological analysis of the Assad personality cult in the 1990s, see Lisa Wedeen, *Ambiguities of Domination: Politics, Rhetoric, and Symbols in Contemporary Syria* (Chicago: University of Chicago Press, 1999). While they were attenuated during the first post-succession years, central notions of the cult lingered on and were reinvigorated after the uprising in 2011.

35. Raymond Hinnebusch, *Syria: Revolution From Above* (New York: Routledge, 2002), p. 85.

36. Volker Perthes, *The Political Economy of Syria Under Asad* (New York: I. B. Tauris, 1995), p. 134. For the concept of corporatism, see Howard Wiarda, *Corporatism and Comparative Politics: The Other Great "Ism"* (Armonk, NY: M. E. Sharpe, 1997).

37. This system of selective inclusion and control was highly efficient for the manage-

ment of everyday challenges and conflicts, but was neither designed nor equipped to handle the dynamics created by the unprecedented wave of mass mobilization and collapsing regimes in neighboring countries in 2011. During the early phase of the uprising in Daraa, negotiations between local leaders and senior regime officials (in particular, Syria's then national security advisor Hisham Ikhtiyar) yielded compromises that included token regime concessions, but failed to stop the escalation (see Barout, *The Last Decade of Syrian History*, p. 187). While the reasons for the failure are naturally contested, the examples of Egypt, Libya, and Tunisia clearly created a horizon of perceived opportunities for protesters and threats for the regime, which differed fundamentally from earlier instances of local uprisings in Syria and made it impossible to contain the situation.

38. "Kalimat as-sayid ar-rais Bashar al-Assad ala madraj Jamiat Dimashq" [Speech by President Bashar al-Assad in the auditorium of Damascus University], website of President Bashar al-Assad, 20 June 2011, http://www.presidentassad.net/index.php?option=com_content&view=article&id=1091:20–2011&catid=303&Itemid=469

39. For instance, even under the most recent electoral law (modified on 17 March 2014), at least 50 percent of parliamentary seats are reserved for "peasants and workers"; see Syrian Ministry of the Interior, Law No. 5, Law for General Elections, § 22 (2014), http://www.syriamoi.gov.sy/FCKBIH/file/Election%20law.pdf

40. See these two accounts concerning the highly ambivalent role of the Christian and Druze clergies in the first phase of the uprising: Mazen Ezzi, "A Static Revolution: The Druze Community" (Sweida, 2013) and Rand Sabbagh, "Attitudes of Christians in the Syrian Capital" (Damascus, 2013), in Stolleis, ed., *Playing the Sectarian Card*, pp. 39–70, 71–89.

41. In an account of sectarian (Sunni-Druze) disturbances in the south of Syria in the fall of 2000, Birgit Schaebler notes that negotiations between the president and the community were conducted through the Druze sectarian elite, cutting out both the governor and the local chapter of the Baath. See Birgit Schaebler, "Constructing an Identity Between Arabism and Islam: The Druzes in Syria," *Muslim World*, vol. 103 (January 2013), p. 76. Along the same lines, Christopher Phillips notes that "where party or union bosses might previously have mediated local disputes, increasingly tribal, religious or sect leaders played this role." (Phillips, "Sectarianism and Conflict in Syria," p. 367).

42. Bishara, *Syria: The Painful Path to Freedom*, pp. 104–5; Thomas Pierret, *Religion and State in Syria: The Sunni Ulama from Coup to Revolution* (Cambridge: Cambridge University Press, 2013), pp. 218–21.

43. See, for instance, the discussion between the author and the Berlin correspondent of the Syrian State News Agency SANA, Husam Ismail, on Deutsche Welle TV, "Revolution in Syria? DW Quadriga 29–04–11 (Part 1) (Arabic)," YouTube video,

posted by "hw," 30 April 2011, https://www.youtube.com/watch?v=m_4_xhy42HU

44. Peter Neumann, "Suspects into Collaborators," *London Review of Books*, vol. 36, no. 7 (3 April 2014).

45. Abbas, "Governance of Diversity in Syria," p. 10.

46. "Syria VP Beaten upon Assad's Order: Report," NOW, 29 June 2015, https://now.mmedia.me/lb/en/NewsReports/565509-syria-vp-severely-beaten-upon-assads-order-report

47. Sabbagh, "Attitudes," in Stolleis, ed., *Playing the Sectarian Card*, p. 80.

48. "Myth No. 7: Alawie is Still a Religious Sect," Syria Exposed (blog), 28 March 2005, http://syriaexposed.blogspot.com.eg/2005/03/myth-no-7-alawie-is-still-religious.html; Phillips, "Sectarianism and Conflict in Syria," p. 365.

49. Joshua M. Landis, "Islamic Education in Syria: Undoing Secularism," Paper prepared for "Constructs of Inclusion and Exclusion: Religion and Identity Formation in Middle Eastern School Curricula," Watson Institute for International Studies, Brown University, November 2003.

50. Brynjar Lia, "The Islamist Uprising in Syria, 1976–82: The History and Legacy of a Failed Revolt," *British Journal of Middle Eastern Studies*, vol. 43, no. 4 (2016), pp. 541–59.

51. Kheder Khaddour and Kevin Mazur, "The Struggle for Syria's Regions," *Middle East Report*, vol. 269 (Winter 2013), p. 2.

52. Balanche, "Géographie de la révolte syrienne," p. 449.

53. Kevin Mazur, "Local Struggles in Syria's Northeast," Monkey Cage (blog), *Washington Post*, 9 September 2014, https://www.washingtonpost.com/news/monkey-cage/wp/2014/09/09/local-struggles-in-syrias-northeast/

54. Khaddour and Mazur, "The Struggle for Syria's Regions," p. 3.

55. Lund, "Chasing Ghosts," pp. 215–17.

56. Such a system of regional autonomy would appear in perfect accordance with the ideological platform of the PKK since the early 2000s. See Heiko Wimmen and Müzehher Selcuk, "The Rise of Syria's Kurds," Sada (blog), Carnegie Endowment for International Peace, 2 February 2013, http://carnegieendowment.org/sada/?fa=50852

57. See George, "Patronage and Clientelism in Bashar's Market Economy."

58. Pierret, "La Syrie d'un soulèvement à l'autre."

59. Khaddour, "The Alawi Dilemma"; Leon Goldsmith, "Alawi Diversity and Solidarity: From the Coast to the Interior," in Kerr and Larkin, eds, *The Alawis of Syria*, pp. 141–58.

60. Raphaël Lefevre, "The Muslim Brotherhood's Alawi Conundrum," in Kerr and Larkin, eds, *The Alawis of Syria*, p. 128. Lefevre puts the number of (Alawite) victims at 83; the official figure was 32.

61. Volker Perthes mentions the broad rejection of the Syrian intervention in Lebanon

and names social inequality and corruption as additional reasons; see Perthes, *Political Economy*, p. 4.

62. For example, after a narrowly failed attempt on the life of former president Hafez al-Assad on 26 June 1980, several hundred alleged Islamists held in the Palmyra prison were summarily shot in their cells. Patrick Seale, *Asad: The Struggle for the Middle East* (Berkeley, CA: California University Press, 1988), p. 329.

63. Members of radical but non-violent leftist groups such as the Communist Action Party were hunted down, severely tortured, and sentenced to long prison terms until the late 1980s, and many were released only a decade or more later.

64. Amartya Sen, *Identity and Violence: The Illusion of Destiny* (New York: W. W. Norton & Co., 2006); Brubaker, *Ethnicity Without Groups*, p. 2.

65. Worren, *Fear and Resistance*, p. 91.

66. Khaddour and Mazur, "The Struggle for Syria's Regions," p. 2.

67. Author's private conversations with Syrian Christians, 1991–2.

68. Arjun Appadurai, "Dead Certainty: Ethnic Violence in the Era of Globalization," *Development and Change*, vol. 29, no. 4 (October 1998), pp. 905–25.

69. Barout, *The Last Decade of Syrian History*, p. 195.

70. Bishara, *Syria: The Painful Path to Freedom*, pp. 321–2.

71. Barout, *The Last Decade of Syrian History*, pp. 211–13.

72. A video is available at "Quwat al-Amn fi-Suriya tadrub al-muataqalin fil-Bayda Baniyas" [Security forces in Syria beating detainees in Al-Bayda/Baniyas], YouTube video (graphic content), posted by "syrianagent2011," 14 April 2011, https://www.youtube.com/watch?v=PVPDZji4-f4&skipcontrinter=1&bpctr=1460570945

73. A video is available at "Qatl ash-shahid Nidal Jannoud" [Killing of the martyr Nidal Jannoud], YouTube video (graphic content), posted by "SYRIALIFE," 21 April 2011, https://www.youtube.com/watch?v=wFHcKm5f41A; see also Bishara, *Syria: The Painful Path to Freedom*, p. 323.

74. Ibid., p. 109; promotional videos for the project are still available: "Homs Dream," YouTube video, posted by "Mohammed Al-tenawi," 15 February 2014, https://www.youtube.com/watch?v=hcCo-hLAKk0; or "Homs Dream Project, Homs City, Syria," YouTube video, posted by "MsSyriano," 23 October 2010, https://www.youtube.com/watch?v=4UOT_GQeIfo

75. Bishara, *Syria: The Painful Path to Freedom*, p. 325.

76. According to Khaddour ("The Alawi Dilemma," p. 14), who quotes a retired Alawite army officer, "the security forces worked to mobilize Alawites, especially the young who were out of work. They mobilized and organized them and sent them to Sunni areas of Homs to lead demonstrations in favour of the regime."

77. According to activists quoted by Bishara (*Syria: The Painful Path to Freedom*, pp. 110–11), the security forces initially tried to convince the protesters to disperse, warning against the danger of sectarian clashes.

78. Khaddour, "The Alawi Dilemma," p. 14.

79. Bishara, *Syria: The Painful Path to Freedom*, p. 114, n. 47.

80. Ibid., p. 117, n. 54.

81. Heiko Wimmen, "Divisive Rule. Sectarianism and Power Maintenance in the Arab Spring: Bahrain, Iraq, Lebanon and Syria," German Institute for International and Security Affairs, March 2014.

82. Venetia Rainey, "Evidence of Massacre as Syrians Demand Assad Exit," *Week*, 20 April 2011, http://www.theweek.co.uk/politics/syria-uprising/6097/evidence-massacre-syrians-demand-assad-exit

83. For a first-hand account of the atmosphere of sectarian violence and retribution reigning in Homs in early 2012, see Jonathan Littell, *Syrian Notebooks: Inside the Homs Uprising* (London: Verso, 2015).

84. Bishara, *Syria: The Painful Path to Freedom*, p. 110.

85. Salwa Ismail, "The Syrian Uprising: Imagining and Performing the Nation," *Studies in Ethnicity and Nationalism*, vol. 11, no. 3 (2011), p. 540. See also the "Covenant Against Sectarianism in Syria," initially signed by more than 600 Syrian intellectuals and published on 10 March 2011, https://www.facebook.com/notes/153001424759618/ (Arabic).

86. Author's private conversations (via Facebook Messenger) with Syrian activists, July–September 2011.

87. Barout, *The Last Decade of Syrian History*, p. 229.

88. During the early phase of the uprising, Syrian activists were in direct contact with Iranian veterans of the Green Movement, advising them on protest tactics and strategies (author's private conversation on Facebook Messenger with a Syrian student activist based in Aleppo, summer 2011). The technique was also applied in Bahrain, with equally ambiguous effects. During the summer and fall of 2011, the intensity of *takbir*, as reported on social media, emerged as something of a yardstick for revolutionary activism and support in specific locations (personal observation of activist and opposition Facebook pages by the author).

89. Khaddour, "The Alawi Dilemma," p. 22.

90. Yassin Hajj Salih, "The Civic and the Traditional Elements in the Syrian Uprising," *Al-Hayat*, 14 June 2011.

91. Mohammed Jamal Barout, "Populist Salafism in Syria and the Revolution of Local Societies," *Al-Hayat*, 17 November 2011.

92. Muriel Asseburg and Heiko Wimmen, "Dynamics of Transformation, Elite Change and New Social Mobilization in the Arab World," *Mediterranean Politics*, vol. 21, no. 1 (October 2015), pp. 1–22; Reinoud Leenders, "Master Frames of the Syrian Conflict: Early Violence and Sectarian Response Revisited," Project on Middle East Political Science, 9 June 2016.

93. Richard N. Haass, "The New Thirty Years' War," Council on Foreign Relations, 21 July 2014; "Joshua Landis on ISIS, Syria and the 'Great Sorting Out' in the

Middle East," YouTube video, posted by "DU Center for Middle East Studies," 7 October 2014, https://www.youtube.com/watch?v=_-roW5Y7vbw

94. Isam al Khafaji, "A Bicameral Parliament in Iraq and Syria," Arab Reform Initiative, 30 June 2016; for an early proposal advocating such a solution, see Stephan Rosiny, "Syria: Power Sharing as an Alternative to Regional Conflagration," German Institute for Global and Area Studies, 2013.

95. Khaled Yacoub Oweis, "Local Dynamics in the Syrian Conflict," German Institute for International and Security Affairs, July 2016.

4. SECTARIANISM AND IRANIAN FOREIGN POLICY

1. See, for example, "The Saudi Blueprint," *Economist*, 9 January 2016, http://www.economist.com/news/leaders/21685450-desert-kingdom-striving-dominate-its-region-and-modernise-its-economy-same; and Ben Caspit, "Israel Fears Return of Persian Empire," *Al-Monitor*, 21 September 2015, http://www.al-monitor.com/pulse/originals/2015/09/israel-fear-persian-empire-iran-shiite-hezbollah-axis-nuke.html

2. See Ray Takeyh, *Guardians of the Revolution: Iran and the World in the Age of the Ayatollahs* (New York: Oxford University Press, 2016); R. K. Ramazani, "Ideology and Pragmatism in Iran's Foreign Policy," *Middle East Journal*, vol. 58, no. 4 (2004), pp. 549–59; and Brenda Shaffer, "The Islamic Republic of Iran: Is It Really?" in her *The Limits of Culture: Islam and Foreign Policy* (Cambridge, MA: MIT Press, 2006). Also see the findings in two recent edited volumes on Iranian foreign policy: Thomas Juneau and Sam Razavi, eds, *Iranian Foreign Policy Since 2001: Alone in the World* (New York: Routledge, 2013); and Shahram Akbarzadeh and Dara Conduit, eds, *Iran in the World: President Rouhani's Foreign Policy* (New York: Palgrave Macmillan, 2016).

3. Mohammad Javad Zarif, "Let Us Rid the World of Wahhabism," *New York Times*, 13 September 2016, www.nytimes.com/2016/09/14/opinion/mohammad-javad-zarif-let-us-rid-the-world-of-wahhabism.html

4. Mohammad Javad Zarif, "Saudi Arabia's Reckless Extremism," *New York Times*, 10 January 2016, http://www.nytimes.com/2016/01/11/opinion/mohammad-javad-zarif-saudi-arabias-reckless-extremism.html

5. Ibid.

6. "Iran: Saudis Face 'Divine Revenge' for Executing al-Nimr," BBC News, 3 January 2016, http://www.bbc.com/news/world-middle-east-35216694

7. Phillip Smyth, "Iran's Martyrdom Machine Springs to Life," *Foreign Policy*, 5 January 2016, http://foreignpolicy.com/2016/01/05/irans-martyrdom-machine-springs-to-life/

8. Adel Bin Ahmed al-Jubeir, "Can Iran Change?" *New York Times*, 19 January 2016, http://www.nytimes.com/2016/01/19/opinion/saudi-arabia-can-iran-change.html.

9. Ibid.

10. Humeyra Pamuk, "Erdogan: 'Iran is Trying to Dominate the Region,'" *Al-Arabiya*, 27 March 2015, http://english.alarabiya.net/en/News/middle-east/2015/03/27/Erdogan-Iran-is-trying-to-dominate-the-region-.html

11. Associated Press, "Arab League Condemns Iranian 'Meddling' in Arab Affairs," *Al Jazeera*, 10 January 2016, http://america.aljazeera.com/articles/2016/1/10/arab-league-condemns-iranian-meddling-in-arab-affairs.html

12. R. K. Ramazani and Joseph A. Kechichian, *The Gulf Cooperation Council: Record and Analysis* (Charlottesville: University Press of Virginia, 1988), pp. 6–8.

13. Shahram Chubin and Charles Tripp, *Iran and Iraq at War* (Boulder, CO: Westview Press, 1988), p. 140.

14. Dilip Hiro, *The Longest War: The Iran-Iraq Military Conflict* (New York: Routledge, 1991), pp. 155–9.

15. See, for example, David Hirst, "Arab Leaders Watch in Fear as Shia Emancipation Draws Near," *Guardian*, 26 January 2005, https://www.theguardian.com/world/2005/jan/27/iraq.davidhirst

16. Robin Wright and Peter Baker, "Iraq, Jordan See Threat to Election from Iran," *Washington Post*, 8 December 2004, http://pqasb.pqarchiver.com/washington-post/doc/409726489.html

17. I discussed this issue in an earlier essay: Afshon Ostovar, "And for the Middle East, a Cold War of its Own," *Lawfare* (blog), 24 January 2016, https://www.lawfareblog.com/and-middle-east-cold-war-its-own; also see the findings from Afshon Ostovar, "Deterrence and the Future of U.S.-GCC Defense Cooperation: A Strategic Dialogue Event," CNA, July 2015, http://calhoun.nps.edu/bitstream/handle/10945/45796/Deterrence%20and%20the%20Future%20of%20U.S.-GCC%20Def%20Cooperation_DCP-2015-U-010969-Final.pdf

18. Thomas Juneau, "No, Yemen's Houthis Actually Aren't Iranian Puppets," *Washington Post*, 16 May 2016, https://www.washingtonpost.com/news/monkey-cage/wp/2016/05/16/contrary-to-popular-belief-houthis-arent-iranian-proxies/

19. See for example, this story published by an IRGC news website that claims Ansar Allah was able to hack into the control system of a Saudi drone and bring it down with Iran's help: "Ansar Allah Brought Down a Saudi Drone With Iran's Help" [Ansar Allah pahpad-e Saudi ra ba komak-e iran bar zamin neshanad], *Basij Press*, 22 February 2016, http://basijpress.ir/fa/news-details/70820

20. Shaffer, "The Islamic Republic of Iran"; see also James Berry, "Brothers or Comrades at Arms? Iran's Relations with Armenia and Azerbaijan," in Akbarzadeh and Conduit, eds, *Iran in the World*, pp. 59–74.

21. The nature and extent of Iran's links to al-Qaeda are far from clear. However, a detailed analysis of the issue, drawn from interviews with, and memoirs and let-

ters of former al-Qaeda prisoners in Iran, can be found here: Cathy Scott-Clark and Adrian Levy, *The Exile: The Stunning Inside Story of Osama bin Laden and Al Qaeda in Flight* (New York: Bloomsbury, 2017); see also Don Rassler et al., "Letters From Abbottabad: Bin Ladin Sidelined?", Combating Terrorism Center, 3 May 2012, https://www.ctc.usma.edu/posts/letters-from-abbottabad-bin-ladin-side-lined; and Daniel Byman, "Unlikely Alliance: Iran's Secretive Relationship With Al-Qaeda," IHS Defense, Risk and Security Consulting, July 2012.

22. See Trita Parsi, *Treacherous Alliance: The Secret Dealings of Israel, Iran, and the United States* (New Haven, CT: Yale University Press, 2007).

23. Takeyh, *Guardians of the Revolution*, p. 89.

24. Speech by Khomeini in Jamaran, Iran; see "Khomeyni Tells World Prayers Leaders to Politicise Sermons," BBC Summary of World Broadcasts, 15 May 1984.

25. Fred Halliday, "Three Concepts of Internationalism," *International Affairs*, vol. 64, no. 2 (Spring 1988), pp. 187–98.

26. On the concept and conduct of exporting the revolution, see Afshon Ostovar, *Vanguard of the Imam: Religion, Politics, and Iran's Revolutionary Guards* (New York: Oxford University Press, 2016), pp. 102–20; Ali Alfoneh, *Iran Unveiled: How the Revolutionary Guards is Turning Theocracy into Military Dictatorship* (Washington, DC: AEI Press, 2013), pp. 204–37; and R. K. Ramazani, "Iran's Export of the Revolution: Politics, Ends, and Means," in John L. Esposito, ed., *The Iranian Revolution: Its Global Impact* (Miami, FL: Florida International University Press, 1990), pp. 40–62.

27. *Payam-e Enqelab*, no. 4 (1980), pp. 32–4.

28. Falah A. Jabar, *The Shi'ite Movement in Iraq* (London: Saqi Press, 2003), pp. 235–59.

29. On why support for foreign activities declined among Iran's leadership during the 1980s, see Ostovar, *Vanguard*, pp. 118–20.

30. Ayatollah Ruhollah Khomeini, *Islam and Revolution: Writings and Declarations of Imam Khomeini (1941–1980)*, trans. Hamid Algar (Berkeley, CA: Mizan Press, 1981), p. 302.

31. Ostovar, *Vanguard*, pp. 104–17.

32. "Montazeri's Guidelines for the Revolution Guards," BBC Summary of World Broadcasts, 19 May 1982.

33. Roschanack Shaery-Eisenlohr, *Shi'ite Lebanon: Transnational Religion and the Making of National Identities* (New York: Columbia University Press, 2008), pp. 89–118.

34. Ibid., p. 47.

35. Emmanuel Sivan, "Sunni Radicalism in the Middle East and the Iranian Revolution," *International Journal of Middle East Studies*, vol. 21, no. 1 (February 1989), pp. 1–30.

36. Ibid.; also Ostovar, *Vanguard*, pp. 104–7.

37. Moojan Momen, *An Introduction to Shi'i Islam* (Oxford: George Ronald, 1987),

pp. 295–7; Elvire Corboz, *Guardians of Shiʿism: Sacred Authority and Transnational Family Networks* (Edinburgh: Edinburgh University Press, 2015), pp. 166–72.

38. Khomeini's thesis of clerical rule (*velayat-e faqih*) remains unpopular among the most senior clerics outside Iran. See for example Hayder al-Khoei, "Post-Sistani Iraq, Iran, and the Future of Shia Islam," *War on the Rocks*, 9 September 2016, http://warontherocks.com/2016/09/post-sistani-iraq-iran-and-the-future-of-shia-islam/

39. Ostovar, *Vanguard*, pp. 102–18; Shaery-Eisenlohr, *Shiʿite Lebanon*, pp. 95–118; also Jabar, *Shiʿite Movement in Iraq*.

40. Ahmad Nizar Hamzeh, *In the Path of Hizbullah* (Syracuse, NY: Syracuse University Press, 2004), pp. 22–6; Augustus Richard Norton, *Hezbollah: A Short History* (Princeton, NJ: Princeton University Press, 2007), pp. 32–4.

41. Niamatullah Ibrahimi, "The Failure of a Clerical Proto-State: Hazarajat, 1979–1984," Crisis States Research Center, London School of Economics and Political Science, September 2006.

42. Mohsen M. Milani, "Iran's Policy Towards Afghanistan," *Middle East Journal*, vol. 60, no. 2 (Spring 2006), pp. 235–56.

43. Ebrahim Gilani, "Iran's Ungrateful European Friend," Institute for War and Peace Reporting, 6 August 2010, https://iwpr.net/global-voices/irans-ungrateful-european-friend

44. See Daniel Byman, *Deadly Connections: States that Sponsor Terrorism* (Cambridge: Cambridge University Press, 2005), p. 115; and Ostovar, *Vanguard*, pp. 169–78 and 204–34 (*passim*).

45. Phillip Smyth, "Should Iraq's ISCI Forces Really be Considered 'Good Militias'?", Washington Institute for Near East Policy, 17 August 2016, http://www.washingtoninstitute.org/policy-analysis/view/should-iraqs-isci-forces-really-be-considered-good-militias

46. Ostovar, *Vanguard*, pp. 171–4.

47. "President Delivers State of the Union Address," White House Office of the Press Secretary, 28 January 2002, https://georgewbush-whitehouse.archives.gov/news/releases/2002/01/20020129–11.html

48. Joseph Felter and Brian Fishman, "Iranian Influence in Iraq: Politics and 'Other Means,'" Combating Terrorism Center, 1 October 2008.

49. Edward Wong and Sabrina Tavernise, "Sectarian Bloodshed Reveals Strength of Iraq Militias," *New York Times*, 25 February 2006; Ches Thurber, "From Coexistence to Cleansing: The Rise of Sectarian Violence in Baghdad, 2003–2007," *Al Nakhlah* (Spring 2011), https://www.ciaonet.org/attachments/17899/uploads; and James D. Fearon, "Iraq's Civil War," *Foreign Affairs*, vol. 86, no. 2 (March–April 2007), pp. 2–15.

50. Alireza Nader et al., *Iran's Influence in Afghanistan: Implications for the U.S. Drawdown* (Santa Monica, CA: RAND Corporation, 2014), pp. 14–16.

51. Ali Khamenei speech in Qom, Iran, January 2007, cited in Karim Sadjadpour, "Reading Khamenei: The World View of Iran's Most Powerful Leader," Carnegie Endowment for International Peace, 10 March 2008, p. 26.
52. "Iran Leader Advisor: No Sectarian Agenda Followed in Bahrain," BBC Monitoring Middle East, 15 March 2011.
53. Ibid.
54. Toby Matthiesen, *Sectarian Gulf: Bahrain, Saudi Arabia, and the Arab Spring that Wasn't* (Stanford, CA: Stanford University Press, 2013); and Frederic Wehrey, *Sectarian Politics in the Gulf: From the Iraq War to the Arab Uprisings* (New York: Columbia University Press, 2013), pp. 73–102.
55. "A Karbala in Bahrain and Different Outcomes" [Karbali-ye bahrayn va peyamad-haye motafavet], *Javan*, 17 March 2011, http://javanonline.ir/fa/news/443704/
56. Ibid.
57. "We Will Support Syria to the End..." [ta akhar az suriyeh hemayat mi-konim], Fars News Agency, 4 September 2013, http://farsnews.com/newstext.php?nn=13920613000905
58. Mohammad Safari, "There is No Longer Any Need for Relations with Saudi Arabia; Mobilizing the Capacity of the People in the Region Against Al Saud," *Siyasat-e Ruz*, 13 January 2014, BBC Monitoring Middle East, 19 January 2014.
59. "Velayati: Daesh, al-Qaeda Are 'Exports' of Wahhabism," *Tehran Times*, 6 May 2016, http://www.tehrantimes.com/news/301168/Velayati-Daesh-al-Qaeda-are-exports-of-Wahhabism
60. "Iran Takes Deliberate and Precise Actions in Syria" [Iran dar suriyeh raftari-e san-jideh va daqiq dasht], Fars News Agency, 20 January 2016, http://www.farsnews.com/newstext.php?nn=13941003000154
61. "The Head of the Judiciary Requests the IRGC and Ministry of Information to Prevent the Infiltration of Takfiris into the Country" [Dar khast-e qovveh-ye qazai-yyeh az sepah va vezarat-e ettelaat/jelogiri az vorud-e jariyan-haye takfiri be kesh-var], Mehr News Agency, 15 January 2014, http://mehrnews.com/news/2215145/
62. Cole Bunzel, "The Kingdom and the Caliphate: Duel of the Islamic States," Carnegie Endowment for International Peace, 18 February 2016, http://carnegieendowment.org/2016/02/18/kingdom-and-caliphate-duel-of-islamic-states/iu4w
63. Ben Hubbard, "Iran and Saudi Arabia Squabble as Millions of Muslims Begin Pilgrimage," *New York Times*, 6 September 2016, http://nytimes.com/2016/09/07/world/middleeast/hajj-saudi-arabia-iran.html
64. "No Country but Iran is Capable of Leading the Muslim World" [Hich keshvari joz Iran qader beh rahbari-e jahan-e eslam nist], Fars News Agency, 13 February 2014, http://www.farsnews.com/newstext.php?nn=13921124000724
65. Ibid.
66. Ibid.

67. "Daesh Believes that the Shia Must Be Annihilated for Them to Achieve Victory" [Daesh aqideh darad baray-e movaffaqiyyat bayad shiiyan ra nabud konad], *Entekhab*, 28 August 2015, http://www.entekhab.ir/fa/news/223019/

68. Heydari's comments are recorded in the 2013 BBC documentary, "Iran's Secret Army," available as YouTube video, posted by "Darius Bazargan," 22 November 2013, https://www.youtube.com/watch?v=ZI_88ChjQtUy

69. "Shamkhani Meets with Leaders of Palestinian Groups" [Didar-e shamkhani ba rahbaran-e goruh-haye felestini], *Tabnak*, 1 October 2014, http://www.tabnak.ir/fa/news/438746/

70. "Syria and Lebanon are Iran's Frontline" [Khat-e moqaddam-e Iran, suriyeh va lobnan ast], Fars News Agency, 15 May 2016, http://www.farsnews.com/newstext.php?nn=13930225000092

71. See Ostovar, *Vanguard*, pp. 121–40.

72. "'Fatimaiyun' Were the Vanguard of the Syria Conflict" ["Fatemiiyun" pish-qaravol nabard-e suriyeh budand], *Bultan News*, 24 July 2016, http://www.bultannews.com/fa/news/385539/

73. Farnaz Fassihi, "Iran Pays Afghans to Fight for Assad," *Wall Street Journal*, 22 May 2014, http://online.wsj.com/articles/SB10001424052702304908304579564161508613846

74. Shelly Kittleson, "Islamic Front Control Staves Off Opposition Infighting in Aleppo," *Al-Monitor*, 4 November 2014, http://www.al-monitor.com/pulse/originals/2014/11/cooperation-prevents-syria-opposition-infighting-aleppo.html

75. Farzin Nadimi, "Iran's Afghan and Pakistani Proxies: In Syria and Beyond?", Washington Institute for Near East Policy, 22 August 2016, http://www.washingtoninstitute.org/policy-analysis/view/irans-afghan-and-pakistani-proxies-in-syria-and-beyond

76. Ibid.

77. "Sardar Falaki, One of the Commanders of the Syrian Front, in an Interview with Mashregh News Site" [Sardar Falaki, az farmandehan-e jebhe-ye suriyeh dar goftogu ba saiyt-e khabari Mashreq], *Bultan News*, 24 July 2016, http://www.bultannews.com/fa/news/385539/

78. Ibid.

79. "A Commander from Zaynabiyun: I Was Supposed to Go to Pakistan to Get Married, but Deemed It More Necessary to Defend the Shrine" [Yeki az farmandehan-e Zaynabiyun: qarar bud baray-e ezdevaj be Pakestan beravam ama defa az haram vajeb-tar didam], Fars News Agency, 25 July 2016, http://www.farsnews.com/newstext.php?nn=13950503001442

80. Ibid.

81. "Iran's Secret Army."

82. See, for example, the funeral of Ruhollah Qorbani, who was killed near Aleppo: "Three Details of the Commemoration of Ruhollah Qorbani, Martyr in Defense

of the Shrine" [Joziyyat-e 3 marasem-e bozorgdasht-e shahid modafe-e haram, ruhollah qorbani], Tasnim News Agency, 5 November 2015, http://www.tasnimnews.com/fa/news/1394/08/16/909280

83. See, for example, the placard honoring the IRGC martyrs killed in Syria: "Farewell Ceremony and Procession of Martyrs in Defense of the Shrine 'Mosafer' and 'Rezi' Was Announced" [marasem-e veda' va tashiy'-e shahidan-e modafe'-e haram "Mosafer" va "rezi" e'lam shod], *Langar News*, 3 April 2016, http://langarnews.ir/51692/

84. See, Ostovar, *Vanguard*, pp. 204–29.

85. "Iraq Crisis: Battle Grips Vital Baiji Oil Refinery," BBC News, 18 June 2014, http://www.bbc.com/news/world-middle-east-27897648

86. See, for example, the placard memorializing martyred IRGC commander Hamid Taqavi: "Commemoration Held for Chief Martyr Taqavi" [Marasem-e bozorgdasht-e sardar shahid Taqavi bargozar shod], Fars News Agency, 5 January 2015, http://www.farsnews.com/newstext.php?nn=13931015001155

87. Mehdi Jedinia and Noor Zahid, "Iran's Launch of Shia Army Threatens to Escalate Sectarian Tensions," Voice of America, 29 August 2016, http://www.voanews.com/a/iran-launch-shia-army-escalate-sectarian-tensions/3485547.html

88. "Sardar Falaki," *Bultan News*.

89. Ibid.

90. Toby Matthiesen, "Transnational Diffusion Between Arab Shia Movements" (memo prepared for "Transnational Diffusion, Cooperation and Learning in the Middle East and North Africa," Project on Middle East Political Science, George Washington University, 8–9 June 2016), http://pomeps.org/2016/08/16/transnational-diffusion-between-arab-shia-movements/

91. Ostovar, *Vanguard*, p. 218.

5. SHIA-CENTRIC STATE-BUILDING AND SUNNI REJECTION IN POST-2003 IRAQ

1. For the purposes of this chapter, sectarian dynamics refer specifically to Sunni-Shia relations as distinct from other intergroup relations such as Arab-Kurdish relations (which may be better phrased in "ethnic" rather than "sectarian" terms).

2. These concepts should be taken broadly as referring to dominant or salient outlooks rather than absolute positions subscribed to by all Sunnis and Shias. As is always the case with sectarian dynamics, nothing can be said about all Sunnis or all Shias.

3. The term "sectarianism" appears in quotation marks throughout, the reason being that the term has no definitive meaning. Until one is able to define "sectarianism," a more coherent way of addressing the issue would be to use the term "sectarian" followed by the appropriate suffix: sectarian hate, sectarian unity, sectarian discrimination, and so forth.

4. This was aptly illustrated in late 2012 when then prime minister Nouri al-Maliki moved against two public figures in short succession: governor of the Central Bank Sinan al-Shibeebi and then vice president Tariq al-Hashimi. The former is a fellow Shia, and hence Maliki's attack against him was perceived as a power move aimed at consolidating the prime minister's grip on power; the latter, however, is Sunni, which immediately lent the episode an unavoidable sectarian dimension in popular perceptions. As is inherently the case in a sectarian environment, political disputes cannot escape sect-coding so long as the protagonists are of different sectarian backgrounds.

5. This has been vividly demonstrated by the reactions to the conflict in Yemen in 2015. Despite the complex and local drivers behind the conflict, some commentators seem content to frame it as part of a broader sectarian, Sunni-Shia conflict. The most breathtaking example of this reductionist logic may be Thomas Friedman's assertion that "the main issue [in Yemen] is the 7th century struggle over who is the rightful heir to the Prophet Muhammad—Shiites or Sunnis." See Thomas Friedman, "Tell Me How This Ends Well," *New York Times*, 1 April 2015, http://www.nytimes.com/2015/04/01/opinion/thomas-friedman-tell-me-how-this-ends-well.html. For more nuanced analysis on the conflict in Yemen, see Susanne Dahlgren and Anne-Linda Amira Augustin, "The Multiple Wars in Yemen," Middle East Research and Information Project, 18 June 2015, http://merip.org/multiple-wars-yemen; International Crisis Group, *Yemen at War*, Middle East Briefing No. 45 (Brussels: International Crisis Group, 27 March 2015), http://www.crisisgroup.org/en/regions/middle-east-north-africa/iraq-iran-gulf/yemen/b045-yemen-at-war.aspx. On how sectarian identity inheres in popular perception toward the conflict, see Maria Abi-Habib and Sam Dagher, "Sunnis Cheer Saudi-Led Battle for Yemen," *Wall Street Journal*, 27 March 2015, http://www.wsj.com/articles/sunnis-cheer-saudi-led-battle-for-yemen-1427507176

6. See Joel Rayburn, "The Sunni Chauvinists," in *Iraq After America: Strongmen, Sectarians, Resistance* (Stanford, CA: Hoover Institution Press, 2014); Shireen T. Hunter, "The Real Causes of Iraq's Problems," *LobeLog*, 14 June 2014, https://lobelog.com/2014-06-the-real-causes-of-iraqs-problems/

7. For more details, see Fanar Haddad, "A Sectarian Awakening: Reinventing Sunni Identity in Iraq After 2003," *Current Trends in Islamist Ideology*, vol. 17 (August 2014), pp. 145–76.

8. For details of Sunni political participation, see Stephen Wicken, *Iraq's Sunnis in Crisis*, Middle East Security Report 2 (Washington: Institute for the Study of War, May 2013), http://www.understandingwar.org/sites/default/files/Wicken-Sunni-In-Iraq.pdf; International Crisis Group, "Make or Break: Iraq's Sunnis and the State," Middle East Report 144 (Brussels: International Crisis Group, 14 August 2013), http://www.crisisgroup.org/~/media/Files/Middle%20East%20North%20Africa/Iraq%20Syria%20Lebanon/Iraq/144-make-or-break-iraq-s-sunnis-and-the-state.pdf

9. See Fanar Haddad, "Sectarian Relations and Sunni Identity in Post-Civil War Iraq," in Lawrence Potter, ed., *Sectarian Politics in the Persian Gulf* (New York: Oxford University Press, 2014).

10. Ali Allawi, *The Occupation of Iraq: Winning the War, Losing the Peace* (London: Yale University Press, 2007), p. 438.

11. For a summary of recent polls on several issues, including the basis of identity and secular politics, see Mansoor Moaddel, "Is Iraq Actually Falling Apart? What Social Science Surveys Show," *Informed Comment* (blog), 20 June 2014, http://www.juancole.com/2014/06/actually-falling-surveys.html

12. This was especially pronounced among major Shia political actors who ran jointly in 2005 under the banner of the UIA. By 2014, many of the constituent parts of the UIA were running under their own newly formed lists. On the two elections held in 2005, see Kenneth Katzman, *Iraq: Elections, Government, and Constitution*, Congressional Research Service Report for Congress RS21968 (Washington: Congressional Research Service, 20 November 2006), http://fpc.state.gov/documents/organization/76838.pdf. On the election of 2014, see Ahmed Ali, *Iraq's 2014 National Elections*, Middle East Security Report 20 (Washington: Institute for the Study of War, April 2014), http://www.understandingwar.org/sites/default/files/AhmedAliIraqElections.pdf

13. On the election of 2014, see Ahmed Ali, *Iraq's 2014 National Elections*, Middle East Security Report 20 (Washington: Institute for the Study of War, April 2014), http://www.understandingwar.org/sites/default/files/AhmedAliIraqElections.pdf

14. For example, see Sami Ramadani, "The Sectarian Myth of Iraq," *Guardian*, 16 June 2014, http://www.theguardian.com/commentisfree/2014/jun/16/sectarian-myth-of-iraq

15. For example, see Peter W. Galbraith, *The End of Iraq: How American Incompetence Created a War Without End* (London: Simon & Schuster, 2006). This line of argument may be valid with regard to the Kurds—particularly since 1991, when they first attained a measure of self-rule. However, it would be inaccurate to conflate the drivers of Arab-Kurdish dynamics with those of the Sunni-Shia divide.

16. Several explanations can be proposed for this. Anticolonial activism may have led some political figures to prescribe a clearly defined and distilled "us" against the colonizer. Related to this, the manner in which Arab nationalism manifested in the early and mid-twentieth century, making "Arab" credentials a central criterion for inclusion in the nation-state, certainly contributed to the problem. Perhaps most relevant is the ever-intensifying authoritarianism of the twentieth-century Iraqi state.

17. The Nationality Law divided Iraqis into "original" and "non-original," "original" meaning those that had been registered as Ottoman subjects. This followed the precedent set by the first Iraqi constitution of 1921 and the Law for the Election

of the Constituent Assembly of 1922, both of which similarly divided Iraqis into original and non-original. The Arabization policies targeted Kurds, Turkomans, and Assyrians in northern Iraq. See Hania Mufti and Peter Bouckaert, "Iraq: Forced Expulsion of Ethnic Minorities," *Human Rights Watch*, vol. 15, no. 3 (March 2003), http://www.hrw.org/sites/default/files/reports/Kirkuk0303.pdf; and Hania Mufti and Peter Bouckaert, "Claims in Conflict: Reversing Ethnic Cleansing in Northern Iraq," *Human Rights Watch*, vol. 16, no. 4 (August 2004), http://www.hrw.org/reports/2004/iraq0804/iraq0804.pdf. Another divisive concept was *shuubiyya*, which refers to an eighth-century movement that challenged the privileged position of Arabs in the early Islamic empires, arguing that Islam does not differentiate between believers on the basis of ethnicity. In the twentieth century, the term was revived by pan-Arabists to describe internal enemies of the Arab world. It was most notably used to discredit Iraqi communists. See Sami A. Hanna and George H. Gardner, "Al-Shu'ubiyyah Up-Dated: A Study of the 20th Century Revival of an Eighth Century Concept," *Middle East Journal*, vol. 20, no. 3 (Summer 1966), pp. 335–51. *Tabaiyya* is commonly translated as "dependency." In recent Iraqi history, the term has been shorthand for *tabaiyya Iraniyya*, meaning those who are of "Iranian dependency"—that is, registered as Persian rather than Ottoman subjects—as stipulated by the Nationality Law of 1924. The charge of *tabaiyya* was used to justify the deportation of hundreds of thousands of Shias. See Ali Babakhan, "The Deportation of Shi'as During the Iran-Iraq War: Causes and Consequences," in Faleh A. Jabar, ed., *Ayatollahs, Sufis and Ideologues: State, Religion and Social Movements in Iraq* (London: Saqi Books, 2002).

18. As one Sunni politician put it: "We awoke one day and suddenly discovered that we are all Sunnis." Quoted in International Crisis Group, *Make or Break*, pp. 4–5.

19. To illustrate, in 1985, Ofra Bengio lamented the fact that "The extent to which the regime has suppressed the [Shia] issue can be gathered from the fact that the term Shi'i itself has become almost taboo in the Iraqi media. This in itself poses tremendous difficulties for the analyst." Ofra Bengio, "Shi'is and Politics in Ba'thi Iraq," *Middle Eastern Studies*, vol. 21, no. 1 (January 1985), p. 13.

20. This explains Shia representation in the upper reaches of government and the civil service in pre-2003 Iraq, despite the existence of a Shia issue. More recently, it also explains how Ayad Allawi—who is from a Shia background—became the Sunni electorate's candidate of choice in 2010.

21. Peter Sluglett, *Britain in Iraq: Contriving King and Country, 1914–1932* (New York: Columbia University Press, 2007), p. 224.

22. Ibid., pp. 103–5; Hanna Batatu, *The Old Social Classes and the Revolutionary Movements of Iraq*, 2nd edn (London: Saqi Books, 2004), pp. 327–8.

23. For full text, see Abdul Razzaq al-Hasani, *Tarikh al-Wizarat al-Iraqiyya* [The History of the Iraqi Cabinets], 7th edn, vol. 4 (Baghdad: Dar al-Shu'un al-Thaqafiyya al-Ama, 1988), pp. 92–4.

24. Memorandum written by Faisal in March 1932 addressing Iraq's political elite, in which he gave his personal assessment of the state of the country. The memorandum can be found in full in Salih Abd al-Razzaq, *Masharee' Izalat al-Tamyeez al-Ta'ifi fi al-Iraq: min mudhakarat Faisal ila Majlis al-Hukm, 1932–2003* [Plans for the Elimination of Sectarian Discrimination in Iraq: from Faisal's Memorandum to the Governing Council, 1932–2003] (Beirut: al-Ma'arif, 2010), pp. 16–27.

25. Amatzia Baram, *Saddam Husayn and Islam, 1968–2003: Ba'thi Iraq from Secularism to Faith* (Baltimore, MD: Johns Hopkins University Press, 2014), ch. 3.

26. On the disturbances of 1979, see Faleh A. Jabar, *The Shi'ite Movement in Iraq* (London: Al Saqi, 2003), pp. 228–31. On the disturbances of 1977, see Jabar, *The Shi'ite Movement in Iraq*, pp. 208–15; Marion F. Sluglett and Peter Sluglett, *Iraq Since 1958: From Revolution to Dictatorship*, (London: I. B. Tauris, 2001), pp. 198–9.

27. For more on the impact of the 1991 uprisings on sectarian relations, see Fanar Haddad, *Sectarianism in Iraq: Antagonistic Visions of Unity* (London: Hurst & Co., 2011), chs 4–6.

28. This was by no means restricted to Sunni Arab Iraqis; however, given that the sect-centricity in question is Shia sect-centricity, suspicion was more likely to emanate from Sunni quarters, in the same way that sympathy was more likely to emanate from Shia ones.

29. Allawi, *The Occupation*, p. 75.

30. Haddad, *Sectarianism in Iraq*, chs 4–6.

31. For the opposition in exile during the sanctions era, see Tareq Y. Ismael and Jacqueline S. Ismael, *Iraq in the Twenty-First Century: Regime Change and the Making of a Failed State*, Durham Modern Middle East and Islamic World Series 34 (Oxford: Routledge, 2015), pp. 84–9.

32. The principle was adopted at the Iraqi opposition conferences of Vienna in June 1992 and Salah al-Din in October 1992. See Ibrahim Nawar, "Untying the Knot," *Al Ahram Weekly*, 19 February 2003; Allawi, *The Occupation*, p. 50; Ismael and Ismael, *Iraq*, pp. 86, 88. Hayder al-Khoei has argued that the idea of ethnosectarian quotas dates to an opposition conference held in Tehran in 1987; Hayder al-Khoei, "The Construction of Ethno-Sectarian Politics in Post-War Iraq: 2003–05," Master's thesis, International Studies and Diplomacy, School of Oriental and African Studies, 2012, p. 12.

33. Perhaps the most cited example demonstrating this fact is the "Declaration of the Shia of Iraq," July 2002. Full text can be found on http://www.al-bab.com/arab/docs/iraq/shia02a.htm

34. Nicolas Pelham, *A New Muslim Order: The Shia and the Middle East Sectarian Crisis* (London: I. B. Tauris, 2008), p. 17.

35. Juan Cole, "Shiite Religious Parties Fill Vacuum in Southern Iraq," Middle East Research and Information Project, 22 April 2003, http://www.merip.org/mero/mero042203

36. See, for example, Joel Roberts, "Triumphant Return of Shiite Leader," CBS News, 11 May 2003, http://www.cbsnews.com/news/triumphant-return-of-shiite-leader/; Associated Press, "Iraqi Opposition Leader Returns Home," *USA Today*, 10 May 2003, http://usatoday30.usatoday.com/news/world/iraq/2003-05-10-shiite-leader_x.htm; "Prominent Iraqi Shi'ite Leader Returns From Exile," *Irish Times*, 10 May 2003, http://www.irishtimes.com/news/prominent-iraqi-shi-ite-leader-returns-from-exile-1.476266

37. International Crisis Group, *The Next Iraqi War? Sectarianism and Civil Conflict*, Middle East Report 52 (Brussels: International Crisis Group, 27 February 2006), p. 29. The report adds: "Already in early 2004, a secular Shiite academic had told Crisis Group that at the end of day, confronted with the choice to vote for a secular or an overtly Shiite party, he would vote for the latter out of 'Shiite solidarity'—to ensure the realisation of the Shiite majority's dream of ruling Iraq." Ibid., p. 29, ftn. 204.

38. The argument commonly made by Sunni Arabs is that they constitute 42 percent of the Iraqi population, while the Shia account for 41 percent; hence, according to this logic, alongside the mostly Sunni Kurdish north, Iraq is a Sunni-majority country. Many Sunni figures have publicly stated their rejection of any notion that they are a numerical minority: from religious leaders such as Harith al-Dhari (former general secretary of the Association of Muslim Scholars); to politicians such as Khalaf al-Ulayan, Muhsin Abd al-Hamid (former head of the Iraqi Islamic Party), and Osama al-Nujaifi; to extremists such as Taha al-Dulaimi. In fact, as early as August 2003, Dulaimi was calling the idea that Sunnis are a minority a lie. See "Al Haqiqa: Awal Kitab Makhtoot an Ti'dad al Sunna wal Shia fil Iraq" [The Truth: The First Written Book on Sunni and Shia Enumeration in Iraq], October 2003, *Islam Memo*, http://www.islammemo.cc/2003/10/02/2626.html

39. Allawi, *The Occupation*, p. 136.

40. Harith al-Qarawee, "National Reconciliation and Negotiation: The Path Forward in Iraq and Syria: Panel 1," YouTube video, from the "National Reconciliation and Negotiation: The Path Forward in Iraq and Syria" event at School of Advanced International Studies, Johns Hopkins University, 15 December 2014, posted by "SAIS events," 16 December 2014, https://www.youtube.com/watch?v=Na5tfj OiB3M

41. Rayburn, *Iraq After America*, p. 130.

42. Initially there were two broad tendencies among Sunni Arabs: one that clung to the sect-averse political frames of reference of the pre-2003 world, and another that essentially tried to catch up with Shias in terms of building a politicized sectarian identity. Although this divergence still exists to some degree, the latter trend quickly gained ground, as evidenced by the December 2005 election in which the Sunni Islamist coalition, Tawafuq, secured the majority of Sunni seats. See International Crisis Group, *Make or Break*, p. 5; Wicken, *Iraq's Sunnis*, p. 36.

43. Benjamin Bahney, Patrick B. Johnston, and Patrick Ryan, "The Enemy You Know and the Ally You Don't," *Foreign Policy*, 23 June 2015, https://foreignpolicy.com/2015/06/23/the-enemy-you-know-and-the-ally-you-dont-arm-sunni-militias-iraq/

44. These paradoxes of Iraqi Sunni identity are discussed in more detail in Haddad, "A Sectarian Awakening," pp. 153–65.

45. This was particularly noticeable in 2009 (which incidentally was an election year). For example, see Ahed Wahid, "Suwar rijal al-din al-siyasiyin tufariq al-manazil wa al-sayarat" [Pictures of political religious figures leave houses and cars], *Al-Hayat*, 22 September 2009.

46. Writing in 2009, Reidar Visser provides an overview of the reasons for optimism and also why optimism needed to be cautious. Indeed, while the January 2009 election was largely peaceful, there were several instances of questionable electoral tactics, such as the use of de-Baathification to exclude rivals from the elections. See Reidar Visser, "Post-Sectarian Strategies for Iraq," Historiae.org, 18 March 2009, http://historiae.org/post-sectarian.asp

47. For an analysis of Maliki's second term and of Iraqi politics during that period, see Marc Lynch et al., *Iraq Between Maliki and the Islamic State*, POMEPS Briefing no. 24 (Washington: Project on Middle East Political Science, 9 July 2014), http://pomeps.org/wp-content/uploads/2014/07/POMEPS_BriefBooklet24_Iraq_Web.pdf

48. On the Hashd, see Fanar Haddad, "The Hashd: Redrawing the Military and Political Map of Iraq," Middle East Institute, 9 April 2015, http://www.mei.edu/content/article/hashd-redrawing-military-and-political-map-iraq. On Sistani's statement, see Luay Al Khatteeb and Abbas Kadhim, "What Do You Know About Sistani's Fatwa?", *Huffington Post*, 10 July 2014, http://www.huffingtonpost.com/luay-al-khatteeb/what-do-you-know-about-si_b_5576244.html

49. On the Hashd's impact on and possible role in politics, see Mustafa Habib, "The Next Rulers of Iraq?", *Niqash*, 30 July 2015, http://www.niqash.org/en/articles/politics/5067

50. For example, after the fall of Mosul, then speaker of parliament Osama al-Nujaifi used the term "revolution" (a term whose positive connotations imply legitimacy) to describe the renewed insurgency, while accepting that "terrorists are taking advantage of it." See Abigail Hauslohner, "Iraq's Crisis Won't be Resolved by Fighting, Sunni Leader Says," *Washington Post*, 12 July 2014, https://www.washingtonpost.com/news/worldviews/wp/2014/07/12/iraqs-crisis-wont-be-resolved-by-fighting-sunni-leader-says/. Similarly, the Mufti of Iraq, Sunni cleric Rafii al-Rifaii, rejected the label of "terrorist," referring instead to "rebels" or "revolutionaries"; see his comments to *Al-Taghyeer*, "Mufti Rafii al-Rifaii's response to Mahdi al Karbalais' statements," YouTube video, posted by "pressnews10," 14 June 2014, https://www.youtube.com/watch?v=kl9XO63TGAM

51. This view was widely shared across the Arab world: soon after news of Sistani's statements emerged, Twitter was awash with tweets carrying the hashtag "Sistani orders our death" (*al-Sistani yafti bi qatlina*).

52. One of the more widely publicized examples of this is Yazan al Jabouri, a Sunni Arab native of Salah al Din province who commands a unit of fellow Salah al Din locals in the Hashd. Noor Samaha, "Iraq's 'Good Sunni'" Foreign Policy, 16 November 2016, http://foreignpolicy.com/2016/11/16/iraqs-good-sunni/

6. THE UNRAVELING OF TAIF: THE LIMITS OF SECT-BASED POWER-SHARING IN LEBANON

1. Seats were reserved for Maronites, Greek Orthodox, and Greek Catholics (or Melkite Uniates) on the Christian side; and for Sunnis, Shia, and the Druze on the Muslim side.

2. See Carol Hakim, *The Origins of the Lebanese National Idea: 1840–1920* (Berkeley, CA: University of California Press, 2013).

3. The Arabic term for the relationship between Lebanonism and political Maronitism is *al-Maruniyya as-Siyassiyya*, coined by the late Lebanese intellectual Munah al-Solh, to designate a diffuse set of political attitudes and behaviors that Maronites displayed toward power and politics. With time, it came to designate the resulting domination that this led them to exercise over the apparatus of the state and a wide array of social and other political resources.

4. See Kamal Salibi, *A House of Many Mansions: The History of Lebanon Reconsidered* (Berkeley, CA: University of California Press, 1989).

5. During a parliamentary session in November 1943, Khoury and Solh made pledges regarding the way they envisaged governance of the country if it were to become independent. The National Pact's principles are found in the record of this legislative session.

6. Salibi, *A House of Many Mansions*.

7. Political sectarianism was not something in which to take pride, even by those who conceived it and have lauded it. That is why it has always been regarded as a temporary arrangement, and the necessity to move beyond it one day was viewed as a desirable objective. Article 95 of the Constitution (amended on 8 November 1943) regulates the distribution of cabinet seats and positions in the civil service by stating: "As a *provisional* measure, and in keeping with the desire for justice and harmony, the religious communities shall be adequately represented in the civil service and in the cabinet, *provided that it does not harm the interests of the state*" (emphasis added). See Theodor Hanf, *Coexistence in Wartime Lebanon: Decline of a State and Rise of a Nation* (London: I. B. Tauris, 1993), p. 72.

8. One of the founding figures of the school of consociational democracies is Arend Lijphart, author of *The Politics of Accommodation: Pluralism and Democracy in the Netherlands* (Berkeley, CA: University of California Press, 1968); "Consociational

Democracy," *World Politics*, vol. 21, no. 2 (1969); and *Democracy in Plural Societies* (New Haven, CT: Yale University Press, 1977).

9. Another condition for consociational democracies to function in a lasting way is one relating to intra-sectarian competition and politics.

10. The presidency of Fouad Chehab (1958–64), for example, was relatively transformational in terms of sectarian equilibrium and interaction as well as economic readjustment and distribution.

11. The first document addressing constitutional changes was the Constitutional Document (*Al-Wathiqa al-Dusturiyya*) in 1975. It was followed by draft documents published after a 1983 national dialogue conference in Geneva and one in Lausanne the following year. The same applies to the so-called Tripartite Agreement signed between the warring militias in Damascus in 1985.

12. The most powerful political proposal seeking fundamental change, put forth by a coalition of Muslim political forces, leftist political parties, and figures close to the Palestinian national movement, called for the abolition of political sectarianism, with the exception of the presidency of the republic, which was to be reserved for a Christian, though not necessarily a Maronite, and the post of prime minister for a Muslim, though not necessarily a Sunni.

13. See Hanf, *Coexistence in Wartime Lebanon*, p. 587.

14. The tentacular Syrian-Lebanese web of corruption was a crucial part of Lebanon's and Syria's political economies between 1992 and 2005. See Reinoud Leenders, *Spoils of Truce: Corruption and State-Building in Postwar Lebanon* (Ithaca, NY: Cornell University Press, 2012).

15. In addition to "Hanoi and Hong Kong," other metaphors were also used, such as Nadim Shehadi's reference to the "citadel" and "the Riviera," in "Riviera vs Citadel: The Battle for Lebanon," *openDemocracy*, 13 July 2007.

16. See Joseph Bahout, *Les entrepreneurs Syriens: économie, affaires et politique* [Syrian entrepreneurs: economics, business, and politics] (Beirut: CERMOC, 1994).

17. Nicholas Blanford, *Killing Mr. Lebanon: The Assassination of Rafik Hariri and its Impact on the Middle East* (London: I. B. Tauris, 2006).

18. See Joseph Bahout, "Liban-Syrie: Une alliance objective franco-américaine?" [Lebanon-Syria: A Franco-American alliance objective?], Paper presented at French Institute for International Relations conference, Paris, 5 September 2005.

19. See Nicholas Blanford, *Killing Mr. Lebanon*. Opponents of Syria regard Rafik Hariri's assassination as a joint Syrian-Hezbollah venture, with all the sectarian repercussions entailing from this.

20. Seth Wikas, "The Damascus-Hizballah Axis: Bashar al-Asad's Vision of a New Middle East," Washington Institute, 29 August 2006, http://www.washingtoninstitute.org/policy-analysis/view/the-damascus-hizballah-axis-bashar-al-asads-vision-of-a-new-middle-east

21. Nadim Ladki, "Clashes Bring Lebanon Death Toll to 81," *Mail and Guardian*,

12 May 2008, http://mg.co.za/article/2008-05-12-clashes-bring-lebanon-death-toll-to-81

22. Hilal Khashan, "The Rise and Growth of Hezbollah and the Militarization of the Sunni-Shiite Divide in Lebanon," Middle East Institute, 26 January 2016, http://www.mei.edu/content/map/rise-and-growth-hezbollah-and-militarization-sunni-shi%E2%80%99-divide-lebanon; and Michael Young, "The Consequences of a Hezbollah-Led Opposition Victory in Lebanon's Elections," interview by Bernard Gwertzman, Council on Foreign Relations, 28 May 2009, http://www.cfr.org/lebanon/consequences-hezbollah-led-opposition-victory-lebanons-elections/p19512

23. The term *aqalliyyat* is now flourishing. It both denotes a feeling of demographic, and therefore political, decline; and signals an implicit call for protection, something the international community, whether in Syria or Iraq, has echoed and reinforced.

24. Two sarcastic Lebanese terms, "Shia Christians" and "Sunni Christians," have been used to describe the polarization and alignment of what is supposed to be still, at best, a community making up "half" of the political system, but already melting, politically at least, into the agendas of the principal Muslim sects.

25. The Arab Awakening was the intellectual, and later political, tradition that developed in Mount Lebanon, then a part of Bilad al-Sham, and in Egypt at the turn of the nineteenth century. The Arab Awakening strived for an Arab Renaissance.

26. "And Then There Were None," *Economist*, 2 January 2016, http://www.economist.com/news/middle-east-and-africa/21684795-fed-up-and-fearful-christians-are-leaving-middle-east-and-then-there-were

27. See Perry Anderson, "The Antinomies of Antonio Gramsci," *New Left Review*, vol. 1, no. 100 (November–December 1976), pp. 5–78.

7. TWITTER WARS: SUNNI-SHIA CONFLICT AND COOPERATION IN THE DIGITAL AGE

1. Aaron Zelin and Phillip Smyth, "The Vocabulary of Sectarianism," *Foreign Policy*, 29 January 2014, http://foreignpolicy.com/2014/01/29/the-vocabulary-of-sectarianism/

2. Geneive Abdo, *The New Sectarianism: The Arab Uprisings and the Rebirth of the Shi'a-Sunni Divide* (Washington, DC: Saban Center for Middle East Policy, Brookings Institution, April 2013), http://www.brookings.edu/~/media/research/files/papers/2013/04/sunni%20Shi'a%20abdo/sunni%20Shi'a%20abdo; Aya Batrawy, "Saudi-Iran Rivalry Over Yemen Deepens Mideast Sectarianism," *Yahoo! News*, 16 April 2015, http://news.yahoo.com/saudi-iran-rivalry-over-yemen-deepens-mideast-sectarianism-172524040.html

3. Abdo, *New Sectarianism*; Geneive Abdo, *Salafists and Sectarianism: Twitter and Communal Conflict in the Middle East* (Washington, DC: Saban Center for Middle

East Policy, Brookings Institution, March 2015), http://www.brookings.edu/~/
media/research/files/papers/2015/03/26-sectarianism-salafism-social-media-
abdo/abdo-paper_final_web.pdf; Batrawy, "Saudi-Iran Rivalry."

4. Ronald Deibert, John Palfrey, Rafal Rohozinski, and Jonathan Zittrain, eds, *Access Controlled: The Shaping of Power, Rights, and Rule in Cyberspace* (Cambridge, MA: MIT Press, 2010), p. 43.

5. Frederic Wehrey, *Sectarian Politics in the Gulf: From the Iraq War to the Arab Uprisings* (New York: Columbia University Press, 2013).

6. Twitter search: #,»‰_«Ê_·Ã—_Ê·", https://twitter.com/search?q=%23%D9
%82%D8%A8%D9%84_%D8%A7%D9%86_%D8%AA%D9%81%D8%AC%
D8%B1_%D9%86%D9%81%D8%B3%D9%83, conducted on 8 August 2015.

7. Ruth Sherlock and Louisa Loveluck, "Warnings of Bloody Sectarian Conflict as Shia Militias Fight Back Against ISIL in Ramadi," *Daily Telegraph*, 26 May 2015, http://www.telegraph.co.uk/news/worldnews/islamic-state/11631595/
Warnings-of-bloody-sectarian-conflict-as-Shia-militias-fight-back-against-Isil-in-
Ramadi.html

8. Unless otherwise cited, all tweets referenced in the remainder of this paper are taken from the data set of 7 million Arabic tweets collected between 3 February and 17 August 2015, through NYU's Social Media and Political Participation (SMaPP) lab. Because these tweets were collected using Twitter's Streaming API, stored in a MongoDB database, and then filtered and aggregated into one data set, links to individual tweets are not available. For a more complete description of the data collection and processing, see the SMaPP Lab's documentation at: https://github.com/SMAPPNYU/smapp-toolkit

9. Abdo, *Salafists and Sectarianism*; Zelin and Smyth, "Vocabulary."

10. @abdulaziztarefe: https://twitter.com/abdulaziztarefe?lang=en

11. @abdall7aliali5: https://twitter.com/account/suspended

12. @moonor27: https://twitter.com/moonnor27/

13. @thebahraini: https://twitter.com/thebahraini

14. Abdo, *Salafists and Sectarianism*; Zelin and Smyth, "Vocabulary."

15. @akramiraq007: https://twitter.com/akramiraq007.

16. @suuigff: https://twitter.com/suuiigff.

17. Twitter search: #,»‰_«Ê_·Ã—_Ê·", https://twitter.com/search?q=%23%D9
%82%D8%A8%D9%84_%D8%A7%D9%86_%D8%AA%D9%81%D8%AC%
D8%B1_%D9%86%D9%81%D8%B3%D9%83, conducted on 5 August 2015.

18. @falarbash: https://twitter.com/falarbash.

19. The exact keywords used to filter the data set are listed in Appendix A.

20. Yabing Liu, Chloe Kliman-Silver, and Alan Mislove, "'The Tweets They Are a-Changin': Evolution of Twitter Users and Behavior" (8th International AAAI Conference on Weblogs and Social Media, Ann Arbor, MI, 2014), http://www.
aaai.org/ocs/index.php/ICWSM/ICWSM14/paper/viewFile/8043/8131

21. "Social Networking Popular Across Globe," Pew Global Research Center,

12 December 2012, http://www.pewglobal.org/2012/12/12/social-networking-popular-across-globe/

22. Racha Mourtada and Fadi Salem, "The Arab Social Media Report 2014," Mohammed Bin Rashid School of Government, Governance and Innovation Program, March 2014, http://www.mbrsg.ae/getattachment/e9ea2ac8–13dd-4cd7-9104-b8f1f405cab3/Citizen-Engagement-and-Public-Services-in-the-Arab.aspx

23. Abdo, *Salafists and Sectarianism*.

24. Ahmed Al-Haj and Hamza Hendawi, "Turmoil in Yemen Escalates as Saudi Arabia Bombs Rebels," *Yahoo! News*, 26 March 2015, http://news.yahoo.com/saudi-air-strikes-targeting-rebel-military-bases-yemen-062700530.html

25. Bader al-Rashed, "Saudi Elites Divided on Yemen War," *Al-Monitor*, 21 April 2015, http://www.al-monitor.com/pulse/originals/2015/04/saudi-arabia-elite-yemen-operation-decisive-storm.html

26. Batrawy, "Saudi-Iran Rivalry"; Frederic Wehrey, "Into the Maelstrom: The Saudi-Led Misadventure in Yemen," *Syria in Crisis* (blog), Carnegie Endowment for International Peace, 26 March 2015, http://carnegieendowment.org/syriaincrisis/?fa=59500

27. Giorgio Cafiero and Daniel Wagner, "Yemen Conflict Raises Sectarian Temperatures Across the Gulf," *LobeLog*, 4 July 2015, http://www.lobelog.com/yemen-conflict-raises-sectarian-temperatures-across-the-gulf/

28. Batrawy, "Saudi-Iran Rivalry."

29. Madeleine Wells, "Sectarianism and Authoritarianism in Kuwait," *Monkey Cage* (blog), *Washington Post*, 13 April 2015, http://www.washingtonpost.com/blogs/monkey-cage/wp/2015/04/13/sectarianism-and-authoritarianism-in-kuwait/

30. Arabic Network for Human Rights Information, "Bahrain: Renewing Incarceration of Human Rights Defender 'Nabeel Rajab' is Flagrant Violation of International Charters, ANHRI Says," ANHRI Statement, 26 April 2015, http://anhri.net/?p=143741&lang=en

31. William Maclean, "Saudi Arabia Says Military Push Will Last Until Yemen Stable," Reuters, 31 March 2015, http://www.reuters.com/article/2015/03/31/us-yemen-security-saudi-minister-idUSKBN0MR0TP20150331#tL0Uxv1srGtB6RBG.97

32. Batrawy, "Saudi-Iran Rivalry."

33. @naseralomar: Twitter status from 14 April 2015, https://twitter.com/naseralomar/status/587890310832754689

34. @naseralomar: Twitter status from 14 April 2015, https://twitter.com/naseralomar/status/588019475603132420

35. Brian Murphy, "Saudi Shiites Worry About Backlash From Yemen War," *Washington Post*, 8 April 2015, https://www.washingtonpost.com/world/middle_east/saudi-shiites-worry-about-backlash-from-yemen-war/2015/04/07/10b01be2-dc7e-11e4-b6d7-b9bc8acf16f7_story.html

36. Ibid.

37. Saif Hameed, "Iraqi Forces Slowed by Snipers and Bombs in Tikrit," Reuters, 12 March 2015, http://www.reuters.com/article/2015/03/12/us-mideast-crisis-iraq-idUSKBN0M810X20150312; "Iraq Tikrit: Looting and Lawlessness Follow Recapture," BBC World News, 4 April 2015, http://www.bbc.com/news/world-middle-east-32181503

38. Michael Weiss and Michael Pregent, "The United States is Providing Air Cover for Ethnic Cleansing in Iraq," *Foreign Policy*, 28 March 2015, http://foreignpolicy.com/2015/03/28/the-united-states-is-providing-air-cover-for-ethnic-cleansing-in-iraq-shiite-militias-isis/; Anne Barnard, "Iraqi Campaign to Drive ISIS from Tikrit Reveals Tensions with U.S.," *New York Times*, 4 March 2015, http://www.nytimes.com/2015/03/04/world/middleeast/iraq-drive-against-isis-reveals-tensions-with-us.html

39. Ben Wedeman and Laura Smith-Spark, "Iraqi Forces Push Toward Tikrit as They Seek to Dislodge ISIS," CNN, 4 March 2015, http://www.cnn.com/2015/03/04/middleeast/iraq-tikrit-battle/

40. @ahlulbayt_says: https://twitter.com/ahlulbayt_says

41. "Syrian Rebels Capture Border Crossing with Jordan," Voice of America News, 2 April 2015, http://www.voanews.com/content/syrian-rebels-nusra-front-capture-jordan-border-crossing/2703815.html

42. "Iraqi Forces Make Gains Against ISIS in Key Town of Ramadi," *Huffington Post*, 22 April 2015, http://www.huffingtonpost.com/2015/04/22/iraq-isis-ramadi_n_7118088.html

43. Juan Cole, "Shiite Militias Announce 'Here I Am, O Husayn' Campaign for Sunni Ramadi," *Informed Comment* (blog), 27 May 2015, http://www.juancole.com/2015/05/militias-announce-campaign.html

44. Ben Hubbard, "Grisly ISIS Video Seems Aimed at Quashing Resistance," *New York Times*, 23 June 2015, http://www.nytimes.com/2015/06/24/world/middleeast/grisly-isis-video-seems-aimed-at-quashing-resistance.html

45. @ab_krar: https://twitter.com/ab_krar

46. "ISIL Claims Responsibility for Saudi Mosque Attack," Al Jazeera, 23 May 2015, http://www.aljazeera.com/news/2015/05/saudi-Shia-mosque-suicide-bomb-150522101–150522131614062.html

47. "Deaths in Blast Near Shia Mosque in Saudi City," Al Jazeera, 30 May 2015, http://www.aljazeera.com/news/2015/05/deadly-car-explosion-Shia-mosque-saudi-arabia-dammam-150529102343732.html

48. Angus McDowall, "Attacks on Shi'ites Create Pivotal Moment for Saudi State," *Yahoo! News*, 4 June 2015, http://news.yahoo.com/attacks-shiites-create-pivotal-moment-saudi-state-140600002.html

49. Colin Freeman and Andrew Marszal, "At Least 142 Killed in 'Isil' Bombings of Yemen Shia Mosques," *Daily Telegraph*, 20 March 2015, http://www.telegraph.

co.uk/news/worldnews/middleeast/yemen/11485080/Dozens-killed-in-Yemen-Shia-mosque-bombings.html

50. Freeman and Marszal, "142 Killed."

51. "ISIL Claims Responsibility for Kuwait Shia Mosque Blast," Al Jazeera, 27 June 2015, http://www.aljazeera.com/news/2015/06/isil-claim-responsibility-kuwait-Shia-mosque-attack-150626124555564.html

52. Lora Moftah, "Shiite Mosque Attack: Kuwait Engulfed in Regional Sectarianism with Suicide Attack Against Minority Sect," *International Business Times*, 26 June 2015, http://www.ibtimes.com/shiite-mosque-attack-kuwait-engulfed-regional-sectarianism-suicide-attack-against-1986143

53. Robert Hatem and Derek Gildea, "Kuwaiti Shi'a: Government Policies, Societal Cleavages, and the Non-Factor of Iran" (IMES Capstone Paper Series, Elliot School of International Affairs Institute for Middle East Studies, George Washington University, May 2011), https://imes.elliott.gwu.edu/sites/imes.elliott.gwu.edu/files/downloads/documents/Capstone-Papers-2011/Gildea%20Hatem.pdf

54. This network (as well as the networks in Figures 6 and 7) was created with Gephi, an interactive network visualization program, using a force-directed layout algorithm.

55. The ring of very small dots around the outside is unconnected to the core of the network and represents people who tweeted messages that contained anti-Shia keywords and were retweeted, but not by anyone in the core of the network. Additionally, these people did not retweet anything from anyone inside the core during the period under study.

56. Erin Saltman and Charlie Winter, *Islamic State: The Changing Face of Modern Jihadism* (London: Quilliam Foundation, November 2014), http://www.quilliamfoundation.org/wp/wp-content/uploads/publications/free/islamic-state-the-changing-face-of-modern-jihadism.pdf

57. @saudalshureem: https://twitter.com/saudalshureem; @abdulaziztarefe: https://twitter.com/abdulaziztarefe; @naseralomar: https://twitter.com/naseralomar;@mohamedalarefe: https://twitter.com/mohamadalarefe

58. @wesal_tv: https://twitter.com/wesal_tv; @safa_tv: https://twitter.com/safa_tv

59. @dr_khalidalsaud: https://twitter.com/dr_khalidalsaud

60. @AlkamiK: https://twitter.com/alkamiK

61. @BANDR_ALRAJHI: https://twitter.com/bandr_alrajhi

62. @Savafi_risks: http://twitter.com/savafi_risks; @risks_IR: http://twitter.com/savafi_risks; @bo_khaled100: https://twitter.com/bo_khaled100

63. @sul535: https://twitter.com/sul535

64. @adnaan_aa: https://twitter.com/adnaaan_aa

65. @KazrajSamar: https://twitter.com/KazrajSamar

66. @hassansharif50: https://twitter.com/hassansharif50

67. @kuwlawyer: https://twitter.com/kuwlawyer
68. @abo_ahmad_al_fh: https://twitter.com/abo_ahmad_al_fh/
69. @yahtadon: https://twitter.com/yahtadon
70. @Liberalih: https://twitter.com/liberalih
71. @ddsunnah: https://twitter.com/ddsunnah
72. @heekmmm: https://twitter.com/heekmmm
73. @vipwaffa: https://twitter.com/vipwafaa
74. "A Week After Kuwait Bombing, Sunnis and Shi'ites Pray Together for Unity," Reuters, 3 July 2015, http://www.reuters.com/article/2015/07/03/us-gulf-security-idUSKCN0PD1JX20150703
75. @princess_2882: https://twitter.com/princess_2882
76. https://marcowenjones.wordpress.com/2016/06/21/the-automation-of-sectarianism/

8. THE POLITICAL ECONOMY OF SECTARIANISM: HOW GULF REGIMES EXPLOIT IDENTITY POLITICS AS A SURVIVAL STRATEGY

1. According to the Saudi Interior Ministry, quoted in "Saudi Arabia executes 47 on terrorism charges," Al Jazeera English, 2 January 2006, http://www.aljazeera.com/news/2016/01/saudi-announces-execution-47-terrorists-160102072458873.html
2. "Saudi Arabia: Appalling death sentence against Shi'a cleric must be quashed," Amnesty International, 15 October 2014, https://www.amnesty.org/en/latest/news/2014/10/saudi-arabia-appalling-death-sentence-against-shi-cleric-must-be-quashed/
3. Quoted in "Iran: Saudis face 'divine revenge' for executing al-Nimr," BBC News, 3 January 2016, http://www.bbc.com/news/world-middle-east-35216694
4. "Saudi Arabia hikes petrol prices by 40% at the pump," Al Jazeera English, 28 December 2015, http://www.aljazeera.com/news/2015/12/saudi-arabia-hikes-petrol-prices-40-pump-151228154350415.html
5. Justin Gengler and Laurent A. Lambert, "Renegotiating the Ruling Bargain: Selling Fiscal Reform in the GCC," Middle East Journal, vol. 70, no. 2 (2016), pp. 321–9.
6. Max Fischer, "The cold war between Saudi Arabia and Iran that's tearing apart the Middle East, explained," Vox, 4 January 2016, http://www.vox.com/2016/1/4/10708682/sunni-shia-iran-saudi-arabia-war
7. Larry Potter, ed., Sectarian Politics in the Persian Gulf (London/New York: Hurst/Oxford University Press, 2014); Frederic Wehrey, Sectarian Politics in the Gulf: From the Iraq War to the Arab Uprisings (New York: Columbia University Press, 2013); Toby Matthiesen, Sectarian Gulf: Bahrain, Saudi Arabia, and the Arab Spring That Wasn't (Palo Alto, CA: Stanford University Press, 2013); Steven Heydemann, "Syria and the Future of Authoritarianism," Journal of Democracy, vol. 24, no. 4 (2013), pp. 59–73.

8. Daniel Brumberg, "Transforming the Arab World's Protection-Racket Politics," *Journal of Democracy*, vol. 24, no. 3 (2013), pp. 88–103.

9. Galal Amin, *The Modernization of Poverty, A Study in the Political Economy of Growth in Nine Arab Countries, 1945–70* (Leiden: Brill, 1974), pp. 49–50, quoted in Dirk Vandewalle, "The Rentier State in the Arab World," in Giacomo Luciani, ed., *The Rentier State: Nation, State and Integration in the Arab World*, Vol. 2 (London: Routledge, 1987).

10. Hossein Mahdavy, "Patterns and Problems of Economic Development in Rentier States: The Case of Iran," in M. A. Cook, ed., *Studies in the Economic History of the Middle East: From the Rise of Islam to the Present Day* (London: Oxford University Press, 1970), pp. 428–67.

11. On monarchism, see Michael C. Hudson, *Arab Politics: The Search for Legitimacy* (New Haven, CT: Yale University Press, 1977); Daniel Brumberg, "Sustaining Mechanics of Arab Autocracies," *Foreign Policy*, 19 December 2011; Victor Menaldo, "The Middle East and North Africa's Resilient Monarchs," *Journal of Politics*, vol. 74, no. 3 (2012), pp. 707–22; Sean L. Yom and F. Gregory Gause III, "Resilient Royals: How Arab Monarchies Hang On," *Journal of Democracy*, vol. 23, no. 4 (2012), pp. 74–88; F. Gregory Gause III, "Kings for All Seasons: How the Middle East's Monarchies Survived the Arab Spring," Brookings Doha Center Analysis Paper No. 8, September 2013.

On Islam, see Ronald Inglehart and Pippa Norris, "Islamic Culture and Democracy: Testing the 'Clash of Civilizations' Thesis," *Comparative Sociology*, vol. 1, no. 3 (2002), pp. 235–63; M. Steven Fish, "Islam and Authoritarianism," *World Politics*, vol. 55, no. 1 (2002), pp. 4–37; Daniela Donno and Bruce Russett, "Islam, Authoritarianism, and Female Empowerment: What are the linkages?" *World Politics*, vol. 56, no. 4 (2002), pp. 582–607.

On the ruling family, see Michael Herb, *All in the Family: Absolutism, Revolution, and Democracy in the Middle Eastern Monarchies* (Albany, NY: State University of New York Press, 1999).

On tribal custom, see Katja Niethammer, "Persian Gulf States," in Ellen Lust, ed., *The Middle East*, 13th edn (Los Angeles, CA: CQ Press, 2013), pp. 717–45; and the arguments of former Qatari prime minister Sh. Hamad bin Jassim Al Thani, reported in Habib Toumi, "Reforms best way to avoid uprisings, Qatar premier says," *Gulf News*, 11 November 2011.

On arts, culture, and education, see Alanoud Alsharekh and Robert Springborg, eds, *Popular Culture and Political Identity in the Arab Gulf States* (London: Saqi Books, 2008); Miriam Cooke, *Tribal Modern: Branding New Nations in the Arab Gulf* (Berkeley, CA: University of California Press, 2014).

On international prestige, see Mehran Kamrava, *Qatar: Small State, Big Politics* (Ithaca, NY: Cornell University Press, 2013); David Roberts, *Qatar: Securing the Global Ambitions of a City-State* (London: Hurst & Co., 2017).

12. Justin Gengler, "Understanding Sectarianism in the Persian Gulf," in Potter, ed., *Sectarian Politics in the Persian Gulf.*

13. In this sense, the electoral reforms that took effect in 2012 can be seen as aiming, ironically, to encourage rather than stifle the emergence of programmatic coalitions—at least in tribal-dominated districts. Kuwait's earlier parliamentary engineering worked only *too* well.

14. Bethany Shockley and Justin Gengler, "Qualification or Affiliation? Determinants of Candidate Evaluations among Arab Voters," Paper presented at the Annual Meeting of the American Political Science Association, Philadelphia, 1–4 September 2016.

15. Bahrain actively recruits Arab and non-Arab Sunnis for police and military service, and more generally as a demographic hedge against its indigenous Shia majority.

16. Anh Nga Longva, "Nationalism in Pre-modern Guise: The Discourse on *Hadhar* and *Bedu* in Kuwait," *International Journal of Middle East Studies*, vol. 38, no. 2 (2006), pp. 171–87.

17. Justin Gengler, "Royal Factionalism, the Khawālid, and the Securitization of 'the Shī'a Problem' in Bahrain," *Journal of Arabian Studies*, vol. 3, no. 1 (2013), pp. 53–79.

18. Madawi Al-Rasheed, "How united is the GCC?", *Al-Monitor*, 3 April 2015, http://www.al-monitor.com/pulse/originals/2016/04/gulf-nationalism-regime-survival-saudi-qatar-uae.html

19. Habib Toumi, "Saudi Mufti calls for mandatory military service," *Gulf News*, 11 April 2015, http://gulfnews.com/news/gulf/saudi-arabia/saudi-mufti-calls-for-mandatory-military-service-1.1489839

20. Leila Hatoum, "All the Kings' Men," *Newsweek Middle East*, 12 November 2015, http://newsweekme.com/all-the-kings-men/

21. Al-Rasheed, "How united is the GCC?"

22. Gengler and Lambert, "Renegotiating the Ruling Bargain."

23. "Transcript: Interview with Muhammad bin Salman," *Economist*, 6 January 2016, http://www.economist.com/saudi_interview

24. Quoted in Gengler and Lambert, "Renegotiating the Ruling Bargain."

25. Adam Bouyamourn, "Get ready for taxes, Christine Lagarde tells UAE and other Gulf nations," *The National*, 22 February 2016, http://www.thenational.ae/business/economy/get-ready-for-taxes-christine-lagarde-tells-uae-and-other-gulf-nations

26. In the Kuwait and Qatar surveys, the sequence of these response options was randomized to avoid ordering effects. The Oman survey was administered by paper-and-pencil and thus could not implement randomization.

27. Mark Tessler, Amaney Jamal, Abdallah Bedaida, Mhammed Abderebbi, Khalil Shikaki, Fares Braizat, Justin Gengler, and Michael Robbins, *Arab Barometer:*

Public Opinion Survey Conducted in Algeria, Morocco, Jordan, Lebanon, Palestine, Yemen, and Bahrain 2006–2009, ICPSR26581-v4 (Ann Arbor, MI: Interuniversity Consortium for Political and Social Research [distributor], 2016). Data available at http://www.icpsr.umich.edu/icpsrweb/ICPSR/studies/26581

28. One might wonder whether this result is partially or mainly an artifact of a selection effect, whereby respondents who cite stability as their top national goal are disproportionately well-off economically, since poorer and/or less economically satisfied citizens will naturally be more likely to choose "boosting economic development." In fact, however, the highest correlation between stability preferences and economic status (as measured by reported household income) is a mere 0.08 in the case of Kuwait.

29. Justin Gengler, "Bahrain's Sunni Awakening," Middle East Research and Information Project, 17 January 2012.

30. Justin Gengler, "Sectarian Backfire? Assessing Gulf Political Strategy Five Years after the Arab Uprisings," Middle East Institute, 17 November 2015.

31. This contrast has been noted, though not specifically treated, by Kristin Smith Diwan. See, e.g., Kristin Smith Diwan, "Bahrain Faces Austerity, Without Protest," Arab Gulf States Institute in Washington, 20 April 2016; and Courtney Freer, "Kuwait Oil Workers' Strike: Domestic and Market Reactions," Arab Gulf States Institute in Washington, 21 April 2016.

32. Personal interview, former Bahraini member of parliament, Doha, May 2016.

33. Ibid.

34. Habib Toumi, "Bahrain MPs ban mixing of politics and religion," *Gulf News*, 18 May 2016, http://gulfnews.com/news/gulf/bahrain/bahrain-mps-ban-mixing-of-politics-and-religion-1.1830097

35. "MOI warns against division, sedition," Bahrain News Agency, 26 March 2015, http://www.bna.bh/portal/en/news/660794

9. THE ROOTS OF SECTARIAN LAW AND ORDER IN THE GULF: BAHRAIN, THE EASTERN PROVINCE OF SAUDI ARABIA, AND THE TWO HISTORICAL DISRUPTIONS

1. Egon Bittner, *The Functions of the Police in Modern Society* (Cambridge, MA: Oelgeschlager, Gunn & Hain, 1970/1979), p. 30.

2. Robert Reiner, *The Politics of the Police* (Brighton: Wheatsheaf, 1985).

3. Jean-Paul Brodeur, *The Policing Web* (New York: Oxford University Press, 2010).

4. Ibrahim Sharif, "A trial of thoughts and ideas," in Ala'a Shehabi and Marc Owen Jones, eds, *Bahrain's Uprising: Resistance and Repression in the Gulf* (London: Zed Books, 2015), pp. 43–60; Staci Strobl, "Policing the Eastern Province of Saudi Arabia: Understanding the role of sectarian history and politics," *Policing and Society* (2015), http://www.tandfonline.com/doi/abs/10.1080/10439463.2014.989153

?journalCode=gpas20; Frederic M. Wehrey, *Sectarian Politics in the Gulf: From the Iraq War to the Arab Uprisings* (New York: Columbia University Press, 2013); Toby Matthiesen, *Sectarian Gulf: Bahrain, Saudi Arabia, and the Arab Spring that Wasn't* (Stanford CA: Stanford University Press, 2013); Staci Strobl, "From Colonial Policing to Community Policing in Bahrain: The Historical Persistence of Sectarianism," *International Journal of Comparative and Applied Criminal Justice*, vol. 35, no. 1 (2011), pp. 19–37; Vali Nasr, *The Shia Revival: How Conflicts Within Islam Will Shape the Future* (New York: W. W. Norton & Co., 2006).

5. Hala Al-Dosari, "Sending a Message to Saudi Shia," *Sada*, Carnegie Endowment for International Peace, 5 November 2015, http://carnegieendowment.org/sada/?fa=61878; International Crisis Group, *Popular Protests in North Africa and the Middle East (III)*, 6 April 2011, http://www.crisisgroup.org/en/regions/middle-east-north-africa/iraq-iran-gulf/bahrain/105-popular-protests-in-north-africa-and-the-middle-east-iii-the-bahrain-revolt.aspx; Sean Foley, *The Arab Gulf States: Beyond Oil and Islam* (Boulder, CO: Lynne Reinter Publishers, 2010); Vali Nasr, *The Shia Revival: How Conflicts Within Islam Will Shape the Future* (New York: W. W. Norton & Co., 2006).

6. Al-Dosari, "Sending a Message to Saudi Shia"; Marc Owen Jones, "Rotten Apples or Rotten Orchards: Police deviance, brutality and unaccountability in Bahrain," in Ala'a Shehabi and Marc Owen Jones, eds, *Bahrain's Uprising: Resistance and Repression in the Gulf* (London: Zed Books, 2015), pp. 207–38; Bahrain Independent Commission of Inquiry, *Report of the Bahrain Independent Commission of Inquiry*, 23 November 2011, http://www.bici.org.bh/BICIreport EN.pdf; Brian Dooley (with Staci Strobl), "Four Years On, U.S Should Push Bahrain to Reform Security Forces," *Huffington Post*, 13 February 2015, http://www.huffingtonpost.com/brian-dooley/four-years-on-us-should-p_b_6680326.html

7. Zainab Al-Khawaja, "Bahrain, a Brutal Ally," *New York Times*, 25 December 2012, https://www.questia.com/newspaper/1P2-36296158/bahrain-a-brutal-ally; Human Rights Watch, "Saudi Arabia: 5-Year Sentence for Rights Defender: Increasing Crackdowns on Activists," 23 June 2013, https://www.hrw.org/news/2013/06/22/saudi-arabia-5-year-sentence-rights-defender

8. See Toby Matthiesen, *The Other Saudis: Shiism, Dissent and Sectarianism* (New York: Cambridge University Press, 2015), for a study of the Shia of Saudia Arabia as a long-standing internal "other," who at times, including contemporary ones, have been constructed as an "enemy within" (p. 23).

9. Wehrey, *Sectarian Politics in the Gulf*.

10. Charles Tilly, "War Making and State Making as Organized Crime," in P. Evans, D. Rueschmeyer, and T. Skocpol, eds, *Bringing the State Back In* (Cambridge: Cambridge University Press, 1985), pp. 169–87.

11. William Sewell, *Logics of History: Social Theory and Social Transformation* (Chicago: University of Chicago Press, 2005).

12. Gayatri Chakravorty Spivak, *A Critique of Postcolonial Reason: Toward a History of the Vanishing Present* (Cambridge, MA: Harvard University Press, 1999); Homi K. Bhabha, *The Location of Culture* (New York: Routledge); Partha Chatterjee, *Nationalist Thought and the Colonial World: A Derivative Discourse* (London: Zed Books, 1986).

13. Frederick Anscombe, "The Ottoman Role in the Gulf," in Lawrence G. Potter, ed., *The Persian Gulf in History* (London: Palgrave Macmillan, 2009), pp. 261–76.

14. Edward Said, *Culture and Imperialism* (London: Vintage Books, 1993); Spivak, *A Critique of Postcolonial Reason.*

15. Gayatri Chakravorty Spivak, "World Systems and the Creole," *Narrative*, vol. 14, no. 6 (2006), pp. 102–12.

16. M. Rheda Bhaker, "The Cultural Unity of the Gulf and the Indian Ocean: A *Longue Durée* Historical Perspective," in Potter, ed., *The Persian Gulf in History*, pp. 163–72.

17. Lawrence G. Potter, "Introduction," in Potter, ed., *The Persian Gulf in History* pp. 1–26.

18. Dionysius Agius, *Seafaring in the Arabian Gulf and Oman: People of the Dhow* (London: Routledge, 2005).

19. William O. Beeman "The Zar in the Persian Gulf: Performative Dimensions," *Anthropology of the Contemporary Middle East and Central Eurasia*, vol. 3, no. 1 (2015), pp. 1–12.

20. Agius, *Seafaring in the Arabian Gulf and Oman.*

21. Abdul Sheriff, *Dhow Culture of the Indian Ocean: Cosmopolitanism, Commerce and Islam* (New York: Columbia University Press, 2010).

22. Toby Matthiesen, "Shi'i Historians in a Wahhabi State: Identity Entrepreneurs and the Politics of Local Historiography in Saudi Arabia," *International Journal of Middle East Studies*, vol. 47, no. 1 (2015), p. 31.

23. Nelida Fuccaro, *Histories of City and State in the Persian Gulf, Manama since 1800* (Cambridge: Cambridge University Press, 2009), pp. 117–20.

24. Reidar Visser, "Britain in Basra: Past Experiences and Current Challenges," 11 July 2006, http://historiae.org/cosmopolitanism.asp

25. Sir Charles Belgrave, *Personal Column* (London: Hutchinson, 1960).

26. Potter, ed., *The Persian Gulf in History*; Agius, *Seafaring in the Arabian Gulf and Oman.*

27. Peter Lienhardt, *Shaikhdoms of Eastern Arabia* (New York: Palgrave, 2001).

28. Potter, ed., *The Persian Gulf in History*; James Onley, *The Arabian Frontier of the British Raj* (Oxford: Oxford University Press, 2007).

29. H. R. P. Dickson, *The Arab of the Desert: A Glimpse into Badawin Life in Kuwait and Saudi Arabia* (London: George Allen & Unwin Ltd, 1949).

30. Anscombe, "The Ottoman Role in the Gulf."

31. Lienhardt, *Shaikhdoms of Eastern Arabia.*

32. Fuad Khuri, *Tribe and State in Bahrain* (Chicago: Chicago University Press, 1980).

33. James Onley and Suleyman Khalaf, "Shaikly Authority in the Pre-oil Gulf: An Historical-anthropological Study," History and Anthropology, vol. 17, no. 3 (2006).

34. Lienhardt, *Shaikhdoms of Eastern Arabia*.

35. N. Yassine, "Arab Political Dispute Resolution," Doctoral dissertation, Detroit, MI: Wayne State University (1999), p. 7.

36. Faoud Ibrahim, *The Shi'is of Saudi Arabia* (London: Saqi Books, 2006).

37. Frank Anscombe, *The Ottoman Gulf: The creation of Kuwait, Saudi Arabia and Qatar* (New York: Columbia University Press, 1997). It should be noted here, however, that not all branches of the Bani Khalid were anti-Shia. Some parts of the Bani Khalid converted to Shiism, and they are depicted positively in Shia historical narratives. See Matthiesen, "Shi'i Historians in a Wahhabi State," p. 33.

38. Wehrey, *Sectarian Politics in the Gulf*; Fuccaro, *Histories of City and State in the Persian Gulf*, pp. 20–24.

39. Lienhardt, *Shaikhdoms of Eastern Arabia*.

40. Mahdi Abdall Al-Tajir, *Bahrain 1920–1945: Britain, the Shaikh and the Administration* (London: Croom Helm, 1987), p. 2.

41. Fuccaro, *Histories of City and State in the Persian Gulf*, pp. 20–24.

42. Major Clive Daly, "Note on the Political Situation in Bahrain," Report to Political Residency, India Office Records, British Library, 15/2/131, 1921.

43. Despatch no. 90, C. A. Gault to Selwyn Lloyd, Papers of Charles Dalrymple Belgrave, 1926–1947, University of Exeter, 148/2/1, 1956.

44. Confidential Report no. 28/c by Major Clive Daly to the Political Residency, India Office Records, British Library, 15/2/131, 11 February 1923.

45. Letter, 15 June 1923, Political Resident Stuart Knox to King Abdul Aziz Ibn Saud, explaining British policy in the Gulf: Papers of Charles Dalrymple Belgrave, 1926–1947, University of Exeter, 148/2/2.

46. Sir Denys Bray, Foreign Secretary to the Government of India, "Notes on Reforms in Bahrain," India Office Records, British Library, 15/2/131, 6 November 1927.

47. Fuccaro, *Histories of City and State in the Persian Gulf*, pp. 53–5.

48. Al-Tajir, *Bahrain 1920–1945*, p. 57.

49. Madawi Al-Rasheed, *A History of Saudi Arabia* (Cambridge: Cambridge University Press, 2002/2010), pp. 2–3.

50. Glen Balfour-Paul, *The End of Empire in the Middle East: Britain's Relinquishment of Power in its Last Three Arab Dependencies* (Cambridge: Cambridge University Press, 1991).

51. Fuccaro, *Histories of City and State in the Persian Gulf*, p. 55.

52. Letter, Political Agent Hugh Weightman to Political Resident Col. Trenchard Fowle no. C/720–1.b/5, India Office Records, British Library, r/15/1/343, 26 November 1938.

53. File r/15/2/100, India Office Records, British Library.

54. Letter from Major T. H. Keyes to the Political Resident, India Office Records, British Library, r/15/1/299, 20 May 1915.

55. Al-Tajir, *Bahrain 1920–1945*.

56. Government of Bahrain Notice no. 26/1357, "Shia Kadis," India Office Records, British Library, r/15/1/343, 27October 1938; Letter no. 404/25 from Adviser Charles Belgrave to Shaikh Ali bin Jafar bin Muhammad, India Office Records, British Library.

57. Belgrave, *Personal Column*, p. 28.

58. Undated note in "Sheikh Khalaf" file, India Office Records, British Library, r/15/2/112.

59. Letter from King Faisal to Sheikh Hamad, 24 July 1928, India Office Records, British Library, r/15/2/112.

60. Article 14(1) of the Bahrain Orders-in-Council.

61. S. A. Amin, *Middle East Legal System*s (Glasgow: Royston Publishers, 1985).

62. Amin, *Middle East Legal System*s; Belgrave, *Personal Column*, p. 28.

63. Belgrave, *Personal Column*.

64. Al-Tajir, *Bahrain 1920–1945*, p. 69.

65. Confidential Report no. 209/8/1 by Major Clive Daly to the Political Residency, India Office Records, British Library, 15/2/131, 31 August 1924.

66. Zoe Holman, "On the side of Decency and Democracy: The History of British-Bahraini Relations and Transnational Contestation," in Ala'a Shehabi and Marc Owen Jones, eds, *Bahrain's Uprising: Resistance and Repression in the Gulf* (London, Zed Books, 2015), pp. 175–206.

67. Letter no. c/84 from Captain C. G. Prior, Political Agent to the Political Resident, India Office Records, British Library, r/15/2/307, 29 June 1929.

68. Al-Tajir, *Bahrain 1920–1945*, p. 37.

69. Despatch no. 90, C. A. Gault to Selwyn Lloyd, Papers of Charles Dalrymple Belgrave, 1926–1947, University of Exeter, 148/2/1, 1956.

70. Major Clive Daly to the Political Resident, India Office Records, British Library, r/15/2/100, 18 June 1921.

71. Despatch no. 90, C. A. Gault to Selwyn Lloyd, Papers of Charles Dalrymple Belgrave, 1926–1947, University of Exeter, 148/2/1, 1956. It should be noted that one of the sticking points for Sheikh Isa in the OiC reforms was the abolishment of slavery; and indeed, this was one of the reasons the British undertook a forced removal. Letter from Political Residet C. G. Knox to Political Agent Percy Cox, India Office Letter, British Library, r/15/1/299, 1 April 1914.

72. Al-Tajir, *Bahrain 1920–1945*.

73. Ibid.

74. Ibid.

75. Belgrave, *Personal Column*.

76. Telegram Report no. 60/c, India Office Records, r/15/2/86, 13 May 1923.
77. Ibid.
78. Major Clive Daly, Confidential Memorandum no. 62A/c, India Office Records, British Library, 13 May 1923.
79. Al-Tajir, *Bahrain 1920–1945*.
80. Belgrave, *Personal Column*.
81. Letter from Political Resident Cyril Barrett to the Foreign Secretary to the Government of India, India Office Records, British Library, r/15/1/307, 23 August 1929.
82. Amin, *Middle East Legal Systems*.
83. J. E. Peterson, "The Arabian Peninsula in Modern Times: A Historiographical Survey," *American Historical Review*, vol. 96. no. 5 (1991), pp. 1435–49.
84. Al-Rasheed, *A History of Saudi Arabia*.
85. Ibid.
86. Ibid.
87. Nasr, *The Shia Revival*.
88. Toby Matthiesen, *The Other Saudis: Shiism, Dissent and Sectarianism* (New York: Cambridge University Press, 2015), pp. 64–5.
89. Ibid., pp. 34–5.
90. Sir Charles Belgrave, diaries, entries in 1927.
91. Al-Rasheed, *A History of Saudi Arabia*.
92. Ibid.; H. al Hasan, *The Shi'a in the Kingdom of Saudi Arabia* [Arabic] (Mu'assat al-Baqi li Ilhya al-Turath, 1993).
93. Letter from Political Agent Cyril Barrett to the Foreign Secretary to the Government of India, India Office Records, British Library, r/15/1/307, 23 August 1929.
94. F. R. Lawson, *The Modernization of Autocracy* (Boulder, CO: Westview Press, 1989).
95. "Full of Sound and Fury," *Economist*, 22 August, 2015, pp. 39–40.
96. Staci Strobl, "From colonial policing to community policing: The historical persistence of sectarianism," *International Journal of Comparative and Applied Criminal Justice*, vol. 35, no. 1 (2011), pp. 19–37.
97. Although in colonial times care was taken to provide judges of the same sect as plaintiffs and defendants in the personal status courts, several informants indicate that assignments in contemporary times have become randomized, leading to public dissatisfaction with the court.
98. Jones, "Rotten Apples or Rotten Orchards."
99. Strobl, "From colonial policing to community policing."
100. Staci Strobl, "Women and Policing in Bahrain," Doctoral dissertation, City University of New York, 2007.
101. Ibid.

102. Strobl, "From colonial policing to community policing."

103. Dooley and Strobl, "Four Years On."

104. Americans for Democracy and Human Rights in Bahrain, "Bahrain: Abusing Anti-Terror Legislation and Increased Death Sentences," 25 March 2016, http://www.adhrb.org/2016/03/9395/

105. An equivalent force does not exist in Bahrain.

106. Al-Dosari, "Sending a Message to Saudi Shia."

107. Ibid.

108. Sunni politicians and historians often use the word "unification" (*tawhid*) to refer to the Saudi expansion to territories outside the Nejd. Shia historians, meanwhile, question this label and prefer the term "conquest" (*ihtilal*) to depict the same historical event (Matthiesen, "Shi'i Historians in a Wahhabi State," p. 35).

109. Lt. Gen. Sheikh Rashid bin Abdullah Al-Khalifah, in "H.E. Minister: No Compromise on National Security," *Al Amn*, no. 43 (May 2013), pp. 12–15.

110. Lt. Col. Muhammad bin Dana, "Civilized Behavior is the Road to a Better Future," *Al-Amn*, no. 41 (March 2013), p. 38.

111. Lt. Col. Muhammad bin Dana, "Our Belief in Dialogue Remains Firm," *Al-Amn*, no. 42 (April 2013), p. 38.

112. Nasr, *The Shia Revival*, p. 234.

113. Human Rights First, "How to Achieve Stability in Bahrain," 11 February 2015, http://www.humanrightsfirst.org/resource/how-bring-stability-bahrain.

114. See Staci Strobl, Emanuel Banutai, Susanne Duque, and Maria (Maki) Haberfeld, "Nothing to do about them without them: The Slovenian National Police and Roma joint-training program," *International Journal of Comparative and Applied Criminal Justice*, vol. 38 no. 2 (2014), pp. 211–13.

115. Matthiesen, *The Other Saudis*, p. 23.

10. THE KINGDOM AND THE CALIPHATE: SAUDI ARABIA AND THE ISLAMIC STATE

1. Peter L. Bergen, *The Osama bin Laden I Know: An Oral History of al Qaeda's Leader* (New York: Free Press, 2006), p. 116.

2. Abu Bakr al-Baghdadi, "Wa-law kariha l-kafirun" [Though the unbelievers be averse], Muassasat al-Furqan, 13 November 2014, https://archive.org/details/wlwCareha21

3. Bernard Haykel, "On the Nature of Salafi Thought and Action," in Roel Meijer, ed., *Global Salafism: Islam's New Religious Movement* (London: Hurst & Co., 2009), pp. 33–57.

4. Cole Bunzel, *From Paper State to Caliphate: The Ideology of the Islamic State* (Washington, DC: Brookings Institution, March 2015), pp. 10–11, http://www.brookings.edu/~/media/research/files/papers/2015/03/ideology-of-islamic-state-bunzel/the-ideology-of-the-islamic-state.pdf

5. See, for example, Brahma Chellaney, "Saudi Arabia's Phony War on Terror," *Project Syndicate*, 21 December 2015, http://www.project-syndicate.org/commentary/saudi-arabia-war-on-terrorism-by-brahma-chellaney-2015–12; and Maajid Nawaz, "Saudi Arabia's ISIS-Like Justice," *Daily Beast*, 2 January 2016, http://www.thedailybeast.com/articles/2016/01/02/saudi-arabia-s-isis-like-justice.html

6. Kamel Daoud, "Saudi Arabia, an ISIS That Has Made It," *New York Times*, 20 November 2015, http://www.nytimes.com/2015/11/21/opinion/saudi-arabia-an-isis-that-has-made-it.html

7. Salman ibn Abd al-Aziz Al Saud, *al-Usus al-tarikhiyya wal-fikriyya lil-Dawla al-Saudiyya* [The historical and intellectual bases of the Saudi state] (Riyadh: Darat al-Malik Abd al-Aziz, 2011/2012), pp. 26, 35. While Wahhabis generally do not call themselves "Wahhabis," the main tenets of their version of Islam are apparent. These include, among other things, the affirmation of *tawhid* (God's unity), the eschewal of *shirk* (idolatry, or association of something with God), the practice of *al-wala wal-bara* (associating exclusively with Wahhabi Muslims and dissociating from non-Wahhabi Muslims), and identification with the mission begun by Muhammad ibn Abd al-Wahhab.

8. Muharib al-Juburi, "al-Ilan an qiyam Dawlat al-Iraq al-Islamiyya" [The announcement of the Islamic State of Iraq], 15 October 2006, in *al Majmu li qadat Dawlat al-Iraq al-Islamiyya* [The anthology (of statements) of the leaders of the Islamic State of Iraq], Nukhbat al-Ilam al-Jihadi, 2010, https://archive.org/download/Dwla_Nokhba/mjdawl.doc, 222

9. Uthman ibn Abd al-Rahman al-Tamimi, *Ilam al-anam bi-milad Dawlat al-Islam* [Informing mankind of the birth of the Islamic State], Muassasat al-Furqan, 2007, p. 41, https://ia801901.us.archive.org/31/items/OZOOO67/DAWLA_ISLAMIA.pdf

10. Ibid., p. 8.

11. Ibid., p. 75.

12. Hamadi Redissi, "The Refutation of Wahhabism in Arabic Sources, 1745–1932," in Madawi Al-Rasheed, ed., *Kingdom Without Borders: Saudi Arabia's Political, Religious and Media Frontiers* (New York: Columbia University Press, 2008), p. 157.

13. Quoted in Alawi ibn Ahmad al-Haddad, *Misbah al-anam wa-jala al-zalam fi radd shubah al-bidi al-Najdi allati adalla biha l-awwam* [Enlightening mankind and illuminating darkness in refutation of the errors of the Najdi heretic by which he misled the multitude] (Cairo: al-Matbaa al-Amira al-Sharafiyya, 1907/8), p. 82.

14. Abd al-Rahman ibn Qasim, ed., *Al-Durar al-saniyya fi l-ajwiba al-Najdiyya* [The glistening pearls of Najdi responsa], 8th edn (n.p.: Warathat al-Shaykh Abd al-Rahman ibn Qasim, 2012), vol. 1, pp. 95–6.

15. Ibid., vol. 9, p. 253.

16. Husayn ibn Ghannam, *Tarikh Ibn Ghannam* [Ibn Ghannam's history], ed.

Sulayman al-Kharashi (Riyadh: Dar al-Thuluthiyya, 2010), vol. 1, p. 412. The Rejectionists (*al-Rafida* or *al-Rawafid*) is a derogatory term for the Shia used by Sunnis since early Islam. It refers either to the Shia's rejection of Islam or to their rejection of the first two Rightly Guided Caliphs, Abu Bakr and Umar.

17. Ibid., vol. 2, pp. 899–900.

18. Uthman ibn Bishr, *Unwan al-majd fi tarikh Najd* [The mark of glory in the history of Najd], ed. Abd al-Rahman ibn Abd al-Latif Al al-Shaykh (Riyadh: Darat al-Malik Abd al-Aziz, 1982), vol. 1, pp. 257–8.

19. *Al-Durar al-saniyya* [The glistening pearls], vol. 9, p. 284.

20. Sulayman ibn Sihman [Poem inciting to jihad against Ha'il], ms. Riyadh, King Salman Library, 3422, 95.

21. Guido Steinberg, "The Wahhabiyya and Shi'ism, from 1744/45 to 2008," in Ofra Bengio and Meir Litvak, eds, *The Sunna and Shi'a in History: Division and Ecumenism in the Muslim Middle East* (New York: Palgrave, 2011), pp. 172–3.

22. Turki al-Binali, *al-Salsabil fi qillat saliki l-sabil* [The fountain of the few following the path] (2012), Minbar al-Tawhid wal-Jihad, pp. 4–5, https://archive.org/details/Salsabil_201309. On Binali, see Cole Bunzel, "The Caliphate's Scholar-in-Arms," *Jihadica*, 9 July 2014, https://web.archive.org/web/20151213140850/http://www.jihadica.com/the-caliphate%E2%80%99s-scholar-in-arms/; and Cole Bunzel, "Binali Leaks: Revelations of the Silent Mufti," *Jihadica*, 15 June 2015, https://web.archive.org/web/20151217164430/http://www.jihadica.com/binali-leaks/

23. Turki al-Binali, "al-Tarjama al-ilmiyya lil-shaykh al-mujahid Turki ibn Mubarak al-Binali" [The intellectual biography of the mujahid Shaykh Turki ibn Mubarak al-Binali], Muassasat al-Battar, 4 March 2014, p. 3, http://ia700708.us.archive.org/16/items/s_shykh_bin3li/Llbj1.pdf; Binali, "Jabr al-rayn fi ritha al-Jibrin" [The force of death in the elegy of al-Jibrin], Minbar al-Tawhid wal-Jihad, June/July 2009, pp. 1–2, https://archive.org/download/abu-hamam-alathary/38.pdf

24. An image of the recommendation is available in Abu Usama al-Gharib, *Minnat al-Ali bi-thabat shaykhina Turki al-Binali* [The Most High's bestowal of steadfastness on our Sheikh Turki al-Binali] (2013), p. 58, https://archive.org/download/minato.alali001/minato.alali001.pdf

25. Turki al-Binali, "Sharh Nawaqid al-Islam" [Commentary on the nullifiers of Islam], part 1, al-Ribat Mosque, Sirte, Libya, 6 April 2013, http://archive.org/download/Islamic_enty/01.mp3, 42:30–42:50.

26. Turki Binali, *Tabsir al-mahajij bil-farq bayn rijal al-Dawla al-Islamiyya wal-Khawarij* [Showing the divergent paths of the men of the Islamic State and the Kharijites], Muassasat al-Ghuraba, 19 January 2014, pp. 5–6, https://archive.org/download/tabsir.almahajij.l/tabsir.almahajij.l.pdf

27. Muhammad ibn Abd al-Wahhab, *Mufid al-mustafid fi kufr tarik al-tawhid* [Informing the inquirer about the unbelief of the abandoner of God's unity]

(Maktabat al-Himma, July/August 2015), pp. 3–4, http://justpaste.it/
MoFeDTwheeD

28. "Arba qawaid muhimma" [Four important principles], Maktabat al-Himma, April/
    May 2015, https://ia601300.us.archive.org/35/items/Qwaed-4/Qwaed4_0.pdf.
    On this text, see Michael Cook, "Written and Oral Aspects of an Early Wahhabi
    Epistle," *Bulletin of the School of Oriental and African Studies*, vol. 78, no. 1
    (February 2015).

29. Included in "Masail muhimma fi l-aqida" [Important issues in creed], Maktabat
    al-Himma, October/November 2014, https://archive.org/details/Mas2il-002

30. "Min al-zulumat ila l-nur" [From darkness to light], al-Maktab al-Ilami li-Wilayat
    al-Khayr, 16 April 2015, transcript available at http://justpaste.it/bttar-tf-tonor

31. Additional works of the Wahhabi canon printed by the Islamic State include *al-
    Dalail fi hukm muwalat ahl al-ishrak* [Proofs concerning judgment of association
    with the people of idolatry] and *Awthaq ura l-iman* [The firmest bonds of faith],
    by Sulayman ibn Abdallah, a grandson of Muhammad ibn Abd al-Wahhab (https://
    ia601504.us.archive.org/21/items/DlailP3/%D8%A7%D9%84%D8%AF%D9
    %84%D8%A7%D8%A6%D9%84%20%D9%81%D9%8A%20
    %D8%AD%D9%83%D9%85%20%D9%85%D9%88%D8%A7%D9%84%D8
    %A7%D8%A9%20%D8%A3%D9%87%D9%84%20%D8%A7%D9%84%D8
    %A5%D8%B4%D8%B1%D8%A7%D9%83.pdf), and *al-Intisar li-hizb Allah al-
    muwahhidin* [Support for the monotheist partisans of God], by Abdallah Aba
    Butayn (https://ia601505.us.archive.org/3/items/IntesarP/Entesar.pdf).

32. *Muqarrar fi l-aqida* [A precis of creed] (Hayat al-Buhuth wal-Ifta, 2014/2015),
    text (along with translation by Aymenn Jawad Al-Tamimi) available at http://
    www.aymennjawad.org/17633/islamic-state-training-camp-textbook-course-in

33. Al-Nabi, "al-Shaykh al-Baghdadi ala khuta l-imam Muhammad ibn Abd al-Wah-
    hab: al-tashabuh bayn al-dawlatayn al-Wahhabiyya wal-Baghdadiyya" [Sheikh
    Baghdadi in the footsteps of Muhammad ibn Abd al-Wahhab: The resemblance
    between the Wahhabi and Baghdadi States], Muassasat al-Minhaj, 31 December
    2014, http://justpaste.it/ioez. (This is the original title of the work as it first
    appeared on the forum alplatformmedia.com on 26 June 2014.)

34. Abu Hamid al-Barqawi, "al-Dawla wa-zaman aimmat al-dawa" [The (Islamic) State
    and the period of the imams of the (Wahhabi) mission], Muassasat al-Battar, 6 June
    2014, https://azelin.files.wordpress.com/2014/06/abc5ab-e1b8a5c481mid-al-
    barqc481wc4ab-22the-islamic-state-and-the-time-of-the-imams-dawah22.pdf

35. Gharib al-Sururiyya, "Sirat aimmat al-Islam fi hadm mawadi al-shirk wal-tughyan"
    [The way of the imams of Islam in destroying places of unbelief and oppression],
    23 July 2015, http://ghareeb-assourouria.blogspot.com.tr/2015/07/blog-
    post_23.html?m=1

36. Ahlam al-Nasr, *Bilad al-Haramayn wal-haram al-hakim* [The land of the two holy
    places and the forbiddenness that reigns], Muassasat al-Sumud, 10 January 2016,

https://ia801503.us.archive.org/31/items/biladalharamayn/%D8%A8%D9%8
4%D8%A7%D8%AF%20%D8%A7%D9%84%D8%AD%D8%B1%D9%85%
D9%8A%D9%86%20%D9%88%D8%A7%D9%84%D8%AD%D8%B1%D8%
A7%D9%85%20%D8%A7%D9%84%D8%AD%D8%A7%D9%83%D9%85%
D8%8C%20%D8%A8%D9%82%D9%84%D9%85%20%D8%A3%D8%AD%
D9%84%D8%A7%D9%85%20%D8%A7%D9%84%D9%86%D8%B5%D8%
B1.pdf. On Ahlam al-Nasr, see Bernard Haykel and Robyn Creswell, "Battle Lines,"
New Yorker, 8 June 2015, http://www.newyorker.com/magazine/2015/06/08/
battle-lines-jihad-creswell-and-haykel

37. On the influence of Abu Abdallah al-Muhajir, see Muhammad Abu Rumman,
"Min ayna jaa hadha l-fiqh al-damawi" [Whence came this bloody jurisprudence?],
al-Ghadd, 3 October 2014, http://www.alghad.com/articles/829105; Hasan ibn
Salim, "Man huwa l-marji al-ruhi li-fiqh Daish al-damawi?" [Who is the spiritual
reference for Daesh's bloody jurisprudence?], *al-Hayat*, 21 October 2014, http://
alhayat.com/Opinion/Hassen-Bin-Salam/5181915; and Hasan Abu Haniyya,
"Marjiiyyat Tanzim al-Dawla al-Islamiyya: min *al-Tawahhush* ila *Fiqh al-dima*"
[The Islamic State group's wellspring: From *Savagery* to *The Jurisprudence of Blood*],
Arabi 21, 26 October 2014, http://arabi21.com//story/784474.

38. I say mainstream because Juhayman al-Utaybi's movement, resulting in the siege
of Mecca in 1979, was both Wahhabi and apocalyptic.

39. William McCants, *The ISIS Apocalypse: The History, Strategy, and Doomsday Vision
of the Islamic State* (New York: St Martin's Press, 2015).

40. On this website, which continues to move from domain to domain, see "Isdarat.
tv: ISIS's Answer to YouTube," *MEMRI*, 19 August 2015, http://cjlab.memri.org/
lab-projects/tracking-jihadi-terrorist-use-of-social-media/isadarat-tv-isiss-answer-
to-youtube/

41. Thomas Hegghammer, *Jihad in Saudi Arabia: Violence and Pan-Islamism Since
1979* (Cambridge: Cambridge University Press, 2010), pp. 199–202.

42. "Akhriju l-Rafida al-mushrikin min Jazirat Muhammad" [Expel the rejectionist
idolaters from the peninsula of Muhammad], *al-Maktab al-Ilami li-Wilayat Najd*,
29 May 2015, transcript available at http://justpaste.it/bttar-tf-rafdh; "Innama
l-mushrikun najas" [The idolaters are indeed unclean], *al-Maktab al-Ilami li-
Wilayat Najd*, 12 October 2015, transcript available at http://www.csnn.
tk/2015/10/0m.html

43. Abu Musab al-Zarqawi, "Hal ataka hadith al-Rafida?" [Has news of the rejectionists reached you?], part 1, al-Haya al-Ilamiyya li-Majlis Shura l-Mujahidin fi l-Iraq,
1 June 2006, transcript available in *Kalimat mudia* [Enlightening speech],
Shabakat al-Buraq al-Islamiyya, June 2006, pp. 525–9, https://archive.org/down-
load/fgfrt/1a.pdf

44. Tweet from "Manfi 14," @CkjaYeociuxc0ze (account since suspended), 17 October
2015.

45. "Risala ila Ahl al-Sunna fi Bilad al-Haramayn" [Message to the Sunnis in the land of the two holy places], al-Maktab al-Ilami li-Wilayat Halab, 15 July 2015, transcript available at http://justpaste.it/bttar-tf-hrmen

46. Tweet from @wikibaghdady, 13 November 2014, https://twitter.com/wikibaghdady/status/532898687718932480; Shiv Malik, Ali Younes, Spencer Ackerman, and Mustafa Khalili, "How Isis Crippled al-Qaida," *Guardian*, 10 June 2015, http://www.theguardian.com/world/2015/jun/10/how-isis-crippled-al-qaida. The *Guardian* report claims to have confirmed the rumors.

47. On the Shuaybi school, see Hegghammer, *Jihad in Saudi Arabia*, pp. 83–98, 147–55; and Saud al-Sarhan, "The Struggle for Authority: The Shaykhs of Jihadi-Salafism in Saudi Arabia, 1997–2003," in Bernard Haykel, Thomas Hegghammer, and Stéphane Lacroix, eds, *Saudi Arabia in Transition: Insights on Social, Political, Economic and Religious Change* (Cambridge: Cambridge University Press, 2015), pp. 181–206.

48. Hegghammer, *Jihad in Saudi Arabia*, p. 222.

49. Angus McDowall, "Inside the Saudi Prison That's Home to New Wave of Jihadis," *Reuters*, 6 July 2015, http://www.reuters.com/article/us-saudi-security-prison-idUSKCN0PG1CO20150706

50. Saud al-Masud, "Tanafur bayn munazziri l-fikr al-dall dakhil al-Hair bi-sabab Daish wa-l-Nusra" [Conflict between the theoreticians of wayward thought inside al-Hair (Prison) on account of Daesh and (the) Nusra (Front)], *al-Riyad*, 7 September 2014, http://www.alriyadh.com/973935

51. Sulayman al-Ulwan, "Nasihat al-shaykh Sulayman al-Ulwan li-Abi Bakr al-Baghdadi wa-tanzim al-Dawla al-Islamiyya fi l-Iraq wal-Sham" [Sheikh Sulayman al-Ulwan's advice to Abu Bakr al-Baghdadi and the Islamic State in Iraq and Sham Group], 14 January 2014, https://www.youtube.com/watch?v=eapGxmDk9f8 (video removed)

52. See "al-Nusra al-Hayiriyya lil-Dawla al-Islamiyya" [The support of al-Hair for the Islamic State], 11 March 2014, http://justpaste.it/hayer; "al-Baya al-Hayiriyya lil-Dawla al-Islamiyya fi l-Iraq wal-Sham" [The al-Hair *baya* to the Islamic State in Iraq and Sham], 11 April 2014, http://justpaste.it/f23o; and "Jalla l-khatb an al-itab" [The matter is beyond reproach], 22 April 2014, http://justpaste.it/f75q

53. Muayyad Bajis, "al-Zahrani wal-Tuwaylii wal-Humaydi abraz man adamathum al-Saudiyya" [Zahrani, Tuwaylii, and Humaydi most prominent of those executed by Saudi Arabia], *Arabi 21*, http://arabi21.com//story/880276. For more on Zahrani, see Joas Wagemakers, "Al-Qa'ida's Editor: Abu Jandal al-Azdi's Online Jihadi Activism," *Politics, Religion and Ideology*, vol. 12, no. 4 (December 2011).

54. "Al-Saudiyya tunaffidh hukm al-qisas bi-haqq 47 shakhsan min al-fia al-dalla" [Saudi Arabia carries out judgment of reprisal against 47 persons of the wayward faction], *al-Sharq al-Awsat*, 3 January 2016, http://aawsat.com/node/534056

55. Abu Bakr al-Baghdadi, "Infiru khifafan wa-thiqalan" [Go forth, light and heavy],

Muassasat al-Furqan, 14 May 2015, transcript available at http://justpaste.it/
bttar-tf-enferoo

56. Nasir al-Fahd, "al-Shaykh Nasir al-Fahd yubayi al-khalifa" [Sheikh Nasir al-Fahd
    gives *baya* to the caliph], Muassasat al-Battar, 25 August 2015, http://justpaste.
    it/n9i0

57. "Risala ila Ahl al-Sunna fi Bilad al-Haramayn" [Message to the Sunnis in the Land
    of the Two Holy Places]. The book is a commentary on a book by Ibn Abd
    al-Wahhab.

58. Abu l-Maali Aqil ibn Ali al-Ahmad, *Nahim al-Fahd wa-nubah al-kilab* [Al-Fahd's
    cry and the barking of dogs], Muassasat al-Sumud, 25 October 2015, https://
    archive.org/details/nahim_fahd

59. McDowall, "Inside the Saudi Prison."

60. Tweet by @wikibaghdady, 20 August 2014, https://twitter.com/wikibaghdady/
    status/5021627676299910016

61. See numerous tweets by @wikibaghdady between April and October 2014.

62. Hegghammer, *Jihad in Saudi Arabia*, pp. 217–19.

63. Ahmed Al Omran, "Saudi Arabia Arrests 431 People with Suspected Islamic State
    Links," *Wall Street Journal*, 18 July 2015, http://www.wsj.com/articles/saudi-
    arabia-arrests-431-people-with-suspected-islamic-state-links-1437227998

64. "Akhtar khalaya Daish min al-Qasim ... khattatat lightiyalat wa-tafjir mujammaat"
    [The most dangerous of Daesh's cells is from al-Qasim ... planned assassinations
    and exploding complexes], *MBC*, 28 April 2014, http://fw.to/OruobGY. Likewise,
    the account @WikiBaghdady has stressed the importance of the former al-Qasim
    network.

65. Hegghammer, *Jihad in Saudi Arabia*, pp. 38–58.

66. Baghdadi, "Wa-law kariha l-kafirun" [Though the unbelievers be averse].

67. The entire collection of videos and essays is available at https://archive.org/details/
    AstiwanahAlharmyncc

68. "Al-Malik Abdallah: samt al-mujtama al-dawli an safk al-dima fi Filastin wa-ma
    yajri fil-mintaqa bi-asriha laysa lahu ayy tabrir" [King Abdallah: There is no excuse
    for the international community's silence on the shedding of blood in Palestine
    and what is happening in all the region], *al-Riyad*, 2 August 2014, http://www.
    alriyadh.com/957314

69. "Khadim al-Haramayn: fikum kasal wa-samt ... utruduhuma" [Custodian of the
    Two Holy Places: There is laziness and silence in you ... expel them], *Al Arabiya*,
    2 August 2014, http://www.alarabiya.net/ar/saudi-today/2014/08/02/http://
    www.alarabiya.net/ar/saudi-today/2014/08/02/%D8%AE%D8%A7%D8%A
    F%D9%85-%D8%A7%D9%84%D8%AD%D8%B1%D9%85%D9%8A%D9%
    86-%D9%84%D9%80-%D8%A7%D9%84%D9%85%D8%B4%D8%A7%D8
    %A6%D8%AE-%D9%81%D9%8A%D9%83%D9%85-%D9%83%D8%B3%
    D9%84-%D9%88%D8%B5%D9%85%D8%AA.html

70. Stéphane Lacroix, *Saudi Islamists and the Arab Spring*, Kuwait Programme on Development, Governance and Globalisation in the Gulf States, London School of Economics, May 2014, pp. 4–5, http://eprints.lse.ac.uk/56725/1/Lacroix_Saudi-Islamists-and-theArab-Spring_2014.pdf; Jon Alterman and William McCants, "Saudi Arabia: Islamists Rising and Falling," in Jon Alterman, ed., *Religious Radicalism After the Arab Uprisings* (Washington, DC: Center for Strategic and International Studies, 2015), pp. 169–70.

71. "Al-Amir Abdallah mukhatiban al-mashayikh fi l-Saudiyya: al-zuruf al-asiba tatatallab al-hikma wal-way lil-taamul maaha wa-la guluww fi l-din wa-la musawama ala l-watan" [Prince Abdallah speaking to the sheikhs in Saudi Arabia: Difficult circumstances require wisdom and awareness to handle, no extremism in religion, and no bargaining over the country], *al-Sharq al-Awsat*, 15 November 2001, http://archive.aawsat.com/details.asp?article=66504&issueno=8388#.VhabiqIbWAw. The mufti of the kingdom, it should be noted, did strongly condemn the 11 September attacks five days after the event. See "al-Mufti al-amm: ahdath al-tafjirat fi Amrika darb min al-zulm wal-jawr wal-baghy la tuqirruhu Shariat al-Islam" [The head mufti: The events of the explosions in America are a strike of oppression, injustice, and wrong, which the Islamic Sharia does not sanction], *al-Riyad*, 16 September 2001, http://www.alriyadh.com/Contents/2001/09/16–09–2001/page13.html#10

72. See, for example, Khalid al-Dakhil, "Liqaat Wali al-ahd al-Saudi ma qiyadat al-nukhba: mulahazat yaqtadiha siyaq al-hadath" [Meetings of the Saudi crown prince with the leaders of the intelligentsia: Observations require context], *al-Hayat*, 11 November 2001, http://daharchives.alhayat.com/issue_archive/Hayat%20INT/2001/11/18/%D9%84%D9%82%D8%A7%D8%A1%D8%A7%D8%AA-%D9%88%D9%84%D9%8A-%D8%A7%D9%84%D8%B9%D9%87%D8%AF-%D8%A7%D9%84%D8%B3%D8%B9%D9%88%D8%AF%D9%8A-%D9%85%D8%B9-%D9%82%D9%8A%D8%A7%D8%AF%D8%A7%D8%AA-%D8%A7%D9%84%D9%86%D8%AE%D8%A8%D8%A9-%D9%85%D9%84%D8%A7%D8%AD%D8%B8%D8%A7%D8%AA-%D9%8A%D9%82%D8%AA%D8%B6%D9%8A%D9%87%D8%A7-%D8%B3%D9%8A%D8%A7%D9%82-%D8%A7%D9%84%D8%AD%D8%AF%D8%AB.html

73. Nabil Mouline, *The Clerics of Islam: Religious Authority and Political Power in Saudi Arabia* (New Haven, CT: Yale University Press, 2014), pp. 255–6.

74. Robin Wright, *Rock the Casbah: Rage and Rebellion Across the Islamic World* (New York: Simon & Schuster, 2011), pp. 183–4.

75. Mansour al-Nogaidan, "Telling the Truth, Facing the Whip," *New York Times*, 28 November 2003, http://www.nytimes.com/2003/11/28/opinion/telling-the-truth-facing-the-whip.html

76. Elizabeth Rubin, "The Jihadi Who Kept Asking Why," *New York Times Magazine*, 7 March 2004, http://www.nytimes.com/2004/03/07/magazine/the-jihadi-who-kept-asking-why.html

77. See, for example, the comments of Sahwa leader Awad al-Qarni in Adwan al-Ahmari, "Tatwir al-manahij yanbaghi an yakun an qanaa wa-laysa stijaba li-dughut Amrika" [The development of programs must be done with conviction and not in response to American pressure], *al-Watan*, 5 January 2004, https://web.archive.org/web/20070516070008/http://www.alwatan.com.sa/daily/2004–01–05/first_page/first_page13.htm. On the Sahwa, see Stéphane Lacroix, *Awakening Islam: The Politics of Religious Dissent in Contemporary Saudi Arabia* (Cambridge, MA: Harvard University Press, 2011).

78. Madawi Al-Rasheed, *Contesting the Saudi State: Islamic Voices From a New Generation* (Cambridge: Cambridge University Press, 2006), pp. 220–23.

79. Hasan ibn Farhan al-Maliki, *Daiya wa-laysa nabiyyan* [Preacher, not a prophet] (Amman: Dar al-Razi, 2004), pp. 23–4.

80. David Commins, *Islam in Saudi Arabia* (Ithaca, NY: Cornell University Press, 2015), p. 57.

81. Hamza ibn Muhammad al-Salim, "al-Salafiyya ala firash al-mawt" [Salafism on its deathbed], *al-Jazirah*, 12 September 2013, http://www.al-jazirah.com/2013/20130912/lp3.htm

82. Hatim al-Awni, "al-Mashayikh al-kusala" [Lazy sheikhs], 3 August 2014, http://www.dr-alawni.com/articles.php?show=171

83. Turki al-Binali, *Sharh shurut wa-mawani al-takfir* [Explanation of the necessary conditions and prohibitive conditions of excommunication] Muassasat al-Ghuraba, 2014, https://docs.google.com/viewer?a=v&pid=sites&srcid=ZGVmYXVsdGRvbWFpbnxuYXNyM2E5aWRhhfGd4OmRiZjlkNDhiOD. This is a transcript of lectures given in Sirte, Libya, in April 2013. Binali's teacher, Abu Muhammad al-Maqdisi, was likewise heavily influenced by *al-Durar al-saniyya* [The glistening pearls]. He has related how powerful was the effect of encountering this book in Saudi Arabia in the early 1980s and how he fashioned his ideas from its contents. See Abu Muhammad al-Maqdisi, *Wa-lakin kunu rabbaniyyin* [Rather, be you masters], Muassasat al-Tahaya, 2015, http://www.up-00.com/?3TxY, 7–8; and Joas Wagemakers, *A Quietist Jihadi: The Ideology and Influence of Abu Muhammad al-Maqdisi* (Cambridge: Cambridge University Press, 2012), p. 36.

84. "Al-Awni lil-Hayat: inkar alaqat al-takfir bi-Salafiyyat *al-Durar al-saniyya* khiyana lil-umma wal-watan" [Awni to *al-Hayat*: Denying the link between excommunication and *The Glistening Pearls* is a betrayal of the community and the country], *al-Hayat*, 29 August 2014, http://alhayat.com/Articles/4347097

85. Bassam Nasir, "al-Sharif al-Awni hakadha nastankir hadith al-Qudayh" [Sharif Awni, that's how we condemn the al-Qudayh event], *al-Sabil*, 26 May 2015, http://www.assabeel.net/essays/item/111505-%D8%A7%D9%84%D8%B4%D8%B1%D9%8A%D9%81-%D8%A7%D9%84%D8%B9%D9%88%D9%86%D9%8A-%D9%87%D9%83%D8%B0%D8%A7-%D9%86%D8%B3%D8%AA%D9%8

6%D9%83%D8%B1-%D8%AD%D8%A7%D8%AF%D8%AB-%D8%A7%
D9%84%D9%82%D8%AF%D9%8A%D8%AD

86. "Al-Shaykh Hatim al-Awni dayf barnamaj Liqa al-Juma ma Abdallah al-Muday-
fir" [Sheikh Hatim al-Awni is the guest of the program Friday Meeting with
Abdallah al-Mudayfir], *Khalijiyya*, 12 September 2014, https://www.youtube.
com/watch?v=FPG0inv45–8

87. Abd al-Rahman al-Wabili, "La-nashudd ala yad hadha l-alim al-sharif" [Let us
grab the hand of this noble scholar], *al-Watan*, 5 September 2014, http://www.
alwatan.com.sa/Articles/Detail.aspx?ArticleId=22881; and Khalid al-Dakhil,
"Murajaat lil-Wahhabiyya taakhkharat kathiran" [Revisions to Wahhabism have
lagged considerably], *al-Hayat*, 21 September 2014, http://alhayat.com/Opinion/
Khaled-El-Dakheel/4688398

88. There were several earlier statements, however. See, for example, "al-Shura al-Saudi:
al-irhabiyyun Khawarij" [The Saudi Shura Council: The terrorists are Kharijites],
al-Hayat, 8 July 2014, http://alhayat.com/Articles/3458544; and "Udw Hayat
Kibar al-Ulama fi l-Saudiyya: al-hamalat didd al-mamlaka yaquduha Khawarij"
[Member of the Council of Senior Religious Scholars in Saudi Arabia: The campaigns against the Kingdom are led by Kharijites], *al-Hayat*, 11 July 2014, http://
alhayat.com/Articles/3525208

89. "Al-Mufti: Daish wal-Qaida imtidad lil-Khawarij" [The Mufti: Daesh and al-Qaeda
are an extension of the Kharijites], *al-Riyad*, 19 August 2014, http://www.alri-
yadh.com/962142

90. Abd al-Wahid al-Ansari, "al-Shathri: al-intima ila Daish ridda an al-Islam wa-hum
akfar min ubbad al-asnam" [Shathri: Association with Daesh is apostasy from
Islam and they are more disbelieving than idol-worshippers], *al-Hayat*, 2 September
2014, http://alhayat.com/Articles/4412736

91. "Hayat Kibar al-Ulama: Daish dasisa ala l-Islam sanaatha aydin khafiyya" [Council
of Senior Religious Scholars: Daesh is a plot against Islam created by hidden
hands], *al-Riyad*, 29 September 2015, http://www.alriyadh.com/1086543

92. Ansari, "al-Shathri: al-intima ila Daish" [Shathri: Association with Daesh].

93. Turki al-Sahil and Saud al-Nashmi, "Al al-Shaykh li-duat al-fitna: intaha waqt al-
tabtaba wa-muhakamatukum wajabat" [Al al-Sheikh to the preachers of dissen-
sion: The time of shoulder tapping is over and you must be tried], *al-Watan*,
21 August 2014, http://www.alwatan.com.sa/Local/News_Detail.aspx?ArticleI
D=197883&CategoryID=5

94. "Imam al-Haram: al-irhab saniat mukhabarat dawliyya wa-waquduhu Khawarij
wa-umala muhtarifun" [The imam of the Great Mosque: Terrorism is the product of international intelligence agencies and its fuel is Kharijities and professional
agents], *al-Hayat*, 23 August 2014, http://alhayat.com/Articles/4257146

95. Abdallah al-Dani, "al-Mufti: Daish junud li-Israil wal-tahaluf al-Islami sa-yuwqi-
fuhum" [The Mufti: Daesh is soldiers for Israel and the Islamic alliance will stop

them], *Okaz*, 28 December 2015, http://www.okaz.com.sa/new/Issues/20151228/Con20151228816592.htm

96. "Hayat Kibar al-Ulama al-Saudiyya tujarrim al-indimam lil-jamaat al-irhabiyya wa-tuayyid qital al-dawla laha" [The Saudi Council of Senior Religious Scholars criminalizes joining terrorist organizations and supports the state's fighting them], *al-Sharq al-Awsat*, 18 September 2014, http://aawsat.com/home/article/183416

97. Ansari, "al-Shathri: al-intima ila Daish" [Shathri: Association with Daesh].

98. Sulayman al-Anazi, "Kibar al-Ulama tataharrak bi-thamaniyat mahawir li-muwajahat al-irhab" [The (Council of) Senior Religious Scholars undertakes eight measures to confront terrorism], *al-Watan*, 1 October 2015, http://alwatan.com.sa/Nation/News_Detail.aspx?ArticleID=237184&CategoryID=3

99. Mansur al-Nuqaydan, "al-Fuqaha fi muwajahat Daish" [The jurists confront Daesh], *al-Ittihad*, 5 October 2015, http://www.alittihad.ae/wajhatdetails.php?id=86573; Abir al-Ali, "Hayat Kibar al-Ulama fi muwajahat Daish" [Council of Senior Religious Scholars confronts Daesh], *al-Watan*, 6 October 2015, http://www.alwatan.com.sa/Articles/Detail.aspx?ArticleID=28126

100. Khalid al-Dakhil, "al-Malik wal-ulama: daf al-muassasa" [The king and the religious scholars: The weakening of the [religious] establishment], *al-Hayat*, 17 August 2014, http://alhayat.com/Opinion/Khaled-El-Dakheel/4161255

101. *Al-Durar al-saniyya* [The glistening pearls], 14:379.

102. Yaroslav Trofimov, "New Saudi Monarch Brings Major Change at Home," *Wall Street Journal*, 29 April 2015, www.wsj.com/articles/new-saudi-king-brings-major-change-at-home-and-abroad-1430310152

103. Haykel, "On the Nature of Salafi Thought and Action," pp. 36–7.

11. RELIGIOUS SECTARIANISM AND POLITICAL PRAGMATISM: THE PARADOX OF EGYPT'S AL-NOUR SALAFIS

1. Among the few studies dealing with Egyptian Salafism before and after the revolution are Richard Gauvain, *Salafi Ritual Purity: In the Presence of God* (London: Routledge, 2012); Stéphane Lacroix, "Sheikhs and Politicians: Inside the New Egyptian Salafism," Brookings Institution, June 2012, http://www.brookings.edu/~/media/research/files/papers/2012/6/07-egyptian-salafism-lacroix/stephane-lacroix-policy-briefing-english.pdf; Khalil al-Anani and Maszlee Malik, "Pious Way to Politics: The Rise of Political Salafism in Post-Mubarak Egypt," *Digest of Middle East Studies*, vol. 22, no. 1 (Spring 2013); Jacob Høigilt and Frida Nome, "Egyptian Salafism in Revolution," *Journal of Islamic Studies*, vol. 25, no. 1 (2014); Ashraf el-Sherif, "Egypt's Salafists at a Crossroads," Carnegie Endowment for International Peace, 29 April 2015, http://carnegieendowment.org/2015/04/29/egypt-s-salafists-at-crossroads-pub-59928; Georges Fahmi, "The Future of Political Salafism in Egypt and Tunisia," Carnegie Endowment for International Peace,

16 November 2015, http://carnegieendowment.org/2015/11/16/future-of-polit-ical-salafism-in-egypt-and-tunisia-pub-61871; Stéphane Lacroix and Ahmed Zaghloul Shalata, "The Rise of Revolutionary Salafism in Post-Mubarak Egypt," in Stéphane Lacroix and Bernard Rougier, eds, *Egypt's Revolutions* (New York: Palgrave, 2016); in Arabic, see Ahmed Zaghloul Shalata, *Al-hala al-salafiyya fi masr* [The Salafi situation in Egypt] (Cairo: Madbuli, 2010); Ahmed Zaghloul Shalata, *Al-da'wa al-salafiyya al-sakandariyya: masarat al-tanzim wa malat al-siyasa* [The Alexandrian Salafi Da'wa: The trajectories of the organization and the outcomes of politics] (Beirut: Markaz dirasat al-wahda al-'arabiyya, 2016); Mu'taz Zahir, *Min al-masjid ila al-barlaman* [From mosque to parliament] (Damascus: Takwin, 2014).

2. Author interview with Sa'id Abd al-'Azim and founding members of the Salafi Da'wa, December 2012.

3. Contrary to many of the Salafis found in Saudi Arabia, the Salafi Da'wa refrained from pronouncing *takfir* on Sufis, liberals, and more generally on non-Salafi Sunni Muslims, and justified its stance by arguing that those groups had the "excuse of ignorance" (*al-'adhr bi-l-jahl*).

4. Mohammed Isma'il al-Muqaddim, *Adillat tahrim musafahat al-ajnabiyya* [Proofs that it is forbidden to shake hands with an unrelated woman], 14th edn (Alexandria: Dar al-khulafa' al-rashidun, 1993); Mohammed Isma'il, *Adillat tahrim halq al-lihya* [Proofs that it is forbidden to shave one's beard], 4th edn (Kuwait: Makbtaba Dar al-Arqam, 1985).

5. Sa'id Abd al-'Azim, *Al-dimuqratiyya fi-l-mizan* [Democracy in the balance] (Tripoli, Lebanon: Dar al-iman, 2009).

6. Yasir Burhami, "Al-salafiyya wa manahij al-taghyir" [Salafism and the methodologies of change], *Sawt al-Da'wa* 3, 1412 (corresponding to 1991–2).

7. *Qayyim* is the name traditionally given to the superintendent of a religious school. One of the main medieval scholars from whom Salafis take inspiration is Ibn Qayyim al-Jawziyya, literally the son of the *qayyim* (Hanbali scholar) of Ibn al-Jawzi's school.

8. Abd al-Rahman Abd al-Khaliq, *Mashru'iyyat al-'amal al-jama'i* [The religious legality of collective action] (Riyadh: Dar al-hijra li-l-nashr wa-l-tawzi', 1988).

9. "Hukm al-musharaka fi thawrat yawm 25 Yanayir" [Judgment on participating in the 25 January revolution], anasalafy.com, 21 January 2011, http://www.anasalafy.com/play.php?catsmktba=23685; "Bayan al-da'wa al-salafiyya bi-sha'n al-ahdath" [Statement of the Salafi Da'wa about the events], Sawt al-Salaf, 30 January 2011.

10. Author interview with Imad Abd al-Ghaffour, Cairo, December 2011. It appears that the process took some time. Still, in April 2011, Abd al-Mun'im al-Shahhat, a close associate of Da'wa strongman Yasir Burhami, declared, "We will not present candidates of our own. We will support candidates from different parties under certain conditions." Author interview with Abd al-Mun'im al-Shahhat, Alexandria, April 2011.

11. Stéphane Lacroix, "Yasser Borhami," in Lacroix and Rougier, eds, *Egypt's Revolutions*, pp. 268–71.

12. Ahmed Zaghloul Shalata, "Hiwar ma' Yasir Burhami: al-da'wa laha ru'ya shamila bima fiha al-musharaka al-siyasiyya" [Dialogue with Yasir Burhami: the Da'wa has a complete vision which includes political participation], islamiyun.net, 13 April 2011.

13. Interview with Imad Abd al-Ghaffour, YouTube, 6 December 2011, https://www.youtube.com/watch?v=rnhzbBEVYV4

14. Author interview with Imad Abd al-Ghaffour, Cairo, December 2011.

15. Stéphane Lacroix, "Sheikhs and Politicians: Inside the New Egyptian Salafism," Brookings Institution, 11 June 2012, https://www.brookings.edu/research/sheikhs-and-politicians-inside-the-new-egyptian-salafism, p. 4.

16. Imad Abd al-Ghaffour's interview with al-Jazeera Mubashir Masr, 6 November 2011.

17. Author interview with Hizb al-Nour official Mahmud Abbas, Alexandria, November 2012; author interview with Nader Bakkar (a close associate of Burhami and spokesman of Hizb al-Nour) Cairo, April 2012.

18. Author interview with Mohammed Nour (then spokesman of the Hizb al-Nour), Cairo, October 2011.

19. Author interview with Imad Abd al-Ghaffour, Cairo, December 2011.

20. Author interview with one of the academics who helped draft the program, December 2011.

21. Author interview with Mahmud Abbas (a proponent of Abd al-Ghaffour), Alexandria, November 2012.

22. Spokesman Mohammed Nour, for instance, indicated that he had not been in contact with the Da'wa since 1995 (author interview, Cairo, November 2011). Mohammed Yusri Salama, the party's first spokesman, even claimed that he had always been close to the Da'wa's figures but had never been part of it (author interview, Alexandria, November 2012); Shalata, *Al-da'wa al-salafiyya al-sakandariyya*, p. 156.

23. Lacroix, "Sheikhs and Politicians."

24. At the Salafi Da'wa events I attended in 2012 and 2013, those few words were constantly repeated to justify the party's controversial positions. This was the case, for instance, when the Da'wa organized a gathering in Alexandria in April 2012 to convince its members to vote for Abu al-Futuh.

25. The term was used by Hussam Tammam. See Hussam Tammam, *Al-ikhwan al-muslimun... sanawat qabl al-thawra* [The Muslim Brotherhood: pre-revolt years] (Cairo: Dar al-Shuruq, 2013), p. 128.

26. Author interview with Yusri Hammad, Alexandria, January 2013.

27. "Hawla ta'assuf ra'is Hizb al-Nur 'ala 'adam tarashshuh nasrani fi qawa'im al-hizb" [On the regrets of the president of the Nour Party for the lack of Christians on

the party's lists], Sawt al-Salaf, 1 January 2012, http://www.salafvoice.com/article.php?a=5914

28. *Al-Fath* (official mouthpiece of the Salafi Da'wa), 4 January 2012. See also Lacroix, "Sheikhs and Politicians," pp. 6–7.

29. "Iqaf al-ustadh Muhammad Nur 'an al-tahadduth bi-ism al-hizb bi sabab hudurihi hifl al-safara al-iraniyya" [Suspension of Mohammed Nur as spokesman of the party because of his attendance at an Iranian embassy gathering], forsanhaq.com, 24 February 2012, http://www.forsanhaq.com/archive/index.php/t-298047.html

30. "Khilafat dakhil al-da'wa al-salafiyya bi-sabab al-ihtifal bi-zikra ta'sis al-dawla al-turkiyya" [Disputes within the Salafi Da'wa because of the celebration of the foundation of the Turkish state], *Al-Sharq Al-Awsat*, 6 November 2012.

31. Informal conversation with an associate of Yasir Burhami, Alexandria, May 2012.

32. Author interview with Mahmud Abbas, Alexandria, November 2012.

33. Stéphane Lacroix and Ahmed Zaghloul Shalata, "The Rise of Revolutionary Salafism in Post-Mubarak Egypt," in Lacroix and Rougier, eds, *Egypt's Revolutions*, pp. 163–78.

34. "Salafiyyu masr yarfudun ta'yid al-'Awwa ka-murashshah li-l-ri'asa" [Egypt's Salafis refuse to back al-'Awwa as presidential candidate], *Al-Alam*, 28 March 2012, http://www.alalam.ir/news/1047564

35. A few Da'wa figures, like Sa'id Abd al-'Azim, were against that choice, but later agreed to abide by the "decision of the majority."

36. "Yasir Burhami ya'tarif bi liqa'ihi bi-l-fariq Ahmad Shafiq" [Yasir Burhami confesses he met with Ahmad Shafiq], *Al-Yawm al-Sabi'*, 27 September 2012, http://www.youm7.com/story/0000/0/0/-/798790

37. Noha El-Hennawy, "Sheikhs and the Ballot Box: Internal Rifts Emerge Within Salafi Nour Party," *Egypt Independent*, 25 September 2012, http://www.egyptindependent.com/news/
sheikhs-and-ballot-box-internal-rifts-emerge-within-salafi-nour-party

38. Author interview with Mahmud Abbas (who was one of the leaders of the Reform Front), Alexandria, November 2012.

39. Author interview with Yusri Hammad (one of Hizb al-Watan's founders), Alexandria, January 2013.

40. "Abd al-Ghaffur wa-l-Zarqa wa 'Alam al-Din... min manabir al-da'wa ila salun al-ri'asa" [Abd al-Ghaffour, al-Zarqa and 'Alam al-Din... from the pulpits of the Da'wa to the salon of the presidency], *Al-Shorouk*, 28 August 2013, http://www.shorouknews.com/news/view.aspx?cdate=28082012&id=0f678981-0256-4536-b4e0-ffe7065d4d0f

41. Patrick Haenni, "The Reasons for the Muslim Brotherhood's Failure in Power," in Lacroix and Rougier, eds, *Egypt's Revolutions*, pp. 19–39.

42. "Al-da'wa al-salafiyya: qanun al-du'a yahdaf li-akhwanat al-manabir" [The Salafi Da'wa: the law on preachers aims at Brotherhoodizing the pulpits], *Al-Mesryoon*, 13 May 2013.

43. "Hizb al-Nur al-salafi: muhawalat akhwanat al-dawla al-masriyya ghayr maqbula" [Salafi Hizb al-Nour: the attempts to brotherhoodize the state are unacceptable], *Al-Arabiyya*, 29 January 2013, http://www.alarabiya.net/articles/2013/01/29/263205.html

44. "Hizb al-Nur yuhaddid bi-kashf tasafil malaff akhwanat al-dawla" [Hizb al-Nour threatens to reveal the details of the file on the Brotherhoodization of the state], *Al-Watan*, 28 February 2013, http://www.elwatannews.com/news/details/139133

45. "Hizb al-Nur yatahaffaz 'ala ziyarat Nijad li masr: Iran ra'iya li-madhabih ahl al-sunna" [Hizb al-Nur criticizes Ahmadinejad's visit to Egypt: Iran is behind the massacres of Sunnis], *Al-Masry al-Yawm*, 5 February 2013, http://www.almasryalyoum.com/news/details/281836

46. "Ihtijaz Burhami bi-matar Burj al-'Arab wa Bakkar:kull wasa'il al-tas'id mutaha" [Burhami detained in Burj al-Arab airport; Bakkar: we are ready to escalate the issue with all possible means], *Rassd*, 30 May 2013, http://rassd.com/62952.htm

47. "Bawwabat al-Ahram tanshur bunud ittifaq jabhat al-inqadh wa Hizb al-Nur li-l-khuruj min al-azma al-haliyya" [Al-Ahram publishes the articles of the agreement between the Salvation Front and Hizb al-Nour to solve the current crisis], *Al-Ahram*, 30 January 2013, http://gate.ahram.org.eg/News/302717.aspx

48. "Yasir Burhami: idha kjaraja al-malayin fi 30 yunyu sa-atlub Mursi bi-l-istaqala" [Yasir Burhami: if millions of protesters take the streets on June 30th, I will demand Morsi's resignation], *Al-Masry al-Yawm*, 5 June 2013, http://www.almasryalyoum.com/news/details/215693

49. "Wathiqa sirriyya musarraba li-Hizb al-Nur 'an al-ra'is al-maz'ul Mursi" [A secret leaked Hizb al-Nour document about former president Mursi], *Al-Arabiyya*, 20 July 2013, http://www.alarabiya.net/ar/arab-and-world/egypt/2013/07/20/وثيقة-سرية-مسربة-لحزب-النور-عن-الرئيس-المعزول-مرسي.html

50. "Li-madha insahab Bassam al-Zarqa mumaththil Hizb al-Nur min ijtima'at lajnat al-khamsin al-yawm?" [Why did Hizb al-Nour representative Bassam al-Zarqa withdraw from the meetings of the committee of the 50 today?], *Al-Shabab*, 16 September 2013, http://shabab.ahram.org.eg/News/14472.aspx; "Bassam al-Zarqa li-l-Shuruq: Insihabi lam yakun li asbab sihiyya" [Bassam al-Zarqa to al-Shorouk: my withdrawal was not for health reasons], *Al-Shorouk*, 3 October 2013, http://www.shorouknews.com/news/view.aspx?cdate=03102013&id=dcc26cf6-932c-4a2d-b5be-bd9846a2359c&fb_comment_id=451921031592902_23751 10#f27b2d9f48; "Mansour to Replace Bassam El-Zarqa as Nour Party Member in Constitution Committee," *Al-Ahram*, 19 September 2013, http://english.ahram.org.eg/NewsContent/1/64/82029/Egypt/Politics-/Mansour-to-replace-ElZarqa-as-Nour-Party-member-in.aspx

51. A number of complaints were filed after 2013, but none has yet succeeded. See, for instance, "Ba'd rafd al-idara al-'ulya hall al-Nur...narsud 4 da'awi qada'iyya quddimat didd al-hizb al-salafi mundhu 'azl Mursi" [After the refusal of the high

administrative court, we cover the four complaints that were filed against the Salafi party since Morsi was deposed], *Al-Yawm al-Sabi'*, 6 July 2015, http://www. youm7.com/story/2015/7/6/عبد فر ض الا رادلا يم علل اح-ل نا رونلا رن صد-4-د عاوى-ق ضائية 2253936/دض متمق

52. Georges Fahmi, "The Egyptian State and the Religious Sphere," Carnegie Middle East Center, 18 September 2014, http://carnegie-mec.org/2014/09/17/ egyptian-state-and-religious-sphere-pub-56619

53. Amr Ezzat, "Li-man al-manabir al-yawm?" [Who owns the pulpits today?], *Al-mubadara al-masriyya li-l-huquq al-shakhsiyya*, August 2014, http://eipr.org/ sites/default/files/reports/pdf/to_whom_do_minbars_belong_today.pdf, pp. 63–64.

54. Author interviews with Da'wa officials. See, for instance, "Khalid 'Alam al-Din li-Sabahak ya Masr: Sa-uqadi al-ri'asa bi tuhmat al-tashhir bi" [Khalid Alam al-Din to Sabahak ya Masr: I will sue the presidency for defaming me], *Al-Yawm al-Sabi'*, 19 February 2013, http://www.youm7.com/story/0000/0/0/-/951188

55. "Al-Nur yuhajim al-ra'is wa yutalib bi-ijra' tahqiq muhayid fi ahdath fadd i'tisam Rabi'a" [Al-Nour attacks the president and demands a neutral investigation into the Rabi'a events], ONTV, 4 September 2013, http://onaeg.com/?p=1145997

56. "Al-aqbat yuwasilun intifadatahum didd Yunis Makhyun ba'd tasrihatihi hawla tarashshuhihim bi-l-intikhabat" [Copts continue their uprising against Yunis Makhyun after his statements on their candidacy for the elections], *Al-Yawm al-Sabi'*, 13 October 2015, http://www.youm7.com/story/2015/10/13/طاب قألا-ن لوص ا ولن-ان تف اض متهم ص ض-س نوي خم يوي-ن عب د-ت ص رحاته -ل وح-ت رش/2386006

57. "Al-da'wa al-salafiyya tubarrir tarashshuh aqbat 'ala qawa'im al-Nur: dar'un li-l-mafasid" [The Salafi Da'wa justifies presenting Copts on Al-Nour's lists: to prevent from harm], *Al-Watan*, 1 October 2015, http://www.elwatannews.com/ news/details/811432. The Da'wa has previously released a longer religious study to justify its new position: Ahmad al-Shahhat, "Al-mar'a wa-l-nasara fi-l-barlaman al-qadim: ru'ya shar'iyya" [Women and Christians in the next parliament: a religious view], anasalafy.com, 12 February 2015, http://www.anasalafy.com/play. php?catsmktba=54010

58. "Bayan hawla al-mawaqif al-siyasiyya li-Hizb al-Nur" [Statement on Hizb al-Nour's political positions], almoslim.net, 12 January 2014, http://www.almoslim.net/ node/198580

59. "Al-Shaykh Abd al-Rahman Abd al-Khaliq mu'assis al-salafiyya li-Burhami: kunta min junud Iblis fa-artaqa bik al-shirr wa sirta ustadhahu" [Sheikh Abd al-Rahman Abd al-Khaliq, the founder of Salafism, to Burhami: you were one of Satan's soldiers, but you have advanced in evil, and you are now his teacher], *Al-Sha'b*, 1 December 2013, http://www.elshaab.org/news/85266/خلادب ع-ن محرلادب ع-خيي شلا
ق لا-م ؤ س س ل س ف لا-ة ي ب ل ب ره ام ي-ك ن ت-ن م-ج ن د إ ب ل ي س ف ت راف ق ى ب ك-رش لا و ر ص ت أ-ت رذ اته

60. According to an internal poll, 60 percent of Hizb al-Nour members disagreed on

the party's position toward the coup against Morsi and its aftermath. See el-Sherif, "Egypt's Salafists at a Crossroads."

61. "Tafasil hurub qiyadi salafi kabir ila Qatar" [The details of the flight of an important Salafi leader to Qatar], *Veto*, 9 December 2013, http://www.vetogate.com/741765

62. "Masr… al-da'wa al-salafiyya tastab'id Sa'id 'Abd al-'Azim wa-l-Muqaddim" [Egypt… The Salafi Da'wa excludes Sa'id Abd al-Azim and al-Muqaddim], *Islam Memo*, 26 July 2015, http://islammemo.cc/akhbar/locals-egypt/2015/07/26/256200.html

63. "Yasir Burhami yasil al-Suways li-ilqa' muhadara wasat harasa amniyya mushaddada" [Yasir Burhami arrives in Suez to give a conference under heavy security protection], *Sada al-Balad*, 3 January 2014, http://www.elbalad.news/770090

64. Abd al-Mun'im al-Shahhat, "Tahlil nata'ij hizb al-Nur fi-l-marhala al-ula min al-intikhabat 2015" [An analysis of Hizb al-Nour's results in the first stage of the 2015 elections], *Al-Fath*, 29 October 2015, http://www.fath-news.com/Art/1072

65. 'Ala Bakr, "Nazra mawdu'iyya fi nata'ij al-marhala al-ula min al-intikhabat al-barlamaniyya" [An objective reading of the first results of the parliamentary elections], *Al-Fath*, 16 November 2015, http://www.fath-news.com/Art/1083

66. "Al-da'wa al-salafiyya bi-matruh tu'lin i'tizal al-siyasa wa-l-'awda li-l-'amal al-da'wi" [The Salafi Da'wa in Matruh announces its renouncement of politics and its return to preaching], *Al-Yawm al-Sabi'*, 1 July 2014, http://www.youm7.com/story/2014/7/1/الدعوة_السلفية_بمطروح_تعلن_اعتزال_السياسة_والعودة_للعمل_الدعوي/1754163

67. Author interview with Ashraf Thabit, Alexandria, January 2012.

68. For a critical appraisal, see Jillian Schwedler, "Can Islamists Become Moderates? Rethinking the Inclusion-Moderation Hypothesis," *World Politics*, vol. 63, no. 2 (April 2011).

69. Yusri Hammad, a Hizb al-Nour dissident who became a spokesman for Hizb al-Watan, said about Hizb al-Nour's rapprochement with the liberals against Morsi in early 2013: "I don't have a problem with speaking to liberals, but I do with the fact that even when they do this, Hizb al-Nour feel they need to talk about Islam, quote the Koran… Why don't they acknowledge this is simply politics, not a religious issue!"

12. RELIGIOUS AUTHORITY AND SECTARIANISM IN LEBANON

1. See, for example, Max Weiss, *In the Shadow of Sectarianism: Law, Shi'ism, and the Making of Modern Lebanon* (Cambridge, MA: Harvard University Press, 2010); and Benjamin T. White, *The Emergence of Minorities in the Middle East: The Politics of Community in French Mandate Syria* (Edinburgh: Edinburgh University Press, 2011).

2. Other than the Maronites, the other eleven recognized Christian sects include:

Greek Orthodox, Greek Catholic, Latin Catholic, Armenian Orthodox, Armenian Catholic, Syriac Orthodox, Syriac Catholic, Coptic, Chaldean, Assyrian, and Protestant. See the Bureau of Democracy, Human Rights, and Labor, "Lebanon," in *International Religious Freedom Report 2011* (Washington, DC: US Department of State, 2011), http://www.state.gov/documents/organization/193107.pdf

3. See the Associated Press photo available at http://www.msn.com/es-us/noticias/other/in-this-photo-released-by-lebanons-official-government-photographer-dalati-nohra-french-president-francois-hollande-front-row-third-left-poses-with-top-lebanese-religious-figures-at-the-pine-resid/ar-BBrR46Q

4. Mustapha Hamoui, "Do We Need a Lebanese Senate?" *Beirut Spring*, 3 February 2012, https://beirutspring.com/do-we-need-a-lebanese-senate-4e782cf2fc1b#.csih364p4

5. Leila M. T. Meo, *Lebanon, Improbable Nation: A Study in Political Development* (Bloomington, IN: Indiana University Press, 1965), p. 55.

6. Kamal Salibi, *A House of Many Mansions: The History of Lebanon Reconsidered* (Berkeley, CA: University of California Press, 1988), p. 144.

7. For the 1920 photo, see http://alafkar.net/wp-content/uploads/2015/08/.jpg. For the 2016 photo, see http://www.msn.com/es-us/noticias/other/in-this-photo-released-by-lebanons-official-government-photographer-dalati-nohra-french-president-francois-hollande-front-row-third-left-poses-with-top-lebanese-religious-figures-at-the-pine-resid/ar-BBrR46Q

8. This is a quotation from the speech of General Henri Gouraud, high commissioner for Syria and Lebanon, at the Palais des Pins on 1 September 1920. For the French text, see Nagib Dahdah, *Evolution Historique du Liban* [Historical evolution of Lebanon] (Beirut: Librairie du Liban, 1967), p. 133.

9. See "Maronite Patriarch Retires; Successor to Be Elected in March," *Catholic World News*, 28 February 2011, CatholicCulture.org, http://www.catholicculture.org/news/headlines/index.cfm?storyid=9423. See also Antoine Saad, *The Seventy-Sixth: His Beatitude Mar Nasrallah Boutros Cardinal Sfeir, Maronite Patriarch of Antioch and the Entire East, vol. 1, 1986–1992*, trans. N. S. Nasr (Beirut: Entire East, 2005).

10. This kind of situation has arisen with regard to the Druze sheikh al-aql in 1946, 1995, 2000, and 2006, as well as with regard to the Sunni Higher Islamic Council and its appointments to regional offices, such as that of the mufti of Sidon between 2012 and 2014.

11. Jakob Skovgaard-Petersen, "Religious Heads or Civil Servants? Druze and Sunni Religious Leadership in Post-War Lebanon," *Mediterranean Politics*, vol. 1, no. 3 (1996), pp. 337–52.

12. See, for example, Gudrun Kramer and Sabine Schmidtke, eds, *Speaking for Islam: Religious Authorities in Muslim Societies* (Boston: Brill, 2006).

13. Ibid.

14. See, for example, Liyakat N. Takim, *The Heirs of the Prophet: Charisma and Religious Authority in Shi'ite Islam* (Albany, NY: SUNY Press, 2006).

15. Edmond Rabbath, *La Formation Historique du Liban Politique et Constitutionnel* [The historical formation of Lebanon, political and constitutional] (Beirut: L'Université Libanaise, 1986), p. 128.

16. Ihsan A. Hijazi, "Sunni Muslim Chief Killed in Lebanon," *New York Times*, 17 May 1989, http://www.nytimes.com/1989/05/17/world/sunni-muslim-chief-killed-in-lebanon.html

17. "Pope Expresses Gratitude for Retiring Maronite Patriarch," Catholic News Agency, 3 March 2011, http://www.catholicnewsagency.com/news/pope-expresses-gratitude-to-retiring-maronite-patriarch

18. Celestine Bohlen, "Pope Calls on Lebanon to Resume Special Role for Peace," *New York Times*, 12 May 1997, http://www.nytimes.com/1997/05/12/world/pope-calls-on-lebanon-to-resume-special-role-for-peace.html

19. "Une Espérance Nouvelle Pour Le Liban de Sa Sainteté Jean-Paul II aux Patriarches, aux Évêques, au Clergé, aux Religieux, aux Religieuses et à Tous les Fidèles du Liban" [A New Hope for Lebanon, from His Holiness John Paul II to the Patriarchs, Bishops, Clergy, Religious, and all the Faithful of Lebanon], from the Special Assembly of the Synod of Bishops, 10 May 1997, https://w2.vatican.va/content/john-paul-ii/fr/apost_exhortations/documents/hf_jp-ii_exh_19970510_lebanon.html

20. For more on Patriarch Sfeir's role since 1990, see Fiona McCallum, *Christian Religious Leadership in the Middle East: The Political Role of the Patriarch* (London: Edwin Mellen Press, 2010).

21. On the Maronite patriarch, see, for example, Pierre Sarkis, "No Ifs, Ands, and Buts: Patriarch Sfeir Should Resign," *LAU Tribune*, April 2009. On the Sunni grand mufti, see, for example, Najib, "Why Religious Leaders Are Against Legalizing Civil Marriage in Lebanon," BlogBaladi, 28 February 2013, http://blogbaladi.com/why-religious-leaders-are-against-legalizing-civil-marriage-in-lebanon/.

22. Theodor Hanf, "*E Pluribus Unum?* Lebanese Opinions and Attitudes on Coexistence," Letters from Byblos no. 14 (Byblos, Lebanon: UNESCO International Centre for Human Sciences, 2007), p. 16, http://library.fes.de/pdf-files/bueros/beirut/04985.pdf

23. Ibid., p. 15.

24. Gary C. Gambill, "Dossier: Nasrallah Boutros Sfeir," *Middle East Intelligence Bulletin*, vol. 5, no. 5 (May 2003), https://www.meforum.org/meib/articles/0305_ld.htm

25. For Maronite examples, see Antoine Saad, *The Seventy-Sixth*.

26. Robert Fisk, "A Cardinal Error? Maronite Patriarch of Antioch to Meet the Pope in Israel," *Independent*, 24 May 2014, http://www.independent.co.uk/news/world/

middle-east/a-cardinal-error-maronite-patriarch-of-antioch-to-meet-the-pope-in-israel-9432050.html

27. "Hizbullah Slams Assault on Mufti as 'Cheap Attempt at Political Exploitation,'" *Naharnet*, 30 December 2013, http://www.naharnet.com/stories/en/111985

28. Bassam Alkantar, "Druze Spiritual Council: Another Lebanese Divide," *al-Akhbar English*, 8 May 2012, http://english.al-akhbar.com/node/7111

29. Hanf, "*E Pluribus Unum?*" p. 26.

30. Ibid., p. 53.

31. "Immunities, rights, and privileges" is the language used in Lebanese parliamentary decrees concerning religious heads of sects. Its meaning is largely interpreted through precedent, although the post-1990 constitution named this group of leaders specifically for the first time, granting them the right, in article 19, to bring cases before a Constitutional Council, albeit "only on laws relating to personal status, the freedom of belief and religious practice, and the freedom of religious education." See Adnan Ahmad Badr, *Al-Ifta wa-l-Awqaf al-Islamiyya fi Lubnan: Madiyyan wa Hadiran wa Mustaqbalan* [Islamic *ifta* and *awqaf* in Lebanon: Past, present, and future] (Beirut: Al-Muassasa al-Jamiiyya li-l-Dirasat wa-l-Nashr wa-l-Tawzi, 1992).

32. Skovgaard-Petersen, "Religious Heads."

33. Rabbath, *La Formation Historique du Liban Politique et Constitutionnel*, p. 128.

34. Skovgaard-Petersen, "Religious Heads."

35. Interviews with Sunni and Druze officials, 2011–16.

36. Interview with Muhammad Sammak, advisor to all three grand muftis since Hassan Khaled, Beirut, 27 January 2012.

37. Jakob Skovgaard-Petersen, "The Sunni Religious Scene in Beirut," *Mediterranean Politics*, vol. 3, no. 1 (1998), pp. 69–80.

38. Yusri Hazran, "How Elites Can Maintain their Power in the Middle East: The Junblat Family as a Case Study," *Middle Eastern Studies*, vol. 51, no. 3 (2015), pp. 343–69.

39. For more on this, see Rodger Shanahan, *The Shi'a of Lebanon: Clans, Parties and Clerics* (London: I. B. Tauris, 2005), p. 165; and Michael Johnson, *Class and Client in Beirut* (London: Ithaca Press, 1989), p. 149.

40. See, for example, Rola El-Husseini, *Pax Syriana: Elite Politics in Postwar Lebanon* (Syracuse, NY: Syracuse University Press, 2012).

41. For example, Sofia Saadeh, *The Quest for Citizenship in Post-Taef Lebanon* (Beirut: Sade, 2007).

42. This assessment is based on eight years of study of Lebanese religious leaders, especially those of the Maronite, Sunni, and Druze communities. See, for example, Alexander D. M. Henley, "Between Sect and State in Lebanon: Religious Leaders at the Interface," *Journal of Islamic and Muslim Studies*, vol. 1, no. 1 (2016), pp. 1–11.

43. See Alexander Henley, "Religious Nationalism in the Official Culture of Multi-confessional Lebanon," in M. Demichelis and P. Maggiolini, eds, *The Struggle to Define a Nation: Rethinking Religious Nationalism in the Contemporary Islamic World* (Piscataway, NJ: Gorgias Press, 2017).

44. Theodor Hanf, *Coexistence in Wartime Lebanon: Decline of a State and Rise of a Nation* (London: I. B. Tauris, 1993).

45. Interview with Assaad Chaftari, a former Politburo member of the Lebanese Forces militia, in Beirut, 2012.

46. Henley, "Religious Nationalism."

47. Thomas Scheffler, "Neither East nor West: Inter-religious Dialogue and Local Politics in the Age of Globalization," in Leslie A. Tramontini, ed., *"East is East and West is West"? Talks on Dialogue in Beirut* (Beirut: Ergon Verlag, 2006), pp. 87–99.

48. Walid Khalidi, *Conflict and Violence in Lebanon: Confrontation in the Middle East* (Cambridge, MA: Harvard Center for International Affairs, 1979), p. 72.

49. "Lebanon Patriarch and Hezbollah Chief Met to Discuss Presidential Vacuum," *YaLibnan*, 4 May 2016, http://yalibnan.com/2016/05/04/lebanon-patriarch-and-hezbollah-chief-met-to-discuss-presidential-vacuum

50. Qassem Qassem, "Lebanon's Mufti: The Future Movement Wants My Turban," *al-Akhbar English*, 16 August 2012, http://english.al-akhbar.com/node/11163

51. "Qabalan Urges the State to Disarm 'All Factions,'" *Naharnet*, 16 October 2013, http://www.naharnet.com/stories/en/102288

52. Sami E. Baroudi, "Divergent Perspectives Among Lebanon's Maronites During the 1958 Crisis," *Middle East Critique*, vol. 15, no. 1 (2006), pp. 5–28.

53. Ussama Makdisi, "Reconstructing the Nation-State: The Modernity of Sectarianism in Lebanon," *Middle East Report*, no. 200 (1996), pp. 23–30.

54. Sofia Saadeh, "Basic Issues Concerning the Personal Status Laws in Lebanon," in Thomas Scheffler, ed., *Religion Between Violence and Reconciliation* (Beirut: Ergon Verlag, 2002), pp. 449–56; and Saadeh, *The Quest for Citizenship*.

55. Ibid.

56. See, for example, Bassel Salloukh, et al., *The Politics of Sectarianism in Postwar Lebanon* (London: Pluto, 2015).

57. Taha al-Wali, *Bayrut fi al-Tarikh wa-l-Hadara wa-l-Umran* [Beirut: history, culture, and urbanism] (Beirut: Dar al-Ilm li-l-Malayin, 1993).

58. Raphaël Lefèvre, "The Roots of Crisis in Northern Lebanon," Carnegie Middle East Center, April 2014, http://carnegieendowment.org/files/crisis_northern_lebanon.pdf

59. Sofia Saadeh, "Basic Issues"; and Saadeh, *The Quest for Citizenship*. On Qabbani's fatwa against civil marriage, see Mohamed Nazzal, "Mufti on Civil Marriage: 'The Fatwa Is Plain and Clear,'" *al-Akhbar English*, 30 January 2013, http://english.al-akhbar.com/node/14817/

APPENDIX A: METHODOLOGY AND DATA FOR CHAPTER 8, JUSTIN GENGLER

1. E.g. Ronald Inglehart and Christian Welzel, *Modernization, Cultural Change, and Democracy: The Human Development Sequence* (Cambridge: Cambridge University Press, 2005).
2. World Values Survey Wave 6 (2010–2014) Official Aggregate v.2015.04.18, World Values Survey Association, data available at www.worldvaluessurvey.org
3. The survey was made possible by NPRP grant #6–636–5–064 from the Qatar National Research Fund (a member of the Qatar Foundation). The statements made herein are solely the responsibility of the authors.
4. Data on sectarian affiliation and other ascriptive demographics were not available in the surveys.

APPENDIX B: COLE BUNZEL

1. Abu Bakr al-Baghdadi, "Wa-law kariha l-kafirun" [Though the unbelievers be averse].
2. "Akhriju l-Rafida al-mushrikin min Jazirat Muhammad" [Expel the rejectionist idolaters from the peninsula of Muhammad].
3. Translations from the Quran are adapted from the translation by A. J. Arberry.
4. Companion of the Prophet, who died in 687–8.
5. More properly al-Samani, historian and *hadith* scholar from Merv in present-day Turkmenistan, who died in 1166.
6. Abu Zura was a *hadith* scholar from Rayy in Iran who died in 877. Abu Hatim—not Abu Hayyan, as the speaker mistakenly has it—was a *hadith* scholar from Rayy in Iran who died in 890.
7. The author was a Hanbali jurist from Jerusalem, who died in 1233. Aisha was a wife of the Prophet and died in 678. In a well-known story, Aisha was accused of adultery. In Sunni tradition, a revelation from God exonerates her, but not so in Shia tradition. She is traditionally seen by the Shia as a subversive enemy of the Prophet's family.
8. On Ahmad al-Ahsai and the Shaykhiyya, see Toby Matthiesen, *The Other Saudis: Shiism, Dissent and Sectarianism* (Cambridge: Cambridge University Press, 2015), pp. 41–4.
9. Hanbali jurist and theologian from Damascus, who died in 1328.
10. Tirmidhi was a *hadith* scholar who died in 892. Abu Hurayra was a companion of the Prophet and died in 678–80.
11. Saudi-Wahhabi scholar who died in 1930.
12. The speaker gets a few words wrong in this famous quote from Ibn Sihman (*al-Durar al-saniyya* [The glistening pearls], 10:510).
13. Quote attributed to Khalid ibn al-Walid, an early Muslim general and companion of the Prophet.

14. Lines by the Kharijite Arabic poet al-Tarhmah ibn al-Hakim, who died in 742–3.

15. Line by the Shia Arabic poet Abu Firas al-Hamdani, who died in 968.

INDEX

al-Abadi, Haider, 132, 133
Abbasid Empire (750–1258), 212
Abd al-Azim, Sa'id, 279
Abd al-Ghaffour, Imad, 269–75, 278
Abd al-Khaliq, Abd al-Rahman, 267,
    279
Abdullah II, King of Jordan, 91–2
Abdullah, King of Saudi Arabia, 257,
    258, 260, 261
Abdulrahman, Omar, 53
Abdulsattar, Muthanna, 57
Abo-Ahmed, 177
Abou Shaqra, Muhammad, 290
Abu al-Futuh, Abd al-Mun'im, 272
Abu Bakr, Rashidun Caliph, 57, 160
Abu Dhabi, United Arab Emirates,
    187, 190
Abu Idris, 269
Abu Isma'il, Hazim Salah, 272
Abu l-Maali Aqil al-Ahmad, 254
al-Adnani, Abu Mohammed, 47
Afghanistan, 4, 15, 64
    Iran, relations with, 98, 99, 102, 105,
        106, 108
    Soviet War (1979–89), 43, 44, 46,
        58, 98
    Syria, fighters in, 4, 102, 106, 108
ahl-i-hava, 212

Ahlam al-Nasr, 247
Ahmadinejad, Mahmoud, 3, 100, 275
Ahmed, Wafaa, 178
Ahrar al-Sham, 110
Ahul Bayt, 170
Air Force Intelligence Directorate,
    Syria, 69
al-Ajmi, Hajjaj, 53
akhwanat al-dawla, 275
Akrama, Homs, 79
Al al-Sheikh, 261
'Alam al-Din, Khaled, 274, 275
Alawites, 12, 62, 63, 65–9, 72, 73,
    75–83, 92, 102, 109, 147
    assassinations of, 62
    genocide, fear of, 76–82
    hate speech against, 160
    Ibn Nusayr, 160
    in Lebanon, 284
    Popular Mobilization Forces, 108
    predominance, 63, 65–9, 75
    religion, 28, 73, 76, 92
alcohol, 66, 67
Aleppo, Syria, 73, 107, 251, 253
Alexandria, Egypt, 266, 267, 268, 275,
    280
Algeria, 248
Ali ibn Abi Talib, 108, 127

INDEX

389

INDEX

INDEX

INDEX

INDEX